ADAMS and CALHOUN

ADAMS and CALHOUN

From Shared Vision to Irreconcilable Conflict

WILLIAM F. HARTFORD

Published by the University of South Carolina Press
Columbia, South Carolina 29208

uscpress.com

Manufactured in the United States of America

32 31 30 29 28 27 26 25 24 23
10 9 8 7 6 5 4 3 2 1

Library of Congress Cataloging-in-Publication Data
can be found at http://catalog.loc.gov/.

ISBN 978-1-64336-393-6 (hardcover)
ISBN 978-1-64336-394-3 (paperback)
ISBN 978-1-64336-395-0 (ebook)

In memory of my parents,
Francis Joseph and Julia Andras Hartford

Contents

Acknowledgments

As all historians do, I incurred a great number of obligations while preparing this study. I must begin by thanking the many scholars who have written about Adams and Calhoun. Their work not only made my own research much easier than it otherwise would have been but also allowed me to adopt an approach that combined biography with a focused examination of specific topics; any readers seeking a more comprehensive treatment of the two men's lives have a rich and accessible body of literature that they might consult. I am also thankful for the assistance I received from the librarians and archivists at the W. E. B. Du Bois Library at the University of Massachusetts at Amherst and the Massachusetts Historical Society, the latter of which kindly granted permission to quote from its manuscripts.

Not the least of my debts to the University of South Carolina Press stems from a decision made more than sixty years ago to publish a complete edition of John C. Calhoun's papers. Without the resulting twenty-eight volumes of his writings and correspondence that the press made available to scholars, the present study would not have been possible. The book further benefited from the helpful suggestions of two anonymous readers who reviewed the manuscript for the press. In Columbia, acquisitions editor Ehren Foley guided *Adams and Calhoun* through the publication process, while Kerri Tolan, Kimberly Doran, Ashley Mathias, Pat Callahan, and Kemi Ogunji contributed to the book's copyediting, production, design, and marketing. I am extremely grateful to all of them for their work on the study's behalf.

It is a great pleasure to have this opportunity to acknowledge longstanding debts to four teachers at the University of Massachusetts. I am still drawing on the wise counsel that Gerald T. McFarland gave a rough-around-the-edges graduate student many years ago; his teaching continues to inform my approach to doing history. Most of what I know about writing biography I learned from the late Stephen B. Oates. I hope he would have been pleased with this product of his instruction. The work of Leonard L. Richards both stirred my interest in John Quincy Adams and provided a model for studying him: Listen carefully to what he is saying but pay equally close attention to what he is doing. My greatest source of inspiration as a historian has been Bruce Laurie. Over the past forty years, Bruce has read nearly everything I have written, consistently offering advice that saved me from one blunder or another and that improved what I had to say. His reading of the manuscript was the most recent of many acts of assistance for which I am thankful.

INTRODUCTION

At 4:30 AM on April 12, 1861, Confederate artillery opened fire on Fort Sumter in Charleston harbor, initiating a civil war that would claim more than seven hundred thousand lives before it concluded four years later. The conflict had been a long time coming. That it began in South Carolina surprised no one. Palmetto political leaders had been the most radical proponents of southern rights since the nullification crisis of the early 1830s, when they attempted to put John C. Calhoun's doctrine of state interposition to the test by nullifying federal tariff legislation. Calhoun, who died in 1850, did not live to see the start of the Civil War. Yet he had done as much as anyone to exacerbate the intersectional controversies that culminated in the firing on Fort Sumter. In addition to devising ingenious constitutional defenses of southern interests, the South Carolinian had helped marshal opposition to the reception of antislavery petitions in Congress, stepped forward as the nation's best-known exponent of the positive good defense of slavery, encouraged various initiatives to subordinate intersectional party cooperation to the cause of southern unity, and made major contributions to the formation of a slavery national doctrine that left little room for compromising issues that divided North against South. As much as he feared the consequences of secession and civil war, Calhoun would have fully understood the reasons behind South Carolina's decision to leave the Union following Lincoln's election; nearly all of them could be found in his speeches and writings.

When news of the Confederate bombardment of Fort Sumter reached Washington, Charles Sumner wasted little time making his way from the Senate to the Executive Mansion. The Massachusetts solon was one of the most outspoken congressional critics of slavery, and he wanted to show President Lincoln how John Quincy Adams's arguments on military emancipation could be employed to put the South's peculiar institution on the road to extinction; antislavery Republicans in Congress would soon be using the same arguments for the same purpose. All of this would have delighted Adams had he lived to see it. Coming from a state that was home to William Lloyd Garrison, Wendell Phillips, Lydia Maria Child, and other prominent abolitionists, the ex-president and nine-term congressman did not play as conspicuous a role in making Massachusetts a bastion of antislavery activism as Calhoun did in placing South Carolina in the vanguard of southern radicalism. But there could be no question of his hatred of slavery, and, like the South Carolinian, he did much to inflame intersectional tensions. Never entirely satisfied with the free labor protectionism that most of his Northern Whig colleagues relied upon to defend regional interests, he was less hesitant to let people know that slavery posed the greatest threat to national development as well as national unity. Best known for his efforts to uphold the right of petition in the face of southern endeavors to suppress antislavery memorials, Adams also stood in the front ranks of those opposed to the expansion of slavery. The constitutional counternarrative that he fashioned to refute Calhounite contentions about states' rights and the place of slavery in US society became part of a freedom national doctrine that Republicans wielded to combat the slavery national assertions of their southern adversaries.[1]

A leading historian of the period has recently written of "the crooked path to abolition" travelled by Abraham Lincoln. The road to civil war was even less straightforward. There are few better examples than the routes traversed by Adams and Calhoun in their journey from exemplars of national unity to sectional standard-bearers. No one who witnessed their performance as nationalist-minded cabinet secretaries in the Monroe administration would have imagined that they would someday be bitter rivals in an intersectional struggle that threatened to tear the country apart. Although Adams believed the Missouri controversy portended much more serious conflict on the slavery front than the South Carolinian did, he was as just as eager as Calhoun to defer that reckoning. Participation in the nullification crisis sharpened the sectional animus of both men without turning them into uncompromising belligerents. In its wake, neither of them had any wish to renew the struggle. Where Adams hoped to devote his energies to realizing the grand developmental vision that had constituted the programmatic centerpiece of his ill-fated presidency, Calhoun briefly considered retirement, thinking he had done his part to establish a solid foundation for the protection of southern interests. They would soon change their plans. Subsequent developments, beginning in the mid-1830s, ended a much-desired respite from the sectional wars and put them on a course that would conclude in the freedom national-slavery national standoff that formed their most consequential contribution to the mounting tensions that ultimately resulted in secession and a civil war that each of them hoped to avoid.[2]

This is not a standard biography. Adams and Calhoun have attracted the attention of many able biographers, whose comprehensive, full-length treatments contain a wealth of detail about all aspects of their lives. Readers seeking to know more about either man can learn much from these fine works; my debt to their authors is considerable. Instead, this study centers on four topic areas—nationalism and empire, sectionalism and nullification, slavery and antislavery, and party, politics, and the expansion of slavery—that permit a chronological treatment of how Adams and Calhoun responded to major shifts in the evolving sectional crisis. Such an approach allows for a more tightly focused concentration on the development of specific themes than is usually found in biographical works without sacrificing examination of the interplay of personal idiosyncrasies and contextual influences that is one of the great strengths of biography. It should also be noted that the study's comparative dimension seeks to go beyond a simple description of similarities and differences in what the two men thought and did. When, for example, Adams's popular constitutionalism is set beside Calhoun's more legalistic, less democratic, and sometimes counterintuitive pronouncements, it becomes possible to offer an assessment of the relative political efficacy of the two arguments. Comparing their response to major developments of the period can be equally illuminating. All students of the Civil War era are familiar with the spread of more radical and better organized forms of abolitionism during the 1830s. Examining the effect of antislavery initiatives on Adams and Calhoun helps clarify ways in which abolitionists transformed the politics of slavery during that critical decade.

It must be added that there was a certain asymmetry in the pattern of interaction between the two men. On one hand, Calhoun loomed large in Adams's political consciousness. For the Bay State congressman, he was "the High Priest of Moloch. The embodied spirit of Slavery." His frequent allusions to the Carolina doctrine had specific and general denotations—sometimes referring to Calhoun's doctrine of nullification, at other times to everything he deplored about slave power impositions and the South's peculiar institution. By contrast, Adams made far fewer appearances in Calhoun's writings. Yet this hardly meant that the South Carolinian was unaware of the New Englander's presence. Dissatisfaction with the Adams administration and its ambitious developmental program was one of several factors prompting Calhoun's abandonment of the ardent nationalism he had displayed as a War Hawk and cabinet secretary. If he did not directly confront Adams in his later efforts to bar Senate reception of antislavery memorials, he certainly knew of the Bay congressman's activities on behalf of the right of petition in the lower house. Similarly, as a well-informed observer of national affairs, he could not escape learning about Adams's intervention in the Amistad case, his opposition to Texas annexation, or his participation in other antislavery initiatives. That a former president adopted such conspicuously provocative positions on such inflammatory matters could not help but deepen Calhoun's apprehensions about the influence of abolitionism on Northern society and politics. His firsthand knowledge of the intelligence and tenacity that the New Englander brought to his work made Adams's conduct all the more unsettling.[3]

When dealing with two strong-willed individuals of combative temperament who can be easily caricatured, it is necessary to distinguish stereotype from reality. The study thus begins with a look at personal matters such as family influence, religious beliefs, distinctive traits, and conduct of interpersonal relations. Chapter 1 also provides a survey of the state political cultures that shaped their early views on public life. Chapter 2 turns to an examination of their response to the War of 1812 and performance as cabinet secretaries in the Monroe administration, where each man's actions often paralleled and complemented those of the other. As secretary of state, Adams became a leading proponent of a nationalist program that sought to expand the national domain while letting European powers know that the Western Hemisphere was closed to further colonization. As secretary of war, Calhoun not only worked to strengthen national defense by improving military organization and efficiency; he also attempted to facilitate white settlement of the West by urging the adoption of major internal improvement projects and implementing policies that removed Native Americans living east of the Mississippi River from their ancestral homelands. Together, their various initiatives looked forward to the consummation of a grand developmental vision that harnessed the nation's vast human and material resources to create an integrated national polity and economy that benefited people from all regions of the union.

The alliance did not last. Relations between the two men became increasingly strained during Adams's presidency before breaking down entirely in the years that followed. Chapter 3 examines Calhoun's transition from nationalist to the South's leading exponent of a states' rights doctrine that placed the protection of regional interests above all other considerations. His claim that states possessed the power to annul congressional enactments that they found objectionable touched off a serious constitutional crisis when a South Carolina convention passed resolutions nullifying federal tariff laws. The resulting controversy revived Adams's long-standing animus toward landed elites whose arrogant assumptions about the superior virtue of agricultural producers were no more sufferable than their abusive labor practices. Moving a step beyond those opponents of nullification who, in their support of protectionist legislation, championed the interests of free labor without directly attacking slavery, Adams adopted a more confrontational stance, forcefully reminding Southern representatives that their labor system required even greater protection than Northern industry did. Although the nullification controversy stopped well short of a major disruption in intersectional relations, it had important consequences for Calhoun and Adams. The Carolinian's unswerving commitment to the promotion of national unity had largely disappeared, and he would spend the rest of his life seeking ways to create a united South capable of turning back what he saw as Northern efforts to aggrandize regional power and prosperity at the expense of Southern interests. Gone as well were any inhibitions that Adams had about inciting slaveholder fears concerning their peculiar institution. He would not go looking for trouble, but neither would he ignore any provocations that might arise.

In retrospect, the belief that discussion of slavery-related differences could be confined to the margins of political discourse appears almost delusional. It did not seem so at the time. Political moderates from all regions remembered the ferocity of the Missouri debates, and they did not wish to see such scenes repeated on the floor of Congress or anywhere else. The nullification controversy did not change that. What did was the growing presence of an abolitionist movement that demanded steps be taken immediately to begin the process of unconditional and uncompensated emancipation. Chapter 4 explores the influence of abolitionist undertakings on Calhoun and Adams. For the South Carolinian, abolitionism was both a threat and an opportunity. Although fearful of the dangers that antislavery agitation posed to the southern labor system, he recognized that such fears could be exploited to raise slaveholder awareness of the need for southern political unity. Abandoning the widely accepted practice of avoiding public discussion of slavery, Calhoun led Senate opposition to reception of antislavery petitions and played a leading role in efforts to persuade white Americans that slavery was a positive good rather than a necessary evil. Adams responded accordingly. His near decade-long struggle to abolish the gag on antislavery memorials turned what might have been a nasty but short-lived dispute into a protracted encounter that heightened Northern consciousness of slave power impositions while stoking southern suspicions of free-state intentions concerning slavery. As this and related abolitionist-inspired battles played out, fewer and fewer people believed public debate of slavery could be muffled.

One constraint on the influence Adams and Calhoun exercised was the second American party system. Neither man could ever be entirely comfortable in a political environment that made party loyalty the most sacred of all virtues; that the operation of the system hurt both of them politically—depriving Adams of a second term in the Executive Mansion and preventing Calhoun from realizing his presidential ambitions—deepened their aversion to its workings. Yet they understood that they had to make some accommodation if they were to escape political oblivion. How they did so is the main focus of the first two sections of chapter 5. The final section examines their participation in the struggle over slavery expansion and their contributions to the development of conflicting freedom national and slavery national doctrines. Formidable as it was, the second party system had one major weakness: It was ill-equipped to withstand any conflict capable of shattering the intersectional understandings that held the two major parties together. This would become unmistakably clear in the decade following

Adams and Calhoun's deaths. But the main sources of stress were already in place at midcentury, and the role the two men played in aggravating the intersectional tensions that ultimately destroyed the second party system was as great as that of any of the major political figures of the 1850s.

Chapter 1

BACKGROUND

They came from very different worlds. Born in 1767, John Quincy Adams grew up in Braintree, Massachusetts, a small farming community ten miles south of Boston, where, since 1630, successive generations of Adamses had labored diligently as farmers and artisans in an effort to wring a modest prosperity from a slender resource base. His father's career marked a significant departure from this localistic orientation. A Harvard graduate and rising star in the Massachusetts bar, John Adams assumed an increasingly prominent role in the opposition to British impositions and the subsequent struggle for independence. In February 1778, when the Continental Congress selected him to help Benjamin Franklin and Arthur Lee represent American interests in France, he took his eldest son with him. With the exception of one brief interlude, John Quincy would spend the next seven years in Europe, residing for varying periods in Paris, Amsterdam, the Hague, and St. Petersburg, where he served as personal secretary to Francis Dana, minister to the court of Catherine the Great. The precocious youth made the most of the many opportunities that came his way. Not only did he meet and converse with Thomas Jefferson, Benjamin Franklin, the Marquis de Lafayette, John Jay, and other major public figures of the time, but he read widely and developed linguistic skills that surpassed those of many seasoned diplomats. In addition to being a fluent French speaker, which made him an invaluable assistant to Dana, he had a strong command of Dutch and German, possessed some competence in Spanish, and had taken great strides toward acquiring the reading ability in Latin and Greek expected of most college students of the era. His father's claim to the contrary, John Quincy may not have been "the greatest traveler of the age" when he returned to enter Harvard in 1785, but his range of experience dwarfed that of any of his Cambridge classmates.[1]

Fifteen years younger than Adams, John C. Calhoun grew up on a farm in the southwest corner of the South Carolina Upcountry. Less rooted than the Adamses of Braintree, the Calhouns formed part of a Scotch-Irish migration that touched nearly all areas of the late colonial backcountry. The family, after departing Ireland in the mid-1730s, lived for a time in Pennsylvania before moving on to southwestern Virginia and then leaving in 1756 for opportunities farther south and to escape the spreading violence of the French and Indian War. As he had in Virginia, Patrick Calhoun, the man who would become John's father a quarter century later, obtained substantial tracts of fertile land in the Long Canes Creek area of South Carolina's Ninety Six district. And despite a 1760 Cherokee attack that resulted in the deaths of an older brother, two nieces, and Patrick's mother, he made the settlement his permanent home. In the years that followed, he not only added to his landholdings and acquired a growing number of slaves but became a prominent figure in Upcountry politics. At his passing in 1796, fourteen-year-old John assumed management of the home estate and five other farms that Patrick had secured. He might well have devoted the rest of his life to building on this inheritance had other family members not taken notice of his learning abilities and ambition to perform on a broader stage. When his brother James offered to finance a program of instruction that would enable him to expand his limited formal education and enter one of the learned professions, John readily agreed, asking only that his mother's consent be obtained and that the support cover a thoroughgoing seven-year period of preparation. Thus began a lengthy immersion in academic life that took him from Moses Waddel's Upcountry academy to Yale College and Judge Tapping Reeve's highly regarded law school in Litchfield, Connecticut. If he still fell short of John Quincy's scholarly achievements, so did most others in the early republic. What he shared with the New Englander—a tireless capacity for hard work, an inquisitive mind, and an ability to absorb and process large amounts of information—would be much more important to his future growth.[2]

It is important to put some flesh on these bare-bone outlines at the outset because both men can be easily stereotyped—Adams the austere, moralistic elitist who had trouble adapting to a world peopled by individuals less gifted and less upright than himself; and Calhoun the grim, dogmatic ideologue unwilling to consider beliefs and perspectives that differed from his own. Although each can be found behaving in ways consistent with these unflattering images, such impressions do not convey an accurate portrait of who they were. This chapter adopts a twofold approach in an effort to take readers beyond the stereotypes. Section one focuses on personal matters such as family influence, religious beliefs, distinctive traits, and their conduct of interpersonal relations. The final two sections examine their early public lives against the backdrop of their home states' political cultures. That Adams came from Massachusetts mattered a great deal, even though he spent nearly half his life in Europe prior to being appointed President Monroe's secretary of state. The proud bearer of a regional chauvinism that people in less favored parts of the land invariably found insufferable, he had no doubts whatsoever about the significance of Bay contributions to national greatness. When he later told a Boston audience that "New England is the child of that puritan race, whom David Hume, with extorted reluctance, acknowledges to have been the founders of *all* the liberties of the English nation," he was not trying to elicit approving nods from listeners; he unreservedly believed every word he said. That Calhoun hailed from South Carolina mattered even more, and not simply because of the profound impact he had on Palmetto political developments. South Carolina's unique political traditions did much to shape his views of checks and balances in government and the relationship between state and society.[3]

Any comparison of the early lives of Adams and Calhoun necessarily suffers from a disparity in sources. There is little direct evidence about Calhoun's upbringing, and what historians do know comes largely from hearsay and reminiscences published many years later. It is nevertheless possible to draw some informed inferences about family influences on his development. By all accounts, his mother, Martha Caldwell Calhoun, was a studious woman familiar with the world of books, and it has been plausibly suggested that she inspired John's interest in learning. A capable plantation manager as well, Martha almost certainly helped her son shoulder the responsibilities he assumed at his father's death. John's later insistence that her permission be secured before he embarked on his extended course of education is only one of many indications of the close bonds between them. When informed that she had died from a fever in the spring of 1801, he could not find words to express the grief that he felt.[4]

Calhoun's father had an equally great—if not greater—role in molding the person he became. According to one Calhoun biographer, John viewed life as "a competitive struggle in which weakness was more to be feared than strength: a struggle in which eminence would naturally be sought by all but would be achieved, through a process of natural selection, only by those whose talents and will were greatest." Few people in the South Carolina backcountry of his youth better exemplified this approach to human endeavor than Patrick Calhoun. Only five years old when his family reached Pennsylvania from Ireland, Patrick grew up in a series of backcountry settlements. After surviving the Long Canes Massacre of 1760, he amassed an estate that placed him among the wealthiest landholders in the Ninety Six district. His eagerness to improve his condition in life did not stop there. An assertive, outgoing individual, who never shied from sharing his strongly held opinions with others, he soon emerged as a formidable figure in district politics. In 1769 Patrick became the first person from the Upcountry to secure election to the South Carolina assembly, where he would serve nearly continuously from the mid-1770s until his death two decades later. It is not clear when or how John's political ambitions took shape, but there can be little doubt that his father's example influenced him. Nor can there be any doubt that, whatever else he might have learned during these years, he needed no instruction in the importance of family.[5]

The documentary record for Adams's early life is much more extensive. Not only did lengthy separations from both parents produce a rich correspondence, but John Quincy began putting words to paper at an early age and continued to do so throughout his life; indeed, it sometimes seems that he entered the world with a pen in each hand and did not stop writing until he collapsed in his House seat eighty years later. Perhaps the greatest difference in the two men's relations with their parents was the pressure to excel that Adams faced. Where Calhoun's family recognized his abilities and took steps to help him make the most of them, Adams received regular reminders of his many opportunities and the obligations they imposed on him. Few young men of his generation, his mother told him, had seen more of the world, enjoyed easier access to books, or spent more time conversing with major literary and scientific figures than he had. "How unpardonable it would have been in you," she added, "to have been a Blockhead." Even his sister urged him not to make light of "the peculiar advantages" bestowed on him. "Very few at any age of life possess so great a share," she observed in a 1782 letter. "It is your own fault if you neglect to make a right improvement in the talents that are put in your hands; your reflections in a future day will be brightened if you can look back on your past conduct conscious of not having deviated from the path of your duty."[6]

John Quincy learned early what making "a right improvement" of his abilities required. Where Calhoun grew up in an agricultural world in which changes in the seasons largely dictated how long and how hard one labored on a given day, Adams's parents sought to instill a different form of work discipline in their son—one much more responsive to internal promptings than to external factors. There was no greater "moral Precept," his father counseled, than the injunction "[t]o lose no Time." No one who ignored this rule of conduct could expect to succeed in life. "You must measure out your Hours, for Study, Amusements, Exercise and Sleep, and suffer nothing to divert you, at least from those devoted to study." His mother could not have agreed more. "You must consider that every Moment of your time is precious," she wrote, and "if trifled away never to be recalled." An excessive preoccupation with recreational activities "will never afford you that permanent satisfaction which the acquisition of one Art or Science will give you, and whatever you undertake aim to make yourself perfect in it, for if it is worth doing at all, it is worth doing well." Such unremitting didacticism might have crushed the spirit of some young men. John Quincy was made of sterner stuff. He eagerly embraced all these exhortations and then passed them on to his younger brother in even less compromising terms than he had received them. It is no exaggeration, he told Thomas Boylston, to "say that every hour you spend in idleness, is an injury you do to your fellow-men." This was so because, given his many "advantages for improvement," people "will, and they have a right to say in the language of scripture, 'To whom much is given, from him shall much be required.'"[7]

As much as they valued learning, John and Abigail Adams did not believe that academic achievement alone would make their eldest son a responsible citizen of the republic. John Quincy should certainly seek to attain an eminent position in life, his mother wrote, "but above all things support a virtuous character, and remember that 'an Honest Man is the Noblest work of God.'" Family honor dictated that he do no less. And should he ever have any questions about where the path of duty lay, he need look no further than his father's example of "disinterested patriotism and Noble Love of your country, which will teach you to dispise wealth, titles, pomp, and equipage, as mere external advantages, which cannot add to the internal excellence of your mind or compensate for the want of Integrity and virtue." Other family members also had their eyes on John Quincy and expected that he would conduct himself in ways that would make them proud and contribute to the general welfare of the new nation. Her recently deceased father, Reverend William Smith of Weymouth, Abigail observed in another letter, had few greater wishes than that his grandson "become a useful citizen, a Guardian of the Laws Liberty and Religion of our Country, as your Father (he was pleased to Say) had already been."[8]

Calhoun absorbed most of these same values and in later years would express them just as eloquently and assertively as Adams did. What set the New Englander apart was the instruction on self-examination and character assessment that accompanied his introduction to them. The most hazardous form of deception he would encounter in life, his mother warned, was self-deception. To prevent its warping his personal growth and engagement with the world around him, she recommended that John Quincy make "the knowledge and study of yourself" an integral part of his daily routine. As with so much else that Abigail told him, he took the advice to heart and, at his father's urging, began what would become one of the most famous and comprehensive diaries in American history. At the same time, both parents stressed the importance of carefully assessing "Men and Manners," so that he might "be Skillfull in both." It was particularly important that, in doing so, he develop a capacity for critical, independent thought. He should read the "great Masters of Antiquity" closely and learn what he could from them, his father said of classical study, but take nothing they say at face value and "never imitate them," for "it is nature not the Ancients that you are to imitate and Copy." Although Adams consistently displayed a greater self-awareness and willingness to engage in self-criticism than the less introspective Calhoun typically exhibited, his efforts to develop impartial standards for evaluating the conduct of others proved more difficult than he imagined. "Affection or Resentment" too often got in the way, creating biases that invariably resulted in misrepresentation. "The victory over prejudice is a conquest of oneself," he observed in an 1812 diary entry. "It is better than to be a ruler of a City." This was one triumph that forever eluded him as the many bile-laden characterizations of others found in his diary so clearly attest. In addition to exhibiting a quick temper that he never fully succeeded in checking, John Quincy would, as one eulogist later put it, always have trouble making "sufficient allowance for a less favored lot."[9]

A lifetime of self-examination and critical scrutiny of others had a decided influence on Adams's approach to interpersonal relations. In a 1786 letter to his brother Thomas Boylston, then studying at Harvard, John Quincy counseled him to be particularly careful about his selection of companions. Too often, the most obliging and agreeable people turned out to be unworthy of one's confidence and trust. Thomas would do well to seek demonstrable evidence of an "attachment to honour, morality and religion" before getting close to anyone. "I could wish you to be on good terms with all your Classmates," John Quincy wrote, "but intimate with few[;] endeavor to have no Enemies, and you can have but few real friends." We do not know what Thomas thought of this advice, but his brother meant what he said. Few political figures of his generation seemed so determined to demonstrate their inability to ingratiate themselves with others. In public, he often appeared "[c]old and reserved," the future antislavery politician Salmon P. Chase remarked in an 1828 letter. "He is stiff as a crow-bar—No polish is perceptible about him and he goes through his part on these occasions like a man who was sensible it must be done and who is heartily rejoiced when it is done." Behind closed doors, people often found him combatively tactless. "What Adams wants," said an otherwise sympathetic observer, "is acquaintance with the temper & disposition of those around him, manners more accommodating, & a readiness to yield small points, that he may carry the great one." None of these comments would have surprised John Quincy. He was well aware of his social shortcomings and had no wish to alter his conduct. "I am certainly not intentionally repulsive," he told his wife, "and in my public station I have never made myself inaccessible to any human being. But I have no power of fascination, none of the honey which the profligate proverb says is the true fly-catcher; and be assured, my dear friend, it would not be good policy for me to affect it."[10]

Like the New Englander, Calhoun was no glad-hander or hail-fellow-well-met. He could speak knowledgably on a broad range of subjects, but he possessed no perceptible wit and had little talent for the sharp thrust or sprightly retort. Unlike Adams, whose rancorous, penetrating invective left at least one adversary exclaiming that he "would rather die a thousand deaths than again to encounter that old man," the South Carolinian exhibited none of what Robert Barnwell Rhett described as "that acerbity or malignity of temper, which gives wit its sharpest edge and deepest interest in exposing the folly or weakness of others."

A man of enormous self-discipline, he maintained an unshakeable decorum. In an era when people from all stations in life seemed "addicted to habitual smut," another acquaintance observed, "Calhoun was the only one whose conversation was uncontaminated by such impurity." Yet he was anything but boring, and he invariably made a strong impression on everyone he met. Within Monroe's cabinet, Adams found that his capacity for independent thought, "sound judgment, quick discrimination and keen observation" set him apart from other members. "All that he does and utters and imagines," Salmon P. Chase said, "is marked by his grand characteristic energy." His entire discourse struck one perceptive observer as being "but a modified species of Senatorial debate," and it is no surprise that Calhoun is so well remembered for his oratorical performances in the halls of Congress. It is equally unsurprising that, given his aversion to small talk and disinterest in celebratory events, so little attention is paid to anything he said outside them. Where Adams voiced some of his most memorable statements in Fourth of July orations and similar addresses, Calhoun made few such appearances, restricting his participation to occasions that had a clear political purpose.[11]

More significantly, Calhoun's interactions with others underwent a subtle but noticeable change as he assumed the role of leading defender of southern society. As late as the mid-1820s, Josiah Quincy IV recalled, the South Carolinian regularly reached out to people from all regions, going out of his way "to make himself agreeable to young men appearing in Washington who might possibly rise to influence in their respective communities." Although concerns about slavery seemed to influence his opinions on most major issues of the day, he carefully avoided any direct reference to the South's peculiar institution in an effort to promote intersectional amity. "Now, from what I have said to you," he observed at the conclusion of one conversation with Quincy, "I think you will see the interests of the *gentlemen* of the North and of the South are *identical*." Not only did such exchanges become much less frequent in later years—if they did not cease altogether—but Calhoun's discourse became increasingly more didactic. Always self-absorbed, he now showed even less interest in what others had to say. His "talk, deeply interesting as it always was," said the South Carolina poet-legislator William J. Grayson, "took the form rather of monologue than conversation." At such moments he was, in the words of Francis Lieber, "mind, through and through," and at least a few people came to feel that a little Calhoun went a long way. Although he considered the South Carolinian his "principal associate" in the Senate, the Alabama politician Dixon H. Lewis found him "too intellectual, too industrious, too intent in the struggle of politics to suit me except as an occasional companion. There is no *relaxation* with him."[12]

Perhaps the greatest personal challenge Adams and Calhoun faced in their public lives stemmed from the conflict between principle and ambition. Both men viewed themselves as paragons of republican virtue, people who would be guided by their sense of right at all times. Both also aspired to become president, an aim that could only be fulfilled by enlisting the support of others, which, to be done most effectively, required making some compromise or another. For Adams, the period of tension was relatively brief. Prior to 1817, he had, with the exception of an undistinguished five-year stint in the Senate, spent much of his career in the diplomatic service, where his consistently outstanding work garnered high praise from leading figures in three presidential administrations but brought little public notice. As he approached his fiftieth birthday, his chances of becoming chief executive seemed slim indeed, and Adams surely knew it, given his lifelong indisposition to engage in wishful thinking. All this changed when President Monroe appointed him secretary of state. Three of the first five presidents had occupied the office, and anyone holding the position immediately became, as Adams later said, "one of those towards whom the public attention must be turned as a suitable candidate to succeed the President upon his retirement from office."[13]

Adams was as well prepared as anyone to reconcile any resulting tensions between aspiration and principle that might arise. "Ambition," his father had assured him decades earlier, "is a good quality," so long as "it is guided by Honour and Virtue," and John Quincy had few doubts about his ability to keep these competing values and yearnings in proper perspective. "The Selfish and Social Passions are intermingled in the conduct of every man acting in a public capacity," he noted in an 1820 diary entry. "It is right that they should be so, and it is no just cause of reproach to any man, that in promoting to the utmost of his power the public good, he is desirous at the same time of promoting his own." Believing he had no talent for the dark arts of electoral politics or inclination to master them, Adams felt certain that he could withstand whatever temptations a presidential contest might present without sacrifice of integrity. "If that office was to be the prize of cabal and intrigue, of purchasing newspapers, bribing by appointments or bargaining for foreign missions," he observed in a subsequent diary entry, he would have "no ticket in that Lottery." It was far better to put aside one's most cherished political aspirations than to let oneself become a morally vacuous casualty of this ethical obstacle course.[14]

There can be no question that Adams believed every word he ever wrote or uttered on the subject of political depravity. But how well did he handle the challenges he encountered during those years when he had a mount in the presidential derby? Many of his contemporaries would have answered: Not well at all. Their reasons for doing so centered on what political opponents dubbed the "corrupt bargain" of 1824. No candidate obtained a majority of electoral votes in that year's presidential contest, and the House of Representatives decided the winner. When Henry Clay threw his considerable influence in the lower chamber behind Adams's candidacy, and the New Englander afterward made Clay his secretary of state, the appointment enraged supporters of Andrew Jackson, who had secured a larger share of the popular and electoral vote than Adams had in the general election. Efforts to determine whether John Quincy acted improperly remain inconclusive, and their findings can be easily summarized: There is no evidence of a formal pact between Adams and Clay, but opinions vary—and likely always will—as to how much winking and nodding might have occurred. More certain is the effect the controversy had on Adams's presidency and political career. Charges of having made a dishonest agreement with Clay dogged him throughout his four years in office and did much to fuel the mobilization of voters that prevented his reelection.

It has also been argued that political ambition influenced Adams's behavior as secretary of state. The focus here is on his response to Andrew Jackson's 1818 invasion of Florida during the First Seminole War. Acting contrary to orders, the hero of New Orleans captured the Spanish garrison at St. Marks, Florida, drove the territorial governor from his headquarters at Pensacola, Florida, and executed two British citizens for allegedly aiding cross-border Native American raids into Georgia. Alone among the members of Monroe's cabinet, Adams unreservedly defended Jackson's actions, arguing that they constituted a justifiable application of force necessary to protect the national interest. For someone so well grounded in the nuances of the law of nations and so strongly committed to the peaceful resolution of international disputes, Adams's endorsement of conduct so clearly at odds with his beliefs and values demands an explanation. According to historian William Earl Weeks, it can be found in his desire to further his political aims. The New Englander was then seeking to bolster his reputation as a champion of empire by securing a major cession of Spanish lands. Were he to negotiate such a treaty, Weeks has written, "he could present himself as 'the man of the whole nation,'" thereby establishing a solid claim to the presidential succession. That Jackson's Florida incursion gave him the type of leverage he needed to obtain an advantageous settlement provided all the incentive Adams required to place long-standing principles on hold and sanction what he otherwise would have deemed an unlawful act of aggression.[15]

An even more serious lapse of principle was Adams's unwillingness to make his antislavery views public. No one seeking national office could openly denounce the South's peculiar institution without alienating southern voters and sacrificing the support of those Northern politicians who sided with southern colleagues on most issues of the day. Adams acted accordingly, and a good example of what that meant in terms of political relations can be seen in an 1824 meeting with George McDuffie. The South Carolina congressman, Calhoun protégé, and future nullifier was then an ardent nationalist whose strong support of internal improvements legislation made him a potential Adams ally after Calhoun's withdrawal from the upcoming presidential contest. When their conversation turned to the

Missouri controversy of the early 1820s, Adams told the South Carolinian that his position "had been greatly misrepresented in the Southern Country, with a view to excite local prejudices against me." Although he had objected to provisions in Missouri's constitution that barred the immigration of free Black people, Adams assured McDuffie that he had said or done nothing to prevent its admission as a slave state. All this was true enough, so far as it went. Worried about the threat that continued agitation of the issue posed to national unity, Adams had believed it best not to insist on the abolition of slavery in Missouri. What he did not tell McDuffie was what he actually thought of slavery. His diary entries during the Missouri dispute contain some of his harshest condemnations of human bondage. Had he shared them with the South Carolinian, one can be certain that the meeting would not have concluded as amicably as it did.[16]

New Englanders had been grappling with the baneful effects of pride, vanity, and ambition since John Winthrop stepped ashore from the *Arbella* in 1630. Their responses often combined self-criticism, evasion, and, by John Quincy's time, acceptance of the frailties of human nature. A good example of the latter was his father's self-admitted struggle with pride and vanity. Over the years, youthful concerns about these sources of personal corruption gradually abated before disappearing altogether. "They say I am vain," he declared late in life. "Thank God I am so. Vanity is the cordial which makes the bitter cup of life go down." People tended to place too much emphasis on humility, the former president observed on another occasion. "When you see or hear a man pique himself on his Modesty, you may depend upon it he is as vain a fellow as lives, and very probably a great Villain." John Quincy would never be quite so accepting of his own faults, but he generally acknowledged their existence. "Pride, and self-conceit and presumption lie so deep in my natural character," he confided to his diary, "that when their deformity betrays them, they run through all the changes of Proteus, to disguise themselves, to my own heart." Yet, conceding that he harbored certain undesirable traits was one thing; acknowledging a sacrifice of principle was something much different, and much more serious. Perhaps the closest he ever came to doing so was in his 1832 poem, "Dermot MacMorrogh," where he wrote:

> Ambition, when she seeks a certain end,
> Deceives herself with hypocritic art:
> That end obtain'd, her purposes to bend
> Becomes a means, another end to start.
> Such, of the plumeless biped is the fashion
> Ambition is a never ending passion.

By the time he penned these lines, Adams could view his conduct of the previous fifteen years with a detachment not then possible. He no longer had to fear submitting to the soul-destroying temptations of that period in his life; his days in the furnace of presidential ambition had ended.[17]

Calhoun would not be so fortunate. His presidential ambitions took hold early in life and never let go. Few politicians of the era enjoyed the South Carolinian's meteoric rise to national prominence. As a young congressman, he joined a group of assertive nationalists known as the War Hawks and became an outspoken proponent of using military force to combat British maritime depredations, in the process securing the chairmanship of the prestigious House Foreign Relations Committee. Afterward, as Monroe's secretary of war, he brought a tireless capacity for hard work and exceptional administrative skills to the demanding task of reforming an executive department much in need of it. If his subsequent seven and a half years in the vice presidency provided few opportunities to demonstrate his leadership abilities, they did keep him close to the center of national affairs. More important his presence did not go unnoticed. Everyone who met Calhoun during these years came away impressed by his obvious talents, and many believed the future held even greater things in store for him. That the South Carolinian did so as well was hardly surprising.

It was no less surprising that his contemporaries recognized as much. To Adams, who freely acknowledged Calhoun's "considerable talent," his most conspicuous shortcoming was a "burning ambition, stimulated to frenzy by success, flattery and premature advancement." He was, the New Englander added, one of those political figures who rarely missed an opportunity "to seize upon every popular breeze to swell his own sails—Showering favours with lavish hand to make partizans, without discernment in the choice of his instruments, and the dupe and fool of every knave cunning enough to drop the oil of fools in his ear." Recorded in 1828, some years after the two men had ceased to be friends, Adams's observations might be dismissed as the cranky censure of a political rival had not others voiced similar opinions. One New Hampshire congressman felt the Carolinian's greatest fault to be a "want of judgment & moderation—His schemes are too grand & magnificent, & he labours too much for show & effect." A number of Calhoun's fellow Southerners also had their doubts. "Ambition is his ruling passion," said the Virginia lawyer-politician Littleton Waller Tazewell, "and, if I mistake not, he will never be scrupulous in the means of gratifying it." The states' rights ideologue Nathaniel Beverly Tucker had even less faith in Calhoun, grouping him together with a band of political profligates whom he considered "utterly destitute of principle." Echoing Adams, an anonymous correspondent from the Old Dominion told Calhoun that, if he did nothing else, he needed to stop listening to people who inflated his hopes with flattering comments on his abilities and political prospects: "Your want of knowledge of human nature makes you, great man that you are, the dupe of the designing."[18]

The South Carolinian could not have been happy to hear that. He would have been even less happy to learn what Tazewell and Tucker thought of him. Although he occasionally conceded—generally with some reluctance—that he was ambitious, Calhoun resolutely denied that he had ever permitted his aspirations to subvert his principles. Whatever his personal aims might be, he declared in an 1820 letter, "I feel conscious that I can never be swayed, to any considerable extent, by motives of ambition." He believed he could honestly say that his political ideals rested "on certain fixed principles, and to carry them into effect has been my highest ambition." He further believed that anyone levelling charges of ambition against him "will at least be compelled to acknowledge in the end that my ambition is subordinate to my attachment to principles." To the extent that such professions varied over the years, they did so only in their self-righteousness. "I am," he said after his withdrawal from the 1844 presidential contest, "too honest & patriotick to be the choice of anything like a majority." But that was of little consequence. "The great point for me is to *preserve my character*, in these corrupt & degenerate times." When he later spoke of the "attachment to self" that afflicted most politicians of the period, it could be readily inferred that he considered himself one of the virtuous few who had not succumbed.[19]

Even some of Calhoun's friends grew weary of hearing him proclaim his unremitting commitment to principle. One modern biographer who titled his work, *John C. Calhoun—Opportunist,* has dismissed such assertions altogether. Although not inaccurate, the term has misleading connotations. Calhoun did act opportunistically, but no more so than other politicians of the period. Moreover, it truly bothered him that his behavior did not always accord with his principles. His incessant declarations of virtue were intended less to deceive others than to convince himself that he had not strayed from the path of duty while pursuing his presidential ambitions. He never fully succeeded. Having no propensity for introspection, Calhoun was incapable of fashioning anything comparable to the intricate web of self-criticism, evasion, and concession that formed the system of moral casuistry Adams employed to deal with his personal demons. A rigid self-discipline, as one fellow South Carolinian perceptively observed, made it even harder for him to confront inconsistencies in his conduct. Unlike Henry Clay, whose "taste for social pleasures" eased the burden of unrequited ambition, William J. Grayson wrote, "Mr. Calhoun was pure of all vices but the vice of ambition which grew stronger by the virtues that restrained him from other indulgences." The long period that he spent chasing an unrealizable dream must also be considered. Where Adams managed to clear his plate of the poisoned fruits of political ambition during his postpresidential years, they remained an indigestible part of Calhoun's diet throughout the final decades of his life.[20]

A final topic meriting consideration is religion. Although Calhoun said or wrote little about his spiritual life, he and Adams appear to have shared many of the same basic beliefs. In an era of widespread religious ferment, marked by feverish outpourings of evangelical enthusiasm, the Second Great Awakening had no perceptible effect on either of them. When informed—mistakenly it turned out—of an 1806 Lowcountry revival, Calhoun expressed no interest in the wondrous workings of God's spirit among his fellow South Carolinians, observing only that "no people ever so much needed reform as those parishes near Charleston." Raised a Calvinist, he later cast aside the Scotch-Irish Presbyterianism of his youth for what he considered the more logical and rationalistic teachings of Unitarianism. As for Adams, one would no more expect to find him at a camp meeting than in a house ill repute. A lifelong Bible reader who began each day with several chapters of Scripture and who—brief moments of skepticism aside—had few questions about the soundness of his religious principles, he had small need of a second birth in Christ to affirm or strengthen his close relationship with the divine.[21]

It will be no surprise to learn that Adams was a Protestant ecumenicist who had little patience with theological controversy. "There are," he observed while still a young man, "two types of preachers: the one doctrinal, the other, practical." He plainly preferred the latter. "The abstruse points of religion have," he believed, "so long been disputed upon, that it is probable every argument that can be of use on either side, has been repeatedly offered, and the preacher can do little more than give his own opinion." After listening to the "inconsistent absurdities" of a Massachusetts divine of Calvinist inclination who professed "to follow purely the dictates of the bible," he vowed "never to puzzle myself in the mazes of religious discussion, [and] to be content with practicing the dictates of God and reason." When the Unitarian controversy later erupted in Massachusetts, he could not see what good could possibly come from so "unprofitable" a squabble. "The only importance of religion in my mind," he told an acquaintance, "consists in its influence upon the conduct; and upon the conduct of mankind the question of the Trinity or Unity, or of the single or double personal nature of Christ, has or ought to have no bearing whatsoever." Calhoun, who was no more inclined than Adams to insist upon the correctness of his own religious beliefs, doubtless shared the New Englander's views on the main function of religion.[22]

One area where the two men parted company concerned the relationship between religion, politics, and society. One of the few discussions of religious matters in Calhoun's correspondence occurred in an exchange of letters with the SC politician James H. Hammond on Henry B. Bascom's *Methodism and Slavery* (1845). In it, Calhoun paid no attention to the work's religious content, focusing instead on its political utility. Although he agreed that Bascom did not go far enough, the pamphlet did address Hammond's concern that something be done "to deprive Abolitionists of the clap-trap of the 'Golden Rule of Christ,'" and he felt it merited "an encouraging notice from the South," while making some passing mention of the parts that "did not accord with our opinion." Adams strongly disagreed with these sentiments, and not simply because he abhorred human bondage. His own beliefs largely precluded Calhoun's narrow instrumentalism. Rather than a tool of political warfare, religion functioned more as a source of personal inspiration for him, something that might lighten his otherwise dark view of the human condition and give hope that the future would be more humane than the past. If he could not believe the scriptural promises about peace on earth, he observed after listening to an 1840 sermon on the topic, he "should be compelled to reject the whole Book." This did not mean that he thought "the nature of carnivorous beasts shall be changed," but he did look forward to a day when "the murderous and treacherous passions in the heart of man will be so far eradicated or restrained that there shall be no more public or private War." And with war, he added, "Slavery must of course be extinguished" as well. That its ultimate demise "is predetermined in the counsels of omnipotence," he noted in another diary entry, "I cannot doubt," and on more than one occasion he asked that God assist his own antislavery initiatives by shielding him "from the craven Spirit of shrinking from danger in the discharge of my duty."[23]

For the purposes of this study, it is no less significant that Adams's understanding of New England's religious past informed his sense of regionalism. Early Massachusetts settlers, he said in an 1802 oration, displayed no greater heroism or enterprise than colonists elsewhere in the Americas, but they did act from nobler motives. Forsaking the "Avarice" and "Selfish passions" that drove European ventures to populate other parts of the hemisphere, he declared, "It was reserved for the first settlers of New-England to perform achievements equally arduous" and "to dispel dangers equally terrific under the single inspiration of conscience." Even more noteworthy was his invocation in later addresses of the priesthood of all believers—the belief that all Christians were at liberty to proffer their own interpretation of Scripture. This Reformation era breakthrough not only spurred efforts to promote public education but gave rise to "the right of private judgment." And it was here, he told a Braintree audience, that "we find that inseparable connection between knowledge, and virtue and liberty, which characterized your forefathers, the Puritan settlers of New England, beyond every other people upon earth." Such regional chauvinism never became a prominent feature of Adams's public speeches or private writings. But it was always there, a fundamental part of who he was. Even though he spent much of his youth and adult life outside the land of his birth, no one ever mistook John Quincy for anything other than a son of New England. How that heritage shaped his early political development is the subject of the next section.[24]

Over time, Adams would come to accept the combative, participatory popular politics that reached full maturity during the Jacksonian era. But he never fully embraced it. This reluctance can be traced to changes taking place in the political world in which he grew up. John Quincy came of age at a time when an older structure of authority was giving way to a more democratic system of governance in which elite pretensions no longer commanded the same respect they once had. To understand these developments in Bay political culture, it is best to start at the beginning—with John Winthrop and the reasons that prompted a middle-aged member of the Suffolk gentry to begin life anew in a distant land where he would have to forsake many of the comforts to which he had become accustomed. Apart from the well-known religious motives for emigration, several socioeconomic factors also influenced the Bay founder. A demographic surge that began a century earlier had resulted in an inflationary crisis that had a particularly devastating effect on the landless. As food and fuel costs skyrocketed and a growing body of wage workers flooded labor markets, real wages plummeted and crime, vagrancy, and destitution increased. What made all this so troubling for Winthrop was what he saw as the moral destitution of English government and society. As things then stood, anyone seeking justice or fair dealing searched in vain; wherever one looked, avarice and covetousness held sway. No less worrisome was the difficulty he faced upholding his social position without abandoning his moral standards. Money could be made, but making it often required a willingness to take advantage of the less fortunate or engage in some corrupt activity or another. In Massachusetts he hoped to escape this vicious cycle by establishing a society that preserved the class divisions of early modern England without the exploitation that undergirded them—a place where members of the elite could maintain their traditional status and perform their customary duties without having to sell their souls or compromise their principles.[25]

Winthrop's vision helped shape the political culture of Massachusetts, but never to the extent that he desired. Bay colonists subscribed to a consensual ideal buttressed by a hierarchical patterning of social and political relations. At the same time, however, they lived in a society riven by various political, social, and religious divisions, where even the most powerful figures came to recognize that they could not disregard the concerns of those beneath them without some sacrifice of what they hoped to achieve. Efforts to reconcile ideal with reality and prevent those tensions from spilling over into overt conflict produced what might best be described as a politics of conditional deference. Its sources can be found in three major features of Bay society. One was a problem faced by nearly all early modern governments: How to maintain the loyalty and obedience of people living outside centers of political authority. What made the problem so vexing was the relative weakness of law enforcement in areas and communities not under the immediate oversight of the central government. Very often, political leaders had to depend on two institutions of equally questionable reliability: a local constabulary whose unpaid and under-motivated officers understood the perils of carrying out their duties in too zealous a manner; and community-based militia units whose rank-and-file members were just as likely to identify with local dissidents as to see themselves as agents of a distant central authority. Given these constraints, political leaders of at least ordinary prudence had good reason to avoid adoption of measures that might incite local resistance. The more perceptive realized that few people felt that reverence for position that constituted true deference and understood the futility of trying to distinguish between the reality and the appearance of deference. In court cases concerning various civic transgressions, magistrates found it best to accept all but the most manifestly insincere statements of repentance. In the aftermath of disruptive crowd actions, royal governors would later find it equally expedient to acknowledge expressions of regret from local authorities whom they suspected had a hand in fomenting the disturbances.[26]

A second source of the culture of conditional deference was religious. Of particular importance was popular adherence to the doctrine of the priesthood of all believers. The potentially disruptive consequences of basing the discovery of scriptural truths on popular reasoning needs little elaboration, and ministers and magistrates did what they could to discourage the faithful from adopting an expansive interpretation of what that liberty entailed. But they could not dismiss the doctrine altogether without appearing to have abandoned a bedrock element of Protestantism that set it apart from the church of Rome. This was especially so among a people who, though not directly engaged in the confessional struggles of the period, believed they stood in the front ranks of the forces of reformed religion. Even more significantly, the doctrine had implications that extended beyond lay-clerical relations to the political realm. Bay colonists listened patiently each spring to election sermons that made frequent reference to Romans 13:1, with its injunction to obey "the governing authorities," their having "been instituted by God." But they did so in the knowledge that other parts of Scripture modified that declaration and—should the occasion arise—provided justification for ignoring it altogether. John Quincy's allusions to the doctrine reflected this understanding. So did a 1776 statement of his father's cousin Samuel. "Our forefathers," he said, "threw off the yoke of Popery in religion" by "open[ing] the Bible to all, and maintain[ing] the capacity of every man to judge for himself in religion." The time had now arrived to inaugurate "the reign of political Protestantism" by "leveling the popery of politics." That process, as he and John Quincy both knew, had begun much earlier in Massachusetts.[27]

A third factor influencing the emergence of the culture of conditional deference was the social composition of the population. Most early Bay migrants hailed from the middling ranks of English society, and political leaders soon learned that such people had their own ideas about how society should be governed. These artisans and yeomen farmers had no wish to bring magistrates down to their own level. They did, however, believe they had certain rights—rights that could not be protected without some form of power-sharing arrangement with colonial leaders. Their demands did not make John Winthrop happy, but there was no easy way to escape the unwelcome reality that people from the middling classes would not reflexively defer to those whom God and the Massachusetts Bay Company had appointed overseers of this errand into the North American wilderness. And while the Bay founder never fully accepted the legitimacy of popular demands for an ever-greater role in government, he did come to understand that the colony could never realize his vision of that errand without the willing compliance of everyone involved in the enterprise. His most capable successors would follow his example.[28]

The structure of authority that emerged over the next century had—apart from the governors who stood at its apex—three main elements. Town government, as it had since the first decade of settlement, formed the base of this structure. Although outside developments occasionally intruded on local affairs, townspeople for the most part paid little attention to what was happening elsewhere. What most concerned them occurred at annual town meetings, where community leaders made decisions about a host of questions related to the exigencies of daily life. Another element of the structure of authority was the provincial legislature. Given the house's reputation for truculence in its relations with royal governors, it is easy to imagine a body comprised largely of outspoken legislators from the countryside whose political skills had been honed to a fine edge by participation in town-meeting democracy. Such people could be found in the lower house, but they did not play a major policymaking role. The leadership group at most sessions numbered about a dozen or so individuals, half or more of whom hailed from eastern commercial towns and enjoyed educational and social advantages that enabled them to assume places at or near the top of the house hierarchy upon entering the assembly. Although this doubtless caused some resentment among country members, house responsiveness to local demands blunted their discontent. In its dealings with rural communities, the leadership group proved more than willing to mediate the numerous controversies that threatened social harmony in Bay towns.[29]

The third major component of this structure of authority was county government. It became a noteworthy force in Bay politics during the gubernatorial administrations of Jonathan Belcher (1730–1741) and William Shirley (1741–1756). Although royal governors had limited patronage at their disposal, what they did have—appointments of justices of the peace, court officers, and militia commanders—could be distributed in ways that influenced the balance of power in the General Court. The primary recipients were people of greater than average wealth who had demonstrated their commitment to crown interests through loyal service in the house. Within the counties where they resided, this patronage elite assumed a commanding role in political and social affairs. As justices of the peace and members of the Inferior Court of Common Pleas, they helped maintain social harmony by settling disputes in which the intransigence of aggrieved parties rendered the accommodative powers of towns ineffectual; as justices of the Court of General Sessions, they heard most criminal cases and exercised administrative authority on matters ranging from local taxation to road construction; and as militia commanders, their organization and leadership of county military units helped protect communities from attack during a period of frequent warfare. More than simply a means of bolstering royal political support outside Boston, the county patronage system also facilitated the consolidation of power at the county level by augmenting the authority of those political figures able to influence the selection process.[30]

Despite periodic disruptions, this structure of authority worked remarkably well. Towns deferred to county leaders and the lower house of assembly whenever necessary without any serious sacrifice of local autonomy. County leaders served as effective representatives of imperial rule in the countryside. And provincial governors managed to push through policies that kept Whitehall happy without alienating house members whose professions of loyalty never seemed entirely sincere to royal authorities with sufficient wit and experience to recognize how conditional they often were. By the mid-1770s, this system of governance would be in near total ruin, the victim of what historian Ray Raphael has called the "First American Revolution." The Massachusetts Government Act of 1774, in addition to limiting the operation of town government, replaced the province's elected council with crown-appointed mandamus councilors. Most of the appointees came from the ranks of county leaders who had played a critical mediational role in royal administration and now faced the wrath of angry crowd members disturbed by what they saw as a dire threat to their rights and liberties. More important than the individuals involved was what these county leaders had so recently represented: a dependable means of implementing royal policy within an integrated, province-wide structure of governance. When people no longer recognized their authority, Boston-based executive officials had no reason even to attempt sending orders to the countryside. There was no one there to receive, much less enforce, them.[31]

The shift from resistance to revolution after the outbreak of hostilities at Lexington and Concord completed the removal of those elite Loyalists who had dominated county government. Their departure created a political vacuum that exposed tensions between competing factions in many areas of Bay political life. The ensuing struggle for power was much less a conflict between the haves and the have-nots than a contest that pitted the well-connected against the less well-connected—people with ties to outside interests and friends in high places against people whose preoccupation with local developments and lingering resentments toward prewar elites left them reflexively distrustful of external encroachments on town and county affairs. Although the government formed by the Constitution of 1780 met with widespread acceptance, in many cases this assent was provisional, as questions remained about how responsive that government would be to the interests and needs of all citizens of the commonwealth. And when a mercantile-financial elite from the state's most developed towns established a dominant position in the General Court and pushed through tax and debt laws that enriched its members at the expense of less privileged groups, a series of crowd actions culminating in the Massachusetts Regulation of 1786 subjected the new government to its first serious test. As much a political as it was an economic movement, the regulation devoted as much attention to the distribution of power as it did to the distribution of wealth. A contemporaneous county convention movement reinforced the political character of the regulation. While convention attendees had no formal links to arms-bearing Shaysite rebels, the movement in effect functioned as the political arm of the regulation, providing a less confrontational alternative means of achieving the same objectives.[32]

The Regulation of 1786 prompted some of John Quincy's first observations on Bay politics. These comments revealed a strong commitment to an elitist version of the politics of conditional deference. Whatever difficulties Shaysite "malcontents" faced, he noted in his diary, they "must look to themselves, to their idleness, their dissipation and extravagance, for their grievances; these have led them to contract debts, and at the same time, rendered them incapable of paying them." He repeated these views in a college oration of the time, adding that the disturbances underscored the need for responsible elite leadership. It is not enough that public figures "lament our fondness for foreign fripperies, our extravagance, and idleness unless, they recommend, by their precepts and example, the opposite virtues of industry and oeconomy." Should they do so, he believed, "their example would soon be followed by the generality of the People, and all complaints of imaginary grievances, with their lawless and destructive consequences would soon be at an end." Meanwhile, he told his father, his greatest fear was that calls for "a pure democracy" might gain adherents and undermine the state's current form of government.[33]

Concerns about direct democracy remained a major preoccupation for Adams. In a series of articles for Boston's *Columbian Centinel* that marked his public debut as a political actor during the summer of 1791, the young lawyer directed his polemical fire at Thomas Paine's recently published work, *The Rights of Man*. He particularly objected to Paine's argument that no government based on anything less than absolute rule of the majority could hope to meet the needs of the current age. Such a government, Adams contended, would ultimately create more problems than it solved were its powers not constrained by a system of checks and balances that limited executive and legislative authority. Even more revealing of his views at the time was his response to a local controversy arising from elite efforts to replace the Boston town meeting with a ward-based form of government headed by a town council. When Benjamin Austin Jr., who had achieved notoriety some years earlier for a savage assault on the legal profession, declared the plan would "destroy the liberties of the people" and "throw the whole burden of taxation upon the poor," John Quincy could barely contain his indignation. Worse, Austin's objections carried the day. On the final vote, Adams wrote his brother, "seven hundred men, who looked as if they had been collected from all the Jails on the continent, with Ben. Austin like another Jack Cade, at their head outvoted by their numbers all the combined weight and influence of Wealth of Ability of Integrity of the whole Town." This sorry spectacle, he added, confirmed his "abhorrence and contempt of simple democracy as a Government." The outcome of a subsequent confrontation pitting Austin against *Centinel* editor Benjamin Russell over a point of honor made him even less happy. After Russell administered "a severe corporeal bruising," Austin charged that the editor had acted not to avenge a personal insult but to please "a few rich men, who were enraged at seeing the success with which he had advocated the cause of *the people*.—And such was the obsequious servility of the rabble, that in consequence of this suggestion, several hundred of them assembled the same evening; threatening to pull down Russell's printing office, and the houses of the *aristocrats* who wished to enslave the people, and actually paraded the street with clubs, and violent menaces for two or three hours."[34]

Two years later, Adams would be on his way to Europe to take up a diplomatic posting. When he returned in 1801, the Bay political scene had changed considerably. Notwithstanding incidents such as the Boston town meeting controversy, the 1790s was a time of relative quiescence within Massachusetts. This political calm did not last. Indeed, it might be seen as the second summer of the politics of conditional deference—an unseasonably warm period of seeming rejuvenation soon to be obliterated by the icy blasts of winter. The much-protracted demise of this venerable political culture had begun nearly fifty years earlier in sporadic challenges to the system of elite rule established under the late colonial structure of authority. Revolutionary era developments fed the middling-class resentments and aspirations that had prompted those challenges without significantly altering political relations within the state. These hopes and fears afterward found expression in the regulation and county convention movement of the 1780s. Although members of the Bay political elite managed to suppress the regulation and secure ratification of the US Constitution without engaging middling-class concerns about the distribution of power, discontent with the political status quo remained alive and well in the consciousness of those who believed "the richest, most notable or most intriguing" continued to dominate state government. Very often people of some prominence in their communities, these dissidents had no patience with a political system that limited their influence in county and state affairs. All they needed was an effective organizational outlet for their energies and ambitions, and by decade's end they had found it in Thomas Jefferson's Democratic-Republican Party. The elections of 1800 stand out as a turning point. As expected, favorite son John Adams easily captured the presidential vote, but the governor's race proved closer than anticipated, and Federalist retention of the office could not mask the growing strength of Bay Republicans in an electorate characterized by steadily rising voter turnout. Their party's capture of the nation's highest office, which gave Jeffersonians control of federal patronage distribution, added to Federalist anxieties about what the future held in store for them.[35]

Some Federalists sensed that the party had seen its best days even before the 1800 election. But they were exceptions, and it is here that the second summer metaphor breaks down. Where all New Englanders expect the coming of winter and prepare accordingly, few Federalists foresaw the challenges arising from the emergence of organized party opposition. Thrust headlong into the muck and mire of electoral competition, they belatedly recognized the need to strengthen their own party organization and devise means of engaging the general populace. On the organizational front, they formed a legislative caucus in 1800, followed four years later by the establishment of a state central committee to manage party affairs when the General Court was not in session. Party activists also created county and town committees to tighten links between state and local leaders and to coordinate voter mobilization efforts. These reforms gave sorely needed structure to a party that had heretofore functioned as a clique-ridden collection of independent-minded grandees and helped reverse the slide in Federalist fortunes.[36]

Adams took no part in these activities, such work being too clear a refutation of his belief in a politics without electioneering. That did not matter to Federalist leaders. As the son of a former president with a solid record of diplomatic service, he was just the type of person they wanted to put in office, and they persuaded him to run for a seat in the Massachusetts Senate, no doubt expecting that his election would seal the continuance of a long and happy relationship between the Boston lawyer and the party of the wise and the good. That is how things might have turned out but for one unfortunate Adams trait: a compulsion to question the motives of other political actors, whatever their party or social standing. Although John Quincy still hoped to see the establishment of a society governed by exemplars of republican virtue, he no longer felt as confident as he once had that this much-desired state of affairs could be readily achieved. Close contact with people of high status in diverse social settings had taught him that many such people were neither wise nor good. An 1802 bank controversy illustrated what all that meant in practical terms. When a group of wealthy Bostonians representing what Harrison Gray Otis called "all the great and respectable interests of the town" sought to charter a financial institution that restricted stock ownership to people of "respectable character," the initiative prompted widespread resistance from the excluded. Adams did not join critics such as "Public Good" who condemned the bank promoters as "rich purse-proud men" who believed they had a "prescriptive right" to control the local economy and urged the town's "middling interest" to demonstrate that "the people, should not only feel their own importance, but make others sensible of it." But neither could he support a measure that was so plainly the product of "[t]he mammon of unrighteousness."[37]

Federalist leaders were not pleased, and, as Adams later observed, the incident provided a sobering lesson in "the danger of opposing and of exposing corruption." Party bosses learned something as well: Adams bore close watching, lest he become "too unmanageable." Yet, despite their misgivings, they afterward arranged for his elevation to the US Senate when their first choice, Federalist hardliner Timothy Pickering, failed on two occasions to secure requisite support in the state legislature. Many of them came to regret the decision. Their dissatisfaction centered mainly on differences concerning the competing claims of region and nation. Ardent regionalists that they were, Bay Federalists hoped to resurrect their floundering political fortunes by posing as defenders of New England civilization. Adams took a broader view. America was destined to become "a Great and powerfull Nation" if it chose to do so, his mother told him as a young man preparing to enter Harvard. Never be unmindful of "her interests," she added, "but make her welfare your study and spend those hours which others devote to Cards and folly in investigating the Great principals by which nations have risen to Glory and eminence, for your Country will one day call for your services, either in the Cabinet or Field." John Quincy took the advice to heart, and when Federalist leaders condemned the Louisiana Purchase as a plot by "Virginia Lordlings" to undermine New England's wealth and power, he refused to follow their lead. Although not entirely unsympathetic to the regional appeal, Adams felt that securing control of the mouth of the Mississippi outweighed other considerations. "The loss of sectional influence," he later wrote, was a reasonable price to pay for "the extension of national power and security."[38]

Relations between Adams and Bay Federalists did not improve in the years that followed. With the collapse of the short-lived Peace of Amiens in 1803, the decade-old conflict between Britain and France resumed, as did British and French impositions on the nation's maritime commerce. Britain being by far the more formidable naval power, its actions attracted the most hostile notice. Tensions came to a head in June 1807, when HMS *Leopard* attacked the US frigate *Chesapeake* and impressed four of its crew. Wishing to avoid war but believing some response necessary, the Jefferson administration pushed an embargo bill through Congress that barred American vessels from sailing to foreign ports. The measure had a particularly adverse effect on New England towns dependent on transatlantic commerce, and regional Federalists wasted little time mounting a vigorous assault on the act. At its most charitable, the critique charged that Jeffersonians from the South and West, having no understanding of how the New England economy operated, had acted from ignorance. Other critics saw something much more sinister at work, and by the summer of 1808, party newspapers spoke increasingly of "Virginia Tyranny" and the malign intentions of "our Virginia Masters" in letters and editorials that portrayed the embargo as a mortal threat to the liberties and livelihood of New Englanders.[39]

As he had on the Louisiana Purchase, Adams parted company with his fellow Federalists on the issue. Despite serious reservations about the embargo's likely effectiveness, he saw no alternative apart from a recourse to war, which should always be a last resort. Other considerations had an even greater influence on his decision to back the administration. Not only did he feel that Americans had an obligation to support the president in moments of national crisis, but he believed the "party spirit and profligate ambition" motivating Federalist leaders had rendered them incapable of discerning, much less upholding, the national interest. His main adversary in the debate surrounding the question was his Senate colleague, Timothy Pickering—"a man," he later wrote, "of weak judgment, of violent prejudices, of great confidence in his own sagacity, of daring spirit and of turbulent disposition, sore with disappointment personally, and deeply embittered against Mr. Jefferson and his party, and boiling with hereditary hatred of" the Adams family, having once been dismissed from office by John Quincy's father. In a public letter to Harrison Gray Otis concerning statements Pickering made condemning the embargo that included adverse comments on his own position, Adams claimed that the Essex senator's aim was less to prevent war with Great Britain than to reconcile Americans "to the servitude of British protection, and war with all the rest of Europe." In making his case, Adams observed of Pickering, "not only are all the outrages of Britain to be forgotten, but the very assertion of our rights is to be branded with odium. *Impressment. Neutral trade. British taxation*. Everything that can distinguish a state of national freedom from a state of national vassalage, is to be *surrendered at discretion*." In the wake of this effusion, any hope he had of remaining in the Senate disappeared, and he resigned his seat before being formally removed by the Federalist-controlled state legislature. But he did not go quietly. Reviewing a recently published collection of Federalist firebrand Fisher Ames's writings the following year, he declared that they revealed all too clearly the guiding principles of the "petty majority" in the General Court: "SUSERVIENCY to Britain—Abhorrence of France—and contempt of the American people." More than that, he wrote in words dripping with sarcasm, Ames's essays and correspondence "furnished food for that modest and generous opinion which [Federalist leaders] delight to entertain; that all the virtue and all the talents, as well as all the wealth of the American continent, is a monopoly of their own, and the rest of the people are a mere herd of Sodom, to be saved from the fire of Heaven only by *their* transcendent merits."[40]

At this juncture in Adams's political life, several things stand out. One was his partial abandonment of the politics of conditional deference. He would always have reservations about democracy, and no one would ever have occasion to laud him as a champion of the common man. But his Federalist experience removed most traces of the snobbish elitism of earlier years. If he still believed certain people better suited than others to assume the responsibilities of government, he now knew that the talent and wisdom required to carry out those duties were not confined to any single social group. Whatever misgivings he had about the current state of government, he wasted little time in wistful reveries of a golden age of American politics; he understood that the good old days had not been nearly as good as some people made them out to be. Meanwhile, many of his former Federalist colleagues, recognizing that their differences with him went beyond questions of policy, viewed him with the same disdain that he did them. Should Adams ever become president, one of them observed in an 1816 letter, "all of N.E. that is virtuous and enlightened, will be persecuted & degraded; manners, laws, principles will be changed and deteriorated." Adams's later relations with members of the manufacturing and financial elite that came to dominate Whig politics in Massachusetts were generally more amicable but—with a few exceptions—never particularly close. Peter Chardon Brooks, an Adams in-law and reputedly the wealthiest person in Boston, doubtless spoke for many of his social peers when he said that he lived in fear of what John Quincy might do, he being "so apt to act independently" and so "set about everything which he once assumes." Adding to those fears were the ways in which Adams's loose attachment to party organization combined with a zest for partisan warfare. The aversion to party discipline that marked his Federalist years would resurface during his post-presidential return to Congress; so would that rare talent for political invective that he brought to any issue he deemed worthy of his support. All in all, these are not the attributes and conduct typical of a successful politician, and it is no surprise that Adams never became a major power broker in Bay politics. In this, he could not have differed more from John Calhoun, who, for much of his long political career, had no equal in his mastery of South Carolina political culture.[41]

Even more so than with Adams, provincial and state political culture did much to shape Calhoun's views on government and society. Here, too, it is best to start at the beginning, with an examination of the considerable gap between Old World assumptions and New World realities that marked the early development of nearly all colonial ventures. Somewhere between the London council rooms in which the promoters of such enterprises laid their plans and the unfamiliar landscape of the North American continent, something invariably got lost in translation. Where Virginia had its "Starving Time," Bay magistrates soon realized that the rigorous system of labor discipline devised by directors of the Massachusetts Bay Company was hopelessly impractical. South Carolina was no exception to this general rule. The Fundamental Constitutions of Carolina (1669) called for the creation of an elaborate feudal structure unlike anything seen elsewhere in British America. Land distribution was based on a complex system of seignories, baronies, and colonies that gave control of forty percent of Carolina lands to the proprietors and a local nobility of landgraves and cassiques. In terms of government, eight separate courts or councils with well-defined functions would handle major administrative tasks. And members of these courts, together with the eight proprietors, would form a grand council that set the legislative agenda for a unicameral parliament consisting of the proprietors or their deputies, local nobles, and representatives of the freemen. Although unwilling to share power with the freemen, the proprietors were not completely insensitive to their concerns. In an effort to attract settlers, they established a generous land policy and provided for religious toleration—a matter of no small significance during a period when a series of parliamentary measures imposed various civil disabilities on English dissenters.[42]

Such enticements notwithstanding, signs that settlement in Carolina would not proceed according to plan appeared early. Not only did freemen resist repayment of cash advances made by the proprietors, but they ignored instructions to conduct a systematic land survey and refused to settle in compact townships. Worse, political factionalism caused a frequent turnover of governors and hampered the establishment of governmental stability. The main source of disruption was a formidable cohort of Barbadian immigrants whose hard-driving, independent-minded, and avaricious members had no compunction about ignoring or evading rules that impeded fulfillment of their acquisitive schemes. Having moved to Carolina to make their fortune, they had little use for laws or anything else that stood in their way. With the formation of a Commons House of Assembly that sat as a separate body and claimed the right to initiate legislation, their power increased and proprietorial authority suffered a further decline.

In light of these developments, it is less surprising that proprietorial rule came to an ignominious conclusion than that it lasted as long as it did. A major turning point was the Yamasee War of 1715–1717, which, apart from the considerable financial costs it imposed on Carolinians, took the lives of four hundred people, destroyed most coastal settlements south of Charlestown, and forced the abandonment of about half of the province's cultivated land. That fears of sacrificing their charter rights had prompted the proprietors to refuse offers of royal assistance during the conflict, while doing nothing on their own to aid embattled colonists, raised serious questions about the continuing value of proprietorial rule. A bad situation got considerably worse when the proprietors afterward announced plans to raise land prices, insisted on passage of a measure providing for the effective collection of quitrents, and annulled legislation designed to improve electoral practices, pay for the Yamasee War, and promote immigration. Their further demand that no new law be put into effect without their first having reviewed it added to the growing rage of provincial freemen. When, in 1719, the proprietors appeared unprepared to bolster colonial defenses in the face of mounting evidence of an imminent Spanish attack, Carolinians decided it was time to take matters into their own hands and seek royal protection. The bloodless revolution of that year ended an experiment in colonial development that—as even some of the proprietors realized—had failed decades earlier.

Perhaps the most illuminating account of these events was a 1726 pamphlet by Francis Yonge. It was so less because of the author's treatment of specific provincial grievances than the interpretive framework he adopted. To understand the Revolution of 1719, Yonge wrote, one must recognize that some combination of "*Love, Fear,* or *Interest*" served as the foundation of all government. Through their self-seeking conduct, which subordinated the public good to their quest for profit, the proprietors had forfeited any claim they might have had to the affection of Carolinians. Particularly disturbing was their failure "to succor and protect then" from the threats posed by Native American uprisings and Spanish invasion. This not only revealed the proprietors' inability to assuage the legitimate fears of colonists but exposed their own weakness. That being the case, Carolinians "judg'd it plainly their Interest to be under the Crown, who could and would protect them, and also (as they hoped) to put them in the same Circumstances" as other colonies that could rely on royal assistance.[43]

The love, fear, and interest model of political culture has applications that go well beyond South Carolina. To cite but a few examples, the three elements can all be found in the local resolutions on independence issued by various localities during the spring and summer of 1776; and it requires little ingenuity to show how the interaction of love, fear, and interest formed major signposts on the road Massachusetts Federalists travelled from staunch support for the government created by the US Constitution to the discontented sectionalism of the Hartford Convention. Yet the model has special relevance for the political history of the Palmetto State. In addition to providing a framework for examining relations between South Carolina and the national government, it serves as a useful explanatory device for the analysis of political relations within the state; as later chapters will demonstrate, the model can also be employed to furnish insightful perspective on major changes in the political thought of John C. Calhoun. The main reason for the model's broad applicability is no mystery. In few other places on the North American mainland did a people's worst fears and most extravagant material aspirations so tightly cohere in a single institution: chattel slavery. Where, in the quarter century after 1670, Africans—most of them from the West

Indies—constituted about twenty-five percent of Carolina's population, by the 1710s they had become a majority, and an ever-growing proportion of them came directly from Africa as planters turned increasingly to the transatlantic slave trade to meet their labor demands. With the continued expansion of rice production, Africans outnumbered white people by a two-to-one margin province-wide by 1730; in some Lowcountry parishes, the ratio was substantially greater.[44]

As Carolina made the transition from a frontier to a plantation economy during the early decades of the eighteenth century, it became one of the wealthiest provinces in British North America. And everyone understood the critical role that African slaves played in this transformation. With "few exceptions," one writer observed in a 1763 tract, they "do all the labour or hard work in the country, and are a considerable part of the riches of the province." John Drayton went even further in his later study of state resources. "With as much propriety might we expect [planters] to dismiss their horses from the plough; as for us to dismiss these people from labour," he observed. "For in both cases, lands of excellent quality, which are cultivated by them, would revert to a state of nature." Indeed, he added, "had not this agricultural strength been furnished South-Carolina, it is probable, in the scale of commerce and importance, she would have been numbered among the least respectable states in the union." Various commentators explained why this was so. The South is "scarcely surpassed in fertility by any region in the world," a speaker told members of the state agricultural society in an 1829 address, "but wherever the principal sources of national wealth—Cotton Rice and Sugar—flourish, it is physically impossible for a white man to cultivate them." Unlike white Southerners, for whom arduous manual labor "has always proved fatal," African slaves could withstand the harshness of the regional climate "with neither danger nor inconvenience," said another defender of South Carolina's peculiar institution: "The torrid sun has no terrors for him; and the hot breath of the South, before which the white labourer faints and perishes, is found to be accordant with the constitution of the black." Perhaps recognizing that he had taken his racist mythologizing a step too far, this writer hastened to assure readers that none of this diminished the need for slavery, it being "vain and idle to pretend, that in a hot and sultry climate, where every thing invites even the more diligent white to indolence, that the slothful negro would labour without compulsion."[45]

However South Carolinians framed their defense of human bondage, interest could never be divorced from fear. As the author of the 1763 tract cited above wrote, slaves "are in this climate necessary, but very dangerous domestics, their number so much exceeding the whites." The latter knew this all too well. Large as the province's slave population was in fact becoming, white South Carolinians routinely overestimated its actual size. Had this been their only concern, they could have slept more peacefully than they did. But try as one might, nobody could escape the constant reminders of the perils posed by the province's dependence on an ever-expanding slave labor force. Where news of Caribbean slave revolts stirred deep foreboding in the minds of all but the constitutionally unimaginative, events closer to home were much more troubling. Although slave awareness of the suicidal consequences of assaulting white people limited such incidents, the poisoning of masters occurred often enough to raise questions as to whether even house servants could be trusted. No less alarming were the periodic rumors of slave conspiracies and the frequent fires of the period, many of which—particularly those resulting in the destruction of rice barns and planters' homes—occasioned suspicion of slave arson, regardless of whether they could be credibly attributed to any specific culprit. When the great Charleston fire of 1740 engulfed large areas of the town, some feared it might be the prelude to a slave insurrection. They had good reason to do so, as the previous year's Stono Rebellion had taken the lives of more than twenty white settlers. In its wake, a report prepared by the Commons House of Assembly expressed regret that Carolinians "could not enjoy the Benefits of Peace like the rest of Mankind and that our own Industry should be the means of taking from us all the Sweets of Life and of rendering us Liable to the Loss of our Lives and Fortunes." Such was life in a society where fear and interest were so inextricably bound together.[46]

Efforts to resolve the dilemma proceeded along several tracks. One involved the crafting of a revamped slave code that called for stricter enforcement of laws restricting slaves' freedom of movement and assembly, curtailing their ability to grow food and earn money, and curbing slave literacy. Another was to limit slave importations, which declined markedly during the 1740s before rising again afterward. Carolinians also took steps to promote white immigration. These included renewed support for a government-subsidized township scheme begun during the gubernatorial administration of Robert Johnson (1730–1735) that was designed to strengthen frontier defenses and create a middle-country counterweight to the Lowcountry's burgeoning slave population. At the same time, provincial leaders attempted to tap into the growing stream of backcountry settlers moving southward from Pennsylvania into Virginia and North Carolina through the offer of free land in frontier areas. These latter initiatives worked about as well as could be expected. Throughout the 1740s, increasing numbers of white settlers established farms in areas outside the older coastal region of settlement. And by the mid-1760s, many backcountry locales had achieved a modest prosperity marked by increased production for Lowcountry and world markets.[47]

Despite these economic advances, not all was well. Social divisions within the backcountry had caused mounting anger, trepidation, and fear among the region's more successful farmers and planters. The main source of anxiety were local bands of hunters, bandits, and others uncommitted to a settled existence who not only offended their sense of propriety but disrupted their daily lives and threatened the region's future development. According to Charles Woodmason, an Anglican itinerant who emerged as a major spokesperson for the forces of law and order, "the Depredations of Robbers" had taken a major toll on a people who appeared to have no other function than to ease Lowcountry apprehensions by serving "as a Barrier between the Rich Planters and the Indians, to secure the former against the Latter." What made the situation particularly problematic was the weak institutional structure of most backcountry settlements. "Without Laws or Government Churches or Ministers—No Police established—and all Property quite insecure," Woodmason added, "Merchants are fearful to venture Goods as Ministers their Persons—The Lands though the finest in the Province unoccupied, and rich Men afraid to set Slaves to work to clear them, lest they should become a Prey to the Banditti." Faced with such disorder and uncertainty, people had no incentive to undertake further improvements: "No New Plans can take Place—Nothing in the Common Round can be executed, till Legislation is extended to Us."[48]

Much to the dismay and frustration of backcountry leaders, the desired legislation was not immediately forthcoming. They sought the creation of an effective court system that would enable them to deal with lawless elements and establish some semblance of order, but provincial authorities did not take their demands seriously. "How lamentable to think," Woodmason exclaimed, "that the Legislature of the Province will make no Provision—so rich, so luxurious, polite a People!" They wanted the security provided by white settlement of the backcountry, but they appeared to have little interest in establishing the civic and legal infrastructure required to create a solid foundation for such settlement. It almost seemed, Woodmason wrote, that they viewed people of the region "as if We were of a different Species from themselves: Reproaching us for our Ignorance and Unpoliteness, while they themselves contribute to it" by doing nothing to assist backcountry proponents of law and order. The Anglican itinerant was not the only one who felt this way, and as it became clear that they would not receive the assistance they demanded, backcountry leaders donned the cloak of regulators and mounted their own campaign against discordant elements in regional society. In addition to breaking up bandit gangs, Woodmason reported, they "burnt the Dwellings of all their Harbourers and Abettors—Whipp'd and drove the Idle, Vicious and Profligate out of the Province," and, had some of them had their way, "would have proceeded to Charlestown in a Regular Corp of 5000 Men, and hung up the Rogues before the State House in Presence of Governor and Council." As these observations suggest, the regulation had by its later stages shifted its focus from the prevention of criminal conduct to the imposition of work discipline. Never simply a program of bandit suppression, it also represented an effort to turn the "lower people" into productive members of society—the type of respectable, hard-working individuals who could be counted upon to fill any labor shortages that might arise in a growing economy.[49]

The regulation represented an important stage in the evolution of relations between backcountry leaders and Lowcountry elites. Unlike neighboring North Carolina, where a contemporaneous regulator movement mobilized backcountry settlers in armed defiance of the intimidation, exploitation, and oppression of coastal elites and local officeholders, South Carolina regulators did not view provincial leaders as avaricious adversaries intent on self-enrichment at their expense. Nor is there any reason why they should have. Tidewater legislators had no wish to see areas outside the coastal plain become havens for runaway slaves and believed the creation of a stable, flourishing backcountry was in everyone's self-interest. Accordingly, they supported regulator objectives, and their failure to carry them through more expeditiously owed less to indifference than to imperial obstruction. Although they strongly condemned later regulator excesses such as the whipping of magistrates unwilling to deal severely with people considered brigands or layabouts, they nevertheless responded with considerable restraint. And with the passage of the Circuit Court Act, tensions began to abate. This hardly placed relations between the two sections on a cordial basis. On one hand, Lowcountry arrogance and condescension were no figment of Charles Woodmason's imagination; on the other, coastal planters worried about the depth of backcountry commitment to slavery and sound government. At the same time, however, they had learned that they could no longer take the region for granted if it was to fulfill its assigned role in the provision of provincial security.[50]

Despite this new awareness of the need to be more responsive to backcountry grievances, Lowcountry leaders were not prepared to address all regulator demands. This was particularly so on the question of legislative reapportionment. Even though two-thirds of South Carolina's white inhabitants resided in the backcountry, Woodmason observed, regional representatives occupied only six of fifty seats in the provincial legislature. "It is to this Great Disproportion on our Part that our Interests have been so long neglected," he maintained, and Charlestonians would do well to recognize that "it is the Number of *Free Men*, not *Black Slaves*, that constitute the Strength and Riches of a State." This was precisely the kind of argument that tidewater planters found most alarming, and they accordingly dismissed the complaint. Backcountry leaders continued to press the issue, and while the state constitutions of 1776 and 1778 made the apportionment of legislative seats less blatantly inequitable, these changes did not go nearly far enough to quiet agitation of the matter. In 1790, Carolinians gathered for another round of constitutional revision. This time Lowcountry leaders grudgingly submitted to the long-standing demand that the state capital be moved inland from Charleston to Columbia, which made it considerably easier for backcountry representatives to attend legislative sessions. They also made further concessions on the regional distribution of House and Senate seats, but backcountry leaders were still not satisfied. In a 1794 pamphlet signed by prestigious regional figures such as Wade Hampton, Robert Goodloe Harper of the Ninety Six district declared that South Carolina, being a state in which "four fifths of the people are governed by one fifth," met "the very definition of aristocracy" in its willingness to give a relatively small group of wealthy planters "the power of making laws to bind the rest." Speaking to a major concern of coastal elites, Harper agreed that the property of the rich deserved protection; it should never, however, "be directly represented" when doing so accorded certain people "different and more numerous political rights than their neighbours, whose master they would thus become."[51]

Although Charlestonians beat back the challenge of the mid-1790s, some of the more thoughtful defenders of the status quo held out the possibility of reconciliation at some future date. Where the wealthy Lowcountry planter Ralph Izard felt transportation improvements could reduce economic differences between the two sections by creating a basis for increased market exchange, the eminent lawyer Henry William DeSaussure looked to the emergence of a responsible backcountry elite capable of keeping local dissidents in check. Once people of the region were "guided by Men of Education and settled principles of government," he wrote, Lowcountry leaders would be willing to consider plans to establish a more equitable apportionment of legislative seats. As it turned out, economic developments of the next decade removed many of these reservations. The gradual spread of cotton culture throughout large areas of the backcountry following the introduction of an efficient cotton gin in the mid-1790s initiated a major sociodemographic transformation that turned what had been a society with slaves into a slave society. Between 1790 and 1810, inland South Carolina witnessed a major surge in slave population and an equally marked decline in the rate of population increase among white people. If still largely a region of yeoman farmers, it was clear that it would not remain so for long. And if Black-white population ratios in the backcountry would never approach those found in rice-growing areas of the coastal plain, no one could any longer doubt the region's commitment to the state's peculiar institution.[52]

It was during these years that John Calhoun made his debut on the SC political stage. At the time, he was feeling somewhat disillusioned with his chosen profession, having begun the study of law in 1803 with great expectations. His belief that only those possessed of "a strong and comprehensive mind connected with assiduous application" could achieve "any considerable perfection in a science so complicated" made the challenge of mastering it particularly appealing. After all, he asked, "[w]ere the law so simple and concise as to be attainable by every one, with moderate application and abilities, where would be the honour of its application?" This lofty view of the profession did not last. Like Adams, who developed a similar aversion to the legal vocation, Calhoun found the actual practice of law a rather dreary business, and, despite his able representation of a growing list of clients, he soon recognized that a lifetime spent in various courtrooms could never satisfy his ambitions. He needed something more, and in the fall of 1808 he secured election to the South Carolina House of Representatives.[53]

Five months before Calhoun entered the legislature it had approved a constitutional amendment that effectively brought the sectional dispute to a close. The Compromise of 1808 established a system of legislative apportionment based on white population and taxable wealth that provided increased representation to backcountry areas as they acquired the affluence made possible by the adoption of plantation agriculture. Legislative control would thus be in the hands of a backcountry majority that could be counted upon to protect Lowcountry planters from the passage of adverse laws on slavery-related issues. It is unclear what—if anything—Calhoun contributed to debate on the issue, but there can be little doubt that he supported the compromise. If nothing else, beliefs that he had absorbed from his father would have predisposed him to view the settlement in a positive light. In most respects, Patrick Calhoun exemplified what DeSaussure had in mind when he spoke of the need for backcountry leaders with "settled principles of Government." As a strong proponent of law and order, he had championed enactment of a vagrancy law to facilitate the assault on backcountry indolence during the regulation; as an entrepreneurially minded landowner, he had supported passage of a 1785 measure that would have removed obstacles to land speculation in the backcountry; and as a staunch defender of property rights, he had sided with Charlestonians in their opposition to debtor relief legislation during the mid-1780s. This latter concern likely explains why he opposed contemporaneous calls for a constitutional convention because he believed "the general mass of the people were so much bent for a democratical government" that such a gathering "would do more harm than good." Even more important his position as one of the largest slaveowners in the backcountry left no doubt about where he stood on that vital question. The younger Calhoun shared all of these views. That he served his legal apprenticeship in DeSaussure's Charleston law office almost certainly deepened his awareness of Lowcountry sensibilities on major issues of the day.[54]

Over time, principles embodied in the Compromise of 1808 became integral parts of Calhoun's political thought. Nearly four decades later, when political reformers sought to replace the practice of having state legislators choose presidential electors with a general ticket extending the right to all qualified voters, Calhoun's condemnation of the proposal rested squarely on his interpretation of the compromise. The 1808 settlement had established a state of "perfect equality" that, he contended, gave each of the state's two major divisions "the power of protecting itself against the injustice and oppression of the other." Should this balance be disturbed by permitting a numerical majority from one section to impose its will on people in the other section, the ensuing decline of social and political amity would have an adverse effect on the lives of all South Carolinians. "Discord, distraction, parties and factions, with all their machinery and demoralizing consequences, would follow, and sink [the state] far below the level she now occupies." The problem, he explained, was that proponents of the reform mistakenly assumed that numerical majorities represented the state as a whole. This was not so, at least not in South Carolina. "Our State is organized on the far broader and more solid and durable foundation, of the concurrent majority," which enabled minority groups to defend their interests against the impositions of numerical majorities. Rather than increasing political stability within the state, he contended, adopting the general ticket would "introduce a new element, calculated to subvert and destroy the very foundation on which its organization rests."[55]

These and related views will be examined at greater length in later chapters. It is necessary here to underscore the significance that elite South Carolinians attached to the Compromise of 1808. After four decades of sometimes rancorous debate over legislative apportionment that often raised disturbing questions about planter privileges, they had arranged a settlement that permitted them to pose as champions of representative government while retaining the authority to curb democratic excesses on the part of the state's nonslaveholding white population. It may have been as close as they ever came to resolving the fear-interest dilemma. Although nothing short of emancipation could fully eliminate the apprehension engendered by an enslaved Black majority, they had taken a major step toward forging what historian Rachel N. Klein has called "the South's most unified and politically powerful leadership." These developments formed the context for the next stage in Calhoun's political career. In 1811, after his cousin Joseph resigned his seat in Congress to make way for his talented kinsman, the South Carolinian was on his way to Washington. There, during a period of rising international tensions, he would be able to give free vent to his nationalist sentiments without having to worry about the effect federal–state relations might have on South Carolina. There, too, he would have occasion to work together with an expansion-minded New England diplomat to advance their shared interest in empire.[56]

Chapter 2

NATIONALISM and EMPIRE

Few public figures of the early national period were more closely identified with the development of American foreign policy than John Quincy Adams. Training and experience had amply prepared him for the role. A widely read student of historical and contemporary societies who had spent much of his youth in various European capitals, he possessed the analytical and linguistic skills required of a first-rate diplomat. During the presidencies of Washington and his father, he represented the United States in the Netherlands and Prussia. Later service as James Madison's minister to Russia and a member of the delegation that conducted the talks ending the War of 1812 added to his reputation as an authority on international affairs. Afterward, he received the prestigious and critically important post of minister to Great Britain. In all these positions, Adams performed with distinction, doing whatever appeared necessary to uphold US interests and composing the sorts of well-informed, insightful reports that secretaries of state looked forward to reading. When the last secretary under whom he served, James Monroe, made him head of the State Department in his administration, the appointment seemed perfectly natural to all but a handful of presidential aspirants who coveted the job as a means of furthering their own ambitions. Adams, who negotiated the Transcontinental Treaty with Spain and was the primary author of the Monroe Doctrine while at the department, gave the president little reason to regret the choice.

As an exponent of American nationalism, John Calhoun in many respects functioned as a domestic counterpart to Adams. Where the New Englander sought to expand the national domain and prevent further European colonization in the Americas, the South Carolinian worked to promote national unity, strengthen the military, and remove obstacles to white settlement of the continental interior. In Congress during the period preceding the War of 1812, Calhoun assumed a conspicuous place in the front ranks of those legislators calling for the initiation of hostilities with Great Britain. When he subsequently realized how unprepared the nation was to engage one of the world's major powers in an extended conflict, he labored diligently to provide the resources needed to prosecute a war that, on too many occasions, gave greater cause for despair than elation. In the period immediately following the Treaty of Ghent, he did what he could to ensure that the nation would never again be so vulnerable to foreign attack by supporting measures designed to repair the country's shattered financial system, bolster economic self-sufficiency, and forge stronger intersectional linkages through government subsidization of internal improvements. This broad-ranging national perspective, which brought him to Monroe's attention, later informed Calhoun's actions as the Virginian's secretary of war. During his tenure at the War Department, he not only helped implement programs to improve military organization, efficiency, and training, but devoted considerable time to clearing the way for western settlement by implementing policies designed to remove Native Americans living east of the Mississippi from their ancestral homelands.

It has long been a commonplace of American historiography that the period following the War of 1812 witnessed a surge in nationalist sentiment. One might well question how intense or extensive the phenomenon was in a country where a large proportion of the minority of the populace affected by the conflict wanted nothing more afterward than to resume the familiar rhythms of their prewar lives. Yet something of the sort did occur, and historians seeking evidence to support the traditional interpretation need look no further than the writings and addresses of Adams and Calhoun. This chapter reviews some of that evidence, beginning with an examination of their response to the war and the lessons they derived from it. Subsequent sections look at major features of their exertions as cabinet secretaries in Monroe's administration. Throughout, the emphasis will be on the ways in which the beliefs and actions of each of them paralleled and complemented those of the other. Although competing presidential ambitions would have a cooling effect on their initially warm relationship, Adams and Calhoun unfailingly demonstrated a resolute commitment to nationalism and empire during these years.

As countless policymakers and general officers have learned over the years, wars rarely proceed according to plan. Few conflicts better illustrate the truth of this maxim than the War of 1812. Militarily, it was a conflict that changed almost nothing. Successive American efforts to conquer Canada went nowhere, British inland offensives proved equally unsuccessful, and the most decisive battle of the war—Andrew Jackson's destruction of British forces at New Orleans—took place two weeks after the signing of the peace treaty that ended the conflict. When one turns to a consideration of the nation's stated war aims, it is hard to avoid a similarly dispiriting conclusion. The Treaty of Ghent not only restored all lands taken by either side to the original owner, but it made little mention of impressment or any of the other grievances contained in President Madison's 1812 war message to Congress. Although the United States did annex part of Spanish Florida in 1813, the war was for the most part a draw diplomatically as well as militarily.

Adams was not altogether surprised by the conflict's outcome. He had regretted the decision to commence hostilities while there was still a chance to avoid war and wished Congress had given the matter greater consideration. His reluctance did not stem from any lack of patriotism. John Quincy's nationalism had the deep roots one would expect of a son of Abigail and John Adams. As a boy standing beside his mother on a neighboring hillside, he had witnessed the Battle of Bunker Hill, where the Adams physician and close family acquaintance, Dr. Joseph Warren, gave his life in defense of American independence. Nearly three decades later, he could still vividly recall major events of the period. "I remember the melting of pewter spoons in our house into bullets after the 19th of April, 1775," he wrote in an 1813 letter to his son. "I remember the smoke and the flames of Charlestown which I saw from the orchard on Penn's hill. I remember the picking up and the sending away of books and furniture from the reach of Gage's troops while we ourselves were hourly exposed for many months to have been butchered by them." The Fourth of July and the Declaration of Independence would occupy special places in his civic consciousness until the day he died.[1]

What most troubled Adams about the decision for war was the nation's unpreparedness to engage a battle-hardened British military. "Now until a real and respectable force shall be raised, organized, systematically provided for by substantial revenue, and prepared for vigorous action," he observed several months before Madison delivered his war message, "I should hold it impossible to commence war with England, and I hope that no such measure will be taken." When it was, the ensuing debacles went beyond even his dire forebodings. Military operations "have been hitherto conducted in a manner which I wish it were in my power and in that of the whole world to forget," he wrote his father in a January 1813 letter, "but which will be too long and too effectually remembered." Although ready to endure some setbacks, he said several weeks later, "I did not indeed anticipate that within six months from the Commencement of the War" that US land forces would be "the scorn and laughter of all Europe," their ineptitude redeemed "only by the exploits of our Navy upon the Ocean." But, he asked, "with a feeble and penurious government, with five frigates for a navy and scarcely five efficient regiments for an army, how can it be expected we should resist the mass of force that gigantic power has collected to crush us at a blow?" The conflict could, he later concluded, best be seen as a war without winners. "It consisted not merely of battles won and lost, but every incident on one side or the other wounded the pride or mortified the feelings of the nation," he remarked in a somber postmortem. "Our naval victories sting the British to the quick, while the ineffable disgrace of our military discomfitures in Canada, and the shameful disaster at Washington," where an invading army burned much of the city to the ground, "still grate upon every national fibre that we possess."[2]

Whatever his reservations about the decision for war, Adams had no doubt whatsoever about the justice of the American cause. Impressment alone constituted an "ineradicable wound which, if persisted in, can terminate no otherwise than by war." The maritime communities of coastal Massachusetts had long been a vital component of the state economy, and Adams viewed their defense as a matter of regional interest and personal honor. Just as his father had in the talks preceding the Treaty of Paris, John Quincy refused—"as a Citizen of Massachusetts"—to consider any proposal at Ghent that would restrict access to the North Atlantic fisheries. Practices that violated the most fundamental rights of the nation's sailors deeply angered him. Although he did not react quite as strongly to British restrictions on American trade, he did feel the issue needed to be addressed at some point or another. "To forgo the right of navigating the ocean," he observed several months before the declaration of war, "would be a pusillanimity which of itself would degrade us from the rank and rights of an independent nation." And once hostilities began, he temporarily abandoned his lifelong aversion to armed conflict and wondered whether the war might not have been necessary to maintain "the Spirit of Independence." His father certainly believed so. "Had this Nation continued at Peace," the elder Adams remarked in a July 1813 letter, "the American Nation would have been as timorous as a Warren of Hares, and might have been decoyed and Slaughtered like Plovers Pidgeons, or Brants, the Silliest of the Birds of the Air." John Quincy elaborated on the point not long afterward. "There are energies in the Constitution of Man which a long protracted Peace always weakens, and sometimes extinguishes altogether," he told his brother. "Occasional War is one of the rigorous instruments in the hands of Providence to give tone to the character of Nations."[3]

Another such instrument, and one that Adams worried about constantly, was the preservation of national unity. Without it, he believed, the nation might all too easily take on the worst features of what he called "the European *condition of society*"—a land of warring states in which the maintenance of large standing armies needlessly wasted scarce resources and made life miserable for a groaning populace. The need for unity became especially important whenever foreign adversaries decided to test American resolve. "For my own part," he observed during the French troubles of the late 1790s, "I believe that in our country the government can never carry through any war, unless the strong, unequivocal voice of the people leads them into it. The impulse must go from the circumference to the center." From his St. Petersburg vantage point, Adams had no way of determining how effectively the Madison administration had met that condition in the months preceding the onset of hostilities. The lackluster performance of American forces inspired little confidence that it had done enough. Worse, there was at least one influential group that could be expected to do whatever it could to undermine the war effort. Massachusetts Federalist leaders, he believed, had been trying since at least 1804 to establish a Northern confederacy, and he had no doubt they would use the conflict to further their secessionist aims. His fears in this regard were based more on personal malice than on sober analysis, and he could later take some satisfaction in the popular abuse directed at New England Federalists following the Hartford Convention. Even then, Adams continued to suspect his former colleagues, observing that their nefarious designs "will be watered into bloom again by the first shower of public calamity that may occur." And disunion being "the only fatal mischief which in the natural course of events can for many ages befall our country," he "hope[d] that a school not less ardent and zealous, and far more wise and learned, will be reared at the same time to repel and explode [their] errors."[4]

Providing safeguards to check Federalist separatism was the least important of the lessons that Adams drew from the war. With the coming of peace, he worried that Americans would remember only such highpoints as Andrew Jackson's victory at New Orleans and forget the many occasions on which US forces betrayed shocking incompetence or lacked the resources to carry the day in major engagements. "They look too intently to their triumphs, and turn their eyes away too lightly from their disasters," he told his father. "It was a war from which, if the account of disgrace and glory were fairly balanced, we should have something, but not much to boast of." People needed to be asking about how much suffering resulted from the nation's near total lack of preparation and what could be done to prevent recurrences of these calamities. Adams could not "imagine a possible state of the world for futurity in which United States shall not be a great naval and military power," and he believed there would never be a better time than the present to persuade a penurious Congress to make the necessary appropriations. As his father had during and after the revolution, he placed particular emphasis on the formation of a powerful navy. The nation's maritime rights would never be secure without a naval force capable of defending them; it was the only language Great Britain understood. Indeed, he later remarked, the war might never have occurred had Jefferson recognized the importance of developing a strong navy. And this was only the most conspicuous of the various national shortcomings exposed by the conflict. If the country hoped to assume its rightful place in the international order, it would do well to furnish the tariff protection required to promote the growth of domestic manufactures, to establish a basis for a stable financial system through the creation of a national bank, and to finance construction of the roads and canals needed to improve the abysmal state of the nation's transportation network.[5]

As ambassador to Great Britain, Adams was in no position to influence legislation on these and related matters. Those who could do so included a young congressman from South Carolina whose disappointment over the nation's prosecution of the war matched—if it did not exceed—that of the New Englander. Unlike Adams, John Calhoun had viewed the prospect of war without fear and without foresight. An outspoken member of a legislative group that Virginia's John Randolph dubbed the War Hawks, he had no patience with people who thought "national honor and interest" might be upheld through negotiation, nonimportation legislation, or some other form of economic coercion. He had equally little patience with those who questioned the nation's readiness to confront Great Britain on the field of battle. "So far from being unprepared, sir," he told Randolph, "I believe that, in four weeks from the time that a declaration of war is heard on our frontier, the whole of Upper and a part of Lower Canada will be in our possession." Those fainthearted moderates who counseled caution and restraint had no conception of what was at stake, for there could be no question about the justice of the American cause or the necessity of war. "This is the second struggle for liberty; and, if we do but justice to ourselves, it will be no less glorious and successful than the first," Calhoun declared on the floor of Congress. "Let us but exert ourselves, and we must meet with the prospering smile of Heaven."[6]

Although Calhoun doubtless would have been more circumspect had he known how long he would have to wait for that smile, he did not lose the courage of his convictions during the dark days ahead. As reports of military setbacks piled up, consistently overshadowing more positive news, Calhoun labored tirelessly to support the war effort: speaking on behalf of bills for increased appropriations, working to prevent war-weary colleagues from losing faith, monitoring military preparations, and regularly visiting the War Department to see what was being done with regard to recruiting and the acquisition of war materiel. He also sought to rebut the arguments of a growing body of critics who represented the conflict "as unjust in its origin, disastrous in its progress, and desperate in its farther prosecution." It was not an enviable task. He had made too many unwarranted assertions in the months preceding the declaration of war, and political opponents took malicious pleasure in throwing them back in his face. "It was this same bold and false prophet," said one Maryland Federalist, "who led us into Canada to conquer free trade and sailors' rights; and such is the sanguine nature of the late Chairman of the Committee of Foreign Relations, that I have no doubt even now he would contract, if he could find security for the forfeiture, to capture in six weeks, the whole British army and deliver them, bound hand and foot, at the Capitol."[7]

Much to Calhoun's relief, the war finally ended in early 1815. For many Americans of this generation, the coming of peace would forever be associated with Andrew Jackson's exploits at New Orleans. This happy conjuncture not only silenced war critics but obliterated Federalist ranks nearly everywhere outside

New England. It also had an amnesic effect that dimmed memories of wartime reversals and, in Adams's words, left people "inclined to be rather more proud than they have reason of the war from which they have so recently emerged." However much he benefited from these developments, Calhoun did not greet them with quite the same amount of glee that others exhibited. Like Adams, he knew there was much less cause for celebration than many believed. Where some former War Hawks quickly put the conflict behind them as they moved on to deal with other concerns, Calhoun saw that it had exposed major national weaknesses and felt that it would not be truly over until Congress addressed those shortcomings. And where people such as Adams, who had hoped to avoid war, could speak about military disasters without feeling any sense of personal responsibility for their having occurred, the South Carolinian could not, given his repeated assurances that US forces would effortlessly sweep away all that stood in their way. Introspection and self-criticism may not have been notable Calhounian traits, but, without ever admitting it, he understood that his earlier inattention to questions of war readiness had prevented him from providing the sort of leadership the nation demanded during a period of crisis.[8]

In the years immediately following the Treaty of Ghent (1814), Calhoun continued his evolution from war promoter to full-fledged nationalist. In his efforts to strengthen the nation and reduce its vulnerability to foreign impositions, he called for the expansion of officer training programs, supported the construction and repair of military fortifications, and backed other defense initiatives. Not content with harvesting this low-hanging fruit, he also adopted positions that required telling people things they did not always want to hear. If the nation was to realize the founders' vision of creating a government that would serve as a model for all civilized peoples, he said in a speech on the 1816 revenue bill, Americans had to be willing to put aside private concerns and make necessary sacrifices for the public welfare whenever the occasion demanded. This meant recognizing that taxes were not "so much money taken from the people," but, when properly put to use, revenue that could advance the national interest in important ways that went beyond the capacity of individual citizens. "The broad question was now before the House," he declared, "whether the government should act on an enlarged policy, whether it would avail itself of the experience of the last war; whether it would be benefited from the mass of knowledge acquired within the last few years; or whether we should go on in the old imbecile mode, contributing by our measures nothing to the honor, nothing to the reputation of the country."[9]

Even more striking was Calhoun's willingness to support tariff legislation that aided Northern producers at the expense of Southern consumers. Rather than direct attention to the effect higher tariffs might have on the prices farmers and planters paid for imported goods, he instead emphasized the interdependence of manufacturing, agriculture, and commerce. None of them alone, he contended, "is the cause of wealth; it flows from the three combined, and cannot exist without each." Just how much this was so became especially apparent when peacetime prosperity buckled under the dislocations of war. At such moments, restrictions on trade cut off the flow of foreign imports and reduced access to overseas markets, thereby depriving farmers of needed implements of production and preventing the sale of agricultural surpluses. Although the development of a powerful navy would help remedy this situation, it did not provide an altogether satisfactory response. Something more was needed if the nation was to achieve the economic self-sufficiency required to deal effectively with the disruptions of war, and Calhoun believed he knew what it was. "When our manufactures are grown to a certain perfection, as they soon will under the fostering care of Government, we will no longer experience these evils," he assured members of Congress. "The farmer will find a ready market for his surplus produce, and what is of almost equal consequence, a certain and cheap supply of his wants. His prosperity will diffuse itself to every class in the community, and instead of the languor of industry, and individual distress now incident to a state of war, and suspended commerce, the wealth and vigor of the community will not be materially impaired."[10]

The creation of a stable, prosperous manufacturing base, Calhoun believed, would not only enable the nation to respond effectively to war-related economic turmoil. It would also focus attention on the need for internal improvements—"a subject every day so intimately connected with the ultimate attainment of national strength, and the perfection of our political institutions." For all its natural advantages, the United States had one major geographic deficiency that an invading force could all too easily exploit. "We occupy a surface prodigiously great in proportion to our numbers," the South Carolinian observed. "The common strength," as the recent war demonstrated on more than one occasion, "is brought to bear with great difficulty on the point that may be menaced by the enemy." Construction of an integrated network of roads and canals provided the only practical solution to the problem. Once in place, he added, an efficient transportation system that forged links between the country's different regions would markedly reduce the likelihood of an even more serious threat to the national interest: the danger of disunion. As he saw it, "the liberty and the union of the country were inseparably united," and House members had an "imperious obligation" to do whatever they could to promote national unity. "Let us then," he urged his colleagues, "bind the Republic together with a perfect system of roads and canals. Let us conquer space."[11]

The main legislative proposal embodying Calhoun's hopes was the Bonus Bill of 1817—an act that would employ revenue arising from the formation of the Second Bank of the United States to create a fund for the construction of roads and canals. As it turned out, the measure made it through Congress only to be vetoed by James Madison. The president questioned whether the bill's lack of specificity concerning plans and projects would permit achievement of its goal of establishing an integrated transportation network. He also had grave doubts about its constitutionality, arguing that its broad interpretation of legislative authority gave Congress the power to pursue nearly any line of policy it chose that was "not specifically exempted" by the Constitution; and he would not sign such a measure without the passage of a constitutional amendment that added the funding of internal improvements to the legislative branch's enumerated powers. Calhoun had anticipated this objection and did not believe it should be allowed to obstruct so critically important an undertaking. "He was no advocate of refined arguments on the Constitution," he said in defense of the Bonus Bill. "The instrument was not intended as a thesis for the logician to exercise his ingenuity on. It ought to be constructed with plain, good sense." And one need look no further than the opening provision of Article I, Section 8, which gave Congress the power to appropriate funds to "provide for the common defence, and promote the general welfare of the United States," to see what the founders thought. Even were it conceded that the Constitution was silent on the question of using public funds for internal improvements, he asked, "Why should we be confined in the application of money to the enumerated powers?" Not only was there no good reason to do so but also, as initiatives such as the Louisiana Purchase demonstrated, "the habitual and uniform practice of the Government coincided with his opinion." However unavailing, the argument left no doubt about the depth of Calhoun's nationalism.[12]

Historian Alan Taylor has written that postwar "nationalism was, ironically, highly sectional: strongest in the Middle Atlantic and western states and weaker in Virginia and" the South, where "states developed a far stronger bond and shared identity with one another." Although Calhoun's exertions do not fit this generalization, Taylor's observation helps put his motives in perspective. An intensely ambitious man, he may already have been looking forward to his first presidential run; when Calhoun took the step some years later, he rested his hopes on Pennsylvania, a state in which his postwar program had strong appeal for a majority of voters. Yet his willingness to cut against the Southern grain suggests how wrong it would be to view his actions as simple opportunism. He could not forget his blithe indifference to national unpreparedness for a war that he had championed more vociferously than most, and he afterward felt duty bound to make amends for having done so. In an 1825 speech, he attributed his "zealous efforts" of the postwar period to concerns regarding the many people "on whom the experience of the war appeared to be lost." There is no reason to question his sincerity. Even more certain is how closely his beliefs paralleled those of Adams. It is easy to imagine the New Englander delivering addresses very similar to Calhoun's had he been a member of Congress. The language would have been different, given John Quincy's greater penchant for literary and biblical allusions, but the ideas would have been exactly the same. It was altogether fitting that these two ardent nationalists would soon be working together as department heads in Monroe's administration.[13]

After a lifetime as an active participant in the nation's political wars, James Monroe entered the Executive Mansion hoping to reduce partisan and sectional animosities. If his eight years there hardly constituted the "Era of Good Feelings" that a Boston editor declared they would, it was not because of anything the president did. In an effort to show that Republicans sought to govern as a national rather than a Virginia-dominated regional party, he set out to create a national unity cabinet in which a New Englander occupied the top post. Adams was a logical candidate for the position. As secretary of state, Monroe had corresponded regularly with him and knew Adams to be eminently qualified to handle any challenges that the custodian of American foreign policy might encounter. Finding a secretary of war took a little while longer. The president's first choice, Henry Clay, believing someone of his experience and ability unfit for any office less than State, rejected the offer; so did two other selections. His fourth choice, John C. Calhoun, accepted, despite the advice of friends who told him that his talents were best suited to the give and take of legislative debate. Not only did Calhoun welcome the opportunity to demonstrate his administrate skills, but he looked forward to doing so in furtherance of objectives that he deemed critical to the national interest.[14]

Within the cabinet, Adams and Calhoun held each other's abilities in high regard. Nearly everyone recognized the New Englander's command of foreign policy matters, and Calhoun was no exception. Although Adams's ill-tempered assertiveness in cabinet discussions could be off-putting, Calhoun never questioned his competence. Adams, who at his most generous tended to be rather sparing in his disbursement of praise, characterized the secretary of war as "a man of fair and candid mind, of honourable principles; of clear and quick understanding; of cool self-possession; of enlarged philosophical views; and of ardent patriotism." Calhoun's fair-mindedness and freedom from bias particularly impressed him. "He is above all sectional, and factious prejudices, more than any other Statesman of the Union, whom I have met." His only fault—and Adams invariably detected some shortcoming in everyone he met—was his sensitivity "to the transient manifestations of public opinion." The secretary of state nevertheless assured Calhoun that should he have "any preference of views with regard to measures" being considered by the administration, he could be certain of the support of at least one other department head.[15]

As primary author of the Monroe Doctrine and initiator of numerous reforms to improve departmental efficiency, Adams was one of the most influential secretaries of state in US history. His approach to foreign relations rested largely on two principles. The first was neutrality. Like the president who appointed him to his initial diplomatic post, the New Englander strongly objected to entangling alliances or anything else that might lead to US intervention in European affairs. Long service in various European capitals had done nothing to modify this view. However much Old World conditions changed, nothing ever seemed to get better. His observations on the fall of Napoleon were typical. Although the French emperor fully deserved whatever retribution his victorious adversaries visited on him, it was highly unlikely that the people of France or anywhere else on the continent would benefit from the emergence of the Holy Alliance. Europe "has burst asunder the adamantine chains of Bonaparte, to be pinioned by the rags and tatters of monkery and popery," Adams wrote. "She has cast up the code of Napoleon, and returned to her own vomit of Jesuits, inquisitions, and legitimacy of Divine Right. With this state of things it is impossible that Europe should be long contented." Thus it was, he famously observed in an 1821 address, that the United States "goes not abroad in search of monsters to destroy." By doing so, even in conflicts fought under "the banners of independence, she would involve herself, beyond the power of extrication, in all the wars of interest and intrigue, of individual avarice, envy, and ambition, which assume the colors and usurp the standard of freedom. The fundamental maxims of her policy would insensibly change from liberty to force."[16]

The second principle guiding his conduct at the State Department was continentalism. Decades before Democratic editor John L. O'Sullivan coined the term, Adams made the doctrine of manifest destiny an integral feature of his policy. Unlike his onetime colleagues among Massachusetts Federalists, who feared the disruptive consequences of territorial expansion for New England and the nation, John Quincy believed that one of the surest "guarantees of order and tranquility in the United States was the movement of the population westward." Let Great Britain revile America "as a mean low-minded, peddling nation having no generous ambitions and no God but gold," he observed in an 1819 diary entry; its rulers and those of other European colonial powers would, however grudgingly, change their way of thinking as they became accustomed to "the idea of considering our proper dominion to be the Continent of North America." And Adams had no doubt whatsoever that would happen. "From the first time when we became an independent people, it was as much a Law of Nature that this should become our pretension as that the Mississippi should flow to the sea." Spanish and British possessions on US borders must inevitably be added to the national domain—"Not because any spirit of encroachment or ambition on our part renders it necessary; but because it is a physical and moral absurdity that such fragments of territory, with Sovereigns at fifteen hundred miles beyond sea, worthless and burdensome to their owners should exist permanently contiguous to a great, powerful, enterprising and rapidly growing Nation." He retained this vision to the end, on at least one occasion enlarging its scope to include the entire hemisphere. The vast "North American Union," he told members of the Massachusetts Historical Society in an 1843 address, was "an empire already bounded by the Atlantic and Pacific Ocean, and, to the eye of prophetic inspiration, to be hereafter bounded only by the eternal ice of the northern and southern Pole."[17]

The greatest challenge Adams faced as secretary of state was dealing with the implications of Spain's collapsing American empire. Under the best of circumstances, the early nineteenth century would have been a period of mounting unrest in Spanish America. After resuming its traditional alliance with France in 1795, Spain found itself at war with Great Britain, which imposed a blockade that—with only short intervals of relief—lasted more than a decade. By the time it ended, Spanish trade with its American colonies had largely collapsed, and declining state revenue during a period of heavy war expenditures had effectively bankrupted the cash-strapped Spanish government. Political ruin soon followed when, in 1808, Napoleon forced the abdication of Ferdinand VII. That year also witnessed the outbreak of struggles for independence in Mexico and Venezuela, followed two years later by the May Revolution in Argentina, which in turn prompted further uprisings in Bolivia and Uruguay. Ferdinand VII's return to the Spanish throne in 1814 only made a bad situation worse. Unable to create a popular, stable government at home, the self-seeking, narrow-minded reactionary lacked the acuity to recognize—much less address—the changes that had taken place in his American colonies. By the early 1820s, regional independence movements had established functioning governments throughout Latin America.[18]

The Spanish possession of most immediate concern to US policymakers was Florida, which Spain, after trading the province to Great Britain in 1763, had reacquired in the treaty ending the American Revolution. During the two-decade lapse in Spanish rule, British administrators had divided Florida into two parts, and US interest initially focused on West Florida, an area stretching across present-day southern Mississippi and Alabama into the Florida Panhandle. Not only did its rivers provide access to the Gulf of Mexico for settlers in the expanding cotton economy to the north, but the vital port of New Orleans would be vulnerable to foreign attack as long as West Florida remained in Spanish hands. How long that would be was extremely uncertain from the start. Spanish efforts to encourage settlement of the thinly populated Floridas by offering generous land grants to US immigrants weakened rather than strengthened their hold on the region. On at least four occasions between 1788 and 1810, American filibusters sought to overturn Spanish rule. In 1810, they largely succeeded when President Madison, contending that the province formed part of the Louisiana Purchase, issued an executive order annexing all of West Florida outside the Mobile district; three years later, US forces occupied Mobile to complete the conquest.[19]

Although Madison would like to have secured East Florida as well, it eluded his grasp. And when the Monroe administration assumed control of the executive branch in 1817, the province went to the top of its acquisitions list. The president wanted it. So did Secretary of War Calhoun, who considered the province extremely important because of its "position and naval and commercial advantages." With Florida, he observed, the United States would enjoy command of the Gulf trade. At the State Department, Adams needed no persuading whatsoever. Adding East Florida to the national domain not only represented a much-desired application of his expansionist ideology; he also recognized that such an achievement would enhance his stature as a candidate for the presidential succession whenever Monroe decided to step down. As he later confided to his diary, ratification of the Florida treaty was "the most important event of my life." In addition to furthering the national interest, "I had at once disconcerted and stimulated my personal antagonists and rivals. It promised well for my reputation in the public opinion."[20]

Well aware of Spanish weaknesses, Adams fully intended to exploit them. He knew that without foreign assistance Spain could not hope to mount a serious defense of the more far flung reaches of its sprawling North American empire. Accordingly, he sought to isolate Spain diplomatically. These efforts focused on Great Britain, which, with its formidable navy, was the only European power capable of providing effective aid should conflict break out between Spain and the United States. However remote the likelihood of such intervention on Great Britain's part, Adams believed it best that Spain clearly recognize where it stood. And the Rush-Bagot Agreement of 1817 and the Convention of 1818 thus served the dual functions of reducing British-US differences and dispelling any illusions that Spanish officials might have harbored of obtaining British support.[21]

At the same time, Adams had no hesitation about recommending the use of military force where he felt it could be applied short of initiating a broader conflict. The greater the pressure, he believed, the easier it would be to persuade Spanish negotiators to accept US territorial demands. In cabinet discussions about what to do concerning the operations of seagoing guerrillas on Amelia Island—a Spanish possession off the northeast coast of Florida—Adams urged that US forces be dispatched to occupy the island. He adopted a similar position in what would become one of the more controversial episodes of the first Monroe administration. In late 1817, after the attempted expulsion of a small band of Seminoles from a settlement just north of the Florida border met unexpected resistance, Calhoun ordered Andrew Jackson to handle the problem. The hero of New Orleans organized a force of five thousand troops and marched into Florida, where, despite encountering little opposition, he laid waste to a number of villages and destroyed the food supplies of those who fled his approach. None of this excited any concern in Washington; everyone expected as much from a veteran commander who had employed similar tactics in the Creek War. When, however, Jackson seized and executed Scottish merchant Alexander Arbuthnot and British royal marine Robert Ambrister after a hastily convened court-martial and proceeded to occupy the Spanish garrisons of St. Marks and Pensacola, administration leaders took notice. Wreaking devastation on Native Americans and intimidating Spanish colonial authorities were one thing; involving the nation in a major conflict that no one wanted was another matter altogether.[22]

Within the administration, cabinet members had differing views on how the government should respond. On one side of the debate, Calhoun believed Jackson was obligated to follow orders previously issued to General E. P. Gaines, which required the commander of the Florida operation to contact the War Department before continuing his pursuit of any Native Americans who had taken shelter in a Spanish garrison. That he failed to do so, Calhoun argued, undermined civilian control of the military. Were this Calhoun's only grievance, he might have been more willing to overlook Jackson's transgressions, given his own interest in acquiring East Florida. But he had other reasons for wishing to see the general reprimanded. This was not the first time that a senior officer had ignored his orders, and as a relatively young cabinet official seeking to demonstrate that his administrative skills matched his legislative abilities, the secretary did not wish to be seen as someone unable to command the respect and obedience of subordinates. It is not surprising that, as Adams observed, he appeared "to be personally offended, with the idea, that Jackson had set at nought the Instructions of his Department." Calhoun also feared the invasion might lead to a wider conflict. Although US forces could handle Spain easily enough, he wrote Jackson, "such a war would not long continue without involving other parties, and it certainly would, in a few years, be an English war." He had already helped thrust a woefully ill-prepared army into one conflict, and, knowing better than anyone how little had been done to remedy the nation's military weaknesses, he had no desire to do so again: "We want time; time to grow, to perfect our forti[fi]cations, to enlarge our Navy, to replenish our depots, and to pay our debts."[23]

Adams had no such reservations. Jackson was not in his chain of command, and even if he had been, it likely would not have mattered, for the New Englander saw no reason to be apprehensive about the consequences of the general's actions. Like Calhoun, he felt Spain posed no credible threat. But he also believed that the last thing Britain wanted was another war. The various conflicts of the past three-quarters of a century had placed an enormous strain on British resources, and government officials were looking forward to a period of peace that would allow them to reduce the national debt and restore fiscal stability. Adams's diplomacy, which promised a marked expansion of Anglo-US commerce, could certainly help in that regard. Britain particularly wished to avoid another conflict with the United States. For British observers, the able performance of US ships in the War of 1812 had been as unsettling as it was unexpected. Although no one anywhere doubted that Britannia still ruled the waves, the mandarins of Whitehall did not want to do anything that might prompt Washington to begin devoting more of the nation's growing wealth to the construction of a world-class navy, however improbable congressional penuriousness made such a development.[24]

Adams appreciated the dilemma that Jackson's actions presented cabinet members. Should they endorse his conduct, they faced potential charges of having violated the Constitution for initiating a war without congressional approval. Should they condemn it, "they must give offense to all [Jackson's] friends, encounter the shock of his popularity and have the appearance of truckling to Spain." Whatever indecision these choices might cause others, Adams knew exactly where he stood. Not to support Jackson would, he believed, be "weakness, and a confession of weakness." The New Englander had no intention of conducting foreign policy on that basis if he could help it, and he became the general's strongest advocate in cabinet discussions, opposing what he perceived as an inclination to disavow "the bold energy of Jackson" and dismiss "the strong reasons which he alledges for his justification." Jackson had acted defensively throughout, Adams insisted, and he would never have taken Pensacola if the Spanish governor had not threatened to expel him from the province. Placing all the blame on the hero of New Orleans would thus be a grave injustice that weakened the US position in current negotiations with Spain.[25]

Outside the cabinet, Adams's most complete statement on the Florida invasion appeared in a November 1818 letter to George W. Erving, the US minister to Madrid, which was to be conveyed to Spanish authorities. In it, he framed his observations as a response to a declaration by Ferdinand VII ordering that the Florida talks be suspended if the United States did not provide satisfaction for Jackson's conduct. The threat made no impression whatsoever on Adams. Certain that Washington had the upper hand, he took full advantage of the administration's superior position and adopted an unapologetically aggressive stance. The more brazen his assertions, he clearly believed, the greater the likelihood that Spanish policymakers would not only continue the negotiations but accede to US demands. In addition to justifying everything Jackson had done, to include the execution of Arbuthnot and Ambrister, he contended that if anyone was at fault, it was the Spanish governor of Pensacola, who deserved to be punished for failing to honor treaty obligations requiring him to prevent the barbarous assaults of "negro-Indian banditti" on US settlers in the region. Should such attacks recur and American troops again be forced to occupy Spanish garrisons, he ominously concluded, "another unconditional restoration of them must not be expected," for "the United States will be reluctantly compelled to rely for the protection of their borders upon themselves alone."[26]

Within three months, Adams and Don Luis de Onís signed a treaty ceding Florida to the United States. What effect the secretary's dispatch had on the discussions leading to the accord is not entirely clear, there being some evidence that Spanish leaders had decided to relent before receiving the Erving letter. "It was Jackson's assertive action in Florida, not Adams's spirited legal arguments," historian Deborah A Rosen has written, "that pushed Spain to greater flexibility in the negotiations." This may be so, but Jackson's invasion would have had far less influence on the talks if Adams had not worked so hard in cabinet discussions to prevent administration disavowal of the assault. And if Spanish officials had any lingering doubts about the weakness of their position, Adams's communication removed them. Besides demonstrating how strongly the administration supported Jackson, it showed how few scruples Washington had about inventing some pretext to justify another invasion. The combination of Jacksonian aggression and Adams's backing also helped secure Spanish acquiescence in the establishment of a transcontinental boundary on the Pacific Ocean. The secretary had introduced the demand late in the talks, at a time when Onís recognized the administration's readiness to employ military force to obtain its objectives and felt he lacked the leverage required to prevent making the concession. Adams considered the acquisition a major personal accomplishment. Securing "a definite line of boundary to the South Sea," he wrote in his diary, "forms a great Epoch in our History." And he believed he could "record the first assertion of this claim for the United States as my own," the need for such an extensive delineation of the national domain having gone unaddressed in the treaty ending the American Revolution and the Louisiana Purchase.[27]

Adams's last major initiative on behalf of his imperial vision was his contribution to the shaping of what came to be known as the Monroe Doctrine. In August 1823, amid rumors that members of the Holy Alliance (Russia, France, Austria, Prussia) were contemplating a military campaign to restore Spanish rule in its Latin American colonies, British Foreign Secretary George Canning proposed issuing a joint British–US declaration warning against any such venture. Within the cabinet, Calhoun and Adams differed on how to respond. Calhoun urged acceptance of the offer, arguing that Britain alone could not prevent the alliance from successfully carrying out its planned offensive. "She would eventually fall into their view," he feared, "and the South Americans would be subdued." Adams disagreed. He thought members of the alliance incapable of mounting an invasion in the face of British resistance, and should they attempt do so, Britain, with "her command of the seas," had the wherewithal to defeat them. In which case, he added, Latin American independence would rest on British protection, thereby enabling Britain to make those nations "her Colonies, instead of those of Spain." What Calhoun and those who shared his position did not understand, Adams argued, was that Britain was more concerned about containing US expansionism than helping the Latin Americans. The administration needed to "act promptly and decisively," but it should do nothing that might be interpreted as acknowledgement of terms that precluded further territorial acquisitions. It would, he observed, be more in the national interest and "more dignified" to adopt an independent stance and "avow our principles explicitly to Russia and France, than to come in as a Cock-boat in the wake of the British man of War."[28]

Monroe, as he had done during the Jackson controversy, sided with his secretary of state. In a December 1823 message to Congress, the president stated that the United States had and would continue to maintain a strict neutrality in the various conflicts among European powers. It could not, however, take such a detached view of developments in the Americas. "We owe it, therefore, to candor and to the amicable relations between Washington and those powers to declare that we should consider any attempt on their part to extend their system of government" or otherwise interfere with the newly independent states of the Western Hemisphere as "dangerous to our peace and safety" and "the manifestation of an unfriendly disposition toward the United States." The only thing that could have pleased Adams more than this clear statement of national resolve was the president's subsequent tribute to the nation's growth. "This expansion of our population and accession of new States to our Union have had the happiest effect on all of its highest interests," Monroe observed. "That it has eminently augmented our resources and added to our strength and respectability as a power is admitted by all."[29]

Adams's performance as secretary of state from Jackson's invasion to the composition of the Monroe Doctrine put two sides of his diplomatic personality on full display: the knowledgeable foreign service veteran whose keen sense of what government leaders were thinking in major European capitals and the aggressive hardballer who had difficulty restraining his impatience with anyone or anything that threatened to obstruct fulfillment of his expansionist agenda. Yet, for all his policy successes, Adams did not view the future with perfect equanimity. The costs of extending the national domain, he came to recognize, might someday outweigh any conceivable benefits. Particularly troubling was the threat to the Union arising from "the overgrown extent of its territory, combining with the Slavery question." In February 1819, New York House member James Talmadge Jr., had submitted a slavery restriction amendment to a Missouri statehood bill. The ensuing debate—one of the most rancorous in congressional history—exposed sharp sectional divisions before ending in a compromise that admitted Missouri as a slave state and Maine as a free state; it also barred slavery in any territory of the Louisiana Purchase north of the 36°30' parallel. According to one acquaintance, Adams initially supported Talmadge's amendment. If so, he quickly retreated from that position, observing that it would be impossible to enforce restriction any place where slavery had already taken root. The need for slaves in such areas "was not in the Lands but in their inhabitants," he wrote. "Slavery had become in the South and Southwestern Country a condition of existence. They could not live without them."[30]

Although Adams endorsed the compromise, he had serious reservations about whether it had been for the best. What he considered Northern legislators' insufficiently persevering prosecution of their case disappointed the New Englander nearly as much as the heavy-handed bullying of Southern lawmakers angered him. "The Slave drivers, as usual, whenever the topic [of slavery] is brought up," he wrote of the debate, "talk of the white Slaves of the Eastern States, and the dissolution of the Union and Oceans of blood—and the Northern men as usual pocket all this hectoring; sit down in quiet, and submit to the slave scourging Republicanism of the Planters." That the controversy ended as it did was predictable in that slaveholders had "a deeper immediate stake in the issue than the partizans of freedom." He was nevertheless surprised that no Northern member of Congress had proposed to revise the Transcontinental Treaty by adding an amendment barring slavery in Florida whenever it should apply for statehood or taking some other step to curb slave expansionism. During one especially dark moment, he even wondered whether civil war "would not be preferable to an extension of Slavery beyond the Mississippi." The South's peculiar institution was "the great and foul stain upon the American Union," Adams believed, "and it is a contemplation worthy of the most exalted soul, whether the total abolition of it is or is not practicable." As things presently stood, "the contest is now laid asleep," but he had little doubt that similar battles would emerge in the future, and for the most compelling of reasons: "If the Union must be dissolved, Slavery is precisely the question on which it ought to break."[31]

One person who did not share Adams's concerns was John C. Calhoun. Although both secretaries supported the Missouri Compromise, they viewed the controversy from much different perspectives. Unlike Adams, Calhoun never for a moment doubted the morality of slavery. And where the New Englander wished Northern legislators had done more to address questions concerning slavery's place in American society, the South Carolinian wanted to see the debate terminated as swiftly as possible. Believing open discussion of human bondage could not end well for the South, he favored an approach to the politics of slavery that can best be described as the less said, the better. The acrimonious and widely reported congressional exchanges concerning Missouri could hardly have made him happy, and he readily assumed the role of administration peacemaker on the issue. Should the North seek to abolish slavery, he told Southern correspondents, disunion would be unavoidable. But that was not the main point of contention. "The fact is, the Missouri question had no connection with emancipation," he wrote his fellow Carolinian Henry W. DeSaussure: "Its object was political power and preeminence." Once Missouri was admitted as a slave state, he observed in another letter, "the evil effects of the discussion must gradually subside."[32]

Calhoun tended to adopt a more menacing stance when discussing the issue with Northerners, on one occasion informing Adams that should the South secede, it would be compelled to form an alliance with Great Britain. But whatever tension this might have caused did not last long. In the period following settlement of the controversy, concerns about slavery, its morality, and the threat its expansion posed to the Union gradually moved to the margins of Adams's political consciousness; and Calhoun ceased talking about such matters altogether, hoping that others would do so as well. During an 1824 discussion of westward expansion and the Union, Calhoun said he believed the establishment of settlements on the Pacific coast could easily take place without inciting sectional strife. According to Adams, he further observed that "the passion for aggrandizement was the Law paramount of man in Society, and that there was no example in History of the disruption of a Nation from itself, by a voluntary separation." Although the New Englander cited several instances in which this had indeed occurred, he voiced no objection to Calhoun's broader thesis, telling him that he "thought a government by federation would be found practicable upon a territory as extensive as this Continent, and that the tendency of our popular sentiments was increasingly towards Union." That they could so readily agree was not surprising. As an examination of Calhoun's tenure as secretary of war makes clear, the two cabinet members then had much in common.[33]

Calhoun's path to the War Department was anything but straightforward. He was not the first choice of Monroe, who had offered the post to Henry Clay, Isaac Shelby, and William Lowndes before turning to the South Carolinian. And when Calhoun eventually received the offer, a number of his friends urged him to decline the appointment. Not only was Congress "the proper theatre for his talents," they argued, but assuming responsibility for a department with a long tradition of less than stellar leadership and "in a state of such disorder and confusion" as now existed there would surely result in loss of reputation. Although Calhoun had no illusions about the administrative chaos that awaited him, he welcomed the challenges that the position presented. He hoped someday to occupy the highest office in the land, and overseeing the War Department would give him an opportunity to show that he possessed abilities that went beyond the oratorical skills required of an effective legislator. Just as important he had not forgotten how unprepared the nation had been for the recent conflict with Great Britain or the part he had played in promoting the war. He thus had strong personal motives for wanting to reform the department.[34]

In an 1825 letter, Calhoun wrote that not too long ago nearly everyone in Europe believed "that a government purely representative, and consequently having no other support but the popular affection, could only be supported in peace," and would, when faced with war-related impositions, fold "under all the pressure of taxes, inter[r]upted industry and militia services." This was no longer the case, he added, and "it will be the pride and consolation of my life, that I have contributed in some degree to this great revolution in opinion." Whether such a "revolution in opinion" actually occurred is certainly arguable, but the views expressed in the letter do reflect one of Calhoun's greatest concerns as secretary of war. If he did not know it beforehand, he soon learned that maintaining even a reasonably formidable peacetime military establishment was no easy task in a nation where many people considered standing armies a threat to liberty. His work became more difficult after the Panic of 1819 spurred demands for cuts in government spending. Forced to reduce the size of the army by a third, he devised a plan that called for the retention of a large proportion of officers so there would be a structure in place to bring the army up to wartime capability in as short a while as possible should it become necessary. Although Congress rejected his recommendations, Calhoun did successfully implement plans to improve officer training at West Point and to expand and strengthen the organization of the general staff. At the same time, he paid attention to the frequently overlooked needs of people in the ranks. Armies required more than adequate supplies of powder and shot to be effective; no less essential was the maintenance of morale and physical health. Accordingly, he emphasized the importance of instituting hygienic sanitary practices and ensuring that soldiers received regular pay, proper clothing, and ample rations.[35]

Not everyone viewed the secretary's performance as approvingly as he did. Adams, though mindful of the obstacles Calhoun faced, felt his "inexperience and susceptibility of flattery in several instances exposed the country to wasteful expenditures and improvident contracts." The New Englander further observed that in developing plans to reform the army Calhoun had been too deferential to senior officers, who played on his vanity so skillfully that he "imagined himself the author of every improvement, real or imagined, that was suggested to him by more experienced men," while "they in turn were willing to avail themselves of his ambition and official power to accomplish changes which they believed would be at once useful to the service and advantageous to themselves." Although other political adversaries voiced similar criticism, historians have given Calhoun much higher marks for administrative competence. His organizational initiatives and the code of rules he had bureau heads compose "to give uniformity, consistency, and stability to the whole" may not have worked quite as perfectly as a campaign biography later claimed, but they doubtless improved operations in a department that had acquired a well-earned reputation for waste and inefficiency. More impressively, the reduction in unsettled accounts from more than $45 million to less than $3 million that took place during Calhoun's cabinet years suggests that he missed few opportunities to keep costs in check.[36]

Whatever Adams's later comments on Calhoun's conduct as secretary of war, during the Monroe years he considered the South Carolinian his most able cabinet colleague. Listening to Calhoun tell an acquaintance that his central aim as a public servant was promoting "the development morally and physically [of] the mighty resources of this country," one can readily appreciate why the New Englander did so. A major area of agreement was internal improvements. Calhoun fully realized that the advantages of roads and canals went well beyond any military rationale for their construction; they also provided vital assistance to merchants, farmers, manufacturers, and all other participants in the nation's diverse and growing economy. Whether such projects were viewed "in relation to military, civil, or political purposes," he told Henry Clay, "very nearly the same system, in all its parts, is required." His most ambitious public works initiative found expression in the General Survey Act of 1824. For Calhoun, the bill provided the legislative foundation for a mammoth building program to improve navigation on the Ohio and Mississippi Rivers, create "a series of canals connecting the bays north to the seat of government," and unite the entire South Atlantic-Gulf Coast region through the construction of "a durable road" from Washington to New Orleans. "When completed," he wrote Monroe, "it would greatly facilitate commerce and intercourse among the States," remove major obstacles to the interregional transmission of information, and provide "effectual protection to every portion of our widely extended country." Although Calhoun would later oppose appropriation of the funds needed to fulfill the measure's promise, this subsequent change of course does not detract from the grandiosity of the plans "to conquer space" that he envisioned as secretary of war.[37]

If Calhoun occasionally exhibited a more cautious approach to foreign affairs than Adams did, he fully shared the New Englander's ardent nationalism. Not long after assuming his cabinet position, he endorsed a proposal to establish a permanent garrison at the mouth of the Yellowstone River. Duty at such a remote outpost might well prove "unpleasant," but he felt certain that soldiers would rise to the occasion. "Combined with the importance of the service, the glory of planting the American flag at a point so distant on so noble a river, will not be unfelt," he observed. "The world will behold in it, the mighty growth of our republic, which but in a few years since, was limited by the Allegany; but is now ready to push its civilization and laws to the western confines of the continent." The construction of western forts also provided a means of protecting American interests against foreign incursions in the outer reaches of the nation's expanding continental empire. However much he wished to avoid another war with Great

Britain, Calhoun demonstrated a firm commitment to containing the spread of British influence in North America. This was especially so in the still largely unsettled areas of the Northwest. In 1824, he strongly supported a plan for the military occupation of the Columbia River. Were British merchants allowed to operate freely in the region, he contended, "they will in a great measure monopolize the Fur Trade west of the Mississippi to the almost entire exclusion in a few years of our Trade." Needless to say, all of these initiatives were perfectly in line with Adams's vision of national development.[38]

The main function of the posts Calhoun wished to establish was to provide security for settlers on a frontier that was constantly moving westward. Carrying out this task forced secretaries of war to confront the always challenging and sometimes perilous responsibility of overseeing relations with Native Americans. By Calhoun's time, they could draw on a rich history for guidance. The intersection of territorial expansion, military policy, and Native American relations dated back to the beginnings of English colonization in North America and such early conflicts as Virginia's Powhatan wars and New England's Pequot War. Never simple in the best of times, keeping these three variables in balance became much more complicated in the wake of the Seven Years' War. After the uprising known as Pontiac's War spread death and destruction throughout the Old Northwest, Great Britain issued a royal proclamation that established the Appalachian Mountains as a boundary line between white settlement and Native American territory. It did not hold. In the South, British negotiators induced regional Native Americans to cede 5.5 million acres of land in the Treaty of Augusta (1763) and two subsequent negotiations; in the Northwest, the Treaty of Fort Stanwix (1768) pushed the proclamation line considerably westward, spurring the resumption of a conflict between Native Americans and settlers that, with varying degrees of intensity, would persist for decades. Caught in the middle were the British soldiers who assumed the thankless chore of protecting settlers against raids as they tried to prevent colonial encroachment on Native American lands. That Native Americans, as one British writer observed, saw "in every little garrison the germs of a future colony" did not make their lives any easier.[39]

Although the Royal Proclamation did not halt white settlement west of the Appalachians, Native Americans retained control of most of the region for the next two decades. This state of affairs changed dramatically after the Revolution. At postwar treaty conferences, US negotiators claimed possession of all lands east of the Mississippi based on a right of conquest, informing Native Americans that the new nation would dispose of them in any manner it desired. Resistance quickly rendered this position untenable, and during Washington's administration, Secretary of War Henry Knox devised a more accommodating stance that, with some modification, would govern US–Native American relations until the

War of 1812. Knox's policy recognized Native American rights to the soil and the government's obligation to purchase whatever lands it sought; linking expansion to acculturation, it also urged Native Americans to abandon hunting and adopt a more settled existence based on agriculture and household manufactures, which would substantially reduce the amount of land required to meet their subsistence needs. The result, policymakers hoped, would be an orderly frontier advance that gradually dispossessed Native Americans of most of their lands without resort to war. Achievement of these aims proved more difficult than anticipated. Where most Native Americans—particularly those in the Old Northwest—had no wish to give up a traditional way of life that combined hunting and horticulture, nothing the government did could slow the pace of white settlement. Thus, while major hostilities ceased following the Treaty of Greenville (1795), sporadic conflict continued throughout the period.[40]

The War of 1812 marked a major turning point in US-Native American relations. Although the conflict had no winners, it did have losers, and no group lost more than Native Americans living between the Appalachians and the Mississippi River. In the Old Northwest, US forces destroyed Tecumseh's British-supported confederacy, ending the last significant initiative to unite Native Americans of the region against the encroachments of white settlers. In the South, an army led by Andrew Jackson decisively defeated a formidable Creek force at the Battle of Horseshoe Bend; not long afterward, in the Treaty of Fort Jackson (1814), the Tennessee general compelled Creek chiefs—most of them former allies rather than vanquished foes—to accept a 23-million-acre land cession that encompassed large parts of southern Georgia and much of the present-day state of Alabama. By war's end, Native American leaders recognized that trying to prevent the spread of white settlement through military means could end only in further death and slaughter. Their one remaining hope was that US negotiators at Ghent might be induced to consider a British plan to create a Native American buffer zone in the Northwest. Intended to prevent US incursions into Canada as well as to protect Britain's allies, the proposal called for the establishment of a 250,000 square mile Native American state that extended across large areas of Ohio and Minnesota and nearly all of Indiana, Illinois, Michigan, and Wisconsin. As it turned out, members of the US team flatly dismissed the proposition, treating it as a nonnegotiable demand that betrayed a lack of seriousness on the part of the British commissioners.[41]

That Kentucky's Henry Clay—"Harry of the West"—resolutely opposed the proposal was no surprise. But he was not alone. Adams not only shared his hostility but took the lead in voicing US repugnance to the plan. The New Englander subscribed to a developmental ethos that saw little value in the hunting activities he considered the mainstay of all Native American societies. He believed it perfectly justifiable to take immense tracts of land from Indigenous peoples incapable of fulfilling his vision of American greatness. "There is not upon this globe a spectacle exhibited by man so interesting to my mind or so consolatory to my heart.' he observed in an 1813 letter, "as this metamorphosis of howling deserts into cultivated fields and populous villages which is yearly, daily, hourly, going on by the hands of New England men in our western states and territories." These views, coupled with his commitment to realizing the nation's imperial destiny, informed his response to the British demand. Should Native Americans establish fixed settlements and begin working the soil, he told Secretary of State Monroe, the nation would be obligated to respect their possessions. But that was not happening, and consigning "vast regions of territory to perpetual barrenness and solitude, that a few hundred savages might find wild beasts to hunt upon it" would be nothing less than "an outrage upon Providence, which gave the earth to man for cultivation, and made the tillage of the ground the condition of his nature and the law of his existence." Of all nations, Great Britain should understand the impulses driving the movement of settlers across the North American landscape and how futile it would be to attempt restraining them. "Can she believe," he asked crown negotiators, "that the swarming myriads of her own children, in the process of converting a western wilderness to a powerful empire, could long be cramped or arrested by a treaty stipulation confining whole regions of territory to a few scattered hordes of savages, whose numbers to the end of ages would not amount to the population of one considerable city?"[42]

As secretary of war, Calhoun's views concerning Native Americans did not differ appreciably from those of Adams. He sometimes exhibited greater sensitivity than Adams, on one occasion chiding a recently appointed Chickasaw agent for expressing a poor opinion of Native Americans before getting to know them. But in most respects, Calhoun's assessment of Native American culture was unreservedly bleak. Adoption of the acculturation policy developed by his predecessors did little to improve it. The policy's main objectives, he told one subordinate, were "to wean the Indians from their attachment to their barbarous customs and practices," while promoting "cultivation of the arts of civilized life," thereby preparing them for the exercise of the "moral and political rights" enjoyed by white citizens. This did not mean that Native Americans could expect to become equal members of white society anytime soon, however. Should everything go well, he informed Monroe, there was reason to hope "they may receive an education equal to that of the laboring portion of our community." And Calhoun harbored doubts as to whether even that would produce the "state of morality, civilization, and happiness, to which it is the desire of the Government to bring them." Above all else, he added in a letter to Clay, Native Americans "must be brought gradually under our authority and laws, or they will insensibly waste away in vice and misery," it being "impossible, with their customs, that they should exist as independent communities in the midst of civilized Society."[43]

Carrying out his duties as the government's chief administrator of Native American affairs gave Calhoun frequent opportunities to proffer guidance and assume the stance of paternalistic lord that Southern slaveholders found so congenial. "My Children, You should not rely upon your annuity nor upon the kindness of your Great Father in making you presents, for the support of yourselves, your wives and Children," he told one Native American delegation. "Your people must cultivate the Earth, like our people and be industrious, and you will prosper. Your Great Father is willing to help you, but you must help yourselves." Regular calls for Native American uplift notwithstanding, the secretary's conception of his role of great white patriarch drew more heavily on Old Testament precepts than on contemporary notions of Christian benevolence. "The principles on which our conduct towards the Indians should be founded," Jefferson had declared, "are fear and justice." Calhoun fully agreed. "Every suitable occasion," he instructed frontier commanders, "should be used to conciliate the friendship of the Indians, to impress them with a high idea of our justice and humanity, and, at the same time, of our capacity to resist violence and punish injury should any be offered." To ensure that western military units convincingly projected that capacity, he believed it better to establish a limited number of strategic strongholds than to "multiply small posts in Indian Country." Such a policy, he wrote, would "effectually overawe the Savages & repress unfriendly dispositions on their part."[44]

Where fear is fear, justice is a more relative concept, and determining what it entailed presented greater interpretive complexities. In the world of US-Native American relations, even seemingly straightforward cases turned out to be more complicated than they appeared. When white people killed Native Americans, Calhoun found that simply apprehending and prosecuting the murderers seldom satisfied nation leaders; they wanted the government to provide monetary compensation as well. Although the secretary objected to such payments, he did occasionally authorize them on the condition that they not be seen as precedents. When Native Americans killed white people, Calhoun was also forced to address extrajudicial questions. One concerned summary punishment. However "justifiable" the practice might be during periods of armed conflict, he told Colonel Henry Leavenworth, US law required that Native American suspects be accorded their due process rights in peacetime. Another concerned the punishment of entire nations for the transgressions of individual members. Not wishing to turn minor disputes into major conflicts, Calhoun discouraged the adoption of such measures, though he did recommend that chiefs be warned that if they did not exhibit their "abhorrence" of murderers by surrendering them to authorities, they would "be considered as participants of their guilt, and their whole nation made to feel the just vengeance and retribution of the Government."[45]

Growing condemnation of the factory system that governed the Native American trade gave rise to further questions about the meaning of justice in US-Native American relations. Established in 1796, the system consisted of a chain of trading posts intended to supply Native American needs without deceit or extortion. However well traders may have observed this mandate in earlier years, the system's operation left much to be desired by the time Calhoun entered Monroe's cabinet. Proposals for reform took two very different tracks. One was a market-based approach championed by Lewis Cass. Abolishing government posts and throwing the trade open to private merchants, the Michigan territorial governor contended, would create a system that "will regulate itself by the competition of those employed in it," ensuring fair prices and preventing the formation of monopolistic combinations. Superintendent of Indian Trade Thomas L. McKenney could not have disagreed more. Frontier traders hardly stood in the front ranks of nature's noblemen, and McKenney had no wish to see them turned loose in Native American country. To be sure, he wrote Calhoun, "an overthrow of the existing Government system would prove favorable to the individual enterprize; but, it is not less certain, that it would be, in the same proportion, unfavourable to the Indians." Whatever benefits opening the commerce might provide individual entrepreneurs, he added, there could be no justification for a policy that would inevitably produce "an enlargement of the range of poverty, and disease, and want, amongst the Indians, which would result, naturally from [the] excess, licentiousness, and undue exactions" of unregulated private traders. Without close government supervision, current problems could only grow worse.[46]

Calhoun, after carefully weighing the two arguments, sided with McKenney. In an 1818 report, he recommended that the factory system be phased out gradually. He further urged the imposition of high license fees on participants in any new system. Although some might contend that this would make it more difficult to furnish goods at moderate prices, he believed the resulting diminution in the number of traders would make it easier to regulate their operations; and saving a few dollars was much less important than placing merchants "under the control of the Government," so that Native Americans "may be protected against the fraud and the violence to which ignorance and weakness would, without such protection, expose them." Indeed, an even better solution to the trade problem would be the creation of a single, well-capitalized corporation that possessed the resources required to counterbalance the power and influence of large private organizations such as John Jacob Astor's American Fur Company. Doing so would doubtless raise the cry of monopoly, but there was no reason to fear that bugbear: "A nation discovers its wisdom no less in departing from general maxims, where it is no longer wise to adhere to them, than in its adherence to them in ordinary circumstances." And what mattered most was that any alternative to the factory system be capable of "subjecting the trade to the will and control of the Government." These observations reveal much about how Calhoun then perceived the relationship between state and society. If they stemmed in part from a paternalistic view of Native Americans that emphasized their incapacity and helplessness, they also reflected his strong belief in positive government. During this phase of his political career, he had little patience with people who thought government was the problem; he was much more likely to see it as the means of remedying whatever ills troubled the nation.[47]

The real test of justice in US–Native American relations centered on differences related to land possession and ownership. This had been the case since the outset of English colonization, and it was especially so during the Monroe years. The War of 1812 had seriously weakened the defenses of major Native American nations east of the Mississippi, giving added impetus to a flood of white settlement that had shown few signs of abating over the preceding three decades; the forty-one land cessions Calhoun negotiated as secretary substantially exceeded the number secured by any of his predecessors. His conduct of these talks required him to address a range of critical issues. Besides having to decide how comfortable he felt engaging in the double-dealing, subterfuge, and chicanery that normally attended land bargaining sessions, he had to take a position on such contentious matters as the government's responsibility for preventing settler encroachment on Native American lands, the expediency of continuing the focus on initiatives to "civilize" Native Americans, the resolutionof their grievances, and the determination of what constituted fair compensation for Native American landholdings. And he had to do it during a period when the main thrust of government policy was shifting from acculturation to removal.[48]

Government dealings with the Cherokees provide a good prism through which to view Calhoun's response. More so than most Native American nations, the Cherokees believed the acculturation program initiated by Henry Knox had much to offer. During the late eighteenth century, Cherokees endeavored to construct roads and ferries, acquire herds of livestock, purchase farm equipment to boost agricultural productivity, and adopt other forms of improvement recommended by those seeking to promote the "civilization" of Native Americans. But adoption was invariably on their own terms. Cherokees took advantage of the educational opportunities provided by Protestant missionaries, but relatively few of them became Christians; they added wheat growing to the cultivation of their traditional crops of corn, squash, and beans, but retained a gendered division of labor that assigned most agricultural work to women; and they continued to hold their lands in common, resisting all efforts to induce them to distribute land on an individual basis. At the same time, they created an increasingly centralized government, consolidating authority in a National Committee and, in

1817, adopting their first constitution, the Articles of Government. Although the Articles did not give leaders the wherewithal to prevent additional land cessions in 1817 and 1819, US representatives who sat down with Cherokee chiefs quickly learned that they faced some very tough and very able negotiators, whose primary aim was to prevent the further contraction of a homeland that still extended across parts of northeastern Alabama, eastern Tennessee, and northwest Georgia.[49]

Calhoun entered the War Department with no fixed plan for conducting land cession talks. Any approach that promised to reduce Native American landholdings east of the Mississippi was fine, though he clearly favored removal west of the river. This was evident in a July 1818 letter to Joseph McMinn. The Tennessee governor had complained of resistance to a recent treaty by a Cherokee faction that had no desire to emigrate or live on reservations confined to a limited land area. Calhoun found this response unacceptable. "Universal experience proves that people still in a savage state, cannot reside in the immediate neighborhood of a civilized nation, without falling into a state of vice and misery," he wrote McMinn. "By removing to the West, the Cherokee nation will obtain time, before they can be crowded by the whites, to become civilized, and capable of enjoying the advantage of equal laws." Addressing members of a Cherokee delegation some months later, he told them that, should they choose to remain where they were, they would have to make do with considerably less territory than they currently held. "You are now becoming like the white people; you can no longer live by hunting but must work for your subsistence," he said. "In your new condition far less land is necessary for you." Should they refuse to adapt, he warned, they faced two alternatives: emigration or extinction. What the Cherokees wanted really did not matter. They needed to recognize that Washington's views concerning what was best for them—not their own—would be decisive: "You see that the Great Spirit has made our form of society stronger than yours—and you must submit to adopt ours; if you wish to be happy by pleasing him."[50]

Calhoun's arguments made little impression on Cherokee leaders. Least persuasive were his assertions that the Cherokees needed to give up the hunt and adopt the norms of white society. As nation chiefs later informed Monroe, their people had been doing just that, taking advantage of government programs to achieve marked advances in "education, agriculture, manufacture, and the mechanic arts," which "are now progressing as rapidly as reasonably can be expected." Moreover, they had grievances of their own. Despite repeated complaints, white settler encroachment on Native American lands continued, often with the active support of state governments. These and other treaty violations, the chiefs told Calhoun, "certainly constitute a reasonable and just claim against your Government." As far as additional cessions were concerned, they had already given up far too much of their traditional homeland. "Brother," they said in an 1822 statement, "we do now declare to you in words with an unchang[e]able heart that we will never cede away any more lands."[51]

Meanwhile, the administration faced increasing pressure from Georgians to complete the removal of Native Americans from state lands. Although Calhoun assured them that it had been government policy since the summer of 1818 to seek "the gradual, and ultimately, the entire extinguishment of the Cherokee title to" lands "East of the Mississippi," there was little he could do to compel further cessions, given his and Monroe's unwillingness to use coercion against recalcitrant Native Americans. Where attempts to exploit divisions among Native American leaders proved unavailing, the government's "civilization" initiative had become more of a hindrance than a source of support—not because Native Americans ignored it, but because, as historian Michael D. Green has written, it "worked both too well and to [the secretary's] disadvantage." Georgians had always condemned the program, believing that any success it enjoyed would only increase the difficulty of justifying Native American removal and make their negotiators more formidable adversaries at the bargaining table. That is exactly what happened. A major obstacle to obtaining further Cherokee lands in Georgia, Calhoun told Monroe in an 1824 letter, was "their growing Civilization and Knowledge, by which they have learned to place a higher value upon their lands than more rude and Savage Tribes." He confronted similar problems in talks with Chickasaw leaders, who said "their refusal to cede more land is not an act of unfriendliness, but that, instead, it represents their effort to follow the advice given to them by the United States, which was to cultivate their land and to become civilized." Despite such resistance, Calhoun would later claim to be "the author of the plan for removing the Cherokees and all the Southern tribes of Indians to the west of the Mississippi," which had opened untold acres east of the river to white settlement and would shortly "remove the last remains of the aboriginal race" from the region.[52]

Controversy concerning Native American removal carried over into the Adams administration before reaching its grim resolution during the presidency of Andrew Jackson. As secretary of state, Adams took little or no part in shaping Native American policy. His conduct as president indicates that he and Calhoun shared the same general perspective. When Secretary of War James Barbour proposed combining all Native American nations into a single territory west of the Mississippi, Adams approved the plan, despite some skepticism about its practicability. And when the state of Georgia violated federal treaty obligations by encouraging settler encroachment on Creek lands, he limited the government response to a few threatening gestures, despite believing that "we ought not to yield to Georgia because we could not do so without gross injustice." He would later condemn Jackson for supporting state efforts to appropriate Native American lands, but in certain important respects the two presidents different little in their view of Native American rights. In his second annual message to Congress, the Tennessee general asked: Who "would prefer a country covered with forests and ranged by a few thousand savages to our extensive Republic, studded with cities, towns, and prosperous farms, established with all the improvements which art can devise or industry execute, occupied by more than 12,000,000 happy people, and filled with all the blessings of liberty, civilization, and religion?" There can be no doubt how Adams would have answered that query. Like Jackson, he subscribed to what might be called an imperialist variant of the labor theory of value: Those who worked the land, as the dominant culture defined work, owned the land. As he observed in an 1843 address, an individual still in a hunter state "had no permanent right to the soil to renounce," and settlers "did him no wrong by assuming, after compensating him for his right of hunting there, the exclusive right of possession to himself."[53]

One must, however, resist the temptation of positing an equivalence between Adams and Jackson. The New Englander viewed the injustice and hardships imposed on Native Americans with a compassion that Jackson never exhibited. He felt genuine distress over "the expulsion of the southern tribes" that had been "driven like herds of cattle, to a common receptacle beyond the Mississippi, [where] they are already threatened again with expulsion, by their neighbors of Arkansas and Missouri." And he truly wished that the government's acculturation policy had turned out better. "We have," he confided to his diary, "talked of benevolence and humanity, and preached them into civilization; but none of this benevolence is felt when the right of the Indians comes in collision with the white man." Adams particularly regretted the fate of the Cherokees, whom he considered "the most civilized of the tribes of North American Indians." Georgia had overturned treaties made with these people, and in defiance of law, "extended her jurisdiction over these Indian lands, and lavished in lottery tickets to her people, the cultivated fields, the growing harvests, and the furnished dwellings of the Cherokee, imprisoned in a dungeon the pious missionaries preaching among them the gospel of Christ, and set at naught the solemn adjudication of the supreme court of the United States, pronouncing this licensed robbery alike lawless and unconstitutional."[54]

These observations show how Adams's ethnocentrism informed even his most sympathetic statements about Native Americans—the more civilized a people, the more deserving it was of one's empathy. But they reveal something more as well. Where, for Jackson and those who shared his perspective, the invocation of value theory all too often served as nothing more than a pretext for the confiscation of Native American lands, Adams subscribed to a more principled position. Decades earlier, he had stated that whatever land Native Americans have "annexed to themselves by personal labor, was undoubtedly by the laws of nature theirs." He believed that all people, regardless of race, had a right to the fruits of their labor; he further believed that government had an obligation to protect that right. If he sometimes lacked the courage of his convictions—as his failure to respond more forcefully to Georgia's land seizures demonstrates—he never abandoned these beliefs. This would become increasingly apparent in the 1830s as he turned his attention to slavery-related issues.[55]

In March 1825, Monroe's second term came to an end. So did the cabinet service of Adams and Calhoun. As the two secretaries departed their posts—Adams for the Executive Mansion and Calhoun for the vice presidency—neither of them left much in the way of unfinished business on his desk. For Adams, these had been particularly good years. The Transcontinental Treaty, together with the role he had played in shaping the Monroe Doctrine, confirmed his reputation as one of the nation's most astute and influential foreign policy specialists. Although congressional obstruction hampered Calhoun's efforts to reform the army, he could take satisfaction in having achieved some successes under often adverse circumstances. Throughout, he had fought the good fight, working impossibly long hours and demonstrating that he possessed a range of talents that fitted him for the assumption of official duties that extended well beyond the floor of Congress. There was, however, one dark cloud on the horizon that they chose largely to ignore. Their efforts to extend the national domain made future conflict between westward movement and slave expansionism all but inevitable. Where Calhoun wanted to avoid any public discussion of the South's peculiar institution, Adams put aside the dire forebodings that the Missouri controversy had awakened in him, hoping that the catastrophe he saw coming could somehow be evaded. It could not, and when he and Calhoun confronted the problem in coming decades, they would do so as bitter adversaries.

That was still in the future. What is most striking about the conduct of Adams and Calhoun in the decade following the War of 1812 is the degree to which the policy initiatives of each of them paralleled and complemented those of the other. It is easy to understand why Adams thought so highly of Calhoun: They both subscribed to a developmental ethos that looked forward to the establishment of the United States as a leading world power. In effect, Adams acted as a "Mr. Outside" through his endeavors to expand the national domain and prevent further European colonization of the Americas, while Calhoun functioned as a "Mr. Inside" through his efforts to hasten the agricultural development of Native American lands and promote the enactment of internal improvement legislation designed to create an integrated national economy. There can be little doubt that the New Englander approved unreservedly of Calhoun's plans to plant the flag in the far western reaches of the expanding American empire. The only area in which they differed was Native American policy. Where Adams never stopped believing that whoever cultivated the land owned it, the secretary of war retreated from his initial endorsement of "civilization" programs to support Native American expulsion schemes that ignored the land improvement activities of indigenous peoples. Yet even here the two men agreed that whenever Native American land rights conflicted with the dictates of national development, Native Americans had to give way before what they saw as the march of progress.

A final question concerns the effect that events and developments between the War of 1812 and the close of Monroe's administration had on the two men. In the case of Adams, the answer is short and simple: not much. In 1812, he was a seasoned diplomat whose principles had begun taking shape during a precocious youth and evolved gradually in the years that followed. Looking out upon an imperfect world, Adams saw much that disappointed but little that surprised him. This is not to say that he experienced no growth at all during the period. One of the New Englander's most admirable traits was a great sense of curiosity that made the quest for knowledge a lifelong passion that he never fully sated. Yet, apart from such learning, he remained much the same person in 1825 that he had been thirteen years earlier—older and somewhat wiser, but still an ardent nationalist, deeply committed to what Calhoun called the moral and physical development of the nation's immense resources.

Calhoun's case is more complicated. The decade or so prior to 1812 had been a period of unchecked achievement and ascent that took him from the South Carolina Upcountry to the center of national affairs, where, at the relatively young age of thirty, he played a major role in leading the country to war. He was as unprepared for the ensuing setbacks on the field of battle as the army that endured them, and for perhaps the first time in his life he had to acknowledge that his miscalculations had contributed to a serious debacle. Believing that hard work was the most effective remedy for damaged self-esteem, Calhoun labored diligently to repair the shortcomings that afflicted the nation's military. Even here, however, he encountered various disappointments. Some notable accomplishments notwithstanding, penurious legislators, querulous generals, and popular distrust of standing armies and federal authority combined to teach sobering lessons in the difficulty of effecting institutional change. One result of all this was to add a prudential element to Calhoun's thought that had not been there before and that never completely went away. In later years, he often assumed the role of provocateur, while remaining wary of extremist solutions to the South's grievances. Whenever this note of caution surfaced, regional contemporaries of more volatile temperament sometimes attributed it to political ambition. Although not entirely wrong, such criticism overlooked the influence that this earlier period had on Calhoun's development. More so than many Southern political leaders of the coming generation, he knew from hard experience that enthusiasm alone went only so far.

Whatever else Calhoun might have felt during his final days as secretary of war, he had not abandoned the vibrant nationalism that he brought to the post. Considerations of love, fear, and interest all reinforced a belief that federal-state relations, if not already perfect, only needed a little more tightening to become so. Under the current system of government, people from all parts of the union could look forward to the imminent realization of a glorious national destiny. "The time is fast approaching, when this continent must take a lead in the affairs of the world," he wrote in an 1821 letter. "Its position, soil, climate and above all its political character resulting from freedom and exemption from the taint of f[e]udalism, must place it far above Europe." However disturbing the sentiments expressed in the Missouri debate, territorial expansion posed no threat to the South. Since 1812, Louisiana, Mississippi, Alabama, and Missouri had entered the union as slave states; Florida and Arkansas would doubtless do so as soon as they attained sufficient population. Nor did slaveholders have anything to fear from the internal improvement projects that Calhoun championed. The creation of an integrated national market would benefit people in all regions, the South as well as the North and the West. It was a wonderful vision, but it would soon give way to darker thoughts.[56]

Chapter 3

SECTIONALISM and NULLIFICATION

As the 1824 presidential contest approached, relations between Adams and Calhoun became, in the New Englander's words, increasingly "delicate and difficult." To be sure, neither man viewed the other with nearly the same degree of disapprobation that each of them reserved for Secretary of Treasury William H. Crawford, whom both considered an unscrupulous political operator who invariably placed his presidential aspirations before the national interest. But an earlier warmth was clearly missing. Where Calhoun began dropping comments about Adams's sometimes unsteady judgment, former Federalism, and rumored support for restricting slavery in Missouri, while professing his great admiration for the North, the secretary of state spoke disapprovingly of the South Carolinian's ambition, charging that his cabinet colleague "had been laboring incessantly to injure him & advance himself" in ways that were plainly "unworthy of a man of talents & integrity." Even worse was Calhoun's duplicity. "My complaint was," Adams wrote in a diary entry listing the many "acts of insidious hostility" directed at him by the secretary of war and his supporters, "not that attempts were made to tear my reputation to pieces for the benefit of Mr. Calhoun, but that they were preceded and accompanied by professions of great esteem, and with the expression of earnest desires for harmony and good understanding."[1]

Their estrangement widened with Adams's election as president. The new chief executive never lived down accusations that his elevation to the nation's highest office rested on a "corrupt bargain" with Henry Clay, whom, critics asserted, he had agreed to make secretary of state in exchange for the Kentuckian's support in the House voting that decided the contest. Calhoun was one of those who eagerly seized on the allegation, telling acquaintances that the purported deal represented "the most dangerous stab, which the liberty of the country has ever received." "Power improperly acquired," he later observed, "will be improperly used. Those who have thus acquired it, will exercise it, not for the publick good, but to make partisans, and the fearful spectacle will be exhibited of using the power and patronage of the government, as the instrument of bribery."

That Adams was the least inclined of all major political figures of the period to use patronage in such a manner did not matter. As vice president, Calhoun assumed a leading role in an anti-Adams alliance intent on ensuring that the New Englander would be a one-term president. And as president of the Senate, his conduct prompted an acrimonious public exchange with Patrick Henry, a pro-Adams correspondent. Accused of stacking key Senate committees with administration opponents and permitting John Randolph to flay Adams and Clay in interminably long, invective-filled speeches without calling the Virginian to order, Calhoun posed as a defender of popular rights in counterattacks that questioned the legitimacy of Adams's election and raised the specter of authoritarian government. None of this made the president happy. He was even less happy about a rising tide of states' rights sentiment that engulfed his legislative agenda, submerging any hopes he might have had of realizing his vision of national development. "The lurking jealousies of slave-holders were enlisted against the native of a state wholly free," he observed in an unpublished manuscript written shortly after he left office. "The born-bred dislikes of the cavalier race to the scion of the Pilgrim Puritans were summoned to the array against him; and the Virginian and Southern and slave-holding mind was thus predisposed to receive falsehoods for truth, and sophistry for reason, to ruin the reputation and paralyze the power of a" chief executive "already basely slandered by infamous imputations" concerning the circumstances of his election.[2]

Calhoun's emergence as a champion of these views deepened the animus Adams felt toward his former cabinet colleague without causing a complete break between them. Several years later, when the Carolinian sought "a renewal of the intercourse of common civility," Adams did not think it proper to dismiss the advance. But, recognizing that their earlier relationship "can never be fully restored," he responded warily. "Mr. Calhoun's Friendships and Enmities are regulated exclusively by his interests," he wrote in his diary. "His opinions are the spout of every popular blast, and his career as a Statesman has been marked by a series of the most flagrant inconsistencies." However much Adams failed to appreciate the sincerity of Calhoun's convictions, he had good reason to speak of the "flagrant inconsistencies" in his thought. The Carolinian's abandonment of a fervent nationalism powered by a strong and active central government for a position at the polar end of the ideological spectrum caught the attention of many contemporary observers. Adams would soon learn that Calhoun's new beliefs represented something more than an opportunistic response to changes in the political climate. A September 1831 exchange of letters, to which each correspondent appended copies of recent addresses, made it unmistakably clear just how far apart they stood. Where Adams's Quincy oration attacked the "hallucination of state sovereignty," Calhoun's Fort Hill Address presented a logical, carefully reasoned defense of the principle that removed any doubts about how long and hard he had thought about his change of course. The New Englander had hoped that communicating with his former associate would open an avenue to further discussion of their "present Sentiments with regard to the Union." Instead, it only reinforced a growing perception that the Carolina doctrine had replaced the fulminations of Virginia radicals as the most dangerous of the political heresies facing the nation.[3]

This chapter explores the significance of these developments, beginning with an examination of Calhoun's transition from nationalist to advocate of an extreme states' rights position that called for state nullification of objectionable federal laws. As a central figure in the ensuing nullification controversy, Calhoun sought to rally Southern support behind what he deemed a much-needed constitutional defense of Southern interests; and he hoped to do so without letting the debate become an intersectional dispute over slavery. Why he wished to avoid a major confrontation concerning the South's peculiar institution is one of several topics examined in section two, which focuses on Adams's interventions in the controversy. More so than other free labor protectionists who chided planters for their reliance on slave labor but stopped short of a frontal assault on the institution, Adams sought to show that slavery was at the heart of the dispute. A final section looks at the closing stages of the nullification crisis and assesses important changes in the political views of Adams and Calhoun. Where the New Englander adopted an increasingly sectional stance without abandoning his nationalist outlook, the South Carolinian discarded most traces of his former nationalism as he assumed the role of defender of Southern rights and interests.

In late November 1824, members of James Monroe's cabinet gathered to discuss the president's upcoming annual message to Congress. There was general agreement that the draft needed little if any revision. The most serious objection came from the secretary of war and concerned a statement declaring "the agricultural, manufacturing, and commercial interests of the Country to be in a flourishing condition." However customary it might be to include such boilerplate in presidential addresses, Calhoun felt the assertion would not play well in the South, where "a state of great depression" that had begun five years earlier continued to take a heavy toll on the region's planters and farmers. In few places was this more so than in his native state. Where most parts of the nation—including large areas of the South—had by now recovered from the distress caused by the Panic of 1819, South Carolina remained mired in an economic slump that showed little sign of abating. Although most Lowcountry planters had managed to keep their heads above water, despite declines in rice and long-staple cotton prices, conditions in Calhoun's Upcountry homeland could not have been much worse. An unrelenting plunge in short-staple cotton prices hit planters there much harder than it did cotton growers in Alabama, Mississippi, and other western areas, where the availability of large expanses of fresh, fertile land permitted a steady growth in crop yields. No less problematic was the Upcountry's inadequate credit facilities and shortage of circulating currency, which added to the problems of planters trying desperately to retire debts incurred during the boom years of the late 1810s. As the crisis deepened, increasing numbers of Carolinians looked west for salvation.[4]

Hard times also prompted a reassessment of federal-state relations. As late as 1820, Palmetto political leaders continued to back Calhoun's expansive view of federal authority. Asked to consider an anti-tariff memorial that attacked protective duties as a violation of states' rights, a committee of the South Carolina House worried that such legislation might, as the petitioners' charged, have the effect of forcing "those parts of the union which are *still* prosperous to contribute even by their utter ruin, to fill the coffers of a few monopolists" elsewhere. Its members could not, however, accept the "unfortunately too common" belief that the states formed "*distinct* and *independent sovereignties*" opposed to the national government. Whenever "the general welfare of the public is in question," they counseled, South Carolina would be best advised to maintain "those wise, liberal and magnanimous principles by which this state has been hitherto so proudly distinguished." Four years later, economic conditions and the views of Palmetto legislators had changed considerably. Led by Calhoun's longtime political rival William Smith, a substantial majority of the assembly urged a vigorous defense of states' rights in resolutions that condemned protective tariffs and bills that "tax the Citizens of one State to make roads and canals for the citizens of another State" as unconstitutional assertions of federal power. Their adoption, one observer later wrote, represented "a remarkable triumph of the good sense of the people over the most unhappy influence in favour of Messrs. MONROE and CALHOUN's politics, which before had been insensibly carrying on the State, to the maintenance of doctrines, in which any thing but safety was to be sought."[5]

By this time as well, a growing number of commentators had added their voices to the assault on federal power. One of the most erudite and least compromising was "that two-legged library of all knowledge and all science," South Carolina College President Thomas Cooper. An immigrant from Great Britain, where he had been an outspoken proponent of parliamentary reform, Cooper later served six months in prison for his incautious criticism of the Alien and Sedition Acts. Since then, he had adopted a more conservative stance on democracy without moderating his fondness for forthright expression. A pamphlet on the 1824 tariff addressed to South Carolina's congressional delegation combined a careful, point-by-point refutation of arguments for protection with a ringing denunciation of the bill's unconstitutionality and an inflammatory assessment of its likely effect on the South. Cooper could not believe that people had knowingly accorded Congress "the power of unequal and discriminatory taxation, so that at the will of government, one set of citizens may be lightly, and another heavily burthened, or that the industry of one class should be fostered at the expense of another." And that was not the worst of it. Should the measure be enacted, he warned, Southern planters faced consequences that went well beyond the injustice resulting from the imposition of customs duties to protect Northern manufacturers: "They are threatened with an annihilation of their staple commodity—NOT WITH TAXATION, BUT DESTRUCTION."[6]

Cooper's tariff tract made no mention of Calhoun. Another pamphlet he wrote that year did, however. In a biting critique of contemporary politics, Cooper made it clear that he believed the divisions of the past had a continuing relevance that too many public figures were unwilling to acknowledge. As he saw it, talk of an "era of good feelings" that had eliminated party competition and vanquished earlier political heresies was part of an insidious ploy to clothe Federalist principles and practices in respectable Democratic-Republican garb. And Calhoun—whom he later described as being "too pretending, too fond of the brilliant, the magnificent, the imposing, too calculating how all his sayings and doing will work with respect to his own honour and glory"—had played a conspicuous role in the deception. As secretary of war, he had dangled a series of costly internal improvement projects before Monroe's eyes in an effort to accumulate ever greater "power and patronage" through the control of "every cent that would otherwise form a surplus revenue." Anyone reading his report on fortifications, Cooper added, would quickly recognize his embrace of "the fashionable folly of the day, a PATRONIZING GOVERNMENT." Do not be deceived, he told his South Carolina readers. Calhoun's politics, like those of Adams and Jackson, "are not the politics of this state," for all three of them subscribed to a view of government that, "from the very moment of party difference, has decidedly characterized the federal party,—Consolidation is the motto of their flag."[7]

What Calhoun thought of Cooper's effusions is unclear, but one can be certain that he found them upsetting. Nothing disturbed Calhoun more than charges that he placed ambition before principle, and while Cooper did not directly accuse him of having done so, suggestions that he was just another self-aggrandizing politician intent on furthering his own well-being came uncomfortably close to the truth at that particular time. Although Calhoun had noticed the growth of states' rights sentiment as early as 1821, he remained committed to "the purity and wisdom of that system and policy which grew out of the experience of the late war," believing such a course to be in the best interests of both the nation and the South. It was also in his own political interest. He was then considering a presidential run in which his hopes rested largely on how well he did in Pennsylvania, where no candidate who opposed protective duties and internal improvements could expect much in the way of voter support. New York and Pennsylvania, he observed in an 1823 letter, had diversified economies reliant on "commerce, & navigation, agriculture & manufactures," and people there "are consequently deeply interested in all of the measures necessary to protect or enlarge them." Adopting a platform with broad sectional appeal further enabled him to portray his main Southern opponent, William H. Crawford of Georgia, as a small-minded demagogue whose attacks on positive government placed him squarely in the camp of those "few leaders, intriguers and political managers" working "against the whole body of the people." In all of this, Calhoun was perfectly consistent, and these observations would merit little notice had he not attempted to have it both ways. In an August 1823 letter complaining of his treatment by states' rights Virginians, he declared "that so far from being the friend of consol[id]ation, I consider the preservation of the rights of the States, as secured in the Constitution, as essential to liberty." By the following summer, he was contending that nothing in his record "could give offense to the most ardent defender of state rights" in communications seeking to justify his earlier support for measures that such people found repellant.[8]

This last statement can most charitably be described as disingenuous. Whatever Calhoun might have said previously on behalf of the states' reserved powers paled beside his steady support of programs requiring a broad interpretation of Congress's delegated powers. As Adams approvingly noted, he had "no petty scruples about constructive powers, and States Rights." Yet, if Calhoun's professions of principle sometimes rang hollow, he was not the sort of person who discarded long-held beliefs simply because it was politically expedient to do so. Needing to convince himself that the public good necessitated abandonment of his prior position, his movement from nationalist to nullifier took place gradually. Adams's election hastened the process. In addition to his ready acceptance of the "corrupt bargain" explanation of the New Englander's victory, Calhoun felt the expansive vision of national development outlined in the new president's first annual message to Congress called for a much greater degree of federal intervention than he could condone; it also suggested plans for the establishment of a patronage machine designed to consolidate the ascendancy of those currently controlling the executive branch. Were something not done to prevent it, he soon came to believe, the unchecked operation of the Adams-Clay diarchy portended a bleak future for American government. His apprehensions had obvious political implications, and he found a sympathetic listener in Andrew Jackson, who had finished second in the 1824 presidential contest despite winning a plurality of the popular and electoral vote. "An issue has been truly made, it seems to me," he told the general, "between *power* and *liberty*; and it must be determined in the next three years, whether the real governing principle in our political system be the power and patronage of the Executive, or the voice of the people. For it can scarcely be doubted, that a scheme has been formed to perpetuate power in the present hands, in spite of the free and unbiased sentiment of the country."[9]

During the next several years, Calhoun's disenchantment took on a more pronounced sectional cast. He had always been mindful of state and regional interests, but rising Southern opposition to protectionism made him considerably more so. Persisting hard times in cotton country provided the context for these protests. "Never was there such universal, and severe pressure on the whole South excepting the portion, which plants sugar," Calhoun observed. "Our staples hardly return the expense of cultivation, and land and Negroes have fallen to the lowest price, and can scarcely be sold at the present depressed rates." These problems made Southern political leaders extremely resistant to any legislative initiative that threatened to make conditions worse. And when Congress, during its 1827 session, turned its attention to a woolens bill that—if enacted—would have increased the cost of slave clothing without any compensating benefit for planters, people gathered throughout South Carolina and other parts of the South to condemn the measure. At a Columbia meeting that passed resolutions denying Congress had the power to pass revenue laws favoring one branch of enterprise over another, Thomas Cooper warned that this was only the beginning, and that Southerners needed to begin preparing to defend themselves against further assaults on their rights. "Is it worth our while," he asked, "to continue this union of states, where the north demand to be our masters and we are required to be their tributaries?" Cooper did not think so; he further believed the question required more serious consideration than many people realized, for the time was "fast approaching to the alternative, of submission or separation."[10]

Cooper's remarks placed him well in advance of where most South Carolinians then stood. Although Calhoun could not be dismissive of what he had to say, there was no compelling reason why he had to follow his lead. As president of South Carolina College, Cooper was well positioned to shape the views of South Carolina's rising generation of state leaders, but his unorthodox religious beliefs and reputation for oratorical excess detracted from his influence. Other states' rights advocates demanded greater attention. One of them was Robert James Turnbull, a prominent lawyer-planter who in 1827 published a series of essays that, in the words of one contemporary, "struck upon the public ear with a shrill, yet full volume, that aroused us from the deep trance in which we had long slumbered." Like all South Carolina polemicists of the period, Turnbull made clear his hostility to protectionism and its inequities. Where Northern calls for higher duties stemmed from rank avarice, he asserted, Southern opponents, "as they become more and more swelled into honest indignation against the tribute of the Tariff, are actuated by the noblest feelings which can influence the actions of men and societies—an adherence to the principles of Liberty and the Constitution.—The North supports the Tariff from INTEREST, mean, sordid interest. The South resists it on PRINCIPLE." What set him apart from most other South Carolina writers was the heavy emphasis he placed on constitutional issues. Protectionism, he contended, could best be seen as a symptom of a deadly disease eating away at the vitals of the regional economy. Attacking the tariff alone would not cure it. What the South most needed was a leadership class capable of casting aside the distractions of party politics and focusing on the construction of constitutional defenses against federal usurpations.[11]

In developing his case, Turnbull devoted less space to denouncing protectionism than to criticizing internal improvements. A major target of his critique was George McDuffie. As Turnbull doubtless knew, the SC congressman had already adopted a firm anti-tariff stance in a speech likening the duties contained in the 1827 woolens bill to the taxes imposed on American colonists before the Revolution; no measure, the Palmetto legislator added, posed a greater threat to "the harmony and existence of the Union" than this iniquitous proposal. But he was also an outspoken supporter of internal improvements. Even worse were the arguments he had marshaled in defense of such measures. McDuffie had no time for strict constructionists who believed the Constitution left Congress without any discretionary authority. Were the national legislature stripped of its implied powers, he maintained, "the machine of government" would grind to a halt, making it impossible to protect the nation against foreign adversaries or to undertake initiatives designed to promote the general welfare. Nor did he have much respect for states' rights doctrine, on one occasion describing it as "mere sounds, used by misguided or designing men" to confuse the public and advance their own interests; in another statement denouncing the "*false, dangerous, and anti-republican assumption*" that buttressed "all the reasoning in favor of state rights," he declared that states "*have no original, independent rights.*" Turnbull considered these views highly objectionable, if not downright heretical. That someone of McDuffie's stature would utter them in public was especially disturbing, and he urged the congressman to reexamine the Constitution—"not with the visionary eye of an ardent enthusiast," but from the detached perspective of the sober statesman. Upon doing so, he would doubtless see that the document's "whole scheme and design is opposed to constructive powers" and placed sharp limits on what Congress could do, particularly with regard to taxation.[12]

McDuffie's place in the relatively small world of South Carolina's political elite, in addition to making his public statements worthy of rebuttal, gave Turnbull's critique greater significance than it otherwise would have had. Orphaned at an early age, McDuffie had been informally adopted by the vice president's brother and grew up in the Calhoun family. With his election to Congress in 1820, he quickly became one of the House's most forceful advocates of Calhounite nationalism. Turnbull did not make the connection explicit in his essays. Nor did he question the congressman's motives; unlike Cooper, who rarely let considerations of social and political status get in the way of a good argument, the lawyer-planter exhibited a gentlemanly regard for propriety when singling out a fellow South Carolinian for chastisement. But it was unnecessary for him to do so. Although McDuffie did not speak directly for Calhoun, informed observers—particularly among members of South Carolina's political class—considered him a Calhoun protégé and assumed that his views reflected the beliefs of his mentor. They understood that in criticizing the congressman, Turnbull was in effect criticizing the vice president as well. They further recognized that he was putting Calhoun on notice: South Carolina had entered a period of crisis, and if he wanted to maintain his position as the state's most respected political leader, he needed to step forward and let people know where he stood.[13]

Calhoun's response to the challenge began even before Turnbull finished writing. As president of the Senate, he cast the deciding vote against the 1827 woolens bill. And when tariff supporters afterward gathered in Harrisburg, Pennsylvania, he denounced this assemblage of "the great geographical Northern manufacturing interest" as part of a plot "to enforce more effectually the system of monopoly and extortion against the consuming States." But he had greater trouble getting a handle on the constitutional issues at the core of Turnbull's critique. Like any able Southern lawyer of the period, Calhoun had a sound understanding of basic constitutional principles. He had never subjected the document to close analysis, however, and his initial efforts to construct a constitutional defense of Southern rights demonstrated as much. A good example is a July 1827 letter to Maryland politician Virgil Maxcy in which he commented on the general welfare clause of Article I, Section 8. Where all strict constructionists unhesitatingly interpreted the clause in the narrowest conceivable manner, Calhoun still had some doubts about what he thought of it. As to what the term *general welfare* means, he wrote, "I had not gone farther formerly, than to say, that all objects of national importance were comprehended, and no more. But it is obvious the question is not precluded, but still remains, what is meant by nationally important." Any "solution to the question, by the soundest rules of construction," he added, "must lead to the conclusion, that the power of appropriation to the general welfare, or to national objects, is neither more, nor less than, the power to apply the funds of the government to the objects for which it was created." Coming from someone with Calhoun's deserved reputation for clear, logical expression, the statement was remarkably equivocal, if not opaque. He did somewhat better in an August letter discussing the need for a state veto to counter federal impositions. Yet even here, he hesitated, observing that "how far such a negative would be consistent with the general power, is an important consideration" that "I waive for the present."[14]

Calhoun may not have gone appreciably further at this juncture had the period of relative quiescence following Senate rejection of the woolens bill persisted. But this was not to be. Enactment of the 1828 tariff changed everything. Commonly known as the Tariff of Abominations, the measure was the product of a series of legislative maneuvers that went disastrously wrong for anti-tariff forces. The latter had conspired to kill the act by agreeing to substantially higher duties on various raw materials, fully expecting that representatives of the manufacturing interest would find them sufficiently onerous to prevent the measure's passage. When the bill passed anyway and Adams signed it into law, South Carolina and other areas of the South exploded in protest. "The excitement is deep and universal," Calhoun wrote at the time, "but I trust and believe [it] will be restrained within the bounds of moderation." Such hopes quickly gave way to the realization that many South Carolinians were much angrier and much less willing to compromise than he was. The strident assertions of one particularly raucous gathering in the southeastern Lowcountry district of Colleton prompted a letter from Senator Samuel Smith of Maryland, who informed the vice president that the meeting's separatist, "Hartford Convention" principles would "not be sustained by Virginia, Maryland, or any of the States East thereof, nor any one of the West." This was decidedly unwelcome news for someone whose prudential instincts and presidential ambitions made him acutely aware of the importance of coalition building. And over the next several months, Calhoun's correspondence projected a mixed message: on one hand, denouncing the inequitable sectional effects of protective legislation, arguing that federal interference in economic affairs threatened "the duration of the Union and the liberty of the country," and defending state refusal to obey oppressive laws that represented congressional usurpation of power; on the other, providing assurances that South Carolina's "patriotick attachment to the Union remain[ed]" strong, professing his appreciation of the economic contributions of manufacturing establishments, and even conceding that protectionism might be justified as an incidental feature of bills clearly intended to raise revenue or regulate trade.[15]

Despite mounting discontent on the home front, public pressure for bold action had not reached a critical point. In the words of historian William W. Freehling, calling for open resistance to the collection of customs duties "was good politics but not yet necessary politics in South Carolina in 1828." This did not mean that Calhoun could maintain his balancing act indefinitely, however. What other members of the state's political class thought always mattered more to South Carolina political leaders than what the general populace believed, and a number of prominent figures were adopting an increasingly radical stance. In a widely reported October speech, Congressman James Hamilton Jr., went beyond the obligatory condemnation of protectionism and internal improvements to argue that the Kentucky and Virginia resolutions of 1798–1799 sanctioned state interposition to prevent the enforcement of unconstitutional federal legislation. South Carolina, he declared, need only follow Jefferson's counsel: "That the several states who formed the constitution being sovereign [and] independent, have the unquestionable right to judge the infractions; and that a NULLIFICATION by those sovereignties of all unauthorized acts done under the color of that instrument, is the *rightful remedy*." When, shortly afterward, state legislator William C. Preston asked Calhoun to compose a report on state interposition for members of the South Carolina Assembly, the vice president accepted the invitation. He had been giving the question serious consideration for more than a year, and now was as good a time as any to clarify his position. Tensions were on the rise, and without proper guidance, the situation might soon get out of control. South Carolinians needed to develop an effective constitutional remedy for their current woes, he told Preston, but they had to proceed cautiously and avoid alienating potential allies by adopting "such measures as may produce *harmony of opinion among the oppressed States*."[16]

Calhoun's labors resulted in a draft of what came to be known as the *South Carolina Exposition and Protest*. The report had two interrelated aims: to enlist Southern support for South Carolina political initiatives and to propose a constitutional defense of regional rights to which all Southerners could subscribe. And he adopted a two-stage forensic strategy to achieve these objectives. The first consisted of an examination of the ways in which protectionism imperiled Southern economic interests and social organization. It began with the familiar argument that protective tariffs enabled Northern manufacturers to monopolize domestic markets while compelling Southerners to purchase necessary items at advanced prices without any compensating benefit. But Calhoun did not stop there. Protective tariffs, he contended, would inevitably create a state of commercial warfare that seriously curtailed the operation of international markets and limited the "great and once flourishing agriculture" of the South to production for an inadequate home market that could never absorb more than a quarter of the region's products. At this point, he warned, Southerners would have small hope of retaining any of those things that made life worth living, as they futilely attempted to avert an unreservedly bleak future: "Forced to abandon an ancient and favourite pursuit, to which our soil, climate, habits and peculiar labor are adapted, we would be compelled, without capital, experience, or skill, and a population untried in such pursuits, to attempt to become the rivals, instead of the customers of the manufacturing States." As regional agriculture collapsed, there would be a marked deterioration in social and economic relations. The vast majority of those people who did not flee the region would soon find themselves the victims of a vicious struggle between capitalists and working people in which "wages will sink much more rapidly than the prices of the necessaries of life, till the operatives will be reduced to the lowest point, where the portion of the products of their labour left to them, will be barely necessary to preserve existence." In time, he added, workers who benefited from the current prosperity of Northern industry could expect a similar fate, for the overriding tendency of an economic system based on protective legislation was to concentrate wealth in fewer and fewer hands, making the rich richer and the poor poorer.[17]

Having established the existential threat that protectionism posed to Southern society, Calhoun turned to a consideration of what could be done to combat it. The main problem, he contended, was Congress's abuse of its delegated powers, which had facilitated the formation of a political system that enabled a tyrannical majority to impose its self-aggrandizing demands on less powerful interests. To reverse this dangerous trend, states, acting "in their sovereign capacity," needed to reclaim the right of interposition described in the Kentucky and Virginia resolutions. Thus armed, they would be able to protect their "separate & peculiar interests" by vetoing or nullifying any congressional usurpations that they deemed unconstitutional. No less important, recognition of this right would place American government on a more enduring foundation. "No government, based on the naked principle, that the majority ought to govern, however true in its proper sense, and under proper restrictions," he argued, "ever preserved its liberty even for a single generation." Only those governments that had taken effective steps to "provide checks, which limit, and restrain within proper bounds the power of the majority have alone had a prolonged existence, and been distinguished for virtue, patriotism, power and happiness." Although some might assert that state interposition permitted unrepresentative minorities to obstruct the operation of the general government, there was no compelling reason to fear that it would do so. Should Congress wish to override state nullification of a given measure, it could invoke Article V of the Constitution and attempt to persuade three-quarters of the states to support a constitutional amendment giving it authority to exercise the contested power.[18]

As much as he believed all that he had to say, Calhoun did not wish to be publicly identified with the exposition. Should that happen, he told Preston, it would give "a personal character to the great question at issue, which would tend to lower its dignity, and to weaken its influence." He might have added that being exposed as the report's author would also have complicated his political plans. He had just been elected Jackson's vice president and did not want to do anything to jeopardize his relations with the new chief executive. Many political observers expected the aging general to serve a single term, and the South Carolinian recognized that he would be well positioned for the 1832 presidential contest if people came to view him as the anointed successor. Calhoun further hoped that Jackson would relieve South Carolina of the need to adopt state interposition by taking decisive action to resolve the tariff problem. As he wrote the Tennessean several months before the election, the belief that in a Jackson administration "equal distribution of the burden and benefit of government, economy, the payment of the publick debt, and finally the removal of oppressive duties, will be primary objects of policy is what mainly consoles this quarter of the Union under present embarrassment." This expectation provided the basis for a passage in the exposition urging moderation and restraint. Upon assuming office, he confidently assured readers, someone with Jackson's reputation for "justice and patriotism" would almost certainly use his influence to effect "a complete restoration of the pure principles of our Government."[19]

That did not happen. Although Jackson was no friend of protectionism, his administration made little effort to address the issue. As the months passed and hopes for reform faded, those Carolinians who objected most strongly to the Tariff of Abominations became increasingly restless. Their growing demands that the state initiate proceedings to veto the measure soon divided South Carolina into warring political camps. Pitted against the nullifiers was an unwieldy coalition of two groups of unionists: one a Lowcountry faction comprised largely of wealthy scions of prestigious old families with Federalist roots who feared nullification would shatter the union and upset customary patterns of commercial and intellectual exchange; the other an Upcountry faction of hard-money Jacksonians who opposed all forms of government intervention in the economy and embraced what historian Lacy K. Ford has described as "a nationalism of spirit" characterized by "an emotional attachment to the Union and to the glorious republican experiment that it represented." What held them together was a belief that state interposition represented an unconstitutional innovation that would likely end in disunion and an unwillingness to attribute all the state's economic woes to protectionism. None of them had a good word for the tariff; nor, as one unionist speaker remarked, did they "wonder at the indignation which the imposition of such a burden of taxation has excited in our people in the present unprosperous state of affairs." But they believed that attempting to nullify a federal law would only create further problems without doing anything to correct the more fundamental causes of South Carolina's faltering economic performance.[20]

This was not the response that Calhoun had envisioned. Should South Carolinians ever deem it necessary to nullify the tariff or any other measure, maintaining a united front would be absolutely imperative. A leadership group that could not control dissent within its own state could hardly hope to persuade people elsewhere in the South of the righteousness of its cause. Several events in the summer of 1831 made the vice president's position even more uncomfortable. One was a May speech at a Charleston dinner to honor his old friend George McDuffie, who by that point had completed the transition from nationalist to nullifier. Diplomacy had never been one of the congressman's strong suits. With a platform style that one observer likened to that of "a mad man in Bedlam," McDuffie typically spoke in provocative, uncompromising terms that did not invite further discussion; once convinced of the justice of his position, he equated the weighing of alternative arguments with the worst sort of equivocation. All this and more were on full display in a three-hour harangue that he delivered at the Charleston dinner. In addition to dismissing the motives of South Carolina unionists and declaring them "accomplices of our oppressors," he challenged listeners to emulate the manly devotion to liberty of their ancestors, asking whether they could be dissuaded from carrying out their "most sacred duty" by succumbing to idle threats that "even the women of our country laugh to scorn." This was no time for South Carolinians to be worrying about the consequences of their actions, he seemed to be saying: Defense of one's rights was infinitely more important than the peaceful preservation of current comforts.[21]

McDuffie was plainly preaching to the converted, and his remarks had an exhilarating effect on those South Carolinians who worshipped at the church of state interposition. That people who subscribed to other political creeds reacted much differently created a real dilemma for Calhoun. As news of the speech spread, various correspondents told him that he would be well advised to cut ties with McDuffie and those who shared his views. The most insistent was Duff Green, a Washington newspaper editor who had assumed the self-appointed role of political manager for the vice president. Green had been telling Calhoun for some time that the actions of his more radical South Carolina friends threatened to destroy any hopes he might have of political advancement. When he learned of McDuffie's diatribe, he fired off a letter informing Calhoun that his "bittere[s]t political enemy" could not have done him more harm, and that he needed to distance himself from the congressman: "A curse on your Dinners and your nullification—the word is more odious to me than any other in our Language, and I fear that you are destin[e]d to wish from the bottom of your h[e]art that it never had a place in your vocabulary." At the same time, however, leading members of the South Carolina political elite believed Green—who had asked one of them whether they "we were all crazy at McDuffie's dinner"—would "ruin [Calhoun] if he is not checked." According to James Hamilton Jr., the editor was advising the vice president to strike a deal with Northern manufactures on the tariff. Should he do so, Hamilton said, it would cause irreparable injury to Calhoun's reputation, and he hoped the vice president had sufficient "sense to see the essential Weakness of his occupying a double position, Janus-faced, with one expression of countenance for one side of the Potomac and another expression for the other."[22]

Were this not bad enough, Charleston unionists added to the growing pressure on Calhoun when, three weeks after the McDuffie speech, they invited President Jackson to attend their upcoming Fourth of July celebration. Increasingly reckless talk of nullification within South Carolina had raised the specter of disunion, they told the president. That "these fatal errors should be promptly corrected, and the feelings which they engendered thoroughly eradicated" was their greatest wish, and they believed his presence at their commemoration of the nation's birthday would help create the climate of opinion required to achieve these patriotic aims. Although Jackson could not attend, he thanked them profusely for the invitation, providing assurance that he fully shared their concerns. At the same time, he issued a diplomatically phrased but unmistakably firm warning to Carolina nullifiers: "Knowing as I do, the patriotic worth and public virtues of distinguished citizens to whom declarations inconsistent with an attachment to the union have been ascribed, I cannot but hope, that if accurately reported, they were the effect of momentary excitement, not deliberate design; and that such men can never have formed the project of pursuing a course of redress through any other than constitutional means."[23]

The South Carolina legislature later condemned Jackson's letter as "an unauthorized interference in the affairs of this State." Calhoun likely wished that he could have done so as well, but he thought better of it. As his relations with the president had steadily deteriorated over the previous eighteen months, any chance he might have had of becoming Jackson's chosen successor had disappeared in the rancor generated by several major controversies. One concerned the conduct and virtue of Margaret Eaton, the wife of Jackson's secretary of war and personal friend John Eaton. Where the president made the defense of Mrs. Eaton a point of honor, it was widely rumored that the unwillingness of large elements of Washington's elite to extend her basic social courtesies owed much to Floride Calhoun's disapproval of the secretary's wife. Another controversy centered on cabinet discussions regarding the general's actions during the Seminole War. Despite rumors to the contrary, Jackson had believed that Calhoun had fully supported his Florida initiative while secretary of war. Aware of how volatile the general's temper could be, particularly about matters concerning his reputation, the South Carolinian had done nothing to correct the misimpression. Jackson was not happy when he learned what his position had actually been. In the ensuing spat, Calhoun rejected the president's right to question what he had done, telling him that he had been faithfully carrying out his official duties "under responsibility to my conscience and my country only." This was no way to appease an angry Jackson, and he let the vice president know it: "I had too exalted an opinion of your honor and frankness to believe, for a moment, that you could be capable of such deception" and "never expected to have occasion to say of you, in the language of C[a]esar, *et tu Brute*."[24]

By this point, Calhoun felt the South had little reason to hope the administration would be responsive to its needs. "Had he placed himself on principle, & surrounded himself with the talents, virtue and experience of the party," he said of Jackson in a January 1831 letter, "his personal popularity would, beyond all doubt, have enabled us to restore the Constitution, arrest the progress of corruption, harmonize the Union, and thereby avert the calamity which seem[s] to impend over us." That Calhoun thought nothing of the sort had occurred stemmed in part from his bitterness at being displaced by Martin Van Buren as Jackson's favorite and heir to the throne. But it also reflected serious differences between himself and the president concerning federal-state relations that had first surfaced at a Jefferson birthday celebration in Washington the previous April. After Jackson offered a toast affirming his unreserved devotion to the Union, Calhoun modified the president's declaration with a toast of his own: "The Union: next to our liberty, the most dear; may we all remember that it can only be preserved by respecting the rights of the States and distributing equally, the benefit and burden of the Union."[25]

Few people then knew that Calhoun was the primary author of the *South Carolina Exposition and Protest,* though many suspected he had a hand in its composition. Such suspicions deepened and spread following the Jefferson birthday dinner. Those harboring them included the Charleston unionists whose invitation had prompted Jackson's letter. They recognized that Calhoun faced intensifying pressure to be more forthcoming, and a participant at their Independence Day gathering put him squarely on the spot by proposing a toast that left little room for further evasion: "The Vice-President of the United States: His political intimates have declared their sentiments on Nullification,—will he *shrink* from an *open* exposition of his own?" At an Upcountry celebration that same day, Calhoun offered a more restrained version of his Jefferson dinner toast: "The state and general governments—each imperfect when viewed as separate and distinct governments; but, taken as a whole, forming one system, with each checking and controlling the other, unsurpassed by any work of man, in wisdom and sublimity." He doubtless wished that he could have left it there, but he soon realized that was no longer possible if he wanted to maintain his stature and credibility as a public figure. The only remaining question concerned the extent to which he should publicly embrace the views presented in the exposition. Disavowing them was not an option. It would only have exposed him to nullifier contempt without doing anything to curb political extremism within the state. As he had earlier explained to Maryland politician Virgil Maxcy, he did not possess the power "to arrest the current of events" in South Carolina, and those who believed he did "make a great mistake." Calhoun also understood that trying to straddle the issue would do him equally little good. He had numerous reasons for desiring to maintain "a retired & silent position," he said of his decision to come forward: "I regret to be forced from it; but no consideration could induce me in the present crisis to occupy a position, that might be thought equivocal."[26]

The decision resulted in the composition of the Fort Hill Address, a lengthy public letter that Calhoun completed in late July and that appeared in the *Pendleton Messenger* the following week. In it, he reprised major themes from the exposition; and he did so in a manner that he hoped would not alienate readers of moderate political inclination. In addition to eschewing inflammatory language, he avoided use of the term nullification, made an effort to distinguish between state interposition and disunion, and insisted throughout that his proposals had a solid grounding in legitimate constitutional principles. What he could not avoid discussing was the growing sectional conflict and what it meant for the future of American government. Although protectionism was the immediate problem, he observed, the tariff question formed only one element of a system of oppression in which Northern manufacturers and their political allies sought to consolidate their control of government and use it to the disadvantage of planters and farmers whose livelihood depended on cultivation of the nation's major agricultural staples. "The system if continued," Calhoun contended, "must end, not only in subjecting the industry and property of the weaker section to that of the stronger, but in proscription and political disfranchisement." There was still time to avert this disaster, he added, but only if the minority section secured ample means to protect itself against discriminatory federal initiatives. And nothing promised to provide such relief more effectively than the principle of state interposition: the right to veto and prevent the enforcement of unjust and unconstitutional congressional measures.[27]

Calhoun's main objective in the address was to demonstrate the need for state interposition without offending prominent political figures outside South Carolina. It is unlikely that anyone could have threaded that needle, and if Duff Green's response was at all representative, the vice president's effort came up short. Few people had greater hopes for Calhoun than the Washington editor and political strategist. But he had apparently been unaware of the South Carolinian's views on federal–state relations, and reading the address "was like a shock produced by a cold Bath." Calhoun's many well-wishers "had been taught to believe that he was not a Nullifier," he observed, and they could not understand why someone with so promising a political future would not avail himself of an opportunity to "promote his popularity" by condemning the doctrine. His dismay notwithstanding, Green remained a staunch Calhoun supporter; he even used his editorial post to defend South Carolina nullifiers in their struggles with Palmetto unionists. Others were not so forgiving. By publishing the address, the vice president had burned many of his political bridges, and he could not turn back. In the months to come, he urged correspondents to stand firm, assuring them that their cause was the cause of good government everywhere. "Let all be animated by the conviction that they are contending for the Constitution, for the Union, and for liberty," he told one acquaintance. This was no time for cowardly retreat, he declared in another letter: "The hope of the country now rests on our gallant little State. Let every Carolinian do his duty. Those who do not join us now intend unqualified submission."[28]

During the summer of 1832, Adams, acting as chairman of the House Committee on Manufactures, submitted a "compromise tariff" that lowered duties on a broad range of items while retaining the principle of protection. Although the bill drew criticism from people on all sides of the debate, Congress passed the measure by comfortable margins and Jackson signed it into law, hoping that it would attract sufficient support from South Carolina moderates to stall the movement toward nullification. It did not, and as the state edged ever closer to a major showdown with the federal government, Calhoun did his part, elaborating on his doctrine of state interposition in two public letters to Governor Hamilton and preparing drafts of important papers for the South Carolina Assembly and the state nullification convention. In the latter document, which he submitted at the beginning of November, Calhoun wrote that when the mounting impositions on the South reached a point where they no longer left "a sufficient amount of proceeds of labor to remunerate the expense of maintenance and supervision —we cannot but foresee, if the system be not arrested, calamity awaiting us and our posterity, greater than ever befell a free and enlightened people." Convention members felt that point had already been reached, and three weeks later they passed an ordinance declaring the tariffs of 1828 and 1832 "unauthorized by the Constitution" and making it "unlawful for any of the constituted authorities, whether of this State, or of the United States, to enforce the payment of duties imposed by the said acts, within the limits of this State." Nullification had gone from theory to practice.[29]

For many nullifiers, the convention's action represented the fulfillment of hopes that had been building for years. It is unlikely that Calhoun shared their glee. However much he believed it necessary to secure recognition of the right of state interposition, he did not want to provoke a direct confrontation between South Carolina and the federal government. If nothing else, his prudential instincts made him wary of how someone of Jackson's uneven temperament might respond to the evolving crisis. The state lacked the resources to resist the coercive force that the president might unleash in a fit of rage, and Calhoun knew from experience that expecting success without preparing for the worst was a prescription for disaster. At the same time, however, he wanted to see the battle over nullification concluded as swiftly as possible. For reasons partly of his own making, the dispute had entered territory he had no desire to visit. Protection of the South's peculiar system of labor formed an essential, if largely unstated, element of his argument for state interposition. Had the region been much like the rest of the country, states there would have had no compelling rationale to demand the right to annul federal laws. Unfortunately for Calhoun, adopting this tack all but ensured that debate would extend beyond the constitutional issues with which he was most comfortable, and to which he sought to confine the controversy. Why he found this so disturbing is one of several topics to be addressed in the next section of the chapter.

"I consider the Tariff act as the occasion, rather than the real cause of the present unhappy state of things," Calhoun observed in a September 1830 letter to Virgil Maxcy. "The truth can no longer be disguised that the peculiar domestick institution of the Southern States, and the consequent direction, which that and her soil and climate have given to her industry, have placed" the region at odds with the interests of a Northern majority that had no qualms about reducing its people "to utter wretchedness." It was all about slavery, Calhoun was saying; yet here and elsewhere he went out of his way to avoid using the word. In public statements, as well as much of his private correspondence, slaves became the South's "peculiar labor," and slaveholders became the producers of the nation's great agricultural staples. Such evasiveness was not altogether new. The founders had demonstrated a similar reticence in drafting the Constitution, slavery being, in Adams's words, "one of those vessels of dishonor, which, albeit impairing the purity of our political institutions, could not even be named with decency in a compact for securing to the people of the Union the blessing of liberty." Thus it was that they adopted euphemisms such as "person[s] held to service or labor" and "three-fifths of all other persons" to make provisions protecting the South's peculiar institution appear less repugnant than it in fact was. But where the founders feared exposing themselves to charges of blatant hypocrisy, Calhoun had other reasons for wanting to avoid any direct mention of slavery. As someone who had worked tirelessly to organize support for the War of 1812, served nearly eight years as secretary of war, and given considerable thought to coalition building as a presidential contender, the vice president had a strong propensity for strategic thinking. He recognized that the greatest challenge facing South Carolina nullifiers was finding ways to overcome their political isolation, and he knew that openly linking the case for state interposition to the protection of slavery would only make such efforts more difficult than they needed to be. Doing so would also draw attention away from constitutional questions and focus it on matters that were best left undiscussed.[30]

Few places better illustrated how troublesome these problems could potentially become than Virginia. Calhoun could not imagine a Southern political bloc that did not include the Old Dominion. In addition to being the region's largest and most economically diverse state, it was also the land of Jefferson, whose Kentucky resolutions of 1798–1799 formed an indispensable part of the constitutional argument for the right of state interposition. "In this great struggle," Calhoun wrote in an 1827 letter to the longtime champion of state sovereignty, Littleton Waller Tazewell, "I look mainly to Virginia, to her fir[m]ness, her zeal and union. You know, that it [is] almost an axiom with me, that every revolution in favour of liberty in our system, must be effected by the South, and I may add, the South headed by Virginia." Four years later, as the nullification crisis deepened, he told another correspondent that it was absolutely "essential, that our cause, should be vigorously sustained in the oldest, most populous, and most exposed Southern State." Many other South Carolinians felt the same way. "'What will Virginia do?' is in every one's mouth," a writer in the *Charleston*

Courier observed during the nullification winter of 1832–1833. Anything less than the Old Dominion's full support, these people believed, would markedly reduce their chances of achieving a successful outcome.[31]

The likelihood of their obtaining such support was extremely uncertain, however. Not only was Thomas Ritchie, Virginia's most influential newspaper editor, an ardent Jacksonian, but major elements of the populace were locked in a bitter political struggle that pitted people living east of the Blue Ridge Mountains against those living west of the range. The conflict centered on an inequitable system of legislative apportionment that enabled an eastern minority to dominate a state assembly that had wide-ranging powers. That the role of slavery in the two regions constituted the most important difference between them gave the contest a broader significance that attracted the attention of slaveholders throughout the South. These differences came to the fore at an 1829 constitutional convention organized to resolve western political grievances. Whatever topic the delegates chose to discuss, the debate sooner or later touched on slavery. Despite repeated assurances of western commitment to the institution, it was never enough. Eastern planters insisted that, because slavery presented challenges that no one living west of the Blue Ridge could fully understand or appreciate, they could not permit any outside meddling in how they managed their slaves "without the extremest danger." The convention ended in a compromise settlement that satisfied no one. Just how little had been resolved became apparent two years later, when, in the wake of Nat Turner's Rebellion, the General Assembly gathered to consider proposals for taking steps toward the abolition of slavery in Virginia. The Southampton County slave revolt caused sufficient alarm that, for a brief time, Virginians abandoned an unspoken rule against public discussion of the state's peculiar institution. No one questioned the legitimacy of planters' rights to the slave property they currently possessed or the need to compensate slaveowners for any losses they might suffer. What they did not agree about was the effect that the existence of a powerful planter class had on Virginia society. Where some speakers raised questions about the compatibility of slavery and democracy, others complained about the baneful effect slavery had on free white labor and state economic development.[32]

South Carolinians—unionists no less than nullifiers—watched these developments with a mixture of dismay, apprehension, and anger, wondering whether the Virginians had lost their minds. That Governor John Floyd parted company with his fellow westerners and supported nullification only complicated an otherwise thoroughly disagreeable situation. An outspoken proponent of states' rights who vowed to "sustain South Carolina with all my power," the Virginia chief executive nevertheless shared most of his neighbors' social views. "Before I leave the Government," he confided to his diary several months after Nat Turner's Rebellion, "I will have contrived to have a law passed gradually abolishing slavery in this State, or at all events to begin the work by prohibiting slavery on the West side of the Blue Ridge Mountains." Although Floyd retreated from that pledge, he remained hopeful that the spread of an economy based largely on grazing would move the west in the right direction. Calhoun had no clearer an understanding than other South Carolinians did of what he called these "sudden and extraordinary movements" on the part of Virginians, though one can be sure that he did not like what he saw; slaveholding Southerners who could envision a future without slavery posed at least as great a threat to the institution as Northern abolitionists did. What Calhoun did understand was that placing slavery at the center of the nullification controversy could only alienate potential supporters in places like the Valley and Trans-Allegheny regions of the Old Dominion.[33]

Where events in Virginia caught Calhoun by surprise, he likely anticipated the free labor arguments of Northern opponents of nullification. His constant references to the South's peculiar productive system made it all but certain that he would face some pushback along these lines. Although he could not prevent such attacks, he hoped to contain them; he did not want to see the nullification dispute turned into a reenactment of the bitter, invective-filled Missouri controversy, with its acrimonious intersectional exchanges and harsh assaults on slavery and the South. The resulting clash over nullification and protectionism generated more heat than the South Carolinian would have liked, and he heard much that must have displeased and angered him. Yet it could have been worse. The most provocative assertions of an antislavery-based Northern sectionalism never fully cohered and—failing to capture a broad audience—ultimately gave way before a somewhat more restrained free labor critique that, however troubling, did not directly attack slavery. An examination of what leading members of the Massachusetts congressional delegation had to say during the tariff debates of the early 1830s provides one way of drawing out these distinctions; it also furnishes illuminating perspective on important developments in Adams's thought during these years.

Few people had a greater personal stake in the outcome of the tariff controversy than Nathan Appleton. Although the Lowell, Massachusetts, textile manufacturer felt excessively high duties encouraged overproduction and was willing to compromise, he adamantly opposed the sharp reductions sought by South Carolina nullifiers. After defeating Boston free trader Henry Lee in an election that centered on the tariff question, he went to Washington fully prepared to do battle with those seeking to abolish protectionism. In addition to demolishing George McDuffie's forty-bale theory—an argument that operation of the tariff reduced planter proceeds from cotton exports by 40 percent—Appleton presented a slashing commentary on intersectional class relations. Adequate tariff protection, he later observed, was necessary to maintain "a high character and a high reward to the laboring classes." This doubtless explained why "opposition to the tariff is in proportion to the number of slaves compared to whites" in a given state's population. John Davis elaborated on Appleton's observations in a subsequent address. The Worcester, Massachusetts, lawyer represented a growing industrial community in the heart of the commonwealth that was in the process of becoming a major regional bastion of free laborism. When he spoke of the schools, churches, and other institutions that contributed to the "moral comforts" of working people, he had Worcester in mind; and when he declared that "all property is the fruit of labor," he was thinking of the town's mechanics and workshops. Like Appleton, Davis believed that unremunerated labor performed by people who did not work for themselves was not labor at all. He also shared the manufacturer's belief that the "comfort and happiness" of Northern working people depended on the continued protection of domestic industry. "Sir," he said of slaveholder efforts to eliminate it, "let us not, in such a rash and foolish experiment, to gratify the insatiable avarice of the greedy planters, barter away the most precious of God's gifts—the lofty, manly spirit of independence of the enlightened laborer."[34]

Appleton and Davis represented two faces of major social and economic changes taking place in antebellum Massachusetts: the owners of large manufacturing establishments who employed an ever-growing proportion of the state labor force; and the local promoters who sought to remove all barriers to the further release of those entrepreneurial energies currently transforming the economic landscape of the towns and cities in which they lived. They were also exponents of a popular conservatism then in transition from Federalism to Whiggery. This political creed, which had first appeared decades earlier as part of an effort to blunt the appeal of Jeffersonian democracy and arrest the decline of the politics of conditional deference in Massachusetts, rested on two pillars. One was the defense of state and regional interests by respected political and economic elites. So long as these Nehemiahs stood atop the walls of Bay civilization, people could rest assured that they would be protected against any outside threats to their well-being. The second column consisted of repeated declarations concerning the economic interdependence of all major elements of Bay society. That some benefited more than others from economic change was no cause for concern because the prosperity of all groups was inextricably linked. It was a wonderful vision of how the world should work, but perceptive observers could see problems on the horizon. The number of dependent wage earners in the Bay populace had been rising steadily for some time, and the spread of industrialization had accelerated the process; recent signs of labor unrest indicated that not everyone viewed these developments with the same cheerful equanimity that characterized elite proclamations on social and economic matters. For those worried about where such dissent might lead, the nullification crisis provided an ideal context for embedding the basic precepts of popular conservatism in a free labor protectionism.

Comparisons with slave society blurred memories of the region's relatively more egalitarian past, enabling adherents of this political ideology to speak much more persuasively about the interdependence of capital and labor than would otherwise have been the case. Evidence of their success can be seen in the declarations of various county gatherings to promote domestic industry that applauded the high wages that protective duties allowed employers to pay "our mechanics and laborers" and asserted that "the interest of the agricultural community is indissolubly connected with the success of manufactures, since the price of labour is sustained and enhanced by them, and the domestic market essentially improved."[35]

As a political platform, free labor protectionism worked as well as its most optimistic advocates could have wished. It soon became an integral feature of Bay Whiggery, providing the basis for a cross-class electoral appeal that enabled the party to drub Democratic opponents in most state elections of the period. As an antislavery critique, free labor protectionism did not work quite as effectively. That it stopped well short of the full-throated abolitionism of William Lloyd Garrison was no cause for worry; followers of the *Liberator* editor were—and would remain—relatively thin on the ground in antebellum Massachusetts. That it did not adequately give voice to the antislavery convictions of certain people of otherwise moderate political inclination was more problematic. Adams was one such person. The former president had found that retirement did not suit him. When local political activists urged him to seek election to the House of Representatives, he brushed aside the objections of his wife and youngest son and reentered the political fray. Adams had no objections whatsoever to the basic principles of popular conservatism. He had grown up in a political culture that esteemed elite leadership, and, though in later life personally averse to most forms of social snobbery, he never doubted the wisdom of placing government in the hands of the well-educated and the well-bred. He further believed that Bay congressmen had an obligation to protect regional interests and considered interdependence the best of all conceivable frameworks for ordering the activities of a society's major economic groups. There is little question that he listened approvingly to all that Appleton and Davis had to say. Yet, while he would not have changed a word in either of their speeches, his own antislavery critique indicated that he felt something more needed to be said. Because that critique contained the seeds of future divisions within Northern Whiggery, it is worth exploring how Adams differed from most other exponents of free labor protectionism.

By way of preface, some mention must be made of the interaction of the personal and the political in Adams's speeches and writings. Like many politicians, then and now, the Bay congressman did not quickly forget what he considered ill-treatment at the hands of faithless friends and malicious adversaries. Although he never exhibited the ferocious anger that Jackson directed at those he felt had crossed him, perceived slights, injustices, and betrayals lingered long afterward in his capacious memory, nurturing resentments that came swiftly to the fore when combined with the added incitement of some question of principle or major policy difference. Trying to determine where personal grievance ended and objective observation began at such moments is a hopeless task. Adams's enmities—in addition to providing a suitably rancorous foundation for an unmatched talent for personal and political invective that congressional foes came to respect and fear—sharpened the edges of his more penetrating analyses, giving them a depth of insight that a more restrained statement of the case might well have lacked.

In his approach to substantive matters, Adams could draw on a wealth of experience enjoyed by few Americans of the period. He had not only seen much but possessed observational abilities of a high order. How the two combined to shape his antislavery views in ways that set him apart from congressional colleagues can perhaps best be seen in his lifelong antipathy to landed aristocrats. Travelling through Poland as a youth of sixteen, he could barely contain his revulsion when describing the feudal organization of society. "All the farmers are in the most abject slavery, they are bought and sold like so many beasts, and sometimes even chang'd for dogs or horses," he wrote to his father. "Their masters have even the right of life and death over them, and if they kill one of them they are only obliged to pay a trifling fine." Russia, which he characterized as a society of "Princes and Slaves," was no better, for no rational person could honestly "assert that a People can be happy who are subjected to personal Slavery." Although some Russian serfs had acquired great wealth, "they are not free and therefore they are despised, besides they depend upon the Nobles, who make them contribute the more for their riches." Closer to home, Adams found that social relations in New York's Hudson Valley more closely resembled those of Europe than the land of his birth. The region's "extensive manors, which descended by law entirely to eldest sons, promoted an aristocratic spirit, which was very contrary to Liberty." Notwithstanding recent political reforms, he added, people there "have not yet acquired that Republican Confidence, which wise Laws, and a longer enjoyment of their Liberty may inspire them with, and which the inhabitants of N. England possess in an high degree." Nothing good, he was learning, could be expected from societies in which a vast gulf separated rich from poor. The greatest happiness, his mother told him, could be found in a middling state between poverty and extreme wealth. A life devoted to acquisitiveness and self-indulgence, she warned, was a life wasted: "Riches always create Luxery, and Luxery always leads to Idleness Indolence and effeminacy which stifels every noble purpose, and withers the blossom of genious which fall useless to the ground, unproductive of fruit."[36]

These early lessons stayed with Adams throughout his life, informing his views of both labor and slavery. Their influence surfaced decades later in a discussion he had with Calhoun during the Missouri controversy. His cabinet colleague felt there was nothing degrading about manufacturing, artisanal, or farm labor—"He himself had often held the plow"—but he insisted that what he called "manual labor" should be performed by Black people alone, it being "the work of Slaves." Adams disagreed, telling Calhoun "that this confounding of the ideas of servitude and labour, was one of the bad effects of Slavery." Though he did not say it, he further believed that the South Carolinian's observations obscured more than they revealed. Slaveholders often conceded that their peculiar institution had its evils, yet "when probed to the quick upon it they show at the bottom of their souls pride and vainglory in their condition of masterdom." And this sense of superiority colored everything that they thought or did: "They fancy themselves more generous and noble than the plain farmers who labour for subsistence. They look down upon the simplicity of a yankee's manners because he has no habits of overbearing like theirs, and cannot treat negroes like dogs. It is among the evils of slavery that it taints the very sources of moral principle" and "makes the first and holiest rights of humanity to depend upon the colour of the skin." Slavery, he later observed, might well give all white Southerners a sense of "being equally privileged" because of their race. But that feeling of equality came at a price: "We can't conceive how far the idea that work is dishonourable has entered the spirit of the Americans of the south. No enterprise in which negroes cannot serve as the inferior agents can succeed in that part of the Union."[37]

As the above comment on Yankee manners suggests, Adams deeply resented the tendency of landed aristocrats and slaveholders to look down upon people who derived their income from economic pursuits other than agriculture. Nearly all his forebears had cultivated the soil, achieving in the best of times no more than a middling prosperity, and he had the utmost respect for the hard work that marked their lives. But New England could never have thrived on agriculture alone, and it always irritated him when some arrogant land baron spoke derisively of merchants. While serving as minister to Russia, one nobleman told him that all current wars could be attributed to the machinations of money-grubbing merchants who "fatten and grow rich upon the misery, and blood of Nations." Adams had no illusions about mercantile behavior and conceded that his acquaintance made a few telling points. At the same time, though, the speaker betrayed an astonishing lack of self-awareness that was all too characteristic of landed aristocrats. In performing their roles as warriors, diplomats, and courtiers, the New Englander observed, nobles displayed "vices" that were "at least as odious as any that can be imputed to the merchants, and from those vices, the Count himself is by no means exempt." Even more disturbing was slaveholder dismissiveness of mercantile contributions to the general welfare. In his inaugural address, Jefferson had referred to commerce as the "handmaid" of agriculture. The phrase stuck in Adams's mind, and nearly three decades later he wrote that the expression reflected "the deeply rooted sentiment that commerce is in its nature an inferior and ancillary interest" that was "to be encouraged only as it is subservient to the higher and master-interest of agriculture." This arrangement of "two great and *equal* interests of the community in the relative position of master and slave" made Jefferson's observation the kind of statement that "could have originated only on a tobacco plantation." Such a belief, Adams added, "was utterly incompatible with the theory of a government founded upon equal rights, and was peculiarly inapplicable to the government of the United States," which had been formed "certainly not more, but more immediately, for the protection of commerce than of agriculture."[38]

The indifference of landed elites to the misery of those whose labor undergirded their social position, their insufferable assumptions of superiority, the threat their exploitative practices posed to human freedom, the need to protect regional economic interests and uphold basic principles of equal rights—these and related reflections swirled uneasily in Adams's restive consciousness as he set about fashioning a response to the nullification controversy, looking for some provocation that could be used to focus his thoughts and serve as a pretext for intervention in the increasingly heated debate. He found two of them. One was Jackson's 1832 annual message to Congress, which called for the gradual elimination of most protective duties and urged a marked reduction in the price of public lands to promote westward expansion; the money would not be missed, the president said, as the national debt was nearing liquidation and there were serious questions about the constitutionality of using federal expenditures to fund internal improvements. All this deeply troubled Adams, given his commitment to providing reasonable levels of protection to New England manufactures and belief that the developmental vision that formed the core of his political ideology could never be realized without the revenue derived from government land sales. But what particularly angered him was Jackson's restatement of a Jeffersonian maxim that he had never accepted: "The wealth and strength of a country are its population, and the best part of that population are the cultivators of the soil." The message, he noted shortly afterward, "puts my temper and my discretion upon a trial equally severe." Jackson seemed intent on surrendering "the whole Union to the nullifiers of the South, and the Land-Robbers of the West." The entire American system—protective duties and the Bank of the United States as well as internal improvements—was "to be swept away so that there will be nothing hereafter to nullify." To let such policy initiatives go unquestioned would be the worst sort of political cowardice, and as chairman of the Committee on Manufactures, Adams believed he had an obligation to prepare a response showing the pernicious consequences of acting on the recommendations contained in the president's message.[39]

The resulting report presented an aggressive and spirited assertion of the basic principles of free labor protectionism. In it, Adams acknowledged the futility of attempting to eliminate the influence of regional self-interest in national politics. Some degree of conflict was inevitable in a nation as economically and socially diverse as the United States, where one half of the population was entirely free and where slaves comprised a substantial portion of the people living in the other half. The founders had recognized as much when drafting the Constitution and had gone out of their way to address the special needs of slaveholding Southerners. But the latter were never satisfied. Their discontent could be seen in the "falsified history, falsified constitutional law, falsified morality, falsified statistics, and falsified and slanderous imputations upon" free state members of Congress that nullifiers had assembled as part of their effort to take money from the pockets of free working people and deposit it in those of slaveholding planters. Now the president of the United States had weighed in on their behalf, telling Americans that "independent farmers are, every where, the basis of society, and true friends of liberty." Where, the report asked, did this leave the mechanics, factory operatives, and other free workers of the North? Not being "the best part of the population, their equal rights may be trampled upon, their highest interests may be sacrificed, their property may be wrested from their hands, themselves and their families may be driven by measures of national policy, by act of the Government of the Union, to beggary and ruin, for the benefit of independent farmers, the wealthy landowners, the best part of the population." As it concerned the operation of the federal government, the time had surely arrived to discard "the old and exploded doctrine" that a country's landed elites stood head and shoulders above other members of society.[40]

Doing so would enable people to develop a much better appreciation of the differences between free and slave labor and what those differences meant for the nation's moral and material growth. "Among men who subsist only upon the fruits of their own labor, industry and frugality are constantly stimulated by the natural and perpetual impulses of bettering their own condition," the report declared. Sadly, this unceasing commitment to self-improvement was absent in many areas of the South, for in places where "one portion of the community lives in perpetual servitude to another, where master and slave both subsist upon the labor of the slave, industry and frugality not only lose much of their natural influence upon human conduct, but are apt to lose even the name and consideration of virtues." As the report proceeded, one can almost hear the voice of his late mother whispering in Adams's ear: "The master's wants, supplied by another's toil, multiply with the means of gratification, and his natural tendencies will be to spend rather than to hoard. And labor to him will assume the hue and disrepute of servitude, and frugality to his eyes will lose her natural healthy bloom, and fade with the livid complexion of penurious avarice." This was free labor protectionism with a vengeance. Sentiments that received at best partial development in the speeches of legislators such as Appleton and Davis assumed a more aggressive and threatening form in Adams's response to Jackson's message.[41]

Augustus Smith Clayton supplied the second provocation. In a tariff speech comparing the Northern and Southern economies, the Georgia congressman declared that planters' "slaves were their machinery, and they had as good a right to profit by them as Northern men had by the machinery they employed." Adams's eyes must have lit up when he heard this pronouncement; he certainly had no intention of letting such an opening pass. Two days later, he made Clayton's unfortunate metaphor the basis for a lesson on protectionism that the Georgian neither anticipated, nor welcomed. In terms of their political implications, Adams observed, Southern and Northern machinery differed in important ways that slaveholders did not seem to appreciate. One of them stemmed from the Constitution's three-fifths compromise. "Did the manufacturers ask for any representation on their machinery?" he inquired. They plainly did not. But planters did, and the spindles, looms, and forges of Northern mills would never secure the increased number of House seats that the planters' machinery had enabled them to obtain. Southern machinery also had a "self-moving power" unlike anything seen in Northern factories, and slaveholders had received further protection from the Fugitive Slave Law. On a related matter, this unique feature of planter machinery made the South "more liable to domestic violence" than was the case elsewhere; and when such uprisings occurred, as had recently happened in Virginia, slaveowners looked to the Union for additional protection. Southern congressmen would do well to bear all this in mind, Adams concluded, as "his constituents had as much right to say to the people of the South—we will not submit to the protection of your interests; as the people of the South had to address such language to them."[42]

Adams's remarks created an immediate uproar in the House. The Charleston unionist William Drayton, speaking "in a strain of great warmth," accused the New Englander of hurling "a firebrand" into the chamber. Had he intended to inflame "the prejudices and passions" of Southern members, "he could scarcely have accomplished his intention more successfully." Closer to home, people responded much differently. Where one correspondent congratulated him for making slaveholders aware "of their comparative weakness," newspapers throughout Massachusetts showered praise on the congressman for rebuking nullifier demands "without cringing or mincing the matter." Unaccustomed to such public acclaim, Adams expressed surprise that the machinery address was "the most popular thing I ever did or said." He was not being disingenuous. Although he had no illusions about how slaveholding congressmen would react, the speech was relatively brief, and he had no reason to expect that it would receive widespread attention. It nevertheless constituted a noteworthy presentation of his views. Taken together with what he afterward wrote in response to Jackson's annual message, the two statements merit further examination because they so well encapsulate where he stood at the time and can be used to illustrate subtle but significant differences between Adams and most other free labor protectionists.[43]

Adams had two major aims in these interventions. One was to clarify what he thought was at stake in the nullification controversy. Calhoun and his supporters spoke interminably about states' rights and federal impositions on a Southern minority that lacked the political wherewithal to defend its interests. But as Calhoun privately acknowledged, and Adams firmly believed, nullification was actually a "question of the white and the black, the freeman and the slave." The Bay congressman feared that not everyone recognized as much, and he wanted to make sure they did. "The Free System and the Slave System are there in full contrast," he said of the two statements, "and I am anxious that they should be seen and considered throughout New England." Slaveholding politicians had "secured to themselves *all* the organized power of the Union, and they will ultimately bully and cajole the North into a surrender of their rights" if people failed to understand that planter grievances and demands were nothing more than a cover for efforts to strengthen slavery. He hoped that he had "opened the field, upon which in my opinion, the free labour of the country is to be defended against the operation of *Southern Machinery*."[44]

Adams's second objective was to secure the constitutional high ground in the nullification debate. Even though no less an authority than James Madison—the "father of the Constitution" and author of the Virginia resolutions—had rejected Calhoun's rendering of the doctrine, those listening to the South Carolinian could well be pardoned if they came away believing that he possessed a transcription of the founders' innermost thoughts. Adams understood this and felt protectionism had to be placed "under the shield of constitutional right" if advocates of the principle were to have any chance of being heard. By revealing "the superabundant *Protection* enjoyed by the Slave Holding interest, at the expense of the Union," he hoped "the tables of invidious argument might be effectively turned upon the assailants." At the same time, he wanted people to recognize that protection was not simply a device for advancing the interests of a particular group or region but an integral feature of all sound government that had deep roots in English political culture. Governments that ignored this obligation did so at their peril. As he later told his constituents in an address that reprised major themes of the machinery speech, protection formed the basis of civic allegiance: "When a government ceases to protect, it must cease to claim obedience or submission. There is no code upon earth which claims obedience and denies protection but the black code; and accordingly, it is from the land of the black code that the hue and cry comes against protection."[45]

This was not the only instance in which Adams sought to turn questions raised by the nullification debate into a broader discussion of the type of government that the nation needed. Take, for example, his response to Jackson's proposals to reduce government to its least complicated form. "The simplest of all Governments," his report on the president's message declared, "is an absolute despotism; and it may confidently be affirmed that, in proportion that a Government approaches to simplicity," it will be one of "arbitrary power." Citizens of the United States enjoyed greater liberty than other peoples of the world, and they did so, the report added, "because of all the Governments of the earth, theirs is the most complicated."[46]

The ex-president had even less patience with assaults on the general welfare clause of Article I, Section 8 of the Constitution. Proponents of states' rights never tired of condemning Adams and other public figures who urged a loose construction of the clause. If nothing were done to check them, Southern critics claimed, these tyrants in the making would employ the clause to justify initiatives that imposed unnecessary and unconstitutional financial burdens on the people, freed Congress from all restraints, magnified executive power, increased political corruption, and transformed the nation's republican system of government into a despotic monarchy, leaving "no state right or privilege, but may be easily prostrated by the general government," including the right to hold slaves. The Bay congressman considered these assertions pernicious nonsense. For Adams, a government that did not seek to advance the general welfare was no government at all. Raising the revenue required to do so was one of Congress's most important obligations. That the founders considered it so was apparent not only in their acknowledgement of the need to promote and provide for the general welfare in the preamble and Article I of the Constitution, but in their "anxious use of all the words by which the contributions of taxation can be levied—taxes, duties, imposts, and excises." Without this revenue, the nation could never realize what Adams considered its divinely ordained developmental destiny. "Had not the God of heaven given us our country to be improved, and what was the tendency of the contrary system?" he asked. "It led us back to the savage state!" During his presidency, he had tried to prevent such regression and put America on the right track by instituting a comprehensive system of internal improvements. But "the Sable Genius of the South," fearing that region's "own inevitable downfall in the unparalleled progress of the general welfare of the North," had dictated otherwise. It was his greatest fear that he would not live to witness the creation of an effective "system of internal improvement by National means and National energies." And there would, he knew, be little chance of that happening should nullification triumph or Jackson's policies be continued indefinitely. As the report on the president's message observed: "Fearful and hopeless, indeed, would be the condition of the people of the United States, if every grant of power delegated by them, for their own benefit and improvement, to their united national supreme Legislature, should be annulled or struck with impotence by every scruple of doubt which the refinements of metaphysical subtlety, the transient ebullitions of popular sentiment, or the factious instigations of electioneering artifice, have, from time to time, disseminated over different sections of the country." If the government should resolve to "engage in no more works of internal improvement," he said in an earlier speech that made his point unmistakably clear, "this Union will soon break into pieces; and I will add that it will not deserve to be preserved."[47]

Here and elsewhere Adams was attempting to construct what might be called a constitutional counternarrative to combat the claims of states' rights advocates. That this was his intention can best be seen in his response to their arguments concerning the historical bases for state sovereignty. Calhoun and those who shared his views made much of the fact that Article II of the Articles of Confederation assured member states that they "retained [their] sovereignty, freedom, and independence." Because the Constitution derived its legitimacy from state assent, they contended, ratification of the document made no fundamental change in the relative autonomy that states had enjoyed during the Confederation period; nor did it impair their right to reject national initiatives that they deemed unjust and unlawful. To fortify their case, nullifiers pointed to the Kentucky and Virginia resolutions of 1798–1799, which Jefferson and Madison had drafted to justify state annulment of the Alien and Sedition Acts. When Madison refused to affirm their interpretation of the resolutions, they simply ignored his objections and made the more popular and better-known Jefferson their primary torchbearer. By 1830, appeals to the principles of '98 were so ubiquitous in South Carolina that small farmers in the most remote parts of the Upcountry could comment learnedly on their meaning.

How Adams responded to these arguments sheds light on his political adroitness. He recognized that the Kentucky and Virginia resolutions needed to be handled with care. Too vigorous an assault on them could expose him to charges of supporting the suppression of civil liberties that enforcement of the Alien and Sedition Acts so plainly required. It might also prompt attacks on his father's legacy. The elder Adams had not initiated the alien and sedition laws, but he had signed them, and any discussion of the measures would inevitably generate unwelcome reflections on his presidency. Rather than directly criticize Jefferson and Madison's resolutions, Adams chose instead to reinterpret their purpose. Those who saw them as a defense of constitutionally protected freedoms, he contended, misunderstood the intentions of their authors. Jefferson might well be considered "the father of South Carolina Nullification," but in drafting the Kentucky resolutions he was more concerned about advancing his political ambitions than protecting the rights of the people. "The Legislatures of Virginia and Kentucky were electioneering machines," he later wrote, "which Mr. Jefferson used to supplant his Predecessor in the Presidency" by making them platforms for an initiative to turn the highly unpopular alien and sedition laws into "levers of insurrection to array the States against the existing administration of the general Government."[48]

Nullifier pronouncements concerning the confederation were another matter entirely. Unlike assertions regarding the Kentucky and Virginia resolutions, these statements provided Adams with inviting polemical opportunities that could be exploited without fear and without evasion. The governments formed by the Articles of Confederation and the Constitution differed in significant ways that proponents of state sovereignty invariably glossed over in their accounts of the early republic. But these differences marked a major turning point in the nation's development and should not forgotten, Adams argued. Where each of the sovereign states comprising the confederation had possessed "uncontrollable, unlimited, despotic power"—a condition that made the disorder and debility of the immediate post-revolutionary years inescapable—the Constitution established a government in which national unity, grounded in popular consent, provided a sound basis for future growth and prosperity. In light of this history, it was hard to imagine how anybody could claim that the Constitution created "a confederacy of States." One need only examine the ratification process to obtain further evidence of the wrongheadedness of such contentions. The founders had sent the Constitution to Congress, which submitted it to state legislatures for approval; but the latter determined that, "because they could never use the language, 'We the people,'" they had insufficient authority to ratify the document and chose instead to let popular conventions decide whether the new frame of government should be adopted. And it was well they did, Adams added, for "had the States, as States, unanimously ratified it, it would have been a dead letter until the people had acted upon it." In all this, he later observed, the Constitution could rightly be viewed as "the consummation of the Declaration of Independence" and its gleaming "spirit of union, speaking with one voice of the vindication of one People for the act of separating themselves from another, and ascending to the First Cause, the dispenser of eternal justice, for the foundation of its reasoning."[49]

References to the Declaration of Independence were never token gestures on Adams's part. In certain respects he would always be the young boy who, standing at his mother's side, had witnessed the Battle of Bunker Hill, and any mention of the Declaration brought back memories of a heroic past. More important Adams viewed the Declaration "as an abridged Alcoran of political doctrine, laying open the first foundations of civil Society." As such, it furnished a measure for assessing the competing claims of political theorists. In the words of Adams biographer Charles N. Edel, the Declaration was not simply "a historic document that justified the American Revolution" but "a timeless moral standard against which all governments must be judged." Even now, he observed in an

1839 address, "there are still philosophers who deny the principles asserted in the Declaration, as self-evident truths—who deny the natural equality and inalienable rights of man—who deny that the people are the only legitimate source of power—who deny that all just powers of government are derived from the *consent* of the governed." Don't listen to them, Adams warned, for adoption of their malign prescriptions could only bring "a curse" upon the nation. So long as Americans remembered that "the *ark* of [their] covenant is the Declaration of Independence," there would be little chance of that occurring.[50]

Such statements, delivered during a period when celebrations of the Declaration were on the rise everywhere, formed an important part of Adams's constitutional counternarrative. They also illustrate noteworthy differences in how he and Calhoun addressed major political questions. In an 1831 letter to an Ohio newspaper, William Henry Harrison criticized Calhoun's seeming inability to adopt a plainspoken, common-sense approach to political issues: "It may I think be admitted, as generally correct, that any proposition that is to be defended by a complex and abstract argument, is not in unison with our system of government, the principles of which are few, simple and easily understood." Adams put it more bluntly when he wrote that Calhoun's "insanity begins with principles; from which his deductions are ingeniously drawn." Such criticism notwithstanding, the South Carolinian could be very persuasive. Anyone who failed to question his starting premise and then followed his rigorously logical development of an argument would have an extremely difficult time refuting it. Yet Calhoun would always be at a disadvantage when pitted against adversaries such as Adams who rested their case on appeals to broadly accepted popular principles. When Calhoun later made criticism of the numerical majority a central feature of his demands for political reform, several Northern acquaintances urged him to be careful. Nearly everyone he knew, a Cincinnati correspondent wrote, considered the principle of majority rule the "corner stone of free institutions"; anyone who sought to deprive a numerical majority of New Yorkers of their power to govern, another writer added, "would be consigned to an oblivion darker than that which shrouds the name of [Benedict] Arnold." Nobody ever had occasion to issue similar warnings to Adams.[51]

On a related matter, the New Englander, during a moment of deep frustration, would later describe the Constitution as a "menstruous rag." The remark might more appropriately have come from Calhoun. The general welfare and implied powers clauses of Article I, the guarantee of a republican form of government in Article IV that Adams made the basis of comments on slave revolt in his machinery speech, the privileges and immunities clause of the same article that featured so largely in the later stages of the Missouri debate, the supremacy clause of Article VI—these and other constitutional provisions could all be used to challenge slaveholder pretensions, and Calhoun would spend the final two decades of his life trying to construct a constitutional defense of Southern rights that might effectively stop the bleeding. Simply holding Congress to a narrow interpretation of its delegated powers would never be enough. As he said of an article by Richmond editor John Hampden Pleasants: "He appears to be ready to abandon the great right of State interposition, in favour of the phantom of strict construction—a good thing in the abstract, but in practice not worth a farthing, without the right of interposition to enforce it." Adams had a much easier time of it. Although his constitutional counternarrative never came to grips with the document's proslavery compromises, he could more readily assume the offensive than the South Carolinian ever could. And, despite his many gloomy observations on the overwhelming strength of the forces arrayed against him, he could do so confident in the belief that differences over state sovereignty, slavery, and related matters would ultimately be resolved in the court of public opinion, and not by a panel of constitutional lawyers.[52]

For Calhoun, the most disturbing feature of the New Englander's interventions was his effort to give free labor protectionism a more pointed antislavery edge. "I rejoiced," Adams's friend Benjamin Waterhouse said of his machinery speech, "when I found by the papers that you had touched the only *string* which vibrates the heart *strings* of the South"—their slaves. "I am very glad that they have been reminded of their comparative weakness." His only surprise, Waterhouse added, was that the subject "had not been touched strongly before." Calhoun dearly hoped that others would not follow the Bay congressman's lead. "Interest," he had observed in an 1812 speech, "has a wonderful control over sentiment. Even the more refined and elevated, the moral and religious sentiment may be considered as ultimately resting upon it." At the time, he did not give much thought to what that might mean in practical terms. He was now finding out, and he did not like it. Should the tariff debate become a clash over slavery, planter interests would be truly imperiled.[53]

Meanwhile, as the nullification crisis ground slowly to a close, Calhoun had more alarming problems than Adams's constitutionalism to worry about. On October 8 and 9, 1832, white male South Carolinians went to the polls to cast their ballots in what many of them doubtless considered the most important election of their lifetimes. The previous year had witnessed intensifying conflict between Palmetto unionists and nullifiers. In Charleston during the period preceding the election, each side had hired local thugs to carry its message into the streets, where bloody fights between armed bands became everyday occurrences. If nullifiers bore responsibility for a larger part of these disturbances, it was only because of their greater numbers, and not because they felt any more malice toward their adversaries than unionists did toward them; both parties believed that—for better or worse—the state's future would be irrevocably altered by the outcome of the contest. When the votes were finally tallied, it was clear that nullifiers had secured the commanding legislative majority that they sought, winning three of every four seats in the Senate and four of every five in the House. At a special session of the assembly shortly afterward, legislators passed a bill calling for a state convention to address the tariff question. Voters selected delegates in an election held on November 12, and the gathering convened a week later in Columbia.[54]

Leading nullifiers believed the current crisis centered as much on slavery as it did on protectionism, but they had no wish to say it out loud. Doing so, they feared, would not only increase the difficulty of obtaining outside support; anything they said might also reach the ears of South Carolina slaves, with consequences that no one wanted to contemplate. Convention delegates thus observed the state's informal ban on public discussion of slavery. and focused instead on tariff-related constitutional questions. In his draft of an Address to the People of the United States, Calhoun elaborated on themes presented in the *South Carolina Exposition and Protest* and Fort Hill Address, writing that the tariff "now stands for the first time, exclusively on its own basis, as an independent system" that if left unchecked "must continue to expand, till it controls the entire labor and capital of the staple and exporting States, subjecting them completely, as tributaries, to the great dominant and sectional interest, which has grown up at their expense." Senator Robert Y. Hayne, reporting for the Committee of Twenty-One, released the convention's main statement of grievances. It condemned the American system as a "violation of the letter and spirit of the Constitution" that threatened "to transform the present representative system of the United States into a monarchy." Sad experience had shown that it was delusory to imagine that the impositions of the "Tariff majority in Congress" could be contained if some state did not step forward and follow the example set by Thomas Jefferson in 1798. Two days later, the convention passed a nullification ordinance that, in the absence of satisfactory tariff reform, barred the collection of customs duties in South Carolina after February 1, 1833; it further declared that any federal action to compel obedience would provide grounds for secession from the union and the formation of "a separate Government" able to do all those "acts and things which sovereign and independent States may of right do."[55]

In Washington, Andrew Jackson watched these proceedings with mounting anger. The president's devotion to the Union and orthodox reading of the Constitution made him reflexively hostile to nullification doctrine; that its main exponent was Calhoun, someone whom he neither liked nor trusted, only deepened his animosity. He nevertheless had mixed feelings about what to do. Uncertain about how other Southern states might react, he wanted to avoid being put in a position that required a military solution to the crisis. At the same time, he had no intention of letting nullifiers block the enforcement of federal law. "The vain threats of resistance by those who have raised the standard of rebellion shew their madness and folly," he told Charleston unionist Joel R. Poinsett. Nullifiers must understand that, should they resort to force, "the friends of liberty and union will be strong enough to prostrate their enemies." Jackson attempted to balance these considerations in his Proclamation to the People of South Carolina. It began with a lengthy explanation of his reasons for rejecting constitutional arguments for nullification. Then, speaking as a native of the state, the president urged South Carolinians to consider how they had been misled by erroneous economic theories, false constitutional doctrines, and "appeals to your passions." They had just grievances, he said, but changes in public opinion ensured that satisfactory tariff legislation would soon be forthcoming. All they had to do was wait. In the meantime, however, they needed to recognize his determination "to execute laws; to preserve the Union by all Constitutional means; [and] to arrest, if possible, by moderate but firm measures, the necessity of a recourse to force;" for he dearly hoped that "if it be the will of Heaven that a recurrence of its primeval curse on man for the shedding of a brother's blood, should fall upon our land, that it be not called down by any offensive act on the part of the United States."[56]

As the proclamation's title indicated, Jackson's intended audience was the people of South Carolina. He said almost nothing to pacify nullifiers, and a great deal to anger them. If the proclamation's menacing tone and dismissive approach to nullification doctrine were not bad enough, these proud patriarchs could hardly have been pleased by the president's attempt to exert "the influence that a father would over his children whom he saw rushing to certain ruin" by telling Carolinians—"with that paternal feeling" he felt for them—that they had been "deluded by men who are either deceived themselves, or wish to deceive you." This was the kind of language that a chief executive used when addressing Native Americans, and it enraged state leaders. In its reply, the legislature declared Jackson's assertions "erroneous and dangerous, leading not only to the establishment of a consolidated government in the stead of a free confederacy, but to the consolidation of all power in the chief executive." South Carolina could not be intimidated, the reply added, not even by "the concentration of a standing army on our borders." Should hostilities ensue, "the state will repel force by force, and relying upon the blessings of God, will maintain its liberty at all hazards."[57]

All this doubtless fired up some of the more enthusiastic nullifiers, but it did so at a price. The movement comprised people of differing temperament and varying degrees of ideological fervor, not all of whom agreed on how far they wished to push the confrontation with federal authorities. According to Charleston lawyer James L. Petigru, the legislature's reply created considerable uneasiness among nullifiers of more conservative disposition who considered prudence the better part of valor. "Many of them"—particularly those who subscribed to the "constitutional nullification" of Calhoun—"say they have been deceived," the unionist leader wrote. They "had no idea of what has come to pass" and were strongly disinclined to travel any farther down the road marked out by the legislature. How Calhoun felt at this moment is difficult to gauge. Having resigned his vice-presidential post in late November, he now occupied a seat in the US Senate, where he tried to maintain a bold front. His main speech of the period came in mid-February. A month earlier, Jackson had asked Congress to pass a measure popularly known as the "force bill," which established procedures for the collection of customs duties in South Carolina and confirmed his authority to use military force should South Carolinians employ armed resistance to obstruct enforcement of the tariff laws. In his spirted response to the president's message, Calhoun summarized the South's accumulating grievances: describing the deep disappointment Southerners felt at the administration's failure to enact tariff reform; condemning the recent movement toward consolidated government, with its accompanying "growth of faction, corruption, anarchy, and if not despotism itself, its near approach, in the provisions of this bill"; explaining how federal policies impoverished the South by exacting "a large portion of the proceeds of its industry, which it bestows upon the other sections, in the shape of bounties to manufacturers, and appropriations in a thousand forms"; and lamenting the South's emergence as a permanent minority pitted against an aggrandizing North in "a contest in which the weaker section, with its peculiar labour, productions, and institutions, has at stake all that can be dear to freemen." Should "we yield, and permit the stronger interest to concentrate within itself all the powers of the government," he declared, "then will our fate be more wretched than that of the aborigines whom we have expelled."[58]

Calhoun's primary aim in the speech was to rally Southern support for nullification. That he still thought it necessary to do so did not speak well for the strength of his position. The previous month had not been a good time for Calhoun or the Carolina doctrine. On January 12, 1833, the Alabama legislature had approved resolutions declaring nullification "unsound in theory and dangerous in practice," adding "that as a remedy it is unconstitutional and essentially revolutionary, leading in its consequences to anarchy and civil discord, and finally to the dissolution of the Union"; the Mississippi legislature followed suit shortly afterward. Calhoun believed Jackson's force bill message would prompt Southerners to abandon such views and form a united phalanx behind South Carolina in opposition to federal encroachment on states' rights. "The doctrines of 98," he confidently predicted, "will triumph again and will again save the Republick." That was not how things turned out. However alarming they considered Jackson's message, other Southern states showed little inclination to rush to South Carolina's aid. Although Calhoun retained the unflagging support of Governor John Floyd in the Old Dominion, most Virginians simply wanted to see the confrontation ended and appeared ready to turn on anyone who seemed unduly intransigent. Divisions of a somewhat different sort existed in Georgia, where

Governor Wilson Lumpkin's misgivings about nullification and the abiding dislike that backers of William Crawford felt toward Calhoun prevented state nullifiers from mounting any meaningful initiative on behalf of their SC neighbors. Once it became clear that Jackson would do nothing to enforce a Supreme Court decision that could be used to obstruct plans for expropriating Native American lands within the state, any chance that Georgia might join the Carolinians disappeared.[59]

Meanwhile, the situation in South Carolina was daily going from bad to worse. State unionists, under the leadership of Joel Poinsett, had mustered a force of 8,000 volunteers. Although no match for the nullifier army mobilized by Governor Hayne, it was large enough to cause serious concern. The unionists also had much better access to outside reinforcements. In his role as liaison to the Executive Mansion, Poinsett dispatched regular reports on local developments to Jackson, who, notwithstanding his wish to avoid the introduction of federal troops, provided assurance that SC unionists would not be left twisting in the wind if the current war of words gave way to armed struggle. How well Hayne's enthusiastic but poorly organized nullifier units might perform in such a conflict was not a question Calhoun cared to contemplate. He understood South Carolina's growing isolation as well as anyone and viewed the prospect of military confrontation with even greater trepidation than Jackson did. His primary objective throughout had been to establish a credible constitutional defense of Southern rights, and he now worried that some fire-eating radicals seemed intent on moving from nullification to disunion. It would be a serious mistake, he told William Preston, to "think of secession, but in the last extremity. It would be the most fatal of all steps."[60]

Given these pressures, one can well believe those contemporary observers who described the South Carolina senator "as excessively uneasy or agitated." Some even thought he might be losing his vaunted self-control. According to Jackson, "Calhoun finds himself between Scylla and Caribdis and is reckless." Although scarcely the most objective of commentators, the president was half-right. Calhoun recognized that he had been placed in a difficult position and faced hard choices, but anyone who believed he would throw caution to the wind at such a moment seriously misjudged him. Seeing that events had overtaken him and threatened to plunge South Carolina into a war that no sensible person desired, Calhoun understood that the time for compromise had arrived. That meant arranging a tariff that addressed protectionism in a way that provided sufficient cover to deflect any charges of capitulation that might be hurled at him without alienating all Northern support for the bill. Henry Clay was thinking along the same lines, and the Kentuckian produced a measure that placed most unprotected items on the free list and called for biennial reductions in rates on protected goods, the most considerable of which would take place in 1842. Protectionism would be eliminated, but not for another decade.[61]

In a posthumous tribute to Calhoun, one eulogist singled out the Tariff of 1833 as a major turning point in state history. "Before South Carolina had extorted the Compromise act from an unwilling Congress, the streets of our city were overgrown with grass," declared Charleston educator Frederick Porcher. "Charleston owes the dawn of her commercial prosperity altogether to the action of that party, which animated by the counsels of our great statesman, dared to arrest the progress of usurpation, and test the conservative principles of our Constitution." However appropriate such remarks may have been for the occasion, they fail to capture the mixed feelings most people had about the measure in the spring of 1833. With the possible exception of Clay, who received widespread praise for negotiating a peaceful resolution to the nullification crisis, no one expressed complete satisfaction with the compromise tariff. This included Calhoun, who, despite objections to many parts of the bill, said "he was willing to take it with all its faults, as a peace-offering." More important the Palmetto senator recognized that tariff reform and constitutional change were two entirely different things, and he knew that relatively few people outside South Carolina accepted the principle of state interposition. Thus, while he believed he could confidently assert that nullifiers had achieved their immediate aim of eliminating protectionism—itself a debatable claim given all that could happen in ten years—he had to acknowledge that the movement had yet to obtain its broader objective of establishing constitutional safeguards for Southern liberties. Were he asked "whether all had been effected which was necessary to secure the rights of the States," Calhoun told a Charleston audience that November, he could only reply: "*no*, NO! Much—much still remained to be done."[62]

Not all nullifiers considered enactment of Clay's bill a triumph. Addressing a convention assembled shortly after its passage, the future champion of secession Robert Barnwell Smith (Rhett) said the measure came up well short of nullifier demands; and state leaders had an obligation to admit as much, for "the People should be taught, from our tone and our declarations, that the battle was yet to be fought and won, and that preparation—armed preparation—energy unremitted—and vigilance, sleepless and untiring, were absolutely necessary to maintain their liberties." At the time, this was a minority view. Most nullifiers chose instead to adopt Calhoun's more moderate stance: declaring victory while warning of struggles ahead. George McDuffie gave voice to their position when he told convention delegates that the compromise could rightly be seen as a major achievement. "But," he added, "it is only such, if the people now awakened refuse to let it lull them even into an instant's security," there being "in this general government, a proclivity to consolidation, that nothing except the most absolute watchfulness can stay." Although South Carolinians could take satisfaction in this momentary success, they needed to keep their powder dry. As Judge William Harper put it, "We must regard ourselves at the beginning, not at the end, of a contest."[63]

The belief that nullification could best be seen as the first battle in an ongoing struggle was not nearly so common elsewhere in the South, and much less so in the North. There were exceptions, however, the most notable of whom was the former president and junior congressman from Massachusetts. Adams was considerably less pleased than most Carolinians with Clay's compromise. He acknowledged that it was better than the Verplanck tariff, an earlier bill that would have removed most protective duties within two years. Had that "Jackson and Van Buren *nostrum* to save the Union and breed harmony" been enacted, he wrote, it would have sacrificed the free labor of the North to the "living machinery" of the South. But Clay's bill nevertheless did great harm; its "monstrous concessions" gave nullifiers an appearance of victory at a moment when they could have been crushed. And Adams had no doubt that they needed to be crushed. Such people could not be appeased, and anyone who believed they would not be back for more had little understanding of what they represented. To the Bay congressman, proponents of the Carolina doctrine formed the shock troops of a larger sectional movement intent on thwarting Northern development. Its adherents opposed all measures to promote the general welfare, and, if left unchecked, they would use the advantages they derived from the Constitution's three-fifths compromise to create a society that reduced people of the North to "the Hewers of wood and Drawers of water to the Slave driving *best part of the population*" that Jackson had praised in his message. "If the freemen of the North will submit to it and bow their necks to be trampled upon," he wrote, "be the responsibility upon themselves."[64]

By the spring of 1833, Adams was a different person than he had been upon entering Congress. Where he had once condemned the bombastic sectionalism of Massachusetts Federalists as a threat to national unity, he now embraced a conspicuously confrontational version of a free labor protectionism that Bay Whigs would soon make the centerpiece of efforts to confirm their reputation as defenders of regional interests. During the previous decade, political ambition and an unwillingness to incite intersectional conflict had prevented him from elaborating on the harshly critical observations on slavery and planter pretensions that he had confided to his diary during the Missouri controversy. This reticence continued during his first months in the House. When presenting antislavery petitions, he recommended that there be no discussion of their content because he feared that any such exchanges "would lead to ill will, to heart burnings, [and] to mutual hatred" without achieving anything. But that was then. Debate over the Carolina doctrine, together with the memories it stirred of political opposition to realization of his developmental vision for the nation while president, had produced a combustible mixture of violated principle and bitter resentment that shattered earlier inhibitions. Although he was not looking for further provocations at the moment, he had no doubt that they would come his way. Clay's compromise, he told his son, had settled nothing: "The main question is between slave and free labour."[65]

One person who shared Adams's dark view of the future was James Petigru. Unlike many South Carolina unionists, who greeted the compromise tariff with a sigh of relief, hoping that it pointed the way toward restoration of an earlier tranquility, the tough-minded Charleston lawyer saw nullification as the initial skirmish in what promised to be a long and increasingly hazardous conflict. He believed state nullifiers were already planning "to pick a quarrel with the North about negroes." And it would not stop there, he predicted, for nullification "has prepared the minds of men for a separation of States, and when the question is mooted again it will be distinctly union or disunion." However well Petigru may have captured the mood and intentions of radicals such as Rhett, his observations did not apply to Calhoun. Although the Palmetto senator made a half-hearted proslavery appeal in an attempt to rally Southern support during the closing stages of the nullification controversy, he remained wary of the adverse consequences of public discussion of slavery. Much less did he wish to do anything that might encourage thoughts of secession. The nullification struggle had been a grueling contest that left him physically and emotionally exhausted. Mounting an initiative so at variance with his prudential instincts was the last thing he had in mind.[66]

None of this lessens the extent to which Calhoun had changed since leaving Monroe's cabinet. Much more so than Adams, he was truly a different person. Where the Bay congressman's newfound public assertiveness built on long-standing convictions, the SC senator had largely abandoned some of his more heartfelt beliefs. Application of the love, fear, and interest model of political culture makes this unmistakably clear. In a January speech concerning Jackson's message to South Carolina, Calhoun declared that he had since his earliest days "cherished a deep and enthusiastic admiration for the Union. He had looked on its progress with rapture, and encouraged the most sanguine expectations of its endurance." That fervent attachment was now gone. How much fear influenced this change of perspective is hard to determine. Although he had maintained a bold stance throughout the nullification controversy, administration threats almost certainly contributed to the rising levels of stress that he experienced during the closing months of the crisis. It is unnecessary to pursue this question any further, for the exact calculus is not important. During his years in the War Department,

Calhoun could scarcely have imagined that he would ever have any reason to feel apprehensive about the exercise of federal power. That he did so now was what really mattered.[67]

Even more striking was Calhoun's altered perception of interest. Although the South Carolinian never fully embraced Adams's grand developmental project, he had hoped to further the establishment of an interdependent national economy in which the growth of one section contributed to the prosperity of others. He was, in the New Englander's words, "the chosen champion of the national bank, of an efficient navy, of domestic manufactures and of internal improvements[;]" in him, "the nation saw with admiration and favour a statesman from South Carolina whose political survey extended beyond the banks of a rice-farm, and whose estimate of the value of the Union was not regulated by the amount of the impost upon cotton-bagging." That Calhoun had disappeared and would never return. He now viewed the South as a permanent minority locked in combat with an increasingly powerful North that had no qualms about using its gathering strength to advance regional fortunes at the expense of Southern interests. Creating a united South capable of resisting the onslaught had become his main mission in life. The emergence of an even greater threat than that posed by Northern protectionists would soon make fulfillment of the task more urgent than it had ever been.[68]

Chapter 4

SLAVERY and ANTISLAVERY

In this chapter, a third actor joins Calhoun and Adams on center stage. The 1830s witnessed a major change in the struggle against slavery. Outside the slender ranks of Black abolitionists, whose consistently militant message went largely unnoticed, most antislavery organizations before that time subscribed to some form of gradualism. The most prominent of these societies in 1830 consisted of a band of colonizationists who seemed more intent on emptying the country of free Black people than on taking serious steps to end human bondage. Apart from a small group of proslavery radicals who strenuously opposed any initiative that even hinted of emancipation, most slaveholders recognized the harmlessness of such programs and responded accordingly, occasionally applauding the good intentions of colonizationists and other gradualists but otherwise ignoring them. The emergence of immediate abolitionism completely altered the relatively tranquil landscape of American antislavery activity. Its proponents, though not expecting the nation's slaves to be freed overnight, demanded that action be taken at once to begin the process of unconditional and uncompensated emancipation. As immediatism spread from New England to New York and into many areas of the Midwest, worried defenders of the racial status quo viewed the movement with growing alarm. Although always thin on the ground, abolitionists exhibited an energy, enthusiasm, and organizational prowess that made them appear much more formidable than their actual numbers would suggest. And having mastered the art of publicity, their ability to produce and disseminate huge quantities of antislavery literature made a particularly strong impression on those more perceptive Southern leaders who knew their region would be hard pressed to match such publishing feats.[1]

Of the various tactics adopted by the immediatists, none proved more effective than their petition campaign. The practice was not new—opponents of slavery had been petitioning government since the eighteenth century; nor was there anything novel about the topics addressed in abolitionist memorials of the mid-1830s—abolishing slavery in the District of Columbia and preventing the admission of new slave states had been abiding concerns of antislavery activists since the beginnings of the republic. What was new was the extraordinary volume of petitions being submitted. As their numbers grew, political conservatives from all parties and regions worried that they would generate arguments over slavery that increased hostility between free and slave states, shattered intersectional understandings that held the two major parties together, and threatened the stability of the union. When Southern congressmen devised a gag rule that effectively barred discussion of the petitions, many of their colleagues breathed a sigh of relief, believing the measure would put the matter to rest. It did nothing of the kind. In many areas of the North, abolitionists used the gag to recruit new members and gather signatures on a veritable mountain of additional memorials. On the floor of Congress, a group of antislavery House members led by Adams initiated what would become a nine-year struggle to defeat the prohibition. "Here, in fact," historian Don E. Fehrenbacher has written of the ensuing controversy, "was the heart of the sectional conflict, the real issue that would drive the nation to civil war—not the regulation of territories or the recovery of fugitive slaves, but, quite simply, northern denunciation of slavery and whether it could be silenced."[2]

Fehrenbacher's assertion is certainly arguable, given the tensions generated by the fugitive slave question and role that intersectional discord over slavery expansion played in demolishing the second American party system. Yet the statement nevertheless merits serious consideration, and a major aim of this chapter is to show why a distinguished historian of the period would make such a claim. It begins with an examination of Calhoun's response to the challenges presented by the abolitionist insurgency. On one hand, he truly feared the long-term consequences of abolitionist agitation in a world where slavery had fewer and fewer friends; on the other, he recognized that the abolitionist threat gave him just the issue he needed to renew his campaign to create a united South. Standing at the head of a group of Palmetto congressmen that adamantly opposed any compromise on slavery-related matters, the South Carolina senator not only demanded that Congress refuse even to receive antislavery petitions; he also emerged as a leading proponent of the positive good defense of slavery and led efforts to strengthen federal protection of slavery in the District of Columbia and the territories as well as the states. The second section of the chapter focuses on Adams's conduct in the petition contest. According to the South Carolina writer William J. Grayson, the Bay congressman "became the most enraged of abolitionists" during the course of the controversy: "His part was to add bitterness and virulence to every dispute. No man was more acrimonious, extreme, or uncompromising." Grayson's description is not altogether accurate—Adams was never an abolitionist. But in most other respects, the South Carolinian's observations were reasonably close to the mark, and the New Englander's interventions did much to turn what might have been a relatively short if occasionally heated debate into a protracted interregional encounter over the place of slavery in American society and government.[3]

In 1830, the nation's best-known antislavery organization was the American Colonization Society (ACS). Founded in 1816, the society's primary aim was to promote slave manumissions by transporting free Black people to a colony it had established in West Africa. With a membership list that included the names of eminent public figures such as James Madison, James Monroe, John Marshall, John Randolph, and Henry Clay, the ACS had a broad-ranging appeal that reached out to people in all sections of the country. Slaveholders who had moral qualms about holding human beings in bondage but who had no wish to see slavery abolished could support ACS initiatives safe in the knowledge that it would take generations—if not centuries—before emigration made any appreciable dent in the size of the regional labor force. That colonization promised to enhance white safety and reduce pauperism in Southern towns and cities through the removal of free Black people provided further reason for backing the ACS. Northern humanitarians also found much to like in the society's program. Colonization, its advocates contended, would not only encourage voluntary manumissions but give Black people an opportunity to lead more fulfilling lives by permitting them to escape the racism that pervaded American society and that ACS leaders fully embraced, believing as they did that emancipation required separation. Another rich source of ACS patronage was the nation's growing body of evangelicals. Dispatching boatloads of bible-bearing emigrants to Africa held out the alluring prospect of bringing Christianity to the "dark continent" and made colonization irresistibly attractive to Protestant divines inspired by the missionary impulse that fueled Second Great Awakening revivals. All in all, it was a wonderful vision—one that offered people of philanthropic disposition a means of feeling better about themselves without actually changing anything; the only risk and dislocation involved would be shouldered by those Black Americans induced or forced to depart a land they knew for one they did not.

Despite the society's apparent popularity, there were questions about the depth of its support. Although large numbers of people found colonizationist proposals perfectly acceptable, the ACS generated little real enthusiasm outside the ranks of evangelical proselytizers. It also had its share of critics. The warm glow of the society's message rarely proved strong enough to melt the frosty skepticism of those disinclined to take whatever they heard from the wise and the good on faith alone. One such person was Adams, who looked closely at the organization's claims and came away with deep reservations about what he saw. In addition to being wildly "impracticable," he observed, the ACS program would benefit no one even if the society somehow managed to devise means of surmounting the prohibitively expensive cost of implementing it. Not only were emigrants likely to "suffer more and enjoy less than they would if they should remain in the United States," but their removal would deprive the nation's developing economy of a vital labor source during a period when it needed all the help it could get. Adams thus concluded "that the result of the whole"—for Black as well as white Americans—"will be evil and not good."[4]

Such criticism, residing as it did in the safe confines of Adams's diary, created few difficulties for the ACS. More serious were the attacks of Southern opponents. One of the society's strongest claims was that colonization provided the best basis for intersectional consensus on the slavery question. Although generally true, not everyone agreed. The consistent backing that Virginia and other upper South states gave ACS appeals was not matched by lower South slaveholders, who tended to view the society's activities with greater skepticism, if not outright hostility. This was especially so in South Carolina, where tariff-conscious farmers and planters believed ACS efforts to secure federal assistance would only increase pressure for the passage of revenue-enhancing protective duties. Worse, a number of observers saw something much more sinister at work. In his influential "Crisis" essays, Robert Turnbull warned that ACS appeals for aid represented an "ENTERING WEDGE" that, by prompting congressional discussion of the pros and cons of slavery, could all too easily initiate a chain of events that "will cause DEATH AND DESTRUCTION to our negro property." The very nature of slavery made such an outcome more than likely. A slave's value, Turnbull explained, "arises not merely from his bodily capacity for labour"[;] no less important was "his contentment with his condition, and his attachment to his master's household." Should slaves ever come to believe "that Congress was to take them and their whole race, under its special cognizance and care," their resulting restiveness would "create in all of us, whose lot it is to live in this country, a solicitude for future consequences" that no rational person dared contemplate. South Carolinians, as Charles C. Pinckney told members of the State Agricultural Society, would therefore be well advised to monitor colonizationist initiatives "with an eye that never slumbers" and be ready to join forces whenever it seemed necessary to "counteract their injurious effects."[5]

However troubling, the South Carolina assault did not pose a major threat to the ACS. For every slaveholder who shared Turnbull's fears, there was one or more who refused to believe the regional labor system so fragile that it could not withstand congressional discussion of colonizationist requests for aid. A much different critique from a much different source would soon prove considerably more damaging. With the exception of Black abolitionists, who consistently opposed emigration and gradualism but lacked the power and resources to shape the broader antislavery debate, the ACS encountered little criticism from

Northern detractors during the first decade or so of its existence. This changed after 1830 with the emergence of an immediatist movement whose most prominent early leader was William Lloyd Garrison. The Boston printer had closer personal ties to Black Americans than other white antislavery activists typically did, and in his speeches and writings he insisted that emancipation must be accompanied by the establishment of racial equality. Accordingly, he had no use whatsoever for an organization whose popularity "is not attributable to its merits, but exclusively to its congeniality with the unchristian prejudices which have so long been cherished against a sable complexion." And in its first annual report, Garrison's New England Anti-Slavery Society argued that abolition of the ACS was a necessary precondition for the abolition of slavery. By their own admission, the report observed, colonizationists had adopted measures "calculated to save the slave-system from destruction, to remove the apprehensions of slaveholders, to increase the value of slave property, and thus to perpetuate the thralldom of millions of native Americans." Despite such policies, the ACS remained a formidable barrier to progress on the antislavery front because of the success of its "Janus-faced" practice of claiming to seek the elimination of slavery and the slave trade when addressing Northern philanthropists while assuring planters that it wanted only "to remove such free persons of color as wish to emigrate to Africa." People concerned about the evils of slavery and the injustices faced by Black Americans needed to recognize the ACS for what it was: a morally vacuous body with no interest in truly engaging the problems of slavery or racism; "*it neither calls for any change of conduct towards the people of color, on the part of the nation,* NOR HAS IT ANY PRINCIPLE OF REFORM."[6]

From the outset, Garrison worked to create an organization that reached beyond his initial base of operations in Boston's African American community. This meant moving into ACS territory and attempting to enlist the support of various evangelicals outside New England—people such as Arthur and Lewis Tappan, two New York City merchants who had applied their financial resources and managerial abilities to diverse reform causes; and the energetic band of lecturers that had made the revival belt stretching from upstate New York into Ohio's Western Reserve a major center of moral and religious uplift. The formation of the American Anti-Slavery Society (AAS) in December 1833 brought these and other groups together in a single association. By mid-decade, the still small immediatist phalanx had assumed an imposing appearance that belied its actual strength. In an 1835 stocktaking, Garrison proudly observed that the AAS had seven state organizations, more than 500 local societies, and thirty-six newspapers whose editorials and articles advocating immediatist doctrine often appeared in other publications. In addition to maintaining the offensive against colonization, the society sought ways to confront planter power directly and to focus national attention on the slavery question.[7]

One major venture was an 1835 postal campaign designed to flood Southern communities with abolitionist literature. As soon as it came to light, the initiative encountered swift and fierce resistance. Few Southerners had forgotten Nat Turner's Rebellion, which many linked to the emergence of Garrisonian immediatism, and they viewed any development that might expose slaves to abolitionist doctrine as a grievous threat to regional safety and well-being; at the very least, it would cause the sort of slave discontent with bondage that Robert Turnbull feared. In Charleston, Postmaster Alfred Huger reported: "The most respectable men of all parties gather'd about our doors and windows, and in a little time I was formally summoned to give up the 'incendiary publications' which were known to be in my possession, and at the same [time] told with very little ceremony, that they would be taken from me if I did not." When Huger did not immediately hand over the pamphlets, a group of vandals broke into the post office and seized the offending publications. Who they were was anyone's guess, for "Nullifiers and Union men, Jackson men and Clay men, Van Buren men and [Hugh Lawson] White men who differ on all points agree on this"—no abolitionist literature would ever freely circulate in South Carolina. And, Huger added, nothing short of "a military force greater than the Undivided population of Charleston" could prevent these people from responding in exactly the same way should another shipment of antislavery tracts be sent to the state.[8]

Administration officials fully sympathized with Southern opponents of the mail campaign. Postmaster General Amos Kendall let Huger and his regional colleagues know that Washington would do nothing to prevent them from disposing of the tracts in whatever manner they deemed most desirable. In his annual message that December, Jackson repeated the demands of a Charleston public meeting that had called on Northern legislatures to suppress abolitionist societies and urged Congress to pass a bill prohibiting the circulation of incendiary literature through the mails. Discussion of the latter did not get far before Calhoun stepped in to block consideration of the measure. At first glance an unlikely source of opposition, the South Carolinian had perfectly logical reasons for wanting to jettison the bill. According to the Constitution, he argued, the states alone possessed the power to provide for their own internal security "to the entire exclusion of all authority and control on the part of Congress." It therefore followed that, "in the case under consideration, it belongs to the Slave holding States to determine, what is incendiary and intended to incite to insurrection, and to adopt such defensive measures, as may be necessary" to preserve order. Permitting the intervention of some outside body that did not understand the South's peculiar social arrangements was a recipe for disaster that would disrupt existing patterns of master-slave relations and "place the two races in a state of conflict, which must end in the expulsion, or extirpation of one or the other." If the federal government refused to acknowledge the South's constitutional prerogative in this regard and "conflict should ensue between your law and our law," he warned, "the southern States will never yield to the superiority of yours." This was no idle threat: The principle of state interposition gave them just the remedy they needed to protect their interests in the event of such a clash. As it turned out, Calhoun's bill to ban the delivery of mails prohibited by state laws went nowhere. So did the administration's federal censorship measure, and the informal adoption of Kendall's policy of letting local postmasters determine what constituted incendiary literature effectively brought the controversy to a close.[9]

A concurrent AAS campaign had more enduring consequences. For the past three decades or so, various groups had petitioned Congress to abolish slavery and the slave trade in the District of Columbia. Although Congress did not have the authority to interfere with slavery in states where it still existed, the Constitution did give it the power of "exclusive legislation" in the district chosen as the seat of the national government, and antislavery groups sought to take advantage of the provision. The AAS drive began in 1834, led by the women who constituted "the great silent army of abolitionism." As they set about gathering signatures in villages, towns, and cities throughout the North, the number and size of petitions grew steadily. The AAS's central aim was to abolish "slavery *by revolutionizing the public sentiment in regard to it,*" and the canvassers had no doubt that their labors were contributing to its fulfillment. Nor did the society's leaders, whose comments on the campaign reflected the vibrant enthusiasm and grand expectations that characterized all AAS initiatives. Don't let anyone suggest that petitions did not matter, New York abolitionist Alvan Stewart declared. Not only did they represent "the enshrouded glory of our age," but their influence would be felt for generations to come: "If another general deluge were to sweep the earth, these petitions would rise above the flood and float over the wreck of human affairs, as the second ark of freedom and liberty."[10]

The petitions met strong opposition in Congress, where South Carolina congressmen proved particularly intransigent. Laying antislavery memorials on the table and letting them die the death of the friendless and abandoned did not go nearly far enough for James Hammond, who said he could no longer sit back "and see the rights of the southern people assaulted day after day, by the ignorant fanatics from whom these memorials proceed." He therefore moved that the House take steps to eliminate them altogether by refusing to receive any petition that cast the South's peculiar institution in an unfavorable light. Three days later, Waddy Thompson raised the stakes in a speech supporting Hammond's motion. The Palmetto congressman found the petitions' substance and tone equally objectionable. Southern slaveholders and abolitionist petitioners had one thing in common, he declared: Neither saw any difference between emancipation in the District and general emancipation; they both recognized that should the process of abolition recommence, it would not stop until it spread across the entire South. This alone should have been sufficient reason to bar reception of antislavery petitions. That the latter defamed Southern society and culture made it no less urgent that they be quashed. Like Hammond, Thompson had no intention of standing by and allowing the reputation of his native region to be dragged through the mud by people professing a higher morality. "I have not obtained my seat by prating about the Union," he warned: "There are things which I value more, and I tell you gentlemen, in all candor and good feeling, if the people of any portion of the country regard slavery as a national disgrace," men of honor in the South would insist on severing whatever bonds united the two sections.[11]

Calhoun weighed in several weeks later with a demand that the Senate also refuse to receive antislavery petitions. Because reception implied consideration, he argued, deciding which petitions they would receive was the most important right possessed by deliberative bodies; without it, they "become the passive receptacle, indifferently, of all that is frivolous, absurd, unconstitutional, immoral, and impious, as well as what may properly deserve their deliberation and action." As the seizure of slave property was clearly unconstitutional, he added, Congress had a special obligation to block the reception of petitions calling for emancipation in the District of Columbia. When James Buchanan, worried about Northern regard for the right of petition, proposed that the memorials be received and immediately rejected without committee consideration, Calhoun adamantly opposed the compromise. It did not matter how summarily legislators disposed of the petitions following their reception. Let them through the door, and they would inevitably generate discussion of a topic that no Southerner wished to see debated on the floor of Congress. Such exchanges, he warned, would ultimately prove even more dangerous to slaveholder interests than abolitionist misuse of the mails by giving official credence to the destructive intentions of a band of lawless fanatics whose "object is to humble and debase us in our own estimation, and that of the world in general, to blast our reputation, while they overthrow our domestic institutions." The Carolinian failed to persuade his fellow senators, who rejected his non-reception motion by a decisive 36-to-10 margin; when they afterward considered and approved Buchanan's proposal, Calhoun refused to vote and departed the chamber. In practice, the Senate would go beyond Buchanan's motion and adopt the even more restrictive procedure of tabling the question of petitions, which prevented any discussion whatsoever of their content. This did not satisfy Calhoun, but it did allow his complacent, conflict-averse colleagues to ignore the matter.[12]

The House, with its larger, more contentious membership, was a different place altogether. Henry L. Pinckney found this out when he attempted to tamp down the petition controversy. Worried that discussion of the question might ignite a full blown debate over slavery, the Charleston congressman proposed that petitions calling for emancipation in the District be referred to a select committee, which would prepare a report explaining the dangers of abolition in a way "best calculated to enlighten the public mind, to repress agitation, to allay excitement, to sustain and preserve the just rights of the slaveholding States and of the people of this District, and to re-establish harmony and tranquility amongst the various sections of the Union." Pinckney probably anticipated some pushback from his more radical SC colleagues, but he certainly did not foresee how furious the ensuing assault would be. Taking the floor later in the day, Hammond denounced the resolutions as wrongheaded, if not worse. The South could not compromise on this question, he declared; anyone who believed "Tappan, Garrison, and the rest of the gang" would relent once they had "tasted blood" was hopelessly naive. And this was only the beginning. Hammond, Calhoun, and others subsequently attributed Pinckney's action to the political opportunism of a second-rate politician seeking to curry favor with Martin Van Buren, who at that time did not want the slavery issue to complicate his presidential bid. Meanwhile, Edgefield congressman Francis Pickens spoke for many when he expressed the wish that South Carolinians would condemn Pinckney's "betrayal" and see him for the "traitor and dastard" that he was. By all accounts, large numbers of them did.[13]

The Charleston lawyer did not know what hit him and must have wondered what he had done wrong. As an outspoken nullifier who had urged South Carolinians to "crown CALHOUN and MCDUFFIE with our choicest wreath" for their contributions to the struggle, he had every reason to believe that he had earned the trust of Palmetto voters and the state's political elite. Moreover, he truly thought that he had acted in the best interests of the South. He wanted to cut off all discussion of slavery in Congress and assumed that his constituents shared his desire to do so. Barring the reception of antislavery petitions, he afterward told his fellow Charlestonians, would have had disastrous consequences for the slaveholding states. Such a provocation, Pinckney explained, could not help but "*increase the spirit and strength of the abolitionists,* by giving them *constitutional ground to stand on,* by enabling them to cry out that they were persecuted and disfranchised on account of slaves, and by inflaming the whole of the nonslaveholding States, by the unnecessary invasion of what they considered a most sacred and fundamental right." The contest was not about some abstract, theoretical point. The question Southerners needed to be asking themselves was how they could best mobilize a broad, united front against abolitionism. Flatly denying the right of petition was not the way, and they should not permit the issue to become "an engine of sectional divisions and hostilities." Why, given the unlikelihood that Congress would ever attempt to abolish slavery in the District, force the issue and push the House "to take ground against the South, and in favor of the fanatics, when, if left to itself, and its mode of operation, it would take very strong and decided ground in favor of the South, and against the views and objects of the fanatics?"[14]

It was a good question: Why incite conflict when a more compromising stance promised better results? That Pinckney's sound, reasoned defense did little to mitigate the harsh criticism of his detractors raises another question: What had he missed? Five years earlier, an argument emphasizing the need to cut off public discussion of slavery would have received respectful attention, if not widespread assent. What had changed since then? How could an experienced politician of good reputation with a general awareness of popular opinion have so seriously misread the public mood? A good part of the answer lies in Pinckney's belief that "there was never a healthier tone of sentiment in the non-slaveholding States, in reference to the domestic institutions of the South, then at this moment." Although the rise of immediatism made "vigilance and caution" necessary, he added, there remained "abundant reason to rely on the enlightened patriotism of the non-slaveholding States." The Charleston congressman could easily have amassed compelling evidence to support these claims. In the age of Jackson, the House contained numerous Northern Democrats ready to side with the South on all slavery-related issues; these "doughfaces"—as John Randolph dubbed them—would never consider supporting any initiative that even hinted of abolition. Everyone understood as much, and had Pinckney been from Virginia or Kentucky, he likely would have fared much better.[15]

But South Carolina was not the upper South, and the Charleston lawyer would have been well advised to have kept such differences in mind. Although all slaveholders strongly objected to any form of government interference with slavery, Palmetto opinion on the matter was particularly uncompromising. Planters, Robert Turnbull had declared in his "Crisis" essays, must be assured "that a petition shall never be received, and a vote NEVER taken in Congress, on any subject connected with slaves, without it being followed by an immediate dissolution of the Union," if they were to have any confidence that their interests were being protected. The growth of abolitionism during the first half of the 1830s made South Carolinians even less compromising. Public meetings such as the one held in Calhoun's home district a month after the Charleston mail incident should have alerted Pinckney to how little tolerance existed for halfway measures that left the least opening for the expression of antislavery sentiment. The Pendleton gathering, after condemning abolitionist agitation as "subversion of the constitutional compact on which the Union of these States rests," warned that if something were not done "to suppress these outrageous attacks," Southerners would not passively submit to "deadly blows aimed not only at our prosperity and happiness, but at our very existence as a people;" any congressional action that interfered with slavery in the District of Columbia or anywhere else, it further resolved, would be seen "as a signal for the South to take care of itself." That December, at a session held two days before Hammond presented his non-reception motion in the House, the South Carolina legislature passed resolutions echoing many of these views and calling on the Northern states to pass laws barring the printing and distribution of abolitionist literature.[16]

The growing abolitionist threat did not create quite the same sense of alarm in Pinckney that it did in other South Carolina congressmen. Where he believed it serious but manageable, others saw something much more ominous at work. Abolition societies, Hammond said, were "springing up like mushrooms" and having an increasingly stronger influence on Northern opinion. Pickens, who found abolitionist publishing initiatives especially disturbing, feared that antislavery sentiments were seeping into and subtly shaping the content of nearly everything that Americans read. "There is scarcely a common newspaper, a magazine or review, that comes from the North, but what brings something of prejudice and discrimination against us," he lamented. "There is not a school book, nor a common geography, which does not contain something, by innuendo or insinuation, calculated to train up our children to believe that the inheritance of their fathers is full of evil and iniquity." William Preston could not have agreed more. The South Carolina senator was particularly impressed by the industry and zeal of abolitionists—by the men, women, and children who circulated antislavery petitions, by the itinerant lecturers who had turned abolitionism into a religious crusade, by the steadily expanding body of people who "are exhorted by all that they esteem holy," and "by all that can warm the heart or influence the imagination, to join the pious work of purging the sin of slavery from the land." The message here and elsewhere was unequivocally consistent: Southerners who underestimated the abolitionist challenge did so at their peril. As the Charleston unionist William Drayton declared in an 1836 tract: "Let him who takes an interest in the matter examine the open evidence of facts; let him observe the extended and insidious operation of presses, agents and societies; let him mark the progress and results of these efforts for the last few years; and then, if he is still incredulous, and still secure, he may sleep on, until he is roused by the glare of the midnight conflagration, or startled by the whoops of the negro at his chamber door."[17]

Hammond, Pickens, Preston, and Thompson all resided at Mrs. Lindenberger's Washington boardinghouse. So did Calhoun, and at least one Northern congressman charged that he had instructed his fellow lodgers to press the non-reception issue as part of an effort to embarrass Van Buren and advance his own political interests. Although Pickens vehemently denied this "foul and infamous calumny," it is not entirely clear what role Calhoun played in initiating the controversy. Even as a congressional freshman, Hammond displayed the independence of mind that would be a hallmark of his long career in state and national politics; nor is it likely that any of his colleagues needed much prompting to stand as they did. At the same time, however, Calhoun never hesitated to let others know his thoughts about major issues of the day and could be very persuasive in communicating his views. According to the English writer and social theorist Harriet Martineau, the strong impression Calhoun made on others owed as much to his tendency to speak *at* rather than *with* those about him as it did to his formidable knowledge of whatever topic he might be discussing: "He meets men and harangues them, by the fire-side, as in the Senate; he is wrought, like a piece of machinery, set a-going by a weight, and stops while you answer:" then "he either passes by what you say, or twists it into a suitability with what is in his head, and begins to lecture again." His fellow boarders may not have been following Calhoun's orders when they launched the non-reception controversy, but he doubtless influenced their actions. More important, he wasted little time assuming command of the anti-abolitionist campaign. Driven by a combination of personal apprehension, regional pride, and political calculation, he would, during the next several years, do more than anyone to move questions concerning slavery and antislavery from the periphery to the core of Southern politics.[18]

There is a tendency to ascribe a certain knee-jerk quality to Southern anti-abolitionism: All abolitionists were fanatics, and nothing more needed to be said. Although it is easy enough to find many such statements, the anti-abolitionist critique was often much more nuanced. This was especially so with someone like Calhoun. In his attacks on abolitionists, he did not try to argue that they posed an imminent threat to slaveholder interests. Nobody believed the American Anti-Slavery Society was on the verge of becoming a major political force, and as a seasoned polemicist, Calhoun knew it would only damage his credibility to contend that it was. He readily acknowledged that the number of abolitionists remained relatively small, observing that "the enlightened of all parties at the North with little exception" had adopted a sound position on the slavery question; much less, he added, did anyone think that abolition societies would "commence a crusade to liberate our slaves by force." Calhoun further conceded that abolitionists had no hope of persuading Congress to end slavery in the District of Columbia. Yet abolitionists almost certainly understood as much, and one therefore had to ask: Why did they continue to flood Congress with their petitions? It was, he declared, to thrust open the doors of the Capitol and to establish a fixed position within its walls. Garrison, Tappan, and company may have called themselves immediatists, but they were playing a long game. Give them an inch, and they would soon find additional ways to undermine "all the outworks upon which we of the South rely for our defence against their attacks here." That was why "we must meet the enemy on the frontier, on the question of receiving [petitions]; we must secure that important pass—it is our Thermopylae."[19]

No less worrisome was the spread of what Calhoun called the "spirit of abolition." Southerners needed to recognize that this insidious disposition "was not to be trifled with," given the ample resources and organizational strength of abolition societies; it had, he argued, already "taken possession of the pulpit, of the schools, and to a considerable extent of the press, those great instruments by which the mind of the rising generation will be formed." That meant that however well-disposed most Northern leaders might now be toward slavery, Southerners could not rely on their friendship and forbearance forever. It would not be long before a new generation, "taught to hate the people and institutions of nearly one half of this union, with a hatred more deadly than one hostile nation ever entertained towards another," displaced those currently occupying positions of power throughout the North. This was not a contest of arms but a battle of ideas, and what made the problem so disturbing was the North's greater capacity to wage such a conflict. Calhoun's cousin Francis Pickens put it best when he observed that "Old and New England" produced much of the nation's literature, "and this was our danger" because it gave abolitionists a platform from which they could shape public opinion in ways that the South could not easily match.[20]

The experience of William Gilmore Simms sheds light on Southern efforts to engage the spirit of abolition. Like Pickens, the Charleston novelist and critic held the abilities of New Englanders in high regard. Although insufferably narrow-minded and bigoted, he said, they were nevertheless able to achieve "great and permanent national results in most of their undertakings" because of a combination of organizational and cultural factors: their well-established "habit of acting *en masse*," their inordinate self-esteem, and their "conviction that the eye of God was noting [their] progress and smiling upon [their] course." These attributes further explained why they "routinely meddle with our domestic interests—now with our Indians, now with our Slaves—satisfied, as they are, of that degree of mental superiority and moral grace, which should entitle them fairly to control the other nations." Given regional disparities in this regard, Simms worried about the South's capacity to withstand assaults on the cultural front. He knew the region did not lack people of intellectual acumen. Charleston alone provided ample evidence of that. Its vibrant cultural life drew on the contributions of various writers, poets, editors, political essayists, theologians, physicians, naturalists, and the like; it was the sort of place where, had slavery not been at issue, someone of Adams's broad learning and eclectic interests would have felt perfectly at home—indeed, more so than Calhoun, whose concerns were almost exclusively political and constitutional and who seldom visited the city. Channeling all this talent into effective organizations was another matter altogether, however. South Carolinians had formed any number of cultural societies, he observed, but "where are they?" Those that did not expire within a few years of their founding typically limped along exerting little influence on people or groups outside their small membership.[21]

Simms's greatest concern was the South's failure to sustain a periodical dedicated to the development and circulation of a regional literature. With the exception of Richmond's *Southern Literary Messenger,* which had been founded in 1834, the numerous publications that came and went left even less of a trace than the region's cultural societies. Whenever he wrote for a Southern periodical, Simms told one correspondent, he did "so under the enfeebling conviction that my labors and those of the editor are taken in vain—that the work will be little read, seldom paid for, and will finally, and after no long period of spasmodic struggle, sink into that gloomy receptacle of the 'lost and abused things of the earth,' which, I suspect, by this time possesses its very sufficient share of Southern periodical literature." Simms did more than complain about this sorry state of affairs. During the early 1840s, he helped establish the *Southern Quarterly Review,* a Charleston-based publication that promised to defend the South's peculiar institutions whenever they might be "assailed, as they often are, by other sections of the American Confederacy." Later in the decade, he commenced a five-year stint as editor that turned the review into one of the region's most influential exponents of Southern values.[22]

Such initiatives went part of the way toward meeting the challenges presented by the spread of abolitionism. One of the most infuriating aspects of the petition campaign was its unremitting attack on the moral and institutional foundations of Southern identity. Echoing the statements of colleagues in the South Carolina congressional delegation, Calhoun declared that the petitioners' primary aim was to undermine regional self-confidence and irreparably damage the South's reputation as they worked to overthrow slavery. When Henry Clay later observed that the petitions functioned as a safety valve for the expression of Northern moral enthusiasm, Calhoun angrily objected, declaring that the Kentucky senator had no conception of the damage being inflicted on the South. Were Southern legislators to sit back and let their region be "assailed from day to day—denounced by every epithet calculated to degrade and render us odious; and to meet all this in silence, or still worse, to reason with foul slanderers, would eventually destroy every feeling of pride and dignity, and sink us, to the condition of the slaves they would emancipate." Calhoun had his prescriptions for engaging the threat, and Simms had his. Publications such as the *Southern Quarterly Review* would enable Southerners to escape the cultural colonialism of the North that abolitionists had proved so adept at manipulating for their own ends. By providing a forum for the development of an independent regional perspective on social and cultural matters, they would enable people of the South to turn back assaults on their "peculiar interests" and create a positive image of the region that commanded the respect of all objective observers.[23]

Had it been that simple, South Carolina political leaders would have felt less anxious about the abolitionist offensive. It was not. Apart from the financial and operational difficulties that plagued nearly all Southern periodicals, there was the question of slavery itself and changing international opinion on the subject, particularly in Great Britain, which in August 1833 had abolished human bondage in its West Indian colonies. Calhoun alluded to the problem when he claimed that abolitionists were seeking to defame Southerners before "the world in general." Pickens put it more bluntly: "The truth is, the moral power of the world is against us. It is idle to disguise it." In this altered universe, where fewer and fewer people considered slavery justifiable, the traditional necessary evil defense no longer seemed adequate. Even to concede that the South's peculiar institution had certain unavoidable defects placed slaveholders in an untenable position. "If we contend in a cause which our understandings and consciences tell us to be wrong, and which the opinion of the world condemns, or if we are doubtful and vacillating in this respect," jurist Willian Harper told a Columbia audience in an 1835 oration, then "we are clearly prepared for defeat." Planters needed to defend slavery from all criticism, and they needed to do so more openly and more unequivocally. "In thus departing from the usual silence of the South upon this subject, it may be thought that I have gone too far," Hammond remarked in a speech supporting his non-reception motion. "But times have changed." Southerners could not shut their eyes to what was happening around them. "Nor," he added, "can we justify ourselves before the world for the course which we may be compelled to take in order to maintain our rights, without boldly declaring what those rights are, defining them, and showing that they are inestimable."[24]

By the time Harper and Hammond spoke, South Carolinians had been moving away from the necessary evil defense of slavery for at least a decade. No one ever questioned slavery's necessity, then or later. All agreed with Edwin Holland's contention that South Carolina's climate "is inconceivably hostile to the white constitution," and that only Black slaves possessed the physical wherewithal to withstand the "pestilence and disease" found in many parts of the state. More than a few would also have assented to his further assertion that the nation as well as the South "owes almost all of its wealth and prosperity . . . to the labor of this strong and hardy race." But during the 1820s a number of writers began emphasizing what they considered slavery's beneficial contributions without adopting a full-blown positive good defense of the institution. Where Thomas Cooper praised the philanthropic intentions of slaveholders and insisted that Southern slaves lived better than most British working people, Edwin Brown argued that, where it existed, slavery played an important role in limiting class conflict, maintaining social order, and promoting the more refined and advantageous features of civilized society. A decade later, as the need to confront an increasingly aggressive abolitionist movement pushed aside earlier inhibitions, the restrained approbation of the 1820s gave way to full-throated acclamation. "Slavery at the South is no evil—it is a blessing to both master and slave," Edmund Bellinger declared. "It is sanctioned by Religion—it is justified by Law"; preserving it "is a stern necessity which we cannot remove." William Drayton repeated these and other proslavery pronouncements in a lengthy defense of the institution that included an impassioned commentary on the closeness of the master-slave relationship, in which he claimed the slave "shares in his master's pride, partakes in his prosperity, feels, with sensibility, his reverses, sufferings, or his death." In Congress, Hammond also paid tribute to planter paternalism as he informed his fellow legislators that slavery, far from being an evil, was "the greatest of all the great blessings which a kind Providence has bestowed upon our glorious region"; anyone the least bit familiar with the institution's history would know that "it has rendered our southern country proverbial for its wealth, its genius, and its manners."[25]

Like most South Carolinians, Calhoun came slowly to the positive good defense. For many years, he had largely avoided saying anything about slavery. As historian Irving H. Bartlett has written, "it is remarkable how little mention there is of slavery in his private and public papers before 1830," given his later prominence as the South's most renowned defender of regional institutions. Calhoun's position before that date appears to have been much the same as that of most South Carolinians—one that shunned criticism of the institution, while insisting that the South's concentration on staple crop production made the use of slave labor absolutely necessary if the region was to enjoy any measure of economic prosperity. Although tempted to assume a more aggressively affirmative stance as a means of bolstering Southern unity during the closing stages of the nullification crisis, Calhoun thought better of it and maintained the traditional Southern policy of trying to limit direct public discussion of slavery. One reason for his restraint was that the abolitionist threat, though clearly growing, had not yet become the obsessive concern that it soon would; and whatever influence anti-abolitionism had on nullifiers was, in William Freehling's words, more "a measure of South Carolina's anxiety about slavery than a tribute to the strength of the antislavery movement."[26]

All this changed during the petition controversy. As abolitionists bombarded Congress with their memorials, concerns about the security of slave property rose markedly. Yet however much distress the agitation caused slaveholders, Calhoun told his fellow senators, it had one salutary consequence: "It has compelled us to the South to look into the nature and character of this great institution, and to correct many false impressions that even we had entertained in relation to it." For far too long, many people in the region had viewed slavery as "a moral and political evil." This was no longer the case, the South Carolinian declared, for the

Southern response to the abolitionist challenge had done much to remove those misconceptions and show that slavery was "a good—a positive good." In his own version of the defense, he drew on existing themes to erect a structure in which planter paternalism served as the foundation for a stable and orderly set of social relations that played an indispensable part in creating a safe environment for the operation of free institutions. Calhoun considered himself a benevolent slaveowner, someone who, in presiding over the labor force on his Fort Hill plantation, combined the roles of master and protector. Both parties in this master-slave relationship accepted and carried out their respective duties, and each individual plantation functioned as "a little community, with the master at its head, who concentrates in himself the united interests of capital and labor, of which he is the common representative." This state of affairs, he contended, exempted Southerners from the disorder that plagued many areas of the North, where class struggle was all too common and appeared to be steadily increasing. It also enabled the South to provide balance to the American political and social order, the region being "the great conservative power, which prevents other portions" of the nation, "less fortunately constituted, from rushing into conflict." Without the South and its peculiar institution, the maintenance and operation of republican government would be immeasurably more difficult, if not altogether impossible. Succinctly put, "Slavery is necessary for civilization"—a term that in Calhounian usage nearly always had stronger political than cultural connotations.[27]

For Calhoun, the positive good defense of slavery represented much more than a response to abolitionist attacks. Forging a united South had been one of his major aims since his 1828 composition of the first draft of the *South Carolina Exposition and Protest*. Nullifiers made limited progress toward achievement of this objective. Although most Southerners opposed protectionism, relatively few put much stock in the dire forebodings of George McDuffie and other prophets of doom. Even Calhoun must have understood that his state's economic woes owed as much to the capriciousness of cotton markets and the attraction of fertile western lands as they did to the tariff. Most people of the region outside South Carolina found the doctrine of state interposition equally questionable and balked at endorsing a practice that pitted them against a popular Democratic president. But that was then, and Calhoun saw immediately that the abolitionist insurgency of the mid-1830s provided a splendid opportunity to renew the campaign for regional unity. "The indications are," he wrote to Duff Green shortly after the Charleston postal incident, "that the South will be unanimous in their resistance, and that the resistance will be of the most determined character, even to the extent of disunion." Although Calhoun had no wish to encourage secession, he did all that he could to promote such resistance during the petition controversy. He could not have agreed more when Robert Hayne told him that the fight against abolitionism promised to "throw every thing else into the shade," and "all other party questions" needed to be cast aside so that people of the South could be "rallied to the defence of [their] 'altars & [their] fire sides.'"[28]

Questions remained, however, as to whether Calhoun's approach furnished an appropriate vehicle for attaining the unity he desired. John King clearly had his doubts about the Carolinian's non-reception proposal. The Georgia senator believed that refusing to receive antislavery petitions only played into abolitionist hands. He could easily imagine Arthur Tappan saying: "Well, that is precisely what I wanted; I wanted agitation in the South; I wished to provoke 'aristocratic slaveholders' to make extravagant demands on the North," and "under the pretext of securing their own rights, to encroach upon the rights of the American people." Calhoun's response did little to conceal his anger with the Georgian's defection. After declaring that all members of the Southern senatorial delegation had a solemn duty "to avoid every thing calculated to divide or distract our ranks" on this "momentous question," he asked if King was prepared to receive a petition calling for the abolition of slavery in Georgia "couched in the most abusive and slanderous language against the state and its institutions." When King said that he was, Calhoun replied: All "I can say is, that the Senator and myself are so organized as to have feelings directly dissimilar. Rather than receive such a petition against South Carolina, against those whom I represent, I would have my head dissevered from my body."[29]

That did not go well. Nor did a subsequent exchange with William C. Rives concerning the positive good defense of slavery. The Virginia senator, who said he had no intention of going "back to the exploded dogmas of Sir Robert Filmer, in order to vindicate the institution of slavery in the abstract," believed Calhoun had taken his argument much farther than common sense or contemporary conceptions of human rights and good government would allow. He did not see how anyone could plausibly "contend that slavery is a positive good; that it is inseparable from the condition of man; that it must exist, in some form or other, in every political community, and that it is even an essential ingredient in republican government." Resting the protection of Southern rights on such an unstable and indefensible foundation, he added, not only "outrage[d] the spirit of the age" but encouraged opponents of slavery to redouble their efforts in support of emancipation. Initially taken aback, Calhoun claimed that his views had been misinterpreted and denied that he had ever declared "slavery in the abstract good." Although Rives had ably summarized the senator's earlier statements on the subject, Calhoun retreated to a racist position and insisted that his observations applied only to social relations in societies where the white and Black races coexisted. At the same time, not wanting to appear overly defensive, he attempted to turn Rives's remarks into an abandonment of Southern institutions. Unlike the Virginian, he would never concede that slavery was a "moral evil."

That position, Calhoun asserted, formed the primary basis for current assaults on slavery; it "was the spring and well-head from which all of these streams of abolition proceeded."[30]

Yet another exchange—one that involved James Hammond and occurred eight years later—furnishes an illuminating postscript to the Rives confrontation. It centered on a proslavery tract titled *Methodism and Slavery* by Henry B. Bascom, a Kentucky preacher and college president later elected a bishop of the Methodist Episcopal Church, South. Calhoun read the work and recommended it to various acquaintances, telling his son-in-law that it presented "one of the fullest & most powerful vindication[s] of the South & its institutions, which has yet appeared." Hammond also read it but reached a much different conclusion. Were South Carolina Methodists to adopt Bascom's view that slavery was an evil "only *permitted & regulated*, not *ordained* by God," he wrote to Calhoun, it would make them as unreliable and treacherous as their Northern counterparts. "Our greatest danger arises from fear & doubt among ourselves," and any sentiment —be it "the clap-trap of the 'Golden Rule'" or "the laws of nature & natural rights"—that contributed to such self-questioning seriously undermined any effort to mount an effective and sustainable defense of slavery. In his response, Calhoun admitted that he had read the work hastily and was forced to acknowledge the justice of Hammond's remarks, having said many of the same things himself on any number of prior occasions. But he did so reluctantly and with deep reservations. Bascom's anti-abolitionism hit the right note throughout, and he felt "we must not break with, or throw off those who are not yet prepared to come up to our standard, especially on the exterior limits of the slave holding States." After all, he reminded Hammond, South Carolina "was not much sounder 20 years ago," and a decade earlier, most people throughout the South had considered slavery a "necessary evil." Southern unity was more important than ideological purity, he seemed to be saying, and if the progress that had taken place in the last ten years was to continue, it might be best to avoid fights with people such as Bascom—or Rives—and to take whatever they could get.[31]

One reason Calhoun could be relatively forbearing on the matter was that his campaign to promote Southern solidarity did not depend entirely on regional acceptance of the positive good defense. Returning to the more familiar and comfortable terrain of constitutionalism, the South Carolina senator also renewed a line of attack he had pursued during the nullification controversy. His main initiative in this area was a set of six resolutions that he introduced in late 1837. Because abolitionism presented challenges that could not be resolved through unilateral state action, Calhoun made no mention of state interposition. He did, however, include an obligatory reference to the Kentucky and Virginia resolutions in remarks supporting his demands, which he placed on firm states' rights ground, repeating his contention that the Constitution was "a compact between sovereign and independent states, formed for their mutual prosperity and security." These views found expression in the first four resolutions, which proclaimed that the states retained sole authority over their domestic institutions, and that the federal government had an obligation to resist any attempts to undermine them. The last two resolutions were more controversial: The fifth declared that any effort to abolish slavery in the District or territories represented a direct assault on Southern institutions; and the sixth asserted that any measure barring the acquisition of new territory because it might expand slavery violated the constitutional rights of the slaveholding states. Few legislators, particularly Northern Democrats who had no good way of pacifying Southern colleagues without alienating at least some of their constituents, looked forward to voting on the resolutions. As the roll call proceeded, Van Buren Democrats put party loyalty before other considerations and provided the support required to pass the first four resolutions and an amended version of the fifth; the sixth was tabled.[32]

Despite rejection of the final resolution, the vote doubtless pleased Calhoun. His main objective in introducing the resolutions was "to ascertain whether there was any common ground on which all that were opposed to abolition" could come together. Had the Senate dismissed them, he observed, it would have effectively removed "all constitutional barriers in the way of the abolitionists" and exposed the South's domestic institutions to more intense assaults: "The deluded agitators must be plainly told that it is no concern of theirs what is the character of our institutions; and that they must not be touched here [in the District], or in the Territories, or in the States, by them or the government." At the same time, Calhoun found the growing political influence of abolitionists extremely troubling. He believed most Northerners harbored an aversion to slavery that abolitionists could all too easily exploit for their own ends. This trend had to be reversed, and the resolutions provided a way of "carry[ing] the war into the non slaveholding States." Van Buren Democrats might have resented being forced to vote on them, but that was precisely what Calhoun wanted, as it would force these ostensible friends of the South to demonstrate whether they actually embraced the states' rights principles that they so frequently professed. If they did so, the resulting conflict between them and what the South Carolinian called "the abolition and consolidation parties" of the North could only strengthen the South's position in national affairs.[33]

One of the developments that reinforced Calhoun's belief that abolitionists were making great political advances in the North was their successful petitioning of state legislatures. He was particularly disturbed when, during the spring of 1837, the Massachusetts General Court passed antislavery resolutions defending the right of petition and instructing the state's senators and representatives to do all in their power to ensure that Congress did nothing to violate it. Many Southerners, he told an acquaintance, felt an "attachment to that State, notwithstanding the differences in our political principles, and what has occurred in her Legislature will do more to shake the confidence of the South in the North in reference to that all important subject, than any thing which has ever occurred." Calhoun clearly overstated the significance of the resolutions. At that very moment on the floor of the House, an ex-president from Massachusetts was creating greater intersectional discord than the Bay legislature ever would.[34]

"The Subject of Slavery, to my great sorrow and mortification, is absorbing all my faculties." So wrote John Quincy Adams in an April 1837 diary entry. By the early 1840s, antislavery had become his most important concern. After a long and distinguished diplomatic career, followed by four disappointing years in the Executive Mansion, Adams had found another calling. To appreciate why he considered this a matter of such regret, it is necessary to understand the reasons prompting his return to public life. Adams had entered the Executive Mansion intent on realizing a grand developmental vision that would thrust the United States into the front ranks of the world's great powers. An ardent economic nationalist, he aimed to lay the foundation for a self-sufficient, interdependent economy bound together by an expansive network of internal improvements that gave full employment to the nation's vast human and material resources. At the same time mindful of the nation's diverse and conflicting interests, he believed the resulting system would counteract tendencies toward disunion by strengthening ties among the country's different regions. As it turned out, his administration made little headway toward achieving any of these objectives. People from all sections and parties, he observed during the closing days of his unsuccessful presidency, had assailed his "aspirations for improvement," creating insurmountable barriers to progress. However disconsolate he may have been, Adams did not despair: "Passion, Prejudice, Envy and Jealousy will pass. The Cause of Union and Improvement will remain; and I have duties to it and to my Country yet to discharge." When he entered Congress several years later, he did so with every intention of resuming the struggle to create the magnificent structure that he had so signally failed to erect as chief executive. His slavery-related interventions in the nullification crisis were more a distraction than the beginning of a new course of action, and he afterward hoped that, for a time at least, he would be able to devote full attention to his much-cherished program for national improvement. But this was not to be. "My conflict now," he wrote in an 1836 letter, "is with the nullifier and Slave-holder, and with their conjoint system of policy, and this conflict has already commenced." Adams had come to realize that nothing could be accomplished without confronting the obstacles presented by slavery. "The Public Lands, the Bank, Tariff, and Currency controversies, the Indian War and . . . everything down to the Northeastern boundary question," he told his son, "will run into the confluent small-pox of Slavery" and the machinations of a Democratic administration pledged to uphold the institution, whatever the consequences.[35]

Adams's above reference to nullifiers in a letter written three years after the controversy concluded was no slip of the pen. Whenever Adams thought of the threat slavery posed to the union and everything else that he held dear, he often thought of South Carolina and Calhoun's doctrine of state interposition. For reasons that he did not fully understand, South Carolina's proslavery radicals appeared to stand apart from other Southern politicians in their ideological rigidity and readiness to do battle with anyone who differed with them. In a conversation with Oliver Wolcott at the outset of the nullification controversy, the Connecticut Federalist told him that that the South Carolina initiative could be summarily dismissed. The former president did not believe this for a moment. Wolcott, he confided to his diary, held the South Carolinians "rather too much in contempt" and failed to recognize just how dangerous they could be. Coming from a state where slaves outnumbered masters, they possessed a "domineering Sprit" that "is wrought up to its highest pitch of intenseness"; they "are attempting to govern the Union as they govern their Slaves," and given the assistance they would likely receive from "all the Slave-driving interests of the Union," they might well induce complacent, compromise-seeking free-state politicians to "truckle to their insolence." Although the nullification dispute did not end as successfully as Calhoun wished—or Adams feared—its outcome did little to moderate the aggressiveness of Palmetto congressmen. With few exceptions, he afterwards observed, they exhibited a fanatical adherence to the most extreme proslavery and states' rights beliefs. All too typical in this regard was Robert Barnwell Rhett, who, like his South Carolina colleagues, formed "a compound of wild democracy and ironbound slavery combined with the feudal cramp of State Sovereignty—the mongrel brood of doctrinal nullification." On the floor of Congress, he took special delight in skewering Palmetto representatives. Isaac Homes, he wrote of one such encounter, "was galled to the vitals by my expression yesterday of South Carolina, and the true history of nullification."[36]

Where Adams's opinion of South Carolina radicals is easily summarized, his views of another group that would play a central role in the petition controversy were more complicated. As he stated on more than one occasion, the Bay congressman was no abolitionist. He did not believe Congress had the authority to interfere with state domestic institutions, telling one correspondent in an 1836 letter that he could not "support the prayer of any petition for the abolition of Slavery or the Slave trade in the District of Columbia at this time." Nor did Adams approach antislavery matters with the same degree of religious zeal that many abolitionists did. Particularly revealing is an 1839 exchange with Samuel Goodhue concerning enforcement of the fugitive slave law. The Revolutionary War veteran and Whig abolitionist claimed that people in the free states had no obligation to turn over fugitives. Because "a bad promise is better broken than kept," he contended, they "ought to consider that pledge in the Constitution as null and void." In support of his argument, Goodhue cited the "case of St. Paul, who upon his conversion at Damascus, broke his promise to the high priest, to bring all the Christians he could find, in bonds to Jerusalem." Adams did not agree and said that "until we should receive a like command [from heaven], it would be best for us to keep our faith." The aging abolitionist was not amused, and it is not surprising that some antislavery activists did not think the Bay congressman could be trusted. One of them was the two-time Liberty party candidate for president, James G. Birney, who told an acquaintance that nobody had done more than Adams "to deaden the awakening sensibilities of our countrymen against the private iniquity and public disgrace of slavery" or promote "forbearance with a system" that he himself had so often condemned "as against justice—humanity—[and] nature."[37]

Whatever his differences with some antislavery leaders, Adams could scarcely be described as an anti-abolitionist. He viewed the rise of abolitionism as an inevitable outgrowth of the spread of democracy that he saw taking place throughout the Western world. In the United States, the long period of relative quiescence following the Missouri crisis had clearly ended by the mid-1830s, and there was "a great fermentation on the subject of Slavery" everywhere one looked: "The theory of the rights of man has taken deep root in the soil of civil Society. It has allied itself with the feelings of humanity and precepts of Christian benevolence. It has armed itself with the strength of organized association. It has linked itself with religious doctrines and religious fervor." The day after he penned those words, Adams received a visit from Abbott Lawrence, who told him of a planned meeting by Boston's political and economic elite "to put down the Anti-Slavery abolitionists." All the participants agreed that something needed to be done, the woolen manufacturer assured him, and "there was no diversity of opinion" on the need to adopt a firm course of suppression. Adams doubted that. "If the measures are vapouring Resolutions, they will pass unanimously and be inefficient," he wrote in his diary. "If the measures are efficient, there will be diversity of opinion." His skepticism was well taken. According to one local abolitionist, the gathering did the antislavery movement more good than harm. Its organizers had acted at the prompting of Southern political leaders and failed to recognize that, as *Boston Courier* editor Joseph Buckingham observed, "the mere suggestion by a Boston meeting that the legislature should put an end to discussions of slavery, *by the strong arm of the law*, would be the signal for revolution." Adams might not have put it quite that strongly, but he doubtless shared the sentiment.[38]

One way to get a more precise fix on Adams's antislavery position is by juxtaposing his experience and beliefs with those of another prominent critic of human bondage, the Boston Unitarian leader William Ellery Channing. This might, at first glance, strike some as an odd pairing. The two men had very different personalities. Compared with Channing, Adams angered more easily, was considerably less conflict averse, and labored under a much heavier load of personal resentments and political grievances. Unlike the Bay congressman, the Unitarian divine took no pleasure in baiting and ridiculing his adversaries and never had occasion to caution himself against losing control of his passions. In other respects, however they were very similar. Both men had achieved great distinction in their public lives and could command the attention of others merely on the basis of who they were, which was often as important as what they had to say. In terms of ideology, they could best be described as principled conservatives—people who felt one's moral and social values should not be subordinated to personal or class interest, and who believed social and political change, if necessary, should proceed gradually. Both hated slavery, but neither of them would ever become an abolitionist.

Channing's entry into the slavery wars of the period came with the 1835 publication of a book on the subject. *Slavery* was an uneven mix of moral exhortation, guarded commentary, and cautiously phrased admonitions in search of a rapidly disappearing middle ground. On one hand, Channing criticized abolitionist impetuosity, urged Northerners to avoid conduct that might upset slaveholder sensibilities, dismissed calls for immediate emancipation, and recommended the creation of a system of guardianship to provide supervision for slaves making the transition from bondage to freedom. Yet he also wrote that slavery was "radically, essentially evil," declaring that "an institution so founded in wrong, so imbued with injustice, cannot be made a good." Adams, who knew better than Channing just how controversial any public discussion of slavery had become, read the book with interest. He recognized the work's moderate intent, noting how the author depicted slavery "in all its most odious colours" while going out of his way to defend slaveholders against charges of wrongdoing. But this was "an exceedingly nice and difficult line to draw," and he felt Channing would do well to prepare for the worst: "He treats the subject so smoothly that some of the Southern Slave-holders have quoted it with approbation, as favouring their side of the question; but it is in fact an inflammatory, if not incendiary publication." William Lloyd Garrison, who published a biting, twenty-five point critique of *Slavery* in the *Liberator*, reached a similar conclusion, telling an abolitionist colleague that "however cautiously and tenderly" Channing may have treated slavery and slaveholders, "if he does not soon have a hornet's nest about his ears, then it will be because hornets have respect unto the persons of men!"[39]

Adams and Garrison had a much clearer view of what was coming than Channing did. As might be expected, leading South Carolinians had little good to say about *Slavery*. "Instead of standing on his palmy eminence, with the benevolence of an enlightened Christian" seeking to restore calm, Francis Pickens said of the Boston Unitarian, "We find him inculcating sentiments and spreading doctrines calculated to alienate the affection and sympathies of the people of the Union from different sections." Addressing Congress ten days later, his messmate at Mrs. Lindenberger's boardinghouse James Hammond declared the work "a tissue of stale, false, shallow, and declamatory reasoning even on acknowledged facts," while Calhoun considered it a "sad omen of the times" that someone of Channing's prestige "should lend the aid of his talents and character to criminal designs, the direct tendency of which is to work asunder the Union and subvert the Constitution." Closer to home, the Federal Street pastor encountered increasingly harsh criticism from prominent members of his congregation when, following the publication of *Slavery*, he opposed an anti-abolitionist legislative initiative and collaborated with Garrison to organize a memorial tribute to the martyred antislavery editor Elijah Lovejoy. People who "had almost worshiped him as a Saint," Adams wrote, were "now call[ing] him a Jacobin." The Bay congressman, whose relations with elite Bostonian had long been strained, knew better than anyone what the Unitarian divine was experiencing. "There are a great many, and persons of influence and great respectability," more than one correspondent had informed him, "whose equanimity is most disturbed by every incident that has reference to you." Although Adams had learned to take such ill will in stride wherever it appeared, it had not always been easy, even for someone of his combative temperament. "The exposure through which I passed in the late Session of Congress was greater than I could have imagined possible; and having escaped from the fiery furnace it behooves me well to consider my ways before I put myself in the way of being cast into it again," he observed in an 1837 diary entry. Yet, he quickly added, he could not forsake his obligations and hoped that God would shield him "from the craven Spirit of shirking from danger in the discharge of my duty." He doubtless had moments when he wondered how well Channing, who was "deeply sensitive to the change in his worldly fame," would hold up under similar pressure.[40]

He did quite well it turned out, indeed well enough that his conduct left a strong impression on Adams. As his antislavery convictions deepened, the Boston Unitarian not only continued to speak out but began to question elite views on how society should function that he had long taken for granted. He also reassessed his opinion of Garrisonian immediatism and assumptions concerning slaves' capacity to manage their own affairs without white oversight. At his death in 1842, Adams paid him the highest tribute he could bestow on a contemporary when he wrote that he "never flinched or quailed before the enemy." That his adherence to principle cost him a prestigious Boston pastorate and the support of many onetime friends and followers made his actions all the more admirable: "The loss of Dr. Channing to the anti-slavery cause is irreparable." Abolitionists also mourned the Unitarian preacher's passing, but they did so for reasons of their own. Where Adams personally identified with the many challenges that Channing confronted, abolitionists viewed him as an elite fellow traveler who had provided welcome assistance to a group that represented a distinct minority of the Northern populace. A Springfield antislavery activist stated the point well in an 1837 letter that sheds light on the place Adams and Channing occupied within the movement. Abolitionists, Samuel Osgood told Adams, recognized that he, like Channing, was not one of them. But that did not matter, given their willingness to embrace antislavery principles. "We are not all of us so overbearing as to blame or denounce those who cannot see it to be their duty to act with us," Osgood said. "We rejoice in their services in whatever way they are disposed to render them."[41]

Although the value of Adams's services became abundantly clear during the petition debate, it was not immediately apparent that he would play a major role in the controversy. The Bay congressman had repeatedly voiced his opposition to emancipation in the District of Columbia. In addition to considering such petitions futile gestures calculated to incite unnecessary conflict, he believed Northerners had no right to interfere with the domestic arrangements of slaveholding states and territories. But he also had fixed beliefs about the right of petition and what should be done to uphold that right. Congress had an obligation not only to receive petitions but to refer them to a select committee that would issue a report stating why the prayer of a given memorial should or should not be granted. Simply reading a petition was not enough; it also needed to be considered. Those who argued that barring the reception of antislavery petitions would quiet discussion of the subject, he contended, had it all wrong. It was much more likely that the exact opposite would occur. Should he refuse to present such a memorial from his own constituents, they would promptly replace him with someone more strongly inclined to carry out their wishes. What, Adams asked, would happen then? Would the House pass another rule prohibiting congressmen from saying "a word in derogation of the sublime merits of slavery?" Members needed to step back, take a deep breath, and consider the consequences of embarking on such a course: "You suppress the right of petition; you suppress the freedom of speech; . . . and the freedom of religion; for, in the minds of many worthy, honest, and honorable men, fanatics, if you please to call them, this is a religious question, in which they act under what they believe to be a sense of duty to their God." The result would be an outpouring of righteous anger that no Northern representative could safely ignore. And it could all be avoided by treating petitions as they should be treated, for everyone knew that no House committee would ever report favorably on a petition calling for the abolition of slavery in the District of Columbia or anywhere else.[42]

However upsetting Calhoun and his fellow lodgers at Mrs. Lindenberger's boardinghouse may have found Adams's remarks, they hardly constituted a call to arms. His recommendations did not differ appreciably from Henry Pinckney's initial response to the petition issue, and at least one antislavery Whig felt the Bay congressman had been much too conciliatory. When the Charleston representative attempted to form a select committee to deal with the petition question, Adams backed the initiative, believing the committee would arrange an acceptable compromise. That did not happen. Although Pinckney held off the non-reception demands of South Carolina radicals, his gag rule was nearly as bad: Petitions would be received, but, "without being either printed or referred," they would be immediately laid on the table without anything being done to address the petitioners' prayer. Up to this point, Adams had been trying to arrange some intersectional accommodation on the handling of antislavery petitions, so that the House could turn its attention to those national development measures that he found most engrossing. Everything changed with the adoption of the Pinckney gag, which rekindled all his latent animosities about planter arrogance and slaveholder indifference to basic principles of human rights. He considered the rule an outrageous violation of the right of petition that, for all practical purposes, was the equivalent of a complete ban on reception. House committees had a duty to consider the contents of petitions and issue reports addressing the petitioners' prayer; anything less undermined public confidence in the work of standing committees, which were the eyes, ears, and judgment of the House. As things now stood, he predicted, it would not be long before Congress passed another rule calling for the expulsion of any member who dared mention the topic of abolition. "Sir," he defiantly added, "I am ready to be that member whenever the House should come to that decision."[43]

Congressional leaders never attempted to expel members who raised the question of emancipation on the House floor, but Adams did use the gag rule to rattle Southern representatives whenever the opportunity arose. On one occasion, he openly defied the rule by presenting a resolution from New York abolitionists that called for the passage of constitutional amendments abolishing slavery and the slave trade in the District, barring the admission of new slave states, and freeing all children born after July 1842. More often, he helped petitioners evade the gag by introducing memorials that employed devices such as the invocation of the Declaration of Independence or the Constitution's guarantee of a republican form of government to paper over their antislavery intent. Some of the petitions he submitted did not attack slavery directly but targeted the foundations of the proslavery ideology. An 1839 memorial seeking the appointment of a "committee on color" to examine House members' "pedigrees" was clearly intended to ridicule the racist beliefs shared by nearly all representatives of the period: Whenever "the parties shall be found to have the least drop of *colored blood* in their veins," the petition read, "they shall be expelled from office, and their places filled by persons of pure Anglo-Saxon blood." Adams may well have had this petition in mind three years later when he questioned a measure extending suffrage rights to all "free white males of twenty-one years and upward" in the town of Alexandria. He saw no reason "why a man whose skin was not white—but who performed all the duties of a good citizen"—should not be allowed to vote; and to support his argument, he said that he could "bring forward a hundred respectable colored men of the city with complexions whiter than those of twenty members of the House." These were not the only instances in which he used the petition controversy to upset Southern colleagues. When a member who objected to his remarks concerning the 1837 gag resolution told him that if it "ever came to the issue of War," the people of the South "would march into New England and conquer it," Adams dismissed the threat, stating that he "had no doubt they would if they could, and that was what they were now struggling for with all of their might." And when the House later adopted a more stringent gag rule prohibiting the reception of slavery-related petitions, he informed members that the rule relieved the North of any obligation to honor planter requests for assistance in the event of a slave insurrection.[44]

Of Adams's many interventions in the petition controversy, two in particular stand out. Each of them prompted an effort on the part of Southern representatives to censure the Bay congressman. The first occurred in early 1837. For much of the past year, Adams had employed various parliamentary tactics to test the limits of the gag and focus attention on the right of petition. On February 6, when he asked the Speaker whether a memorial from slaves fell within the Pinckney rule, Southern members erupted in anger. The petition—which asked that slavery be protected not abolished—turned out be a hoax, but this did little to soothe the feelings of his adversaries. Adams might think it was great fun, Pinckney said, "but farces of this kind neither suit the humor of the slaveholding States, nor comport with the character and dignity of the Legislature of the nation." And to show just how unfunny they found the matter, Southern congressmen initiated censure proceedings against their Bay colleague. They soon came to regret the decision. Faced with charges of wrongdoing, Adams had the right to speak in his own defense and used the opportunity to defend the right of petition. It was, he declared, "a right belonging to every human creature," one "which does not depend on the condition of the petitioner, and which cannot be denied to man in any condition." Should the House seek to abridge that right by refusing to receive slave petitions, he asked, where would it end? Could anyone be assured that the liberties guaranteed by the Constitution were safe? Adams also used the occasion to condemn Waddy Thompson's statement that he should be hauled before a District of Columbia grand jury for his conduct in the controversy. "I am not to be intimidated by the gentleman from South Carolina," he asserted, "nor by all the grand juries in the universe." House members had a right to speak their minds without fear of being prosecuted for the free expression of their views, and he hoped that when people outside Washington read about this debate, Thompson's "astonishing threat" would not go unnoticed. Adams then went for the jugular. As a congressman, he had heard much "of the great superiority of Anglo-Saxon blood." Sadly, he added, the South Carolinian appeared to have no conception what that meant in political terms: "What, sir! is there a drop of that blood flowing in the veins of any man who will subscribe to such a political doctrine as this? How little does such a person understand of the true principles of freedom in relation to the powers of a legislative body!"[45]

One attribute that made Adams such a dangerous foe was his ability to broaden the context of disputes in ways that enabled him to introduce threats that his adversaries did not see coming. During the slave petition controversy, Francis Pickens described the Bay congressman's "wanton attempts" to defend slave rights as an effort to undermine "the principle that the slave could only be known through his master." Thompson seconded the point, declaring that slaves "are property, not persons; they have no political rights; and even their civil rights must be claimed through their master." Adams took note of these observations and made them the basis of a critique of the slavery petition debate that he prepared for his constituents. Southern society, he wrote, comprised three main classes: masters, slaves, and free white and Black people who did not own slaves. Protecting the right of petition certainly did not harm the slaves who formed "the suffering, the laborious, the *producing* class." Nor did it hurt nonslaveholding free people. But the same could not be said for slaveowners, who viewed the right of petition—at least as it applied to slaves—as a threat to their "rights of *mastery*." What they did not seem to understand was that, while the Constitution afforded them certain protections, there were clear limits to how far their rights of mastery extended. This was nowhere more so than when they attempted to exercise them in ways manifestly "incompatible with the inalienable rights of mankind, as set forth in the Declaration of Independence," not to mention the "the fundamental principles of all the free states of the Union" and the First Amendment to the Constitution. In all such instances planters' rights of mastery needed to be narrowly construed. That being the case, he concluded, the right of petition was, "upon every principle of fair construction, . . . as much the right of the South as of the North, as much the right of the slave as of the master."[46]

This was the type of argument that Calhoun understood all too well. He had followed the slavery petition debate closely from his vantage point in the upper house, and he did not like what he saw and heard. The effort to censure Adams had only created further problems, and he wondered whether Southern representatives possessed the wherewithal to deal adequately with the question. Although it is unclear whether he read Adams's letter to his constituents, no one had to explain the relationship between slave petitioning and the rights of mastery to Calhoun. Granting slaves the right of petition, he told James Hammond, would be the practical equivalent of emancipation: "It would make the masters but overseers, aga[i]nst whom the slaves would have the right to appeal to Congress," which would assume the position of "absolute masters of all." The chance that such an eventuality might ever come to pass made the creation of a united South more important than it had ever been. Something needed to be done, he wrote to a Georgia correspondent, though he did not know exactly what. Organizing a Southern convention would be a good first step, but he feared that too few regional congressmen would agree to attend.[47]

Meanwhile, the gag rule controversy raged on. In 1840, when the House adopted a rule that barred the reception of abolition petitions, Calhoun believed the change could not help but "be productive of good consequences." Adams, thought otherwise, and as his anger and frustration grew, he intensified his efforts to challenge the gag. On January 21, 1842, he presented a memorial from Bay residents that claimed the thirteen slave states had "despotic, onerous, and oppressive" governments and urged Congress to adopt some means of extirpating "this alarming evil" and guaranteeing a "Republican form of Government . . . to each of the States as are now without it." Four days later, he presented another petition that went even further. It came from Haverhill, Massachusetts, and asked that steps be taken "to dissolve the Union" because no national government "can be agreeable or permanent which does not present reciprocal benefits" to all its member states. In introducing the petition, Adams told his fellow legislators that the people whom he represented, "the freemen of the Union," deeply resented Southern efforts to limit their rights and "to force the spirit of slavery upon them." Although he could not support the petitioners' prayer, he did believe it was "time for the Northern people to see if they can't shake [that spirit] off"; and if that meant raising the question of disunion, then so be it. Southern members greeted these remarks with a mixture of anger and expectation. They had been trying to check Adams for years, and his unwillingness to condemn the Haverhill memorial appeared to offer another opportunity to censure the Bay congressman. That their earlier attempt had failed miserably was either forgotten or no longer mattered.[48]

It should have, because the 1842 initiative proved no more successful than its predecessor had. Adams could not have been happier. Taking the House floor in his own defense, he added a few chapters to an already voluminous polemic that he had begun composing years earlier. Should he withdraw the Haverhill memorial, he told House members, he would view "himself as having sacrificed the right of petition, as having sacrificed the right of habeas corpus; as having sacrificed the right of trial by jury; . . . as having sacrificed the freedom of speech; as having sacrificed every element of liberty that was enjoyed by" American citizens. And if slaveholding members believed that censuring Northern representatives for presenting antislavery memorials would end the petition controversy, he assured them that they were mistaken. Any such violation of House rules and the rights of Northern freemen "would have the people coming here (to use the expression of a sublime and lofty poet of England) 'besieging, not beseeching.'" And so it went. By the time he finished, Ohio congressman Joshua Giddings wrote, Adams had shown how the slave power had "crept into our whole policy, subsidized our presses, affected our Literature, invaded the sanctity of the Post office, degraded our patriotism, taxed the free labor of the north, frightened our Statesmen, and controlled the nation." By that point as well, Southern House members had heard enough. Giddings claimed he had seen them "literally shake and tremble through every nerve and joint, while [Adams] arrayed before them their political and moral sins." The Bay congressman's "vigorous and commanding" presence, combined with his "indomitable adherence to his principle," Theodore Dwight Weld added, had "exacted from every slaveholder in the house involuntary *respect*."[49]

However deserving such tributes, they should not be allowed to perpetuate what historian Leonard L. Richards has called the "persistent myth" that Adams acted "virtually alone in his fight against the gag rule." Although he knew better, the Bay congressman liked posing as the intrepid warrior doing lonely battle against the malevolent forces of an omnipotent slave power. Nearly all Southern House members "would crucify me, if their votes could erect the cross," he wrote during the 1842 censure proceeding. There were also forty "representatives of the free in the league of Slavery" who "would break me on the wheel if their votes and wishes could turn it round. And four fifths of the other hundred and twenty are either so cold or lukewarm that they are ready to desert me at the very first scintillation or indiscretion on my part." These observations clearly overstate his isolation. In addition to the much-appreciated research assistance he received from Weld and the abolitionist editor Joshua Leavitt during the censure contest, Adams enjoyed the steadfast support of a small cohort of antislavery Whigs that included Giddings, William Slade of Vermont, and Seth Gates of New York. More significantly a clear majority of Northern Whigs put aside concerns about pacifying Southern party members and consistently backed his position on the gag rule and other slavery-related measures throughout the period.[50]

This is important because it raises the broader question of what effect the gag controversy had on Northern opinion. Letters that Adams received during the 1837 censure contest shed some light on the matter. Not surprisingly many came from abolitionists who appreciated his efforts to combat the gag. More interesting are those from people who viewed the antislavery struggle from a much different perspective. Where William Lee applauded Adams's defense of the right of petition, while expressing regret "that abolition is gaining ground" and "running like wildfire through the Legislature," Joseph Paine wrote that he was "not an abolitionist in the remotest degree" but strongly supported the Bay congressman's actions to uphold the principle of "free discussion." Anthony Collamore adopted a similar position when he wrote that "although I cannot approve all the sentiments of the abolitionists, I regard the right of petition, and the freedom of debate, as main pillars on which rest the security of our freedom and independence." John Marston was even less of an antislavery activist, declaring himself "from principle, as much opposed to the 'Abolitionists,' as any citizen from the South—because they would break the great *Charter* of our Union." Yet he also believed "that every citizen has a right to petition" and congratulated Adams on his "*complete triumph*" in the censure confrontation. None of these people became abolitionists as a consequence of the gag rule controversy. They did, however, represent a growing body of voters who found slaveholder impositions on popular rights intolerable. Northern Whig congressmen, whatever their own views of abolitionism or the gag rule, recognized they could not dismiss such concerns if they wished to avoid alienating constituents angered by these constraints.[51]

Over time, at least some Northern Democrats did so as well. More than a few of them resented the constant pressure from Southern party members to follow their lead on all slavery-related questions. This was especially so among those who represented districts where submitting to such pressure threatened electoral ruin, and in December 1844 enough of them crossed the aisle to provide the votes needed to abolish the gag rule. Repeal did not free any slaves in the District of Columbia; the committee to which abolition petitions were referred routinely dismissed them. Yet the eight-year struggle did make a difference. For Joshua Giddings, who fully understood how Congress continued to treat antislavery memorials, repeal "constituted the first surrender of the democratic party, to the popular feeling of the northern states; and in that point of view marked an era in 'the regime of slavery.'" Some Southerners feared that was all too true. Although Calhoun never moderated his insistence on non-reception, others from the region expressed relief when Congress finally brought the dispute to an end. The South Carolina writer William Gilmore Simms counted himself among the many who were "almost glad" that the House rescinded the gag rule, because it deprived abolitionists of one of their primary "means of excitement." Another of them was Virginia's John Minor Botts, who had long believed the petition controversy "made more abolitionists in one year, by identifying the right of petition with the question of slavery, than the abolitionists would have made for themselves in twenty-five years." His fellow Virginian and Calhoun critic, William C. Rives, felt much the same way. The "fanatics" who opposed reception of antislavery petitions, he told House members, "are likely to do more injury to our cause than five hundred men such as Garrison, Tappan, [George] Thompson, Adams, and Slade."[52]

Of particular interest was the response of Henry A. Wise. The Virginia representative had been Adams's most unrelenting adversary from the moment he entered Congress, behaving in a manner that, in the New Englander's words, made him a worthy "successor to John Randolph, with his tartness, his bitterness, his malignity and his inconsistencies." Wise never regretted his conduct, but he did have second thoughts about the gag rule dispute. "Again and again," he later observed, Adams "said he would not abolish slavery in the District of Columbia if he could; for he would retain it as a bone of contention,—a fulcrum of the lever for agitation, agitation, agitation, until Slavery in the States was shaken from its base." One must reserve judgment on whether Adams actually said any such thing; "blessed ever blessed be the name of God!" was his diary remark on House revocation of the gag rule. But Wise's recollections may not have been altogether mistaken. During the petition debate, the Bay congressman quickly overcame whatever initial reservations he might have had about further interventions in public disputes over the slavery question. More than that, he came to see the necessity of contesting slaveholder claims whenever the opportunity arose. Commenting on a letter he wrote for an 1843 celebration of emancipation in the British West Indies in Bangor, Maine, he expressed concern that there was "no hostile notice of it abroad." This, he added, was "the worst fate that can befall it—for if I can but raise a controversy" on slavery, "it shall be if my life and health admit, a last book for future enlargement and illustrative for the whole remnant of my toilsome days."[53]

The petition controversy presented many such opportunities, and the New Englander took full advantage of them. Wise, whose frequent encounters with the Bay congressman helped him refine his own forensic skills, called Adams "the acutest, the astutest, the archest enemy of Southern slavery that ever existed." But he did not limit his interventions to congressional debates or the gag rule struggle. His public letters and periodic orations of the period provided a means of resuming the constitutional counteroffensive he had initiated during the nullification controversy. Largely a response to Calhounite assertions, at least some of these statements also reflected the distress Adams felt in 1840 when he read James's Madison's notes on the Constitutional Convention, which showed that the document's immersion in "the infection of slavery" had created a contagion that "no fumigation could purify, no quarantine could extinguish." In the Bangor letter, he focused on the three-fifths clause of Article I, Section 2 and the unjust political advantage it gave proslavery forces. Adams had long opposed the provision, believing it responsible for his father's defeat in the 1800 presidential election. As a young senator he had even prepared a constitutional amendment seeking its repeal. Yet again he urged people of the free states to consider this horrible iniquity. "Is it not enough to be told that" one must accept "an overwhelming representation of one species of property, and that the odious property in slaves?" he asked. "It is not enough that by this exclusive privilege of property, confined to one section of the country, an irresistible ascendancy in the actions of the general government has been secured"—and not to the section as a whole, "but to an oligarchy of slave holders in that section, and to the cruel oppression of the poor in that section itself?"[54]

Elsewhere, Adams trained his fire on the morally reprehensible and constitutionally fallacious "tenets of the modern nullification school." In a likely reference to Calhoun, a Fourth of July address to the citizens of Newburyport, Massachusetts, condemned "the master-philosopher" who "teaches you that slavery is no curse, but a blessing!—that Providence—Providence! has so ordered it that this country should be inhabited by two races of men, one born to wield the scourge, and the other to bear the stripes on his back, one to earn through a toilsome life the others' bread, and to feed him on a bed of roses," in the process demonstrating "that slavery is the guardian and promoter of wisdom and virtue." It was little wonder that such people dreaded open discussion of the principles contained in the Declaration of Independence. That document not only exposed the contemptible sordidness of those "master-priest[s]" whose sermons assert "that slavery is consecrated and sanctified by the Holy Scriptures of the old and new Testament." The Declaration also laid waste to the constitutional underpinnings of the states' rights dogma propounded by adherents of the Carolina doctrine. Repeating what for him was a familiar argument, Adams told his Newburyport audience that "the Declaration was itself at once a social compact of the whole people of the Union . . . and a manifesto proclaiming themselves" to be "*one* Nation, possessed of all the attributes of sovereign power"—a power that could in no way be reconciled "with the absolute sovereignty of the separate States." That error was the product of the Articles of Confederation, and to embrace it now would only turn the nation into the "monument of impotence and imbecility" that it had been during the Confederation period. As for the Constitution, Adams said on another occasion, he would not comment on "the captious quibbling" concerning the states' role in its ratification: "These are the cobwebs of Nullification, all spun from the bowels of slavery. The language of the whole document is, 'We the People.'"[55]

Adams also used the Declaration to explore the religious dimensions of antislavery. Abolition, he wrote in the Bangor letter, was "the consummation of the Christian religion." It was "only as immortal beings," he explained, "that all mankind can in any sense be said to be born equal; and when the Declaration of Independence affirms as a self-evident truth, that all men are born equal, it is precisely the same as if the affirmation had been that all men are born with immortal souls." Although no evangelical, Adams could, when speaking of the glorious "day when slavery shall be proclaimed a word without meaning in all the languages of the earth," simulate the cadences of a revivalist preacher: "To share in the jubilant chorus of that day, if my voice could burst from the cerement of the tomb, it should be to shout, hallelujah! for the Lord God omnipotent reigned; let the world rejoice, and be glad!" Commenting on an 1842 sermon on "the spirit of [the]19th century," he noted a serious but all too typical oversight on the minister's part: "The discourse was a rhapsodic declamation upon the moral improvement of the age—Sunday Schools, Bible, Tract, Missionary and Temperance Societies—But no abolition—not even colonization. Not one word on the subject of Slavery or emancipation. Oh! No! we never mention her." It was a telling observation, one that he likely would not have made a decade earlier and reveals the extent to which his long-standing antislavery convictions had deepened in the interim.[56]

To appreciate what all this meant, it is necessary to return to where the chapter began—to the rise and spread of organized abolitionism. The 1830s might well be dubbed the Garrisonian decade. Although the Boston editor would remain a major figure in the antislavery movement into and through the Civil War, his later achievements never matched those of the 1830s. Especially notable was his marginalization of the American Colonization Society. Viewed from today's perspective, this might not seem like much. Given its racism, financially implausible emigration scheme, and lack of major ground support outside conservative evangelical circles, it is easy to dismiss the society as a band of feckless reformers fated for an early end. This viewpoint misses the ACS's many strengths. It was also the type of feel-good, do-nothing organization that, with its impressive list of distinguished members and host of congressional supporters, has always been a formidable obstacle to meaningful action—the type of organization that, in the words of one abolitionist, functioned as a "safety-salve for troubled consciences, and a very sure way to make slavery valuable and perpetual." To his credit, Garrison, influenced by the urgings of the Black abolitionists who formed the bulk of his early backers, understood as much. Had he done nothing more than push colonization to the sidelines, he would merit inclusion in the front ranks of antislavery activists.[57]

As it was, he and other abolitionists from New England and elsewhere did a great deal more. In a later speech the Garrisonian orator Wendell Phillips provided a concise description of the movement's central aims: "To waken the nation to its real state, and chain it to the consideration of one duty, is half the work. To startle the South to madness, so that every step she takes, in her blindness, is one more step toward ruin" was the other half. That abolitionists made such great strides toward achievement of those objectives during the 1830s was particularly significant. The experience of Adams and Calhoun helps us understand why this was so. As noted, the nullification crisis stopped just short of a major public confrontation on the slavery question. Afterward, Adams was perfectly content to put aside his concerns about the issue and focus on the economic measures he considered essential for the realization of his developmental vision for the nation. Calhoun was equally ready to forget that he had briefly considered placing the defense of slavery at the center of efforts to forge a unified South. In a February 1834 letter describing the current political scene, he wrote that the situation could not be better: "The tariff is adjusted; the American system prostrated; [and] Consolidation deeply distrusted, where recently it had the most efficient support." He was so satisfied with how things were going that he was even contemplating retirement—or at least said he was. Abolitionist initiatives changed Calhoun's plans, as they did those of Adams and other participants in the antislavery controversies of the decade. Thus it happened that what started out as a period of general quiescence on the antislavery front gave way to a series of pitched battles that set the stage for greater conflicts in the years to come.[58]

In attempting "to waken the nation to its real state," abolitionists did well to make the petition campaign the centerpiece of their efforts. By the very act "of signing a Petition," the Garrisonian lawyer Ellis Gray Loring persuasively contended, "strength and clearness are called to the convictions of thousands. So much force and definiteness do our principles gain by expression. So much moral vigor does a man acquire by openly taking his side." At the same time, Loring observed, petitioning had done more to expose "the dangerous tendencies of slavery" through the congressional debates it engendered "than we could have instilled for years." It was here that Adams did his part. Commenting on a letter the Bay congressman sent to the 1838 annual meeting of the Massachusetts Anti-Slavery Society, Samuel J. May told his fellow abolitionists: "I read with emphasis one sentence. I repeat. 'Nothing can be effected till the people shall be aroused to see and feel that the contest is for their own freedom, not less than for the freedom of the enslaved.'" Adams elaborated on the point time and again on the floor of Congress. Throughout, he insisted that he was no abolitionist; yet these societies, he added, "were composed, the great mass of them, of men of as much virtue and of as much intelligence, and as much rectitude of principle, and as much patriotism, warm and ardent patriotism, as any member on this floor." Most abolitionists accepted his reservations. Adams, Joshua Leavitt said in a letter to one of the congressman's harshest antislavery critics, "belongs eminently to that class of [men] who *do* much better than they *say*. I think he is more devoted to the cause of liberty than nine-tenths of our liberty men, and that he is all that they are except [for] his non-adherence to the liberty party."[59]

Where Adams played a major role in abolitionist efforts "to waken the nation to its real state," Calhoun was of ten at the center of the movement's campaign "to startle the South to madness." The more loudly Calhoun and other South Carolinians denounced antislavery petitions, the better abolitionists liked it. Their speeches, said one member of the American Anti-Slavery Society, "have so much enlightened the northern mind, that we trust the tables of the next Congress will groan with a tenfold weight of petitions, and these same champions of eternal and unmitigable bondage will have a wider opportunity to recommend and explain their darling system to the free laborers of the North." Calhoun's further assertion that the "well-informed and thoughtful" viewed antislavery literature with "contempt" drew a sharp rebuke. Were that truly the case, said one Garrisonian, "it would voluntarily place Mr. CALHOUN and his associates in the ranks of 'the inexperienced, the ignorant and thoughtless'—for they regard the publications with far different feelings; they cannot despise that which excites so much consternation among themselves." These observations could not have been more pertinent. Only six months earlier, the South Carolinian had written that abolitionism "strikes directly and fatally" at "our existence as people. Should it succeed, our fate would be worse, than the Aborigines whom we have" driven from their lands, "or the Slaves whom we command." These fears informed Calhoun's major initiatives of the period. His uncompromising insistence on non-reception persisted throughout the petition controversy, despite the warnings of Pinckney and others who believed any public discussion of slavery did the South more harm than good; his promotion of a positive good defense of slavery proceeded unrelentingly in the face of mounting Northern derision and the objections of Southerners who had reservations of one sort or another about the region's peculiar institution; and his 1837 proslavery resolutions created tensions in intersectional party coalitions that many Southern political leaders wished to avoid.[60]

Yet in other respects, abolitionists did not understand Calhoun at all. The Garrisonian quoted above was completely off the mark when he added that Calhoun's apprehensions revealed "a state of mind ill at ease, a conscience troubled with its own fearful monitions, an understanding filled with guilty confusion." If Calhoun ever felt any guilt or pangs of conscience about slavery, there is no evidence of it. Nor did he suffer from confusion. He had long harbored the same misgivings about public discussion of slavery that Pinckney voiced and knew the risk he was taking. But he felt the time had come to cast aside such reservations and force the issue. The growing strength of abolitionism not only posed an existential threat that he could not ignore; it also presented a political opportunity that he could not resist. Although widespread wariness of the doctrine of state interposition had crippled his earlier efforts to forge a united South during the nullification crisis, his commitment to strengthening regional solidarity was, if anything, stronger than it had ever been. Where the campaign against protectionism had failed to provide a firm basis for establishing the sort of regional unity he desired, an initiative founded on the defense of slavery promised to be much more effective when linked to the increasing visibility and assertiveness of Northern abolitionists. Not everyone was yet prepared to follow Calhoun's lead; his Virginia adversary William C. Rives described discussion of the "*abstractions*" contained in his 1837 resolutions as "the most schoolboyish scene I have ever witnessed in a Legislative body." But Rives and those who shared his views soon learned that they could not dismiss Calhoun as easily they had during the tariff controversy. As Southern concerns about abolitionism mounted after mid-decade, historian William J. Cooper has written, political candidates seeking national office "found themselves hounded by the omnipresent slavery issue." Whatever they may have thought about the actual dangers facing slaveholders, none of them wanted to say or do anything that might result in their being labeled anti-Southern. Calhoun had still not created the tightly knit Southern confederacy that he believed necessary to protect regional interests, but he had done as much as anyone to further a change in the climate of opinion that would have lasting political consequences.[61]

Only one question remained: Where did the national government fit in to all of this? Championing regional unification was not the same thing as calling for separation, and Calhoun had no serious thoughts of disunion. Although he continued to insist that protection of Southern economic interests required the imposition of sharp limits on federal power, the abolitionist threat raised fears that made the question of federal-state relations more rather than less complicated. Abolition-induced changes in the political climate of opinion may have forced Southern political leaders to be much more careful about how they handled slavery-related issues, but they did not require their adoption of radical solutions to whatever problems might arise. Many of them, William Freehling has observed, "distrusted uncompromising Southerners and relished compromising national parties." They further believed federal authority provided the most secure defense of their peculiar institution. "We could not have kept slavery here a day," Mary Boykin Chesnut's slaveholding father-in-law was often heard to observe, "but the powerful government of the U.S.A. protected it for us." Calhoun's challenge was to find ways of proceeding without sacrificing his own convictions and without inviting the political isolation that open condemnation of regional moderates might bring. Like them, the South Carolinian desired stronger federal protection of slavery. Yet he also hated all forms of dependency—thus the introduction and promotion of his proslavery resolutions as a means of bolstering Southern unity. At the same time he had no wish to concede control of the federal government to Northern legislators who, through personal conviction or political expediency, might submit to antislavery influences—thus his unshakeable opposition to receiving antislavery petitions and readiness to mobilize resistance to any other initiative that hinted of emancipation. Even had these actions been more successful, Calhoun would still have had considerable work to do. Most notably he had not yet come to grips with a political party system that—however much he despised its compromising nature—he could not ignore if he was to retain any influence in national politics. What he and Adams thought of that system and how they attempted to negotiate it is the subject of the next chapter.[62]

Chapter 5

PARTY, POLITICS, and the EXPANSION OF SLAVERY

In January 1827, Martin Van Buren composed one of those rare letters that anticipates a central political development of an entire era. Concerned about what the disappearance of major party competition following the demise of Federalism portended, the New Yorker thought the time ripe to create a new national party capable of rejuvenating a moribund political system that had lost the capacity to absorb the stress likely to result from what he saw as a forthcoming clash of regional interests. In his famous letter, he shared these concerns with Thomas Ritchie, editor of the influential *Richmond Enquirer* and a powerful figure in Virginia politics. The nation, he contended, had in the recent past thrived under a vigorous party system and could do so again. Indeed national well-being demanded the formation of such a system. Without the partisan enthusiasm that attachment to party generated in the politically engaged, he warned, "geographical divisions founded on local interests, or what is worse prejudices between free and slave holding states will inevitably take their place." As things now stood, "this all powerful sympathy has been much weakened, if not destroyed by the amalgamating policy of Mr. Monroe. It can and ought to be revived." Van Buren believed that restoration, with its attendant benefits, could best be achieved by forming a party that brought together "the planters of the South and the plain republicans of the North," and he urged Ritchie to join him in the undertaking.[1]

In certain respects, Van Buren's plan worked out as well as could be expected. His Democratic party came to form one-half of a second American party system that pitted Jacksonian proponents of limited government against National Republican-Whig politicians who believed the state should assume a more active role in the nation's economic development. Their debates over issues such as a national bank, the tariff, and federal funding of internal improvements helped contain intersectional conflict on slavery-related matters without eliminating it. These disputes—often enlivened by Democratic charges of monopoly and class oppression on the part of their adversaries—also gave rise to a "partisan imperative" that energized rank and filers and substantially increased popular participation in the political process. Yet as Van Buren sadly learned, nothing lasts forever. The second party system proved singularly ill-equipped to negotiate controversies concerning the expansion of slavery. By the late 1840s, the system was visibly coming undone; during the following decade, it would collapse altogether.[2]

This chapter looks at the role Adams and Calhoun played in these developments. Neither of them ever felt entirely at home in a system that made party loyalty the greatest of all political virtues; their frequent professions of principle, if occasionally overstated, reflected deeply held convictions that did not always coincide with party dictates. At the same time, however, refusal to make some accommodation meant accepting a degree of political marginalization that both of them found objectionable. The first two sections of the chapter, in addition to examining their changing views of party, describe how they adapted to the new political environment created by Van Buren's innovations. Although they never displayed the New Yorker's mastery of the second party system, they managed to work out ways of surviving within it. The final section turns to an examination of Adams and Calhoun's interventions in the struggle over slavery expansion that ultimately destroyed the second party system. They did not live to witness its final collapse, but their contributions to the formation of conflicting freedom national and slavery national doctrines that left little room for intersectional compromise did much to hasten its passing.

According to one Adams scholar, John Quincy "was congenitally incapable of leading a party or remaining within one." As it concerns his capacity for party management, the statement is certainly accurate. If nothing else, his lifelong aversion to electioneering rendered him unfit to provide the leadership needed in the ever more combative political environment of the early national period and antebellum era. Although Adams recognized the reasons for electioneering, he could never embrace the practice. "That very pimping to the popular passions upon which all the Jacobin cabals are founded is but too well calculated to succeed in a country like ours," he wrote of political campaigning during the 1800 presidential contest in which Jefferson unseated his father. "I despise it from the bottom of my soul, but I have too long witnessed its efficiency not to be conscious of it." His views had not changed a quarter century later during his own run for the presidency when, he noted, it seemed that "every liar and calumniator in the Country was at work day and night to destroy my reputation." What made all this particularly depressing was the effect it had on all too many members of the educated elite whom he never stopped hoping would someday infuse the nation's politics with some semblance of reason. "Men of Intelligence, Talents, and even of integrity upon other occasions," he lamented, during the heat of a political campaign "surrender themselves up to their Passions—Believe every thing with, without, or even against evidence, according as it suits their own wishes." With each passing election cycle, Adams's gloom deepened. And just when it appeared that the situation could not get any worse, the famously raucous "Log Cabin" election of 1840 brought American politics to a new low. Not only did major public figures hit the campaign trail, "holding forth like methodist preachers, hour after hour, to assembled multitudes, under the broad canopy of Heaven," he observed, but a legion of lesser officials was "summoned to the same service, and instead of attending to the duties of their Offices rave, recite and madden round the land."[3]

The New Englander's approach to patronage and low opinion of party newspapers made him even less suitable to assume the role of party leader. Patronage was the glue that held nineteenth-century party organizations together, and as president, Adams's political associates never tired of telling him that he would be wise to make appointments that rewarded friends and punished enemies. Although political considerations did influence some of his administration's selections, Adams largely ignored the advice. Were he to adopt such a policy, he believed, "an invidious and inquisitorial scouting into the personal dispositions, of public officers, will creep through the whole union, and sordid passions will be kindled into activity to distort the conduct and misrepresent the feelings of men, whose places may become the prize of Slander upon them." He was even less inclined to cultivate the support of partisan editors, whom he likened to "a sort of assassins who sit with loaded blunderbusses at the corner of streets, and fire them off for hire or sport at any" passerby who happened to displease them. Adams appreciated the power of the press; he also knew that his political adversaries made the subsidization of friendly editors an integral component of their electioneering initiatives. But he would have no part of a campaign practice that he felt cast truth to the wind in an effort to sway public opinion and called for the open purchase of defamatory invective merely for the sake of adding to one's vote count. Of the many reasons for losing his 1828 bid for reelection, his reservations about electioneering, patronage, and party newspapers rank high on the list. Pitted against a party whose main strategist was Martin Van Buren—a man of far fewer scruples and much greater understanding of the ways of the political world—Adams never had a chance.[4]

To say that Adams lacked the temperament, interpersonal skills, and flexibility required of an effective party manager is not, however, the same thing as to say that he subscribed to an anti-partyism that prevented his remaining within a party. When one turns to his observations and conduct concerning party, the record is not only mixed but inconsistent; and because his behavior did not always comport with his many pronouncements on the subject, it is necessary to pay close attention to what he said and when he said it. This latter point is especially significant. More a creature of circumstance than he would ever admit, Adams's thoughts on party were never static. As new experiences forced him to view familiar problems from changing perspectives, he adapted accordingly. The John Quincy Adams who regularly aroused the ire of slaveholding congressmen in the 1830s and 1840s was a different person than the Federalist senator, diplomat, cabinet member, and chief executive of the period preceding his election to the House. And major consistencies notwithstanding, what he came to believe in his postpresidential years differed appreciably from his earlier views on party.

Prior to the 1830s, Adams considered parties an unfortunate but necessary feature of free government that no principled politician could fully accept. His opinion of the two major parties made this abundantly clear. However preferable Federalists may have been to their Democratic-Republican adversaries in the early 1800s, they shared too many of their opponents' most disagreeable traits to be anything better than the lesser of two evils. The party of Jefferson, he observed, "uses its triumph with all the unprincipled fury of a faction, while the other gnashes its teeth, and is waiting with all the impatience of revenge, for the time when its turn may come to oppress and punish by the people's favour." Given how little room such conflict left for objective statesmanship, he disconsolately added, "I see the impossibility of preserving the dictates of my own conscience, without sacrificing every prospect not merely of advancement, but even of sustaining that character and reputation I have enjoyed." Not surprisingly, Adams never entirely secured the trust of Federalist colleagues during his years in the Senate. Especially troubling was his seeming unconcern about the adverse effects of major Republican initiatives on New England during a period when Bay Federalists were attempting to forge a popular conservatism based on their defense of regional civilization. His support of the Louisiana Purchase angered party elders who feared the acquisition would diminish New England's influence within the Union; and his later unwillingness to heed warnings about the damage Jefferson's embargo would do to regional commerce created pressures that forced him to resign his Senate seat. By this point, Adams could see no difference at all between Federalists and Republicans, interparty rancor having "become so inveterate and so virulent" that "it has totally absorbed the understanding and the heart of almost all the distinguished men among us" and extinguished "that congenial spirit which has always preserved itself pure from the infectious vapors of faction." He could only hope that the nation might yet witness the emergence of what he called "an energy of union sufficient to counteract all the personal interests, all the electioneering passions, and all the paltry geographical jealousies and envies, which constitute the repulsive parts of our political system."[5]

Much to Adams's anger and disappointment, the obstructionist tactics of New England Federalists blocked the release of that "energy of union' during the War of 1812; as late as 1829, he would still be condemning their disunionism in a bitter dispute that generated considerably more heat than light. The war's aftermath did, however, provide hope that partisan warfare might become a receding vestige of a regrettably less enlightened past. With the disappearance of Federalism in most areas outside New England and an accompanying surge in nationalist sentiment, some political figures believed it possible to disband the current party system and place American politics on a more consensual foundation. One of them was James Monroe, the victor in the 1816 presidential election. A battle-scarred veteran of the early republic's political wars, the Virginian wanted to create a less acrimonious politics directed by a single party whose program transcended ideology and region. Convinced that nothing constructive resulted from political discord, he felt that free government had no need of party competition; indeed the undoing of previous republics could in nearly all instances be traced to the destructive effects of party and factional conflict. Adams was a major beneficiary of this vision. As part of his plan to unify the nation, Monroe sought to form a cabinet that fully reflected the country's regional diversity. While serving as secretary of state in Madison's administration, he had read enough of Adams's reports from St. Petersburg, Ghent, and London to appreciate his deep understanding of European affairs. Once in the Executive Mansion, he recognized there could be few better ways of demonstrating his desire to eliminate interregional tensions than by appointing the New Englander to succeed him in the nation's top diplomatic post.[6]

Although never close to Monroe, Adams established a good working relationship with the president. He particularly approved of the Virginian's wish "to draw the parties of the Country together, and unite them all as one People." At the same time, he saw that doing so would be no easy task. People who spoke of an "era of good feelings" doubtless meant well, but such happy talk went only so far. The president would need to watch his step if he were to escape the pitfalls presented by party prejudice among his own supporters and avoid exacerbating the sectional discord that had arisen during the Missouri controversy. When Monroe's second term ended in 1825, much still remained to be done, and Adams fully intended to carry on his predecessor's work. "A politician in this country must be the man of a party," he had confided to his diary several decades earlier. "I would fain be the man of my whole country." Nothing had happened in the intervening years to weaken that conviction, and his "great object" as president, he told an acquaintance not long after his election, "would be to break up the remnant of the old party distinctions, and bring the whole people together in sentiment as much as possible." He would be bitterly disappointed. His ambitious program for national development met stiff resistance in Congress, where efforts to enact it did more to fuel a resurgence of party conflict than to create an enduring basis for national unity. The experience marked an important turning point in his views on party. Several years after leaving the Executive Mansion, an older but wiser Adams penned a tribute to his recently deceased predecessor in which he reflected on Monroe's attempts to subdue party passions and introduce more conciliatory forms of political engagement. The Virginian's evenhanded, judicious conduct, he wrote, helped reduce partisan rancor by applying "the finishing *coup de grace* to the federalism of '98." But, he added, new divisions soon appeared, and Monroe must have come to see that his hopes for establishing a more consensual political order "were opposed to the genius and spirit of the American people, and that until the thought and action characteristic of freemen had degenerated into the most groveling effeminacy, they could not be practically illustrated." One can certainly question whether Monroe thought any such thing, but that is beside the point. Adams was speaking more for himself than for the man he had succeeded as chief executive.[7]

It was no coincidence that the statement appeared at a time when Adams had just entered Congress and was in the process of forging a political alliance with Massachusetts Anti-Masons. Initially a response to events surrounding the alleged 1826 murder of an upstate New York Mason named William Morgan, Anti-Masonry became a serious political force in many parts of the Northeast and Midwest. One such area was Adams's Plymouth congressional district, and while he later contended that his embrace of the party hurt rather than helped him politically, he almost certainly understood that he benefited from the association. At the same time, he found much to like in Anti-Masonic principles and showed no hesitation in echoing the party's condemnation of Masonry as a secret, oath-bound fraternity dedicated to the promotion and protection of its own members with no regard for the rule of law, on one occasion denouncing the organization as "a conspiracy of the few against the equal rights of the many." Nor did it bother him that most Anti-Masons hailed from plebian backgrounds and espoused an outspoken anti-elitism. Masonic depredations could not be tolerated in a free society. Something needed to be done, and the "cry" for reformation "arose, not from the mansions of the wealthy, nor from the cabinets of the learned or the great, not even from the sentinels on the watchtowers of Zion—it arose from the broad basis of the population; from the less educated and most numerous class of the community. So it is with all great reforms." Adams's adoption of this populist stance stemmed in part from a sincere belief that Masonry posed a genuine threat to republican institutions. It also owed much to his long-standing contempt for Federalist pretensions. That Andrew Jackson, his main political nemesis of the moment and reputed champion of the common man, was a slaveholding Mason made it even easier for him to identify with "the broad basis of the population."[8]

Adams's affiliation with Anti-Masonry did not last long. In 1833, he ran for governor on the Anti-Masonic ticket but withdrew from the contest when initial balloting resulted in a three-way runoff that might have ended in the election of a Democratic candidate had he remained in the race. By the following year Anti-Masonry was on the wane and so was Adams's interest in the movement.

His primary aim at that point was to construct an Anti-Masonic-National Republican coalition against Jacksonian Democrats. When state Anti-Masons later decided to support Van Buren for president, he severed all ties with the party. However brief, the Bay congressman's Anti-Masonic interlude left its mark on him. As a diplomat, secretary of state, and president, Adams had moved in a rarefied social universe where the only opinions that mattered were those of other members of the elite. Even his earlier Senate election by the Massachusetts legislature had depended more on the support of state political elites than on his popularity with the general electorate. His association with Anti-Masonry opened up a different world to him. The experience did not turn him into a glad-handing man of the people, but it did, in historian Sean Wilentz's words, help him develop "a newfound appreciation of the possibilities of democratic politics as a vehicle for his overriding political ambition, which was to be considered as a courageous, enlightened, and virtuous statesman, a great and good man in the classical mold."[9]

Whether Adams wished to realize those ambitions in the House is questionable. His 1833 run for governor and eager pursuit of an open Senate seat two years later certainly suggest otherwise. But when a falling out with Daniel Webster blocked his elevation to the upper house, his bitter disappointment soon passed, and he grudgingly accepted that he would likely spend the rest of his political career in the lower chamber. On a theoretical plane, the adjustment came easily. He viewed American constitutional government as a compound of monarchy, aristocracy, and democracy in which none of the three could be trusted to rule on its own. When functioning properly, all free governments "exhibited a perpetual struggle between" the major branches, "each of which was encroaching on the other; and it was the duty of each to resist that encroachment." He had once looked favorably on Alexander Hamilton's proposal to give special status to the monarchical and aristocratic elements of government by electing presidents and senators to lifetime terms. He had also agreed with his father, who, in one of many memorable observations to be found in his writings, asserted that any chief executive without an absolute veto of legislative measures "will be run down like a Hare before the Hunters." But that was then. After nearly a half-century "of inextinguishable war between the democracy of the European race and its Monarchy and Aristocracy," he observed in an 1837 diary entry, "the democracy is yet in the ascendant and gaining victory after victory over the porcelain of the race." As a House member and representative of the democracy, he intended to make the most of that happy development. Not surprisingly, given his background, he still thought presidents should be accorded broad discretion in foreign affairs. But their ability to block domestic legislation was another matter altogether. In 1842, disgruntled Whigs sought to curb John Tyler's actions to prevent passage of their economic program by proposing a constitutional amendment that would enable the House and Senate to override presidential vetoes by majority vote. Although generally opposed to constitutional revision, Adams now wondered "whether it would not have been better for the nation if the [veto] power had not existed" and felt some limitation needed to be placed on its future exercise. Apart from Tylerite obstructionism, he told House members, Jackson's earlier vetoes of bills to promote national development had been "among the most pernicious acts that could have been committed for the people of the United States and their higher interests."[10]

However comfortable he became with his new role as a spokesman for democracy, Adams never entirely overcame what would be a lifelong elitism. Whenever he looked out upon his fellow House members, "the cream of the land, the culled darlings of fifteen millions," the most "remarkable phenomenon they present is the level of intellect and of morals upon which they stand," he wrote in an 1838 diary entry. "And this universal mediocrity is the basis upon which the liberties of the Nation repose." Yet other observations reveal a more appreciative view of his fellow legislators. He had been assessing the character and competence of people he met since his adolescence, and the practice continued as a member of Congress. An 1841 antislavery speech by Joshua Giddings could have been better structured, Adams noted, "but he proceeded step by step citing his documentary proof as he went along to the exquisite torture of the Southern dualists and Slave mongers." "Profitt," he said of another colleague, "with little education, with no learning; with a backwoodsman's roughness of manner, with open hearted candour, and with an instinctive tact in debate, is one of the most powerful speakers in the house." Believing it wise to know one's enemies, Adams was particularly attentive to the strengths as well as the shortcomings of political adversaries, and some of his most bile-laden characterizations of them contained perceptive comments on their effectiveness. Alexander Duncan of Cincinnati was a tall, stocky thug with "no perception of any moral distinction between truth and falsehood" who took far too much pleasure in carrying out his duties as "the prime bully" of the Democratic opposition. Despite being "a thorough-going hack demagogue," Duncan was nevertheless a formidable presence in the House, for he possessed "abundant sagacity to discern and a brazen front to apply that which will be sure to touch the ignorance, the envy, and the malignity of the million."[11]

Such knowledge was important to Adams because, notwithstanding his many assertions to the contrary or his flirtation with Anti-Masonry, he was a dependable party regular throughout much of his congressional career. To be sure, he never stopped complaining of the abuse heaped on anyone who resisted being "hand-cuffed with the manacles of party," insisting that he could never be "a mere partisan," or telling people that he "had always professed not to be a party man and wished to preserve that character to the end." But his voting record differed little from that of National Republican-Whig leaders, and his general conduct on the House floor betrayed a partisanship that he never openly acknowledged. Such behavior was less surprising than it might seem. Temperament alone left Adams ill-suited to resist the temptations of party warfare. Decades earlier, when Madison offered him a place on the Supreme Court, he declined because, he told his brother, he was "too much of a political partisan for a judge, and although I know as well as any man in America how and when to lay the partisan aside, I do not wish to be called so often and so completely to do it, as my own sense of duty would call me, were I seated upon the bench." No less important, he was strongly committed to enactment of the Whig program and knew this could not be accomplished without some degree of party discipline. Moreover, he had long recognized as much. For government to operate effectively, he observed in an 1810 letter, "it is certainly necessary and even indispensable, that individual members of a party should on most occasions, perhaps on all, sacrifice their individual opinions to those of the majority, whenever this acquiescence does not involve a *dereliction of principle*."[12]

None of the major elements of the National Republican-Whig program demanded such a sacrifice. Of them, Adams showed the least interest in party efforts to turn back Jackson's assault on the Second Bank of the United States (BUS). In 1832, the president vetoed a bill to renew the Bank's charter four years before it expired. The following year he sought to starve it of capital by ordering that its federal deposits be removed and distributed to various state banks. The Bay congressman did not want to see the institution destroyed. In addition to being a shareholder in the BUS and friend of its president, he believed it played an important stabilizing role in the nation's financial system. At the same time, however, he never fully understood the intricacies of banking policy; nor did he feel any need to obtain the knowledge required to engage the controversy's finer points, as the Bank War never became a critical issue in Massachusetts, where the Suffolk Bank system effectively provided for the state's credit needs regardless of what happened to the BUS. When he did address questions arising from the dispute, he tended to oversimplify or misrepresent them. But this did not bother Adams, for what he did understand about the controversy was its potential for securing partisan advantage. Dismissing Jackson's anti-bank rhetoric as a demagogic compound of nonsense and duplicity, he asserted that the president's hostility to the institution "was a mere courtship of popular favor" designed "to renew his lease of *the Government*, and to prolong his continuance in power." Distribution of its public funds furnished an ideal means of enlarging the spoils of office, it being "the invariable practice of the President to reward his friends and punish his enemies." Jackson's attack on the BUS might further be seen as an integral part of a plan for "reverting to a hard money currency" that, by depriving traders of the capital needed to carry on their activities, would "prostrate every other interest in the community before the holders of lands and holders of slaves." Were all this not bad enough, he added, presidential usurpation of legislative authority threatened to shatter the division of powers that formed the basis of American constitutional government by subordinating Congress and the courts to the will of the executive. "Representatives of the people of the North American Union," he asked Democratic legislators, "is it for this that you were elected the trustees of their interests? the guardians of their rights? Is there no way but by laying them at the feet of Andrew Jackson that you can support his administration?" How they answered did not really matter to Adams. He had made his point, and he hoped voters would take it into consideration when they next went to the polls.[13]

Although tariff legislation was of greater importance to Adams and the Bay economy, he had little to say on the subject during the period. The Compromise Tariff of 1833 put the issue on hold for nearly a decade, and the Tariff of 1842 contained enough protectionist provisions to satisfy regional manufacturers. But when he did speak about protectionism, he continued to do so with a difference. In making their case, most free labor protectionists focused on the threat that Europe's "pauper labor" posed to the livelihoods and well-being of Northern free labor. If they mentioned slavery, it was generally to illustrate the nature of that threat: Where the slave labor of the South faced no foreign competition, the free working people of the North did, which was why they needed the protectionist measures that permitted their employers to pay them a decent wage. Adams fully agreed with such analyses but did not feel they went far enough. His own remarks on protectionism often exhibited a more pronounced sectional edge. As was the case with the Jackson and Van Buren presidencies, he told one acquaintance, "Slavery was at the root of the whole system of the [Tyler] administration," and "an essential part of this system was hostility to the manufacturers, and to the free labourers of the North." Worse, he added, the slave interest, "in alliance with the mock democracy of the free States," controlled both chambers of Congress and could be expected to use that power to "defeat every measure which could contribute to promote the manufacturing interest or domestic industry of free labour." These beliefs clearly hardened the partisan impulses that influenced Adams's conduct as a House member.[14]

Of the various components of the Whig economic program, none excited Adams more than the party's commitment to internal improvements. The primary aim of his presidency had been to create a network of roads and canals that "would have afforded high wages and constant employment to hundreds of thousands of laborers, and in which every dollar expended would have repaid itself fourfold in the enhanced value of the Public Lands." When speaking of the benefits of internal improvements, he invoked a biblical lyricism rarely found in his remarks on banking, the tariff, or other economic issues. "Friends and fellow-laborers," he told people gathered at the groundbreaking ceremony for the Chesapeake and Ohio Canal, "We are informed by the holy oracles of truth, that, at the creation of man, male and female, the lord of the universe, their maker, blessed them, and said unto them, be fruitful and multiply, and replenish the earth, *and subdue it.*" Calling upon his listeners to join him "in a fervent supplication to Him from whom that primitive injunction came," he asked God to bless "this joint effort of our great community, to perform his will in the subjugation of the earth for the improvement of the condition of man." It was his greatest hope that such projects would "increase and multiply, till, in the sublime language of inspiration, every valley shall be exalted, and every mountain and hill shall be made low; the crooked straight; the rough places plain."[15]

Adams knew that not everyone shared his vision. If nothing else, there was no shortage of politicians who subscribed to the "maxim of leaving money in the Pockets of the People": It "is always the high road to popularity, and it is always travelled by those who have not resolution, intelligence and energy to attempt the exploration of any other." To overcome such obstructionism, he looked mainly to the proceeds from public land sales. Whigs, historian Daniel Feller has written, "viewed the Western domain essentially as a capital fund—not a source of revenue for the Treasury, but an endowment for social and economic improvement." Adams certainly did, having, as he told his constituents, "long entertained and cherished the hope that these public lands were among the chosen instruments of Almighty power" to promote the moral and material improvement of the human condition. That hope was never realized. When Tyler rejected a provision in an 1842 tariff bill to use the revenue from land sales to fund internal improvements—as Jackson had a decade earlier—Adams was bitterly disappointed but not altogether surprised. The Bay congressman viewed all such actions as evidence of the influence of slavery and the Carolina doctrine on public policy. Nullifiers understood all too well "that if the internal improvement of the country should be left to the legislative management of the National Government," the beneficent consequences of such initiatives "would so grapple the affections of the people to the national authority that it would, in process of time, overwhelm that of the State Governments, and settle the preponderancy of power in the free States." And they could not let that happen if they were to protect their peculiar institution, which explained why "Slavery stands aghast at the prospective promotion of the general welfare and flies to nullification for defence against the energies of freedom and the inalienable rights of man."[16]

Taken from an 1842 address, these observations show the lasting imprint that events of the early 1830s had on Adams's thinking. He had initially hoped to put the acrimony of the nullification controversy behind him and resume a less confrontational approach to lawmaking. When the gag rule controversy extinguished those hopes, he saw the hand of South Carolina nullifiers in this and other developments that contributed to the spread of intersectional strife.

Not only had Hammond, Thompson, and other South Carolinians assumed a vanguard position in the effort to block reception of antislavery petitions, but, Adams believed, the Palmetto delegation exercised an influence in Congress that belied its relatively small size. He had good reason for doing so. Compared with their colleagues from other areas of the South, South Carolina congressmen had a more coherent and fully developed sense of the problems facing the region and what to do about them. They did so largely because of the ideological leadership of Calhoun, who, in addition to dominating Palmetto politics, had supporters throughout the region. That many Southern leaders distrusted and disliked him became increasingly less relevant with the passage of time. Calhoun, historian William J. Cooper Jr., has written, "saw with laserlike perception the plight of slavery and the South," and as the politics of slavery moved to the center of Southern electoral life after the mid-1830s, other regional politicians had to pay attention to what he was saying. They might still refuse to follow his lead on a given issue, but they could not ignore him.[17]

Further evidence of how events of the early 1830s shaped Adams's later views can be seen in his repeated invocation of Jackson's 1832 message to Congress. Although Jackson and Calhoun had become bitter enemies, Adams believed their political agendas complemented and reinforced each other. Where the South Carolina senator's doctrine of nullification provided the ideological foundation for the defense of slavery and maintenance of Southern political hegemony, the president's message—with its reference to agriculturists as "the best part of the population"—laid out a program for the realization of those objectives. As Jackson then made clear, Adams observed in an 1834 statement on the Tennessean's removal of the public deposits from the BUS, his policy was based on a "determination to give away all the public lands to the *best part of the population*; to withdraw all protection from domestic industry; to renounce forever all undertaking of internal improvements; and to annihilate the Bank of the United States." Nothing changed when Van Buren succeeded the hero of New Orleans in the Executive Mansion. The New Yorker's first annual message to Congress, Adams wrote in his diary, demonstrated a continued readiness on the part of Democrats to sacrifice "Northern freedom to Slavery and the South" whenever the two came into conflict; it was "the system of Jackson's Message of December 1832 covered with a new coat of varnish." When John Tyler, an apostate Whig and states' rights Virginian who was arguably more committed to Jacksonian principles than the Tennessean or Van Buren, later blocked the use of proceeds from public land sales to fund internal improvements, Adams interpreted the move as a continuation of a project first enunciated in the 1832 message. "The consummation of [Jackson's] Maysville road veto," represented a "substitute for nullification" designed "to perpetuate the institution of slavery, and its dominion over the North American Union." Reflecting on what else might be expected from Tyler's administration, he could only express the forlorn hope that "the omnipotence of God" might somehow "overrule the depravity of man."[18]

Adams's friend and admirer Joshua Giddings later wrote that he "had attained a position which forbade him to look to any party as a guide to his conduct." The New Englander and his closest associates in Congress "stood aloof from political parties whenever subjects involving moral principle were agitated or the rights of humanity were at it." The statement contains a large measure of truth without being wholly accurate. At one time or another, Adams had harsh words for people of all parties, including his fellow Whigs. An analysis of the recent vote on a slavery-related question, he observed in an 1838 diary entry, revealed "the rallying of the whole South to the Van Buren Standard—the close adhesion to it of Northern and Western [Democratic] Serviles, and the total want of settled principle in the Northern and Western opposition Whigs." Such comments notwithstanding, Adams's partisanship was remarkably consistent. In addition to following the lead of party managers on nearly all congressional votes, he received support from most Northern Whigs throughout the petition controversy. Even more important he drew a clear distinction between the relative merits of the two parties. He may never have read Van Buren's 1827 letter to Ritchie in which the New Yorker called for the formation of a coalition between "the planters of the South and the plain Republicans of the North." But he had no need to do so, as the practical consequences of Van Buren's design were unmistakably apparent to anyone who cared to look. They could be seen in the conduct of the Northern men with Southern principles who constituted the "mongrel democracy of the North and West" that, together with the "Slavemonger brood" of the plantation states, had no higher aims than to maintain power and turn back any threats to the South's peculiar institution. Political reprobates of the first order, they were all destined for that special place in hell God had reserved for the least redeemable of officeholding miscreants. With the possible exception of Daniel Webster, whom Adams thoroughly despised, no Northern Whig had descended to a comparable level of degradation.[19]

Adams's response to antislavery political initiatives sheds further light on his attachment to Whiggery. When Massachusetts abolitionists began interrogating political candidates about their positions on slavery during the late 1830s, the Bay congressman considered the practice "vicious" and counterproductive. Such interventions, he told the Garrisonian activist Edmund Quincy, would likely produce more harm than good, for they "tended to break down the barrier between the [two major] parties, the natural consequence of which is to strengthen the administration they abhor." Equally revealing is a conversation he had with a Liberty party member on the eve of the 1844 presidential election. The contest pitted Henry Clay against James K. Polk, and Adams intended to vote for his former secretary of state, notwithstanding the Kentuckian's equivocation on Texas annexation, a policy that Adams unreservedly opposed. When the Libertyite argued that he should support the antislavery candidate because there was no difference between the Whig and Democratic parties, Adams could not have disagreed more: "I thought there was a great difference between them; and that placing them on the same level was to assure the triumph of the worst party." In neither of these instances could Adams be accused of sacrificing principle to party; in both cases, he believed he was seeking to prevent adverse political developments that could only make a difficult situation more problematic. But they were hardly the actions of someone who refused "to look to any party as a guide to his conduct." Rather, they were the calculating decisions of a veteran politician who feared being consigned to the margins of the policymaking process. Whatever his reservations about the integrity of certain colleagues, Adams felt it better to work within a less than perfect political organization than to pursue futile endeavors outside party ranks that had little chance of influencing the national debate.[20]

This did not mean that Adams resisted all efforts to alter the political status quo. His discontent was real. Never entirely satisfied with the free labor protectionism of Northern Whigs, he was constantly seeking ways to provoke a more spirited sectional response to the slaveholder aggression embodied in Calhoun's doctrine of nullification and the political program outlined in Jackson's 1832 message. He would not try to displace the main Northern party of the moment, but he was open to the formation of political coalitions that promised to move the party in the direction he desired. Just as he urged that National Republicanism would benefit from an alliance with Anti-Masonry, Adams appreciated the energy, enthusiasm, and antislavery fervor that Liberty party activists could bring to Northern Whiggery should any of them choose to leave their organization. The growing importance of the slavery expansion issue would, by the mid-1840s, provide heretofore unimagined opportunities along these lines.

"No one appreciates more highly the value of party ties within proper limits, or adheres more firmly to his party within them. He never permits them to influence him beyond the necessary limits." This equivocal statement was probably the most enthusiastic endorsement of party ever issued in Calhoun's name. It is no surprise that it appeared in an 1843 campaign biography designed to promote the South Carolinian's presidential ambitions. He understood that realization of those aspirations required some form of genuflection before the altar of party. If unwilling to drop his knee to the chapel floor, he knew that he had at least to bow his head respectfully if he was to dispel the doubts of skeptical Democratic regulars, few of whom trusted that he could be consistently relied upon to place party objectives before a personal agenda that Calhoun reflexively defended as an expression of the most righteous moral and political principles.[21]

By 1843 they had good reason to be mistrustful. Like Adams, Calhoun's aversion to party stiffened appreciably in the face of Federalist resistance to government initiatives during the War of 1812. Such "moral treason" had throughout history "proved the most deadly foe to freedom," he observed in one wartime speech, and every step must be taken "to guard against the pernicious effect of a factious opposition" that sacrificed "the general welfare" to the avaricious passions of party interest. Similarly, he joined Adams in applauding Monroe's subsequent campaign to subdue party conflict. There could be no doubt, he wrote the Virginian, that his administration had "adopted the course and means best calculated to advance the lasting interest of the country" in attempting to quell the more baneful consequences of partisan warfare. But where the New Englander later negotiated a grudging peace with the second party system, Calhoun never came to terms with either of the two new parties. Despite deep reservations about the growing partisanship of the post-Monroe years, he initially threw his support behind Jackson's fledgling Democratic party in an effort to check what he considered the aggrandizing tendencies of Adams, Clay, and the American system. The affiliation did not last long. Old Hickory's forceful response to nullification and Van Buren's artful political maneuvering at his expense left Calhoun ill-disposed toward the two men and the party they headed. Bad enough alone, Jackson and Van Buren together formed a particularly formidable and treacherous combination. "They are both equally corrupt and insincere," he told an acquaintance, "but one b[r]ought to the common stock force of character, reputation for patriotism and honesty, and great strength of popularity, while the other brought dexterity, cunning and a thorough knowledge of party tactics." Calhoun afterward moved back and forth between the Whig and Democratic camps without finding a comfortable home in either before deciding that the party of Jackson represented the lesser of two evils.[22]

South Carolina political culture was another major influence shaping Calhoun's anti-partyism. Unlike Massachusetts, where Whig leaders forged a popular conservatism to fend off Democratic challenges to their dominant position in state politics, the second party system did not take deep root in South Carolina, and the near extirpation of Palmetto Whigs during the early 1840s ensured that it never would. Historian Richard P. McCormick did not include South Carolina in his study of Jacksonian-era party development because it held no statewide elections for any office before 1860 and exhibited little in the way of party competition. To be sure, large numbers of voters went to the polls each year, turnover in the General Assembly was generally high, and most candidates for seats in the state legislature conducted spirited campaigns. But it was popular participation without parties or the political managers who assumed an increasingly important role in electoral contests elsewhere during the period. According to South Carolina political leaders, curtailing the influence of party encouraged talented people of principle to seek public office and minimized the role of spoilsmen, charlatans, demagogues, and other riffraff in the political process. It also provided a sound basis for creating a harmonious political environment in which vituperation and backstabbing gave way to consensus and unity. This was of particular concern to Calhoun, who believed the absence of strong political parties and the conflict they all too frequently engendered was a major reason that South Carolina possessed the capacity "to interpose & nullify an unconstitutional act of Congress, which no other State can do, except on some local question."[23]

Whenever South Carolinians spoke of the state's vaunted social and political unity, they almost invariably made some reference to the state constitution and the Compromise of 1808. The latter consisted of a constitutional amendment on legislative apportionment designed to address Upcountry grievances about underrepresentation without impairing the ability of Lowcountry planters to protect their interests. No one feared a surge of abolitionist sentiment in the Upcountry, but there was some concern that people there might begin to envision a future without slavery, as occurred in Virginia's Valley and Trans-Allegheny regions during the early decades of the nineteenth century. That such people had no wish to emancipate South Carolina slaves did not matter. Should a sufficient number of them obtain seats in the General Assembly, they might well pass laws that furthered Upcountry interests at the expense of wealthy slaveowners in major plantation areas. To prevent this from happening, the Compromise of 1808 combined white population and taxable property in ways that enabled the Lowcountry to retain control of the Senate and disproportionate power in the lower house; yet it also permitted Upcountry areas to add representatives as they increased their wealth through the adoption of plantation agriculture. The subsequent expansion of cotton culture in the Upcountry thus muted Upcountry complaints about underrepresentation while ensuring that legislators from the region would do nothing to inconvenience leading planters elsewhere in the state.[24]

Few people expressed greater satisfaction with the "happy fruits" of the Compromise of 1808 than Calhoun did. Its successful adjustment of differences between South Carolina's two major regions not only removed a major source of conflict but showed how sagacious political leaders could rise above personal interests and party considerations to advance the general welfare. "The consequence was," he wrote in his *Discourse on the Constitution of the United States*, "the almost instantaneous restoration of concord and harmony between two sections. Party division and party violence, with the distraction and disorder attendant upon them, soon disappeared," to be replaced by a "mutual attachment" that has "continued uninterrupted for more than forty years." Throughout the period, he claimed, South Carolina could be truly said to have escaped the many baneful effects of partisan conflict: "Party organization, party discipline, party proscription—and their offspring, *the spoils principle*, have been unknown to the State." This was not altogether true. As he knew all too well the struggle over state interposition had produced bitter enmities between nullifiers and unionists that some of the combatants nurtured long afterward. Yet Calhoun's broader point was well taken. Palmetto political culture differed sufficiently from the experience of other states—South as well as North—that most people of the time would have accepted his assertions about South Carolina government, however much they disagreed with his views on party.[25]

No less important for Calhoun, he believed the Compromise of 1808 had created a system of government that furnished a practical illustration of the benefits of his doctrine of the concurrent majority. One of the South Carolinian's greatest fears was that population growth was giving the North a commanding position in national politics that would ultimately enable the region to impose its will on the South. Convinced that existing constitutional checks on majority rule lacked sufficient force to arrest this development, he insisted that special steps be taken to provide adequate protection of Southern interests. South Carolina had shown how that could be done. Its constitution, he told Senate colleagues, "respects all the great interests of the State, giving to each a separate and distinct voice in the management of political affairs, by means of which the feebler interests are protected against the preponderance of the greater." The result was a "Government of the people, in the true sense of the term, and not of the mere majority, or the dominant interests." Just as the Compromise of 1808 gave the South Carolina Lowcountry a veto power over any initiatives proposed by representatives of an Upcountry region that contained nearly five times its white population, Calhoun contended, the South could not rest secure until it possessed a similar power vis-a-vis the North.[26]

Calhoun further argued that the concurrent majority provided a safeguard against the potential perils of suffrage extension. When simple numbers dictated policy, the danger always existed that some demagogue, seeking to advance the interests of a corrupt political faction, would rally the invariably more numerous impecunious members of the community against those affluent, talented individuals who constituted its natural leadership class. The likelihood of that occurring in a government of the concurrent majority, where public officials made every effort to achieve consensus, was remote: "There, mere numbers have not the absolute control; and the wealthy and intelligent being identified with the poor and ignorant of their respective portions or interests of the community, become their leaders and protectors." Again, South Carolina provided a model for the attainment of this happy state of affairs. During a period when other states were adopting constitutional reforms that removed barriers to popular influence in the political process, the Palmetto constitution retained slaveholding and property requirements for public office and concentrated power in a malapportioned, elite-dominated legislature that chose presidential electors, appointed governors, and filled numerous state and local offices. From the viewpoint of South Carolina's ruling oligarchy, it was, as James Hamilton Jr., said, a wonderful system—one in which the common people expected their leaders to "think for them" and were "prepared to *act* as their leaders *think*."[27]

Calhoun certainly had no complaints. Any talk of constitutional reform sparked his immediate opposition. Should popular election of governors be permitted, he wrote, conflict between Lowcountry and Upcountry would cleave the state in two, leaving it at the mercy of the federal government: "There would be no need of a force bill to assert federal supremacy" over South Carolina; "our own mercenary divisions & factions would be effectual for that purpose." Allowing voters to choose presidential electors would also upset the balance established by the Compromise of 1808 and have similarly dire repercussions, producing the sort of discord and factionalism that made good government nearly impossible. And such an outcome was inevitable because granting voters the right to select presidential electors would open up a Pandora's box and prompt demands that the general populace be permitted to fill a wide range of offices—governors, lieutenant governors, US senators, judges, and other officials now chosen by the legislature. Nothing good, he added, could result from adopting the "radical" belief "that the majority has the natural, inherent, and indefeasible right of government—an assumption not only unfounded, but of the most dangerous character, and in direct conflict with the Constitution of this State and that of the union." If it was to retain its current stature and reputation for sound government, South Carolina must under all circumstances remain committed to "the far broader and more solid and durable foundation, of the concurrent majority to the exclusion of the numerical."[28]

Apart from ideological considerations, Calhoun had practical reasons for opposing changes in the operation of the South Carolina government. Within the state, he stood atop a governing structure in which he had no peers. Unlike Adams, whose influence on Massachusetts politics did not reach far beyond the boundaries of his congressional district, Calhoun projected a commanding presence that members of the Palmetto political class dared not ignore. Where recently elected chief executives sought Calhoun's counsel on how they should proceed, the New Englander would have been shocked to receive a similar request from any incoming Bay governor. During his lifetime, Alfred Huger later said of Calhoun, "the only lesson taught or comprehended, from the parish schools to the Senate Chamber, was to obey orders," it being widely understood that he had little tolerance for opinions that differed from his own. As Huger's half-brother Daniel derisively remarked: "I am the State says Mr. Calhoun; he who does not fight to make me *first* is a slave, and he who obeys me 'to the death' is a freeman." Yet Calhoun's position was somewhat more precarious than these observations suggest. However much other Palmetto politicians respected and feared him, many came to dislike and resent him. People "hate him for his superiority of mind not less than for his arbitrary will," James Hammond observed, and the list of prominent South Carolinians who broke ranks with him on one issue or another included Henry L. Pinckney, William C. Preston, Waddy Thompson, Hugh S. Legaré, and Francis W. Pickens. That Calhoun managed to maintain his exalted place in SC politics, Hammond added, "arises from the confidence our people have in his devotion to our peculiar interests." But this popular faith in his unflagging dedication to the state's well-being was not unshakeable: "Let them once think he has sacrificed us, as I think he has, to his own ambitious views, and he is prostrated." It did not help that Calhoun's infrequent performances before political gatherings left something to be desired. Hoping to unseat Waddy Thompson, he intervened in a congressional contest on behalf of Thompson's opponent. It did not go well. Notwithstanding "all of his great talents, overshadowing reputation and autocratic power in South Carolina," Benjamin Perry reported, "he proved unequal to General Thompson on the stump. The masses were more pleased with the wit, humor and anecdotes of the General than with the dry logic of Calhoun." It was little wonder that he despised electioneering, hated political parties, resisted all attempts to democratize Palmetto political life, and insisted that any deviation from his ideological formulations and policy prescriptions would place South Carolina on the road to perdition.[29]

In all this, Calhoun strongly influenced the development of a state political culture that in turn shaped his own beliefs. Despite occasional setbacks, he more often than not got his way in South Carolina politics; and despite some grumbling, much of it communicated in private, most members of the Palmetto political class deferred to his leadership. But South Carolina was not the nation. Nearly everywhere outside the state, political leaders dismissed Calhoun's disdain for party and participated enthusiastically in the rituals and activities of an increasingly pervasive second party system. This presented a problem for the South Carolina senator because he spent nearly his entire political career in the nation's capital; and what happened there almost always meant more to him than what took place in Columbia, Charleston, or his home district in the Palmetto Upcountry. This can perhaps best be seen in an 1835 letter he wrote explaining his decision to put off retirement from public life. On one hand, he worried that his departure would disrupt "the harmony of the State & party" by unleashing a struggle to fill his seat. Many able individuals would be competing for the post, but none of them, he immodestly but accurately noted, possessed the stature and experience he brought to the position or so fully enjoyed the confidence of the people of South Carolina. More important he felt that he was particularly well equipped to engage the many challenges that lay ahead. For "the danger is not half over," he warned, and much work remained to be done if Southerners were to preserve "not only liberty & prosperity, but our existence, as a people": That future developments will compel white residents of the region "to abandon the South & leave it exclusively to the black race, without our most strenuous & united efforts, I hold certain."[30]

This was where the problem arose. Calhoun knew he could not head off these threats acting alone. As much as he would have liked to break free from both major parties, he had to choose between them. After a brief flirtation with Whiggery, he opted to go with the party of Jackson. The Democrats at least had the right principles, however much they deserted them in practice, he wrote one correspondent: "I believe that our only recruiting ground, is in their ranks." By contrast, the Whigs were "consolidationists by nature" and could never be expected to support a political program designed to put the country back "on the State-rights Republican track, as was intended by the framers of the Constitution." Calhoun's differences with Adams in this regard went well beyond a preference for the limited government emphases of Democrats. The Carolinian believed abolitionism and the policy initiatives of the American system were inextricably bound together, and his position on major economic issues of the day helps explain why, long after the nullification controversy had ended, the Bay congressman continued to believe that advocacy of the Carolina doctrine imperiled the nation's well-being. "In calling [abolition] a progeny of consolidation, I make the assertion not without due reflection," Calhoun told a group of Georgians. The movement to abolish slavery "has its origin in the same mistaken views of the Constitution with the Bank and the protective system, and other measures of the kind—all of which regard our confederate system of Government as a great national consolidated Republic, with the right to determine, in the last resort, the extent of its power, and to enforce its decision by musket and bayonet, even against the sovereign States from which it derives its existence and all its powers." If steps were not taken to ensure that such measures and the "false principles to which they owe their origin be thoroughly put down, Abolition in the end will do its work."[31]

How these beliefs informed Calhoun's participation in Jacksonian economic debates was evident in his approach to the bank question, a subject on which his views differed substantially from those of Adams in nearly all respects. Where the New Englander considered the extension of loans an essential part of economic development, Calhoun deemed financial institutions the most objectionable feature of modern economic society. Although no one could plausibly accuse him of being a backward-looking agrarian who condemned all commercial endeavors, he felt the banking system degraded everything it touched. Its malign effect, he told Senate colleagues, could be seen in the way "it allots the honors and rewards of the community, in a very undue proportion, to a pursuit the least of all others favorable to the higher qualities, intellectual or moral, to the decay of the learned professions, and the more noble pursuits of science, literature, philosophy, and statesmanship, and the great and more useful pursuits of business and industry"; everyone, the "rising generation" particularly, "cannot but feel its deadening influence." Even more alarming was the inordinate power exercised by banks, particularly when combined with the authority of the federal government. Should this union "be permitted to progress," he contended, "it will elevate the money power above all others—above thrones and principalities, laws and constitutions." Worse, the South would suffer most as a consequence. The concentration of the nation's money supply in Northern banks "has been one of the most efficient means by which that section has governed our commerce." Bank policy was thus "far more a political, than a commercial or money question." Any merger of "the money power and the political power," be it "a league of State banks or a national bank," he warned, would, in addition to destroying regional trade and impoverishing Southern staple producers, put "an end to State rights."[32]

These assertions appeared in various speeches and public letters supporting Martin Van Buren's independent treasury plan. Announced by the president in a September 1837 message to Congress, the initiative proposed to do exactly what Calhoun demanded: separate government and banking by directing that all federal revenue be held either in the US Treasury or in subtreasuries located in major cities throughout the nation and by eliminating the role of all banking institutions in the collection and disbursement of government funds. The Carolinian not only backed the measure but pushed further by introducing an amendment that would have required the Treasury to accept only gold and silver in any transactions with state banks. Although Calhoun subsequently voted against the bill after Congress removed his specie clause, he remained staunchly committed to its principal aim of dissolving the union between the money power and the political power. Van Buren appreciated his stance, despite its deepening of the split between hard-money and soft-money Democrats. Others did not, however. When almost the entire Palmetto congressional delegation rejected the independent treasury concept, Calhoun singled out William C. Preston and Waddy Thompson for retaliation. It was bad enough that such prominent figures adopted a position that could be seen as challenging his role as South Carolina's leading spokesperson in Washington. That they did not seem to recognize the broader ideological import of his views on the relationship between government and banking was truly unforgiveable.[33]

One person who did was Adams. The Bay congressman may not have understood the finer points of banking policy, but he believed he had a firm grasp on the broader implications of a given measure and roundly opposed the independent treasury proposal. "Bedlam seems to me the only place where it could have originated," he told an acquaintance. "A Divorce of Bank and State! Why a divorce of Trade and Shipping would be as wise to carry on the business of a merchant." A product of "ultra-nullification," the scheme was clearly intended to undermine "the Commerce and Merchants of the North." Its roots, he observed in a letter to his constituents, could be traced to "the panic terrors and insatiable thirst for domination in the slaveholding planters of the south, once characterized by [Jackson] under the name of independent farmers, as the *best part of the population*." For these people, the destruction of "all banking credit under the name of capital" formed part of an insidious design to promote class conflict in the North. The slaveholder, he explained, "builds up a theory that confounds poverty with slavery; and he says to the laborer of the north—you are poor, your next door neighbor is rich—you are compelled to hard labor to earn your subsistence and that of your family—you are a laborer, he is a capitalist—you are a slave—there is his banking house—go and burn it down." Thus it was that the slaveholding planter "invokes the *labor* of the north as an auxiliary defence to the *slavery* of the south."[34]

As the exponent of a free labor protectionism that emphasized the interdependence of capital and labor and used comparisons with slave society to blur recognition of growing social inequities in many parts of the North, Adams's interpretation of the motives behind the independent treasury plan is certainly understandable. But to the extent that his remarks were directed at Calhoun, they represented a misunderstanding of a recurrent theme in the South Carolinian's thought. Calhoun did comment on Northern class relations from time to time, but he did not do so for the purpose of inciting conflict between labor and capital. He believed that one element of the community lived off the labor of another in all societies. He further believed the South better able to manage the resulting tensions than was the case in the North, where employers could never achieve the same unity between labor and capital that slavery provided. This was so because slaveowners embodied the shared interests of capital and labor in ways that Northern capitalists could never hope to do. As a result, he contended, planters constituted a conservative balance wheel in the American social system that Northern economic leaders would do well to recognize and embrace if they were to contain labor unrest. This did not mean that he championed slavery in the abstract. When critics accused him of doing so, Calhoun denied the charge, insisting that he had never said "the best and most natural condition of the laboring community was that of slavery, or anything like it." These denials rested on a deeply ingrained racism. Inflexibly committed to the belief that Black people could never be anything other than a subordinate group wherever they mixed with white people, he saw slavery as the most appropriate form of social relations in such societies. "With us," he observed, "the two great divisions of society are not the rich and the poor, but white and black;" and it was this, together with slavery, that made the region the bulwark of social order that Calhoun proclaimed it to be.[35]

Another major economic issue demanding Calhoun's attention was the tariff. It had even clearer sectional overtones than the bank question, and it presented the South Carolinian with much greater challenges. Everyone knew where he stood on the subject. His opposition to protectionism had been a driving force behind the nullification crisis of the early 1830s. That controversy had ended in the Compromise Tariff of 1833, which promised a gradual reduction in duties over a nine-year period, with the most substantial taking place in the final year. This did not happen however. When the Tariff of 1842 canceled the last year's cuts, rates remained at a much higher level than most South Carolinians had anticipated or were willing to accept. Calhoun strongly objected to the measure in Senate debate, condemning it as an assault on Southern prosperity that would make government "the agent of a portion of the community to extort, under the guise of protection, tribute from the rest of the community, and thus defeat the end of its institution, by perverting powers, intended for the protection of all, into the means of oppressing one portion for the benefit of another." No one doubted that the South Carolina senator would denounce the subsequent bill. The only question was how fiercely and how long he would do so. After the South Carolina Democratic Convention issued an address praising his position on protectionism the following May, some of his supporters hoped he would let the issue rest. With a presidential election looming, they told him, continuing to rail against the tariff could only divide the Democrats, enhance Van Buren's prospects, and destroy his reputation within the party. Calhoun neither accepted nor rejected the advice. In a public address to his friends and backers, he declared protectionism "to be another name for a system of monopoly and plunder, and to be thoroughly anti-republican and federal in character." He had labored too long and "suffered too much" in his efforts to promote the free exchange of goods between nations, he added, to "abandon the cause now, when [across the Atlantic in Great Britain] its banner waves in proud triumph over the metropolis of the commercial world." At the same time, he urged state political leaders to stand their ground without giving undue offense to Democratic chieftains: "Conciliate the party, as much as you can, but not at the expense of principle, or in the vain hope, you can compel Mr. V[an] B[uren] and his friends to go right, except through fear."[36]

South Carolina's most powerful political figure and the nation's leading proponent of free trade had spoken, and if anything more needed to be said, he would say it. Or so one would have expected. That it did not turn out that way owed much to Robert Barnwell Rhett, an irascible editor-politician with disunionist inclinations who enjoyed few things more than casting a line into troubled waters. Rhett was an uncompromising critic of the Tariff of 1842 whose bitterness deepened in June 1844 when the Senate rejected a treaty calling for the annexation of Texas. Late the following month in the Lowcountry town of Bluffton, he brought these and other developments that threatened Southern interests together in an inflammatory speech calculated to incite popular unrest. As things now stood, he declared, people of the South had four options: electing Polk president, organizing a Southern convention, seceding from the Union, or nullifying any laws that discriminated against the region. Rhett dismissed the first two responses out of hand, arguing that Southerners could no longer trust the Democratic party, while asserting that nothing positive could be expected from a regional convention; both represented "the embodiment of the vanity of hope." Secession or nullification might work under the right circumstances, however, and he preferred "either of them, or any thing else, . . . to base and cowardly submission." Whatever South Carolina chose to do, its "only hope is resistance—[the state] must commence acting for herself, and others will soon come to her assistance." According to one reporter, Rhett's performance had a mesmerizing effect on his audience: "Youth and old age of both sexes . . . hung breathless upon every word and the whole mass seemed as if moved by a single thought." Nobody knew what the Bluffton gathering portended, but many feared that it would not be good.[37]

Calhoun was one such person. By the time Rhett spoke in Bluffton, he had already received disturbing news of the emergence "of an uneasy & restless spirit" in several districts of the state that if left unchecked "may extend to other parts of the country" and cause considerable harm. This resurgence of South Carolina radicalism, various correspondents warned, not only threatened to increase the state's political isolation but could impair his reputation and contribute to the election of Henry Clay in the upcoming presidential contest. Worse, it might even result in his displacement as South Carolina's undisputed political leader. Some people, upset that he appeared to have gone silent on the tariff after the bold assertions in the address to his political friends and backers, were suggesting that he had abandoned former associates, and that it might be time to find someone else to "to save the State &c." One of these malcontents, Francis W. Pickens informed him, was *Charleston Mercury* editor John A. Stuart, who had told a local representative that Palmetto political leaders needed "to decide whether the State was to lick your toes forever." And he was not alone. Similar comments could be heard from James Hammond and others who had long claimed to be loyal supporters. Rhett, who believed people of the South faced ruin if they did not "act independently of both parties," reportedly had charged Calhoun with softening his stance on the tariff in exchange for promises of support in the 1848 presidential race.[38]

As it turned out, the challenge to Calhoun's authority went nowhere. Whispering behind the great man's back was one thing; openly confronting him was another matter entirely, and none of his critics wished to experience a visitation of his wrath. Even Rhett tried to minimize any differences he had with Calhoun. There was considerable irony in all this. No one had done more than Calhoun to shape South Carolina opinion on two of the main questions in dispute: party fealty and opposition to protectionism. When Rhett declared that South Carolinians should jettison the Democrats whenever the party appeared to forsake its defense of Southern interests, he could plausibly contend that he was only echoing views expressed by the region's leading exponent of states' rights. Similarly, when Rhett insisted that no action should be deemed too radical when opposing protectionist tariff measures, he could argue that he was following a course charted by the father of nullification. To a greater degree than perhaps even Calhoun realized, the equation of protectionism with Northern treachery had taken deep root in the political consciousness of many South Carolinians, where it would continue to linger long after the Walker Tariff of 1846 depoliticized the issue by markedly reducing import duties. A good example can be found in the Civil War diaries of Mary Chesnut. The wife of a moderately inclined US senator, Chesnut had small regard for the rantings of Rhett and other fire-eating secessionists. She did, however, believe that Northern manipulation of tariff legislation had led "Yankees" to "think we belong to them" and turned cotton planters into "good milk cows": "We bore the ban of slavery. They got the money. Cotton pays everybody who handles it, sells it, manufactures it, &c&c—rarely pays the men who make it. Secondhand, they received the wages of slavery. They grew rich, we grew poor."[39]

Of the major economic questions of the period, Calhoun devoted the least attention to internal improvements. What he had to say was nevertheless significant. In addition to revealing the constraints that strict constructionism placed on his political interventions, his shifting views on the issue shed light on another dimension of his sectional thought. Where the South Carolinian had, by the late 1820s, completely disavowed an earlier openness to protectionist tariff legislation, he was less quick to abandon his interest in government initiatives "to conquer space." In an 1831 conversation with Hammond, he suggested amending the Constitution to remove any objections to federal support of internal improvements "and to make the public lands the great fund to be set apart for that purpose." Calhoun never acted on the proposition. Doing so in South Carolina during the 1830s would have exposed him to withering criticism. Yet his reasons for considering such an Adams-like proposal appeared ever more compelling in the years that followed. Creating a transportation system that linked South and West would, he believed, produce a revolution in intersectional relations with wide-ranging commercial and political consequences. "Instead of being shut off from the vast commerce of the West," he observed in an 1836 letter, the South would be able to direct the region's "copious streams to [its] own ports." No less important, closer economic ties between the two regions would establish a solid foundation for mutual action on the political front at a time when the growing power of industrial areas of the North posed an increasingly serious threat to Southern interests. In the words of James Gadsden, bringing the people of the South together with those of the Mississippi Valley would make the latter "feel as allies of the Great commercial and agricultural interests—instead of the Tax gathering and monopolizing interests of the North."[40]

Gadsden's observation appeared in an October 1845 letter to Calhoun concerning an upcoming transportation convention in Memphis, Tennessee. The South Carolinian had been looking for an opportunity to do exactly what Gadsden suggested, and the Memphis gathering presented an ideal forum. Speaking before the convention, he enthusiastically endorsed plans for navigational improvements, canal and road building, and related construction initiatives, on occasion sounding like the nationalist secretary of war who two decades earlier had done so much to shape and push through the General Survey Act of 1824. Strengthening ties between the Mississippi Valley and the Atlantic coast did not go far enough, he declared: "Our great valley must be intimately and closely connected with the valley and lakes of the St. Lawrence, by a canal which will permit the vessels which navigate one to pass, if practicable, to the other." Yet he also warned convention-goers that they should not expect much help from the federal government. Notwithstanding the seeming expansiveness of the general welfare clause, the Constitution did not allow Congress to appropriate funds for programs that went beyond its delegated powers, and he could not approve any measure that violated this fundamental maxim of states' rights doctrine. He did, however, believe some forms of indirect assistance were permissible. In a later report on the convention's memorial to the US Senate, he wrote that the commerce clause—while it did not permit federal construction of harbors and canals—could be interpreted to sanction the removal of obstructions to navigable waterways. He further conceded that land grants might be made to railroads in situations where construction promised to enhance the value of other property held by the US government.[41]

Apart from an unwillingness to contravene his own strict constructionist views, Calhoun had good reason to be cautious. Some commentators, such as a writer in the *Southern Quarterly Review*, applauded his constitutional logic and believed his recommendations provided safe guidelines for government assistance to internal improvements. Others responded much differently. The *Charleston Mercury* declared the convention's demands an unjustifiable raid on public resources that embodied the consolidationist doctrines that Calhoun had so long condemned. Hammond was particularly critical. In a characteristically uncharitable private assessment, he mercilessly flayed Calhoun's constitutional reasoning in the Memphis report: "His argument is the most finished specimen of wire drawing he has yet produced. In many parts it is absurd, in others trivial, in all unsound." Worse, he had abandoned "the whole cause of strict constitutional construction" as part of an effort to endear himself to western voters for a future presidential run, "in which as usual he will fail." To be sure, Hammond added, "the fixed fact remains that one half of the Union will soon be directly interested in the navigation of the Mississippi, and its commerce is almost equal to the whole coasting trade." It was Calhoun's misfortune that he did not seem to understand that "such powerful interests will not be controlled by constitutional scruples."[42]

For all the malice and envy that often colored Hammond's comments on Calhoun, his observation was right on the mark. Calhoun considered his Memphis report a resounding success, which would do much to cement political ties between South and West. Other commentators had similar doubts. The otherwise sympathetic author of the *Southern Quarterly Review* was also skeptical. Could westerners be expected to accept the "high responsibilities" that observing Calhoun's guidelines imposed on them, he asked, or would they use their rising influence to "act only on the blind and greedy impulses of gain" to further their own ends? As this writer knew, to ask the question was to answer it: Of course they would do everything they could to advance their interests without paying the least attention to states' rights contentions concerning the limited scope of the Constitution's general welfare clause. Calhoun's prescriptions can thus be seen as another of what historian Daniel Feller has called the "watery panaceas" that had hobbled earlier Southern efforts to forge a political alliance between South and West on the public lands question. Hedged in as it was by his "constitutional scruples," the South Carolinian's plan for regulating federal spending on internal improvements could never command anything more than yawning notice from people of the West.[43]

More so than any other political controversy of the period, the internal improvements debate reveals a major difference in how Adams and Calhoun approached public policy matters. In certain important respects, the two men could not have been more alike. Each of them reflexively cast policy questions in a North-South framework that emphasized the treachery and perfidiousness of regional adversaries. Even when they avoided the language of conspiracy, their observations often intimated that some corrupt and vicious stratagem was afoot to destroy the prosperity and general well-being of their respective sections. Yet, to a much greater degree than Calhoun ever could, Adams was able to place his defense of Northern interests within a broader nationalist design. Where mounting sectional tensions steadily narrowed the South Carolinian's conception of the national interest, they did nothing to dim the Bay congressman's grand developmental vision for the nation. The significance of these differences would become ever more apparent as the issues of slavery and westward expansion combined to dominate political discourse in the latter half of the 1840s.

The presidential contest of 1844 marked the beginning of a major sea change in national politics. Signs of a new departure first appeared in the Democratic party, where Martin Van Buren seemed to be coasting toward the nomination. The New Yorker likely would have obtained it if had he come out in favor of Texas annexation. When he failed to do so, Southern Democrats blocked his bid to represent the party in the November election. The eventual nominee and next president, James K. Polk, was a zealous expansionist who promised to add Texas and Oregon to the national domain. Not content to stop there, the Tennessean soon made it clear that he also had his eye on large areas of northern Mexico and was willing to go to war to acquire the territory. The questions raised by these developments quickly overshadowed familiar topics of congressional interest, and with the 1846 passage of the Walker Tariff and an independent treasury bill, long-standing economic controversies retreated even further to the margins of political debate. By 1848, few politicians of either party would have disagreed with the New Orleans editor who wrote: "Old party issues are worn out and have nearly disappeared."[44]

Had southwestern expansion been simply a matter of adding territory to the nation's land holdings, it is not entirely clear how Adams would have responded. He had been an ardent expansionist throughout his long career in public life: as a young senator, he had broken ranks with other New England Federalists to support the Louisiana Purchase; as secretary of state, he had negotiated a treaty with Spain that added Florida and areas of the West to the national domain. The beliefs inspiring these actions had changed little during the past four decades. In the debate over whether the Polk administration should insist on a 54°40' dividing line in the Oregon Territory or accept a boundary five degrees to the south, Adams lined up squarely behind the fifty-four fortiers. Adopting language he had first employed in his Plymouth oration of 1802 and that New England's first English settlers had used long before then, he contended that American claims to the region rested on God's words in the first chapter of Genesis, where the Lord said to man: "Be fruitful and multiply, and fill the earth and subdue it." The region, Adams believed, could never prosper under the administration of Great Britain's Hudson Bay Company, or while its most numerous inhabitants were Native Americans who supplied the company with furs. He wanted to see the land settled by industrious pioneers committed to making the wilderness bloom and establishing the "great nation that is to arise there, which must come from us as a fountain from its source, of free, independent, sovereign republics, instead of hunting grounds, for the buffaloes, braves, and savages of the desert."[45]

But Texas was not Oregon. Where the Pacific Northwest had little appeal to land-hungry slaveowners, the Lone Star Republic did; and where Adams continued to champion the acquisition of additional free soil territory, his views on the expansion of slavery had changed noticeably over the years. In 1804 he voted against a proposal for gradual emancipation in Louisiana. Slavery was indeed a moral evil, he observed at the time, "but connected with commerce it has important uses." Later, at almost the exact same time that the Missouri controversy prompted some of his harshest comments on slavery, he was engaged in talks to obtain Florida, which no one doubted would eventually become a slave state. Adams would also claim that, within the Monroe administration, he had strongly urged including Texas in the Transcontinental Treaty, even though he had to have known that it was slave territory and would likely remain so. At the very least, this record raises questions about the consistency of his position on the issue of slave expansionism. But that was then. The nullification controversy had hardened Adams's antislavery convictions, and the emergent struggle over the gag rule made him even more resistant to any initiative that promised to strengthen the institution. In the years to come, he would miss few opportunities to challenge what he considered the insatiable demands of an aggressive, power-mad slavocracy.[46]

The Bay congressman began sounding the alarm on Texas a month after Sam Houston's victory in the Battle of San Jacinto effectively toppled Mexican rule in the province. In a May 1836 House address that featured arguments conspicuously absent from later remarks on Oregon, he not only said the nation had sufficient territory to satisfy the most avaricious of land-jobbers, but voiced concern for the rights of Native Americans of the region: "Have [you] not," he asked his fellow legislators, "Indians enough to expel from the lands of their fathers' sepulchers, and to exterminate?" But the overriding theme of this and subsequent statements was that Texas represented as stark a contrast between the forces of slavery and freedom as one could hope to find. The assertions of Southern congressmen who described Anglo-Texans as a liberty-loving people fully deserving of the nation's support had to be refuted. Should they not and should efforts to annex Texas prove successful, he wanted to know, "where will it end?" The answer to that question was all too apparent. Adding Texas to the national domain formed part of a "slave-breeding conspiracy against the freedom of the North" designed "to obtain a nursery of slave-holding States, to break down the ascendant power of the free States, and to fortify, beyond all possibility, of reversal, the institution of slavery." Under no circumstances, "while health is in my body," the seventy-four-year-old Massachusetts representative told members of Congress in an 1842 speech, "will I consent to the annexation of any foreign State, which is burdened with the curse of slavery."[47]

As demands for Texas annexation grew louder, Adams's opposition intensified, and his rhetoric became even more heated. In March 1843 his name headed a list of thirteen Northern congressmen who issued a public letter instructing people of the free states to unite in expressing their unwillingness to condone annexation. The movement to acquire Texas nevertheless moved forward, and as it did, Adams's despair deepened. "This was a memorable day in the annals of the world," he observed in an April 1844 diary entry. "The Treaty for the annexation of Texas was this day sent on to the Senate; and with it the freedom of the human race." When the Senate rejected the pact, he resumed his denunciations of the annexation campaign, sometimes employing phraseology more commonly associated with the martial patriarchalism of South Carolina orators. In a speech before the Boston Young Men's Whig Club, he urged members to remember their revolutionary ancestors. "Young men of Boston," he declared, "burnish your armor, prepare for the conflict, and I say to you, in the language of Galcagus to the ancient Britons, think of your forefathers! Think of your posterity." At the same time, he fleshed out his thoughts on the slave power conspiracy, seeking to show how it began with planter intrigues to dominate public offices, proceeded to attacks on the right of petition, and was now reaching its culmination in efforts to secure new slave territory, which would enable the South to expand its senatorial delegation "and a corresponding double slave representation in the house, all to rivet forever the chains of slavery" on the rest of the nation.[48]

These assertions reveal linkages between the slave power conspiracy and the constitutional compromise on slavery, which Adams had long considered a "morally and politically vicious" bargain. Although he never questioned constitutional protection of slavery in states where it existed, he believed there were clear limits on how far that protection extended. "We have," he observed in an 1837 letter, "bound our destinies in community with the People of States encumbered with Slavery before we sealed the bond; and by the bond we covenanted to tolerate, to defend, to protect that institution as an offspring of our own, though not as our legitimate progeny." Of the major elements of that contract, Adams most objected to the provision permitting slave states to count slaves as three-fifths of a person for the purpose of representation. When the Massachusetts legislature passed resolutions calling for an amendment to remove the offending clause from the Constitution, he happily submitted them to the House in a speech combining his deep aversion to the three-fifths compromise with a defense of the right of petition. Southerner political leaders, nearly all of whom responded angrily to the proposal, doubtless agreed with the Alabama and Virginia legislatures when they condemned it "as a proposition virtually to dissolve the Union." Adams did not care. Much as the nullification controversy had during the early 1830s, Texas crystallized antislavery notions that had been circulating in his political consciousness for some time, giving them a coherence they had heretofore lacked. He now brought these ideas together by making "Slave representation" the main theme of letters and addresses dealing with other political matters such as the slave power conspiracy, the "contortions of Calhoun," and the secession schemes of South Carolina radicals.[49]

As various historians have shown, there was no slave power conspiracy. One need look no further than Calhoun's often strained relations with other Southern political leaders to appreciate how difficult it would have been for them to muster the organizational wherewithal required for such a project. Yet Northern congressmen of the period could not completely dismiss Adams's contentions. It was not necessary to accept his argument in its entirety, or to peruse the statistics he had gathered on the South's disproportionate political power, to realize that slaveowners' influence in national councils exceeded their actual numbers. And outside the halls of Congress, many Northern voters were even more receptive to the slave power conspiracy thesis. This created a serious problem for John Tyler. The Virginian wanted to annex Texas, but he did not wish to do anything that would give credence to the Bay congressman's charges or to alienate Northern Democrats fearful of being portrayed as agents of slave expansionism. Adams's interventions thus helped slow the movement toward annexation; but they could not stop it. Tylerite procrastination on Texas ended with the May 1843 appointment of the Virginia planter-lawyer Abel Upshur to head the State Department. Much in contrast to his predecessor, Daniel Webster, Upshur was an enthusiastic annexationist who considered slavery a national blessing that benefited all regions of the country. At State, he made annexation his top priority and worked hard to further the cause by initiating treaty negotiations with Lone Star leaders.[50]

By the time the resulting accord was signed, Upshur would be dead, the victim of a March 1844 explosion on the USS *Princeton*. Tyler, now unreservedly committed to acquiring Texas, chose Calhoun to replace the Virginian, sure in the knowledge that the South Carolinian would carry on Upshur's initiatives. Like Adams, Calhoun had recognized the significance of Texas as early as 1836; unlike the New Englander, he believed acquisition of the fledgling republic absolutely essential. He also knew from personal experience that any mention of Texas elicited "long and loud cheering" from Southern audiences. Calhoun was nevertheless hesitant to assume too conspicuous a role in the later campaign for annexation—in part because of the adverse effect South Carolina's reputation for radicalism might have on potential supporters, and in part because of popular suspicions concerning his political motives. When Upshur urged him to adopt a more outspoken position for the sake of promoting Southern unity, the South Carolinian did not think it advisable. "I have taken so prominent a stand on all subjects connected with abolition," he responded, "that any movement at this time, in this State would be" seen "as intended for electioneering, & would do more harm, than good." What seemed perfectly good reasons for maintaining a prudent silence in the summer of 1843 did not appear nearly so compelling the following spring. By then, he had not only withdrawn from the presidential contest but saw that the greater the amount of attention given to Texas, the more it would damage the candidacies of his longtime political adversaries Henry Clay and Martin Van Buren, both of whom dearly wished to avoid saying anything about so divisive an issue. Even more important, increasing numbers of Southerners, alarmed by mounting antislavery attacks on annexation, had come to view the acquisition of Texas as vital to the protection of regional interests: "On it," James Gadsden told Calhoun, "hinges the very existence of our Southern institutions, and if we of the South now prove recreant, we will or must [be] content to be Hewers of wood and Drawers of Water for our Northern Brethren."[51]

Thus it was, Adams acidly observed, that the "long-sighted prince of South Carolina nullification" put aside "his own presidential pretensions to contribute his agency and influence to this nefarious conspiracy against the freedom of his country and of the world." How much that agency and influence actually aided administration efforts to acquire Texas is a matter of some dispute. On several occasions, Calhoun's unwillingness to follow his predecessor's lead did more to hinder than assist the campaign. Although he and Upshur had nearly identical views on all slavery-related questions, the two men differed in at least one important respect: Where the Virginian practiced a quiet, restrained diplomacy, the South Carolinian was more inclined to throw caution to the wind. The best-known instance was an 1844 letter to Richard Pakenham, the British minister to Washington. Responding to a statement by Pakenham's Whitehall superior, Lord Aberdeen, that Great Britain would like to see slavery in Texas abolished, Calhoun declared that realization of that objective would destroy the harmony and well-being of the entire Union, and the administration had a "solemn obligation" to do whatever might be necessary to prevent any such violation of the national interest. Had Calhoun stopped there, his assertions would have constituted nothing new; Brit-bashing had been a favorite pastime of American politicians since the Revolution. But he went on to provide Pakenham with his current version of the positive good defense of slavery. Drawing on flawed census data that purported to show that, compared with Southern slaves, Black people in free states were much more prone to vice, pauperism, mental illness, and physical debility, he contended that wherever abolition had occurred "the condition of the African, has become worse." That being the case, any alteration of established relations between the races in slave states could only have disastrous consequences for all concerned. Proponents of emancipation, he concluded, needed to understand that slavery was, "in reality, a political institution, essential to the peace, safety, and prosperity of those States of the Union in which it exists."[52]

Few people reacted more angrily to this misuse of government documents than Adams, who wrote that Calhoun had "betray[ed] so total a disregard of all moral principle that it can be attributed only to the alternative of absence of honesty or of mental sanity. 'Tis the fanaticism of the Slave-monger." Of greater consequence, the letter stiffened Northern resistance to annexation and doubtless contributed to Senate rejection of the Texas treaty two months later. Congress later approved annexation by passing a joint resolution that required only a majority vote in both houses rather than the two-thirds margin needed for Senate confirmation of treaties. But Calhoun's interventions—by framing the Texas controversy as a contest between slavery and freedom—helped ensure that the dispute would have broader ramifications. When Democrats chose Polk as their 1844 presidential candidate, James Hammond predicted that the nomination would surely divide the party into Northern and Southern factions; it would also, he believed, shatter the union by "arraying the two sections against each other in our national contests," which "event will be precipitated & brought about almost at once by the Texas Question." Although premature, Hammond's prognosis was not altogether wide of the mark. Texas had a decidedly disruptive effect on the second party system. As Hammond observed, this was most apparent among Northern Democratic supporters of Van Buren. Southern use of the party's two-thirds rule to deny the New Yorker the 1844 presidential nomination, even though he had arrived at the convention with a majority of delegates, made many of them more open to talk of a slave power conspiracy than they otherwise would have been. That large numbers of Northern voters opposed the expansion of slavery increased their willingness to question party policies designed to placate Southern political leaders. Differences concerning Texas also had some influence on Whig politics. The clearest example was Adams's home state of Massachusetts, where his son, Charles Francis, played a major role in the formation of a Conscience Whig faction that adopted a more radical stance on annexation than the party's Cotton Whig leadership deemed advisable. No one knew where this might lead, but it could turn ugly, given Conscience Whig inclinations to question the moral consistency of party members who hesitated to follow their lead on slavery-related matters.[53]

What followed made the annexation controversy even more significant. One of Polk's primary aims as president was to obtain possession of Mexican lands in the Southwest and along the Pacific coast. Although he preferred doing so through a negotiated purchase of the desired territory, Polk had no strong objection to the employment of more forceful methods. When Mexico refused to consider his proposals, the president decided to increase the pressure. In the spring of 1846, he ordered General Zachary Taylor to take his army into a disputed area along the Rio Grande. After a Mexican cavalry unit attacked a US reconnaissance patrol in late April, Taylor assembled his troops and engaged Mexican forces in the first major battles of an armed struggle that would drag on for the next two years. The war had barely begun before people of all regions realized that it would be about much more than enlarging the national domain. On August 8, a Pennsylvania Democrat named David Wilmot rose from his House seat to propose an amendment to a special appropriation bill that would bar slavery in any territory acquired in the conflict. One person who had lived in fear of such a moment was Martin Van Buren. He knew that any Democratic-led war between Mexico and the United States would enable Whigs to argue "with plausibility if not truth, that it is waged for the extension of slavery." He also understood that such a conflict could all too easily result in the undoing of the intersectional political alliance that he had done so much to forge two decades earlier. Faced with mounting assaults from Whig adversaries, Northern Democrats would "be driven to the sad alternative of turning their backs upon their friends" in the South "or of encountering political suicide with their eyes open." The strong support they gave the Wilmot Proviso left no doubt as to what their choice was to be.[54]

Of our two protagonists, Adams adopted a surprisingly complacent stance on the Wilmot Proviso. Although adamantly opposed to the expansion of slavery, he did not believe the proviso necessary to prevent that from happening. Mexican law, he argued, already prohibited slavery, and he did not see how the institution could be permitted to exist in any territory acquired from Mexico. By this point, Adams's contributions to congressional debates were becoming increasingly less frequent. Now nearing his eightieth birthday, the years were finally beginning to take their toll. He continued to assume his seat on the House floor every day the chamber was in session, but he was not nearly as active as he had once been. His powers fading and the end fast approaching, he was content to step back and let younger colleagues do the heavy lifting in the ongoing struggle against slavery. Even so, his influence could still be felt. When, in April 1847, Massachusetts Conscience Whigs pushed a strongly worded set of resolutions on the Mexican War through the state legislature, the language they employed could have been lifted verbatim from public letters Adams had written and speeches he had delivered years earlier. After stating that "attention is directed anew to the wrong and enormity of slavery, and to the tyranny and usurpations of the 'slave power,'" the authors declared: "We are impressed with the unalterable conviction, that a regard for the fame of our country, for the principles of morals, and for that righteousness that exalteth a nation, sanctions and requires all constitutional efforts for the destruction of the unjust influence of the slave power, and for the abolition of slavery within the limits of the United States."[55]

Calhoun could not view the Wilmot Proviso with the same equanimity that Adams displayed. Like Van Buren, the South Carolinian saw that war with Mexico might well upend the second party system by widening divisions between North and South. Should this happen, he initially believed, there would be "one consolation; it will be much easier to bring the two parties in the South to act together, than the two in the North." The Northern response to the proviso forced him to reassess its likely consequences. In Congress, many Northern Democrats who had previously endorsed Texas annexation joined their Whig counterparts in voting for Wilmot's amendment. Outside Congress, the general public exhibited even greater enthusiasm for the proviso. As one Cincinnati correspondent told Calhoun, support for the measure was much stronger than he had anticipated, "though thee is aware, I have long insisted that the principles of the Abolitionists were making more progress than was suspected, and were rapidly approaching to ascendancy in the free States." If that was the case in southern Ohio, it was likely even more so elsewhere in the North. Needless to say, this was not what Calhoun wanted to hear, and as he came to recognize that both Northern parties "seem resolved, that we shall be excluded from whatever territory may be acquired," he knew something needed to be done to prevent the Mexican War from becoming a conflict in which Southern soldiers did the fighting and dying and free state settlers established control of the governments formed in conquered territory.[56]

Calhoun adopted a two-pronged strategy in responding to the challenge. One centered on an objective that had been a central aim of his politics since the nullification crisis. In a February 1847 Senate speech directed primarily at Southern colleagues, he renewed his campaign to promote regional unity. Speaking as a Southerner, cotton planter, and owner of slaves, who considered himself "none the worse for being a slaveholder," the South Carolinian admonished members of his intended audience to resist any imposition that sacrificed the equality of the people they represented. The South was already a minority in the House and the Electoral College, he told them, and this latest attack on the region promised a marked reduction in whatever power it still retained in national affairs. Should Northern political leaders succeed in compelling acceptance of the Wilmot Proviso, it would not only enable them to establish control of both houses of Congress, the courts, and the departments and agencies of the federal government; it would also—by shattering the influence of what he called "the conservative portion" of the sectional balance of power—open the way to "political revolution, anarchy, civil war, and wide-spread disaster." At the conclusion of his speech, Calhoun introduced a set of resolutions declaring that Congress had no authority to pass any measure depriving a state of its "full and equal right in any territory of the United States, acquired, or to be acquired" for doing so would violate "a fundamental principle of our political creed, that a people in forming a constitution have the unconditional right to form and adopt the Government which they may think best calculated to secure their liberty, property, and happiness."[57]

The second prong consisted of an effort to rally opposition to the war and the acquisition of new territory. Here Calhoun combined a defense of regional interests with a concern for the national interest. His objections to the conflict were, in part a product of the hard-won knowledge of someone who as a young congressman had helped take the nation to war without asking any serious questions about what the successful prosecution of a war required. "Our people," he told his son-in-law, "are like a young man of 18, full of health & vigour & disposed for adventure of any discription, but without wisdom or experience to guide him, and I fear we shall share the fate" that "usually befal such." Early advances notwithstanding, he contended, further offensive operations would, in addition to raising troublesome questions about how to pay for them, soon encounter increasingly formidable obstacles as US forces moved more deeply into Mexican territory. Although Calhoun overestimated Mexican defensive capabilities, there is reason to believe that US successes owed more to good luck than to good planning. During the previous decade and a half, constant clashes with Native Americans had decimated large areas of northern Mexico, markedly impairing the region's ability to withstand a foreign invasion. Had this not occurred, historian Brian DeLay has persuasively argued, US military units would almost certainly have faced considerably greater resistance than they did. Calhoun did not know this, but neither did Polk or any of his senior advisors.[58]

More worrisome were the ways in which war furthered governmental consolidation. Checking this inexorable tendency and the baneful practices to which it gave rise needed to be the first priority of all true states' rights advocates. Calhoun's commitment to the task never wavered, and he expected those who shared his views to recognize that war, being the greatest of all public works projects, could not help but increase the size and power of the national government. Should the Mexican conflict continue, he observed at its outset, deepening US involvement would "disclose our financial weakness; involve us in a heavy debt; give a strong central tendency to our system, prevent reform, & greatly strengthen the spoils principle," in the process shattering all hope of placing federal fiscal policy on a sound foundation of economy and retrenchment. The war's aftermath could produce even greater problems. If the Polk administration embraced calls to annex all of Mexico, he warned, the precedent "would elevate the power of the President above that of the other departments and the Constitution itself, and end, almost necessarily in establishing despotic authority in that branch of the Government." As this nightmarish scenario played out and an omnipotent imperial government rendered the states powerless, the South would find it nearly impossible to maintain an effective defense of its interests. Being a minority region, it was particularly ill prepared to deal with the threats posed by a "consolidated national government." It certainly could not rely on the workings of a political system based on the principle of the numerical majority, Calhoun declared: "I would rather trust a sovereign, rather an aristocracy—any form of government, than that."[59]

The prospect of large territorial acquisitions in Mexico also gave Calhoun an opportunity to voice his views on race and government. Drawing on racist ethnographic beliefs shared by many white Americans of the period, the South Carolinian placed Anglo-Saxons well above other peoples in the great chain of being. That they merited such distinction could best be seen in their genius for self-government, which clearly set them apart from lesser folk. Throughout human history, he claimed, "there is no instance, whatever, of any civilized colored race, being found equal to the establishment and maintenance of free Government, although by far the largest of the human family is composed of them." It would therefore be as politically disruptive as it was socially deleterious to attempt to incorporate a country with Mexico's large indigenous population. Doing so would, in addition to burdening the nation with the hopeless task of forming a stable government there, force people of a superior race to associate "as equals, companions, and fellow-citizens" with what he considered the mixed races of a lesser civilization. "Ours is the Government of the white man," Calhoun was saying, and those who belonged to that select group would do well to keep it so.[60]

As it turned out, Calhoun's worst fears never came to pass. Polk briefly considered annexing all of Mexico but for his own reasons decided that pursuing the policy would be more trouble than it was worth. He had always been most interested in obtaining California and New Mexico, and the Treaty of Guadalupe Hidalgo added them to the national domain. He also felt confident that their acquisition would cause few political problems. The slavery question "would probably never be a practical one" in the two territories, he confided to his diary, because there was little likelihood that the institution would take root in either of them. That Polk could make such an observation betrayed an astonishing lack of imagination and foresight. A veteran political tactician and former speaker of the house, the Tennessean possessed impressive legislative skills but limited political vision. Calhoun could not have been more different. Pushing bills through Congress was never his strong suit, but as a proslavery ideologue and staunch defender of Southern rights, he thought in strategic terms and was always looking to the future. "Mexico is to us the forbidden fruit," he said in a February 1847 speech, and "the penalty of eating it would be to subject our institutions to political death." He soon learned how well taken his forebodings were. Although California and New Mexico fell within a defensive line that he had proposed in the hope of curbing demands for more extensive acquisitions, debate over the status of slavery in the two territories would convulse the nation during the next several years, widening fissures within both major parties and prompting calls for disunion from the least tractable of Southern fire-eaters.[61]

The immediate problem confronting party leaders was the Wilmot Proviso. They knew that the longer Congress debated whether to bar slavery from the Mexican Cession, the greater the likelihood that their organizations would split along sectional lines. Several proposals emerged to evade the dilemma. One was to extend the Missouri Compromise line to the Pacific. Although Calhoun loathed the compromise because he considered it "highly injurious to the South," he initially backed an extension resolution for the sake of intersectional peace.

But the initiative went nowhere. As would happen time and again in succeeding years, a clear majority of Congress rejected the proposal. Calhoun afterward lost interest as well, mainly because he believed adoption of an extension bill would do nothing to curb Northern assaults on Southern rights. Even if such a measure halted debate over the proviso, he observed during an August 1848 discussion of the question, it could "not stop abolitionism, or prevent it from accomplishing its end."[62]

A second stratagem for getting around the Wilmot Proviso centered on what came to be known as the doctrine of popular sovereignty: empowering settlers in the territories to determine whether a given locale would permit or ban slavery. Calhoun liked this policy even less than he did proposals to extend the Missouri Compromise line to the Pacific. When Daniel Dickinson first suggested the approach, some Southern Democrats supported the New York senator's initiative as a politically expedient way of preserving party unity. Calhoun was not among them. Instead, he condemned the proposal as a treacherous ruse designed to induce Southern acceptance of territories where slaveholders would never comprise a majority of the population. He did not go quite as far as Waddy Thompson, who said "he would consent to be gibbeted, or, if dead, that his bones be dug up and made manure of, if ever a slaveholding State were formed out of any portion of" the Mexican Cession. But he certainly shared the sentiment. Migrating slaveowners could find ways of adapting to unfamiliar climatic and soil conditions, but they could never overcome the demographic advantage of the free states, where annual population growth—fueled by large and growing increases in foreign immigration—so greatly surpassed that of the South. That being the case, letting settlers decide the question of slavery in the territories would only furnish another illustration of how the principle of the numerical majority discriminated against Southern interests. When Lewis Cass made popular sovereignty the centerpiece of his 1848 presidential campaign, Calhoun urged anyone who cared about preserving slavery to reject the Michigan Democrat's candidacy. A vote for Cass, he wrote, "would surrender every thing, as far as the territories are concerned."[63]

Calhoun had reason to be concerned about the doctrine of popular sovereignty. A decade later, its leading proponent, Stephen A. Douglas, would express views that appeared to confirm all the Carolinian's apprehensions. In what came to be known as his Freeport Doctrine, the Illinois senator declared that slavery could exist only where police regulations protected slave property; and because such regulations could only be established by local legislative bodies, "if the people are opposed to slavery, they will elect representatives to that body who will by unfriendly legislation prevent the introduction of it in their midst." Calhoun, drawing on his belief in the anti-majoritarian principle of the concurrent majority, saw this coming in his 1848 critique of popular sovereignty.

Northern Democrats, he argued, sought to secure Southern votes by letting the people—not Congress—decide questions concerning slave expansionism, while assuring their own constituents that slavery would never take hold in the West. As growing numbers of Southerners came to share this point of view during the 1850s, their mounting fury would find release at the 1860 Democratic presidential convention, where opposition to Douglas prompted the walkout of most Southern delegates and their nomination of an alternative regional candidate.[64]

By the late 1840s, Calhoun had lost what little faith he had ever had in the second party system. Some of his objections reflected long-standing grievances that all critics of party have voiced at one time or another. "The only material difference between the two parties," he told a Georgia correspondent, "is, that the democratick look more exclusively to plundering through the finances & the treasury, while the Whigs look more to plundering by whole sale, through partial legislation, Banks, Protection and other means of monopoly." However distressing Calhoun found this state of affairs, he could live with it. What he could not live with was major party indifference to Southern interests during a period of rising intersectional tensions. The Wilmot Proviso had seriously shaken whatever trust he had in the willingness of Northern Democrats to honor their end of the Van Burenite bargain that served as the foundation of North-South cooperation in the second party system. But the problem was much worse than that. As the slavery question became an increasingly important factor in national politics, he declared in a Senate speech on the eve of the 1848 election, leaders of both parties, "North and South," found it advisable "to observe silence and keep out of sight as far as possible, the movements and progress of the Abolitionists and the countenance and support they received from their respective parties in the North." To the extent that these political bosses condemned antislavery provocations, they did so in as "feeble a tone as possible," while thrusting "whatever blame they attach to [them], on the opposite party, and to excuse their own." The most disturbing consequence of all this was that Southern political leaders—the people most responsible for guaranteeing the safety of regional institutions—had "entered into a pitiful contest" to show that their respective presidential candidate was "less hostile to us, than are their opponents, as if nothing was left us, but to choose the least hostile for our protector." "Can," he asked, "degradation go further?" Calhoun did not believe so. The developing crisis, he observed in a letter written a week after delivering the above remarks, had reached a juncture where "we must make up our mind, to give up our slaves, or give up all political connection & association with either of the existing parties at the North, and rely on ourselves for protection."[65]

Calhoun expected nothing good to come from the 1848 presidential contest. Not only did the Democratic nominee base his candidacy on a popular sovereignty plank that the South Carolinian considered a ploy to dupe Southerners into accepting free state control of the Mexican Cession, the election also witnessed the formation of the Free Soil Party, a northern-based political organization whose primary aim was to prevent the expansion of slavery and whose membership included a substantial number of New York Van Burenites. Another source of Free Soil strength was Massachusetts, where Conscience Whigs had finally parted ways with party regulars. Although Adams had died some months earlier, his son Charles Francis—who was then going through the most radical phase of a long political career that in later years would take a marked turn to the right—had stepped in to fill his place. The elder Adams had long been looking for ways to push Massachusetts Whiggery beyond the free labor protectionism that stood at the center of a popular conservatism that enabled the party to appeal to a broad range of Bay voters. As editor of the *Boston Daily Whig,* the state's most prominent exponent of Conscience Whig views, Charles Francis took up the challenge with a bluntness that sometimes made his notoriously plainspoken father look like a model of discretion. In a series of articles attacking Abbott Lawrence, he told the wool manufacturer that he had personally "heard several of the principal politicians of this State affirm, that after all, the Tariff was the only question the people would listen to, and that it was essential to dwell upon." He did not believe that, and his main quarrel with people such as Lawrence was "that you have all along been thinking more of sheep and cotton than of Man." John Quincy fully approved of these and other interventions on the part of Charles Francis, who in turn acknowledged his father's influence. "It has been the fate of three generations of our race to stand as guardians of Liberty in this commonwealth against the corrupting principles of a moneyed combination," he wrote in his dairy after John Quincy's death. And "[s]o long as I live, there shall be another Adams in this commonwealth who will denounce every bargain that shall trade away the honor of his country."[66]

Charles Francis's discontent both reflected and contributed to a growing belief among antislavery Whigs that a political system comprised of two evenly matched parties divided largely over economic issues did little more than provide cover for the insidious machinations of proslavery politicians. The younger Adams clearly thought he saw that happening in Massachusetts, and by late 1847 he had concluded that "nothing can be done with the Old Whig party." It was only a matter of waiting for the right moment to chart an independent course, and Whig leaders provided it when they chose a soldier-slaveholder from Louisiana as their 1848 presidential nominee. In August of that year, delegates to the convention of the newly established Free Soil Party selected Adams as their vice-presidential candidate on a ticket headed by none other than Martin Van Buren, one of the founding fathers of the second party system. In part recognition of Charles Francis's work on behalf of antislavery fusion, the nomination was also a tribute to his father by antislavery Whigs who, in the words of one observer, had arrived at the convention "breathing the spirit of the departed John Quincy Adams." Not unexpectedly, the party did not do particularly well in the election, capturing about fourteen percent of the popular vote in the North and finishing second ahead of Lewis Cass in only three states: Massachusetts, New York, and Vermont. None of this changed how Adams felt. In a postelection commentary that combined regional chauvinism with moral fervor in language that his father surely would have appreciated, he told fellow New Englander John Gorham Palfrey that, for more than three centuries, America's "only pure moral influences" for "regulat[ing] the passions of man" had "come from the land of the Puritans." And so it remained. As long as "some of the race yielded to the temptations of the harlot," their conduct would inspire people of principle to stand "with those who prefer to remain true."[67]

The political activists who gathered at Buffalo, New York, in the summer of 1848 to form the Free Soil Party did more than channel the spirit of John Quincy Adams. They also made one of his most deeply held convictions the centerpiece of the party's appeal. In an 1842 letter to Joshua Giddings, the Ohio antislavery politician Salmon P. Chase summarized the main elements of that appeal: "The principle must be established & acquiesced in that the government is a nonslaveholding government—that the nation is a nonslaveholding nation—that slavery is a creature of state law—local—not to be extended or favored, but to be confined within the states which admit and sanction it." What Chase had in mind was adoption of a freedom national strategy that denied slavery any legal existence outside states where it already existed.

Implementation of the strategy would, in addition to barring slavery in the territories, entail the imposition of other constraints such as abolishing the institution in the nation's capital, prohibiting the employment of slave labor at military installations or other government facilities, and preventing federal intervention on behalf of slaveholders in cases where slave rebels or British authorities seized ships transporting slaves from one locale to another on the high seas. Wherever slavery raised its head, the government would be there to whack it back into place. Giddings loved the idea, later observing that it suggested what he called "*the germ of a party*" with the potential to become a formidable force in national politics. Delegates to the Free Soil convention acted on the suggestion when, following "the example of our fathers in the days of the first Declaration of Independence," they resolved to place themselves "upon the national platform of freedom, in opposition to the sectional platform of slavery." In doing so, they declared it "the duty of the federal government to relieve itself from all responsibility for the existence or continuance of slavery wherever the government possesses constitutional power to legislate on that subject, and is thus responsible for its existence."[68]

It is no surprise that, given his strong antislavery convictions and close association with John Quincy, Giddings proved so receptive to the freedom national appeal. The Bay congressman had long exhibited the type of thinking that gave rise to the doctrine. Decades earlier during a discussion of the Missouri controversy while he was secretary of state, Calhoun and two other members of Monroe's cabinet insisted that the constitutional provision empowering Congress to "make all needful rules and regulations respecting the territory or other property of the United States" did not extend to slavery. Adams disagreed. He argued that the term "needful" must be interpreted in relation to some principle stated in the Constitution's preamble such as the injunction "to establish justice." That being the case, he asked, "What can be more needful to the establishment of Justice than the interdiction of Slavery where it does not exist[?]" When Secretary of the Treasury Crawford said that territories north of the Missouri Compromise's 36° latitude line could sanction slavery after securing admission to the Union, Adams again dissented. "The Declaration of Independence," he contended, "not only asserts the natural equality of men, and their inalienable right to Liberty, but that only the *just* powers of government are derived from the consent of the governed. A power of one part of the people to make Slaves of the other can never be derived from consent, and is therefore not a just power" but a "wrongful and despotic power." Congress thus had the authority to cast any state seeking to "establish [slavery] de novo" outside "the pale of the Union," stripping it of "all the rights and privileges of that connection."[69]

These were extremely provocative views in 1820, and Adams, who then harbored strong ambitions for higher office, did not go public with them. But he did not abandon them either. This could be seen in his later performance as cocounsel for the defense in the Amistad case—the era's most widely publicized trial of a slave seizure of a ship at sea—where he vigorously upheld another element of the freedom national argument: the contention that the Constitution nowhere recognizes the principle of property in man. It could also be seen in his defense of abolitionists' right of petition. Their memorials had "nothing to do with the institution of slavery in the Southern States," he told his fellow legislators. "What they demanded is, that the Congress of the United States should liberate them from all connection whatever with it. They asked to be relieved from the burden of carrying such laws into effect, which they find to be onerous upon them." That Adams unreservedly supported the Massachusetts legislature's initiative to pass a constitutional amendment repealing the three-fifths clause further demonstrated a readiness to take the freedom national doctrine into areas not yet sanctioned by the nation's founding document.[70]

Some Southern political leaders, hoping to maintain intersectional party unity and dampen talk of secession, chose to dismiss the freedom national appeal as the rantings of a fanatical minority, if they did not ignore it altogether. Calhoun had nothing but contempt for such complacency. Although he saw no major difference between Free Soilers and abolitionists, he considered the former to be "the worst and most dangerous" of the two. Their disavowal of any intention to interfere with slavery where it existed disguised a program capable of rallying the North behind the antislavery cause and leaving "the South more derided, distracted and debased than ever." Believing those who did not take the freedom national strategy seriously lacked the foresight to protect regional interests, he made resistance to the doctrine the focus of what would be his last major initiative to create a unified South. In the January 1849 Address of the Southern Delegates in Congress to their Constituents, the South Carolina senator directed attention to various "measures of an aggressive nature" that had recently been introduced in Congress and Northern legislatures. Should these attacks on Southern rights be allowed to continue unchecked, he warned, they could well "end in emancipation, and that at no distant day." This was so, he explained, in words that could have been taken from the correspondence of Salmon Chase, because not much "would be left to be done after we have been excluded from the Territories, including those to be hereafter acquired; after slavery is abolished in the District and the numerous places dispersed all over the South, where Congress has the exclusive right of legislation, and after the other numerous measures are consummated." Given the enormity of the threat, the time had clearly passed when Southern politicians could subordinate such concerns "not merely to questions of policy, but to the preservation of party ties and ensuring of party success." If people of the South failed to present a bold, united front at this critical moment, Calhoun declared, "the North will not believe that you are in earnest in opposition to their encroachments, and they will continue to follow, one after another, until the work of abolition is finished."[71]

"Poor old dotard," Robert Toombs said of Calhoun's latest attempt to make regional unity the basis of Southern politics, "to suppose he could get a party now on any terms! Hereafter treachery itself will not trust him." Convinced that "the Union of the South was neither possible nor desirable until we were ready to dissolve the Union," the Georgia Whig said as much to Calhoun and predicted that the Southern Address would have little or no effect on what people of the region thought about the current political situation. Toombs spoke much too soon. Large numbers of Southerners—Democrats especially—viewed the address as a call to arms. Even people who had deep reservations about Calhoun recognized that the South Carolina senator could not be ignored. One correspondent told Georgia Democrat Howell Cobb that, while "Calhoun is no favorite with me" and he would not follow him, it was nevertheless necessary to "cooperate with him in resisting [Northern] encroachment." Meanwhile, public meetings throughout the region endorsed the Southern Address, many of them in language similar to that of the Virginia gathering that declared the territorial question transcended party politics and asserted that "all who are not with us are . . . foes to our rights, to our honor, to our peace, to our safety, to our Federal equality, to our Federal Constitution, and to our Federal Union."[72]

Forging a united South was only part of the challenge facing Calhoun. He also felt the need to fashion a constitutional defense of Southern rights that effectively addressed the current crisis. The problem, as he saw it, was that the operation of the numerical majority had enabled one section to achieve political dominance in a nation comprised of two major regions with different institutions and interests. Reliance on the doctrine of state interposition offered little help in meeting the threat; territorial expansion and protectionism were two entirely different matters, and if South Carolina nullified a congressional measure permitting the legislatures of California or New Mexico to bar slavery, it would be of no consequence whatsoever. Something more was required. If Southerners were to maintain their rights, they needed to embrace a slavery national doctrine capable of countering the freedom national appeal that was steadily gaining traction in the North. Calhoun had foreseen as much at least a decade earlier in his 1837 resolutions, which asserted that Congress had no power to pass legislation concerning domestic institutions in the territories. Since then, he had developed a "common property" argument that denied slavery was a local institution, declared the states "joint and common owners" of the territories, and contended that Congress, as the joint agent of the states, had no right to exclude slaveowners or their property from these lands. All this and more came together in a Senate speech on March 4, 1850, delivered a month before his death. In it, Calhoun elaborated on the many Northern encroachments that made adoption of a slavery national standard necessary. To avoid disunion, he warned, the North must accord the South equal rights in the territories, suppress antislavery agitation, and support passage of a constitutional amendment that would "restore to the South in substance the power she possessed of protecting herself, before the equilibrium between the sections was destroyed by the actions of this Government." Enforcement of these prescriptions would violate basic democratic norms, but that was the whole point of the slavery national doctrine and the principle of the concurrent majority on which it rested. If the South acceded to the rules of democratic majoritarianism, Calhoun repeatedly insisted, the region could not hope to defend its interests in a polity where it formed an irreversible minority.[73]

It was a fitting close to a long and often contentious political career. For Calhoun and Adams, the emergence of the freedom national-slavery national division marked the culmination of a clash of ideas and values that had begun nearly two decades earlier. The role they played in its formation was their most significant contribution to the developing intersectional crisis and the accompanying disintegration of the second party system. Although the Compromise of 1850 ended the battle over slavery in the Mexican Cession, it did not relieve the underlying tensions that had made the controversy so acrimonious. Because neither North nor South consented to the terms that the other desired, historian David Potter has written, "there really was no compromise—a truce perhaps, an armistice, certainly a settlement, but not a true compromise." Disputes over slavery and its expansion would continue to arise, and each time one did recourse to the freedom national and slavery national doctrines would make the question at hand less negotiable and remove another of the wobbly props holding up a party system whose existence depended on intersectional cooperation. The system's total collapse in 1860 ushered in a civil war that both Adams and Calhoun had wished to avoid but had long predicted.[74]

CONCLUSION

It is fair to say that few deaths had a greater impact on a single state than Calhoun's passing in the spring of 1850 did on South Carolina. For more than two decades, he had been the dominant figure in Palmetto politics. Despite much grumbling and occasional challenges to his position on a given issue, no one had mounted a serious initiative to remove him from the throne. If he did not get his way all the time, he got it often enough to leave little doubt as to who set the state's political agenda. Not everyone believed this had been a good thing. "It was the unfortunate effect of Mr. Calhoun's influence here, to dwarf all the men about him," William Gilmore Simms observed. "As the great tree of the forest makes shrubs of all within its shadows, so has his ascendency deprived of their proper growth & stature those who might have succeeded him on his departure." During his lifetime, Alfred Huger wrote, Carolinians had become much too accustomed to following orders. Worse, Francis Lieber added, Calhoun's efforts to suppress "any issue whatever that might lead to the formation of two opposing bodies in South Carolina" had given rise to an ideological conformity that limited people's ability to assess and confront threatening developments. On all matters of any significance, they fell back on the maxim, "I go with my State," regardless of the consequences. Where people of the North did "their own thinking," Mary Chesnut lamented in the closing months of the Civil War, "we let one man do ours—Mr. Calhoun. We let things drift, and now we are in this snarl." Although such observations overstated Calhoun's actual influence, they accurately reflected his larger-than-life image in the eyes of most South Carolinians. There was nothing feigned about the shock and grief so many displayed upon hearing of his death.[1]

The reaction to Adams's 1848 passing was different. He had never been a powerful presence in Bay politics, but his accomplishments outside Massachusetts more than compensated. As great men were then defined—and still are—Adams checked all the boxes: US senator, minister to major European countries, secretary of state, president of the United States, and nine-term member of the House of Representatives. This extraordinary public career, which had begun more than a half-century earlier during the administration of George Washington, gave eulogists ample scope to expound on his many contributions to the nation's political and social development. There were, to be sure, some discordant notes. Adams's relations with the Bay elite had never been entirely congenial, and Boston financier Thomas Wren Ward, who tired quickly of listening to tributes to Adams's character and religiosity, expressed dismay that anyone could bestow such accolades on "a man who had not a particle of the spirit of Jesus Christ and whose life was a war against friends and foes, who had no personal friends and the worst temper in the world, and great want of tact and judgment." Perhaps the most illuminating of the Adams testimonials came from Theodore Parker. An outspoken Unitarian minister and abolitionist who had as little use for platitudinous equivocation as Adams did, Parker attempted a careful evaluation of the ex-president's strengths and shortcomings, describing his various departures from principle and noting that he often exhibited "a certain vindictiveness of spirit" toward adversaries, invective having been "his masterpiece of oratic skill"—as it was with Parker himself. Such deficiencies notwithstanding, the Boston clergyman believed Adams deserved the thankful praise of all good citizens: "He loved his dollars as most men—but he loved justice more; honor more; freedom more; the Unalienable Rights of man far more."[2]

By the time Adams and Calhoun died, most people who knew anything about them knew them best as combatants in an increasingly bitter intersectional struggle over slavery. Where Calhoun had by his final days become the living embodiment of Southern rights and the positive good defense of slavery, Adams had, in Parker's words, seen "from afar the plots of Southern politicians . . . for narrowing the area of freedom" and done more than anyone to expose them. It was thus no surprise that some observers hoped their departure from the political scene might make intersectional compromise more attainable. "I regard his death as fortunate for the country & his own fame," the Upcountry unionist Benjamin Perry wrote of Calhoun's passing. "The Slavery question will now be settled. He would have been an obstacle in the way." Francis Lieber, then a professor of history and political economy at South Carolina College, also believed "Calhoun's death will be healing rather than otherwise." The South was gradually losing its dominant place in national affairs, he observed, "and such changes never take place without struggle"; having one less extremist in the debate might reduce the "pangs and heartburning" that invariably accompany major shifts in power. In his eulogy for Adams, Parker imagined major political figures of diverse outlook drawing similar consolation from the New Englander's death. "Strange men will meet with mutual solace at his tomb," he caustically remarked, "wondering that their common foe is dead, and they are met! The Herods and Pilates of contending parties may be friends above his grave, and clasping hands may fancy that their union is safer than before."[3]

They would all be disappointed, Parker hastily added, for "there will be a day after to-day." History did not stand still, and the forces unleashed by the struggle over slavery could not be contained by the death of any single individual, regardless of how prominent that person may have been. In Calhoun's case, it might even have made a bad situation worse. That, at least, was the opinion of one Palmetto politician. James Hammond knew Calhoun as well as any of his political associates. If sometimes too quick to accuse the senator of sacrificing principle to ambition, he had a good understanding of how the state's senior statesman operated. Better than most, he recognized that a sense of caution often tempered Calhoun's most aggressive initiatives; what he said and the tone he adopted in saying it did not necessarily indicate how far he was willing to push a given policy pronouncement. The effect of all this, Hammond believed, could be seen in the influence Calhoun had on South Carolina politics: "He kept her in check. He held up her high pretensions. He put his foot upon her evil passions and restrained her dangerous tendencies." With his passing, Hammond observed, a "flood of passion, pretension, folly, and corruption has broke lo[o]se from its barriers and pours in on all sides, sweeping every thing before it."[4]

However arguable this last assertion, Hammond's observations raise an interesting question: How would Calhoun have responded to the secession crisis of 1860? We know that he had a deeply pessimistic view of the future. "The Union is doomed to dissolution," he told Virginia Senator James M. Mason during his final illness, "there is no mistaking the signs." Even were the current controversy over the status of slavery in the Mexican Cession satisfactorily resolved, he believed, "it would not avert, or materially delay, the catastrophe." Northern efforts to obstruct enforcement of the Fugitive Slave Act of 1850, the formation of a sectional party committed to halting the spread of slavery in the wake of the Kansas-Nebraska Act, Northern unwillingness to accept the Supreme Court's decision in the Dred Scott case, and the election of a Republican president in 1860—these and related developments of the coming years would, in addition to stoking Calhoun's anger, have removed any lingering doubts he had about the possibility of keeping the Union intact. But what would he have done when the decision concerning secession finally arrived? Would he have joined Robert Barnwell Rhett and other South Carolina fire-eaters in demanding immediate withdrawal following Lincoln's triumph? Or would he have adopted a more deliberate approach and urged Palmetto leaders to consult with other Southern states before taking action?[5]

Although these questions cannot be directly addressed, there are ways of teasing out suggestive answers to them. One is by looking at the response of notable southern leaders who shared Calhoun's perspective on the sectional crisis. Jefferson Davis had a greater regard for the Democratic party than the South

Carolinian ever did, but in most other respects his actions and beliefs reflected a strong Calhounite influence. Not only did he support Calhoun for president in 1844 and sign the Southern Address five years later, he also demonstrated an unwavering commitment to states' rights constitutionalism and insisted that the South could not protect its interests if it settled for anything less than equal status within the Union. In February 1860, he submitted a set of Senate resolutions on the territorial issue that one historian has characterized as "Calhoun brought up to date." Yet Davis did not embrace immediate secession following Lincoln's election. Concerned that the South respond in unison, he saw no reason to act precipitately and adopt a course that foreclosed all hope of compromise. He thus returned to the Senate to see if some settlement could be arranged that would ensure the protection of Southern rights under the new regime. It is likely that, however reluctantly, Calhoun would have followed a similar course, and for many of the same reasons that Davis did. A West Point graduate, combat veteran of the Mexican War, and former secretary of war, the Mississippian possessed Calhoun's capacity for strategic thought and knew that the South could never match the human, material, and financial resources that the North could bring to bear in an extended conflict. Enthusiasm alone was not enough when pitted against the manufacturing might of a rising industrial power whose population was expanding by leaps and bounds.[6]

South Carolina's political leaders felt none of this hesitancy. They did, however, continue to hold Calhoun's constitutionalism in high regard. In December 1860, a state convention passed a secession ordinance and issued a Declaration of Causes Which Induced the Secession of South Carolina. In making their case for disunion, the latter document's authors cited the justification for abandoning allegiance to an oppressive government presented in the Declaration of Independence and the provision in the Articles of Confederation that proclaimed, "each State retains its sovereignty, freedom and independence, and every power, jurisdiction and right" not "expressly delegated to the United States in Congress assembled." The Constitution, they conceded, placed certain restraints on the states, but it did not bar secession because it was based on the "law of compact" that Calhoun had made the centerpiece of his constitutional reasoning. This "law," they argued, establishes mutual obligations between contracting parties; and the failure of one of those parties to uphold its end of the agreement cancels out "the obligation of the other," leaving it to its "own judgment to determine the fact of failure, with all its consequences." In terms of specific grievances, the Declaration had little to say about the territorial question. Instead, its authors focused on the unwillingness of free states to assist slaveholders seeking the rendition of fugitives, while condoning the spread of abolition societies committed to undermining the peace and taking away "the property of the citizens of other States." The election of a president who represented a sectional party intent on restricting Southern rights was the last straw. Once Lincoln took office, they asserted, the slaveholding states will have lost whatever claim they had to equality within the Union, and, without "the power of self-government, or self-protection," would be at the mercy of a chief executive who had declared the nation "cannot endure permanently, half-slave, half-free." These contentions, much more so than any reservations he might have had about the wisdom of secession, would be Calhoun's final testament.[7]

Adams's views on the nation's founding document never exhibited the theoretical sophistication of Calhoun's constitutional thought, but he did have important things to say. Where the South Carolinian's constitutionalism contributed to the coming of the Civil War, Adams's arguments would be used by antislavery politicians to broaden the conflict's purpose. The New Englander had never been happy about the founders' compromise over slavery, and his search for ways to evade its constraints led him to the war powers clauses in Article I, Section 8 of the Constitution. He readily acknowledged that as long as slaveholders could maintain their peculiar institution without assistance from other parts of the Union, the national government had no authority to interfere with slavery where it existed. But should the slave states become a theater of war and find themselves in need of such aid, he contended, there would be no question about the right of Congress "to interfere with the institutions of the South, inasmuch as the very fact of the people of a free portion of the Union, marching to the support of the masters would be an interference with those institutions." Once the "laws of war" were invoked, he added, all of a nation's "laws and municipal institutions [are] swept by the board, and martial law takes the place of them." Although none of this had any practical meaning during the Bay congressman's lifetime, the Civil War changed everything. The Confederate bombardment of Fort Sumter had barely ceased before Charles Sumner was presenting Adams's arguments to President Lincoln; within Congress, Republican legislators employed them to support passage of laws sanctioning the confiscation of slaves in rebel areas. In time, these and subsequent initiatives such as Lincoln's Emancipation Proclamation would turn a war to preserve the union into a struggle to abolish slavery.[8]

Of the many differences between Adams and Calhoun, one of the more interesting concerned their view of the future. Although always looking for some positive development, the South Carolinian was much too perceptive not to know that he lived in a world where slavery was in retreat everywhere. His fears about mounting threats to Southern rights and interests drove him to devote substantial time and energy to devising constitutional defenses and promoting the formation of regional organizations designed to protect the South's embattled peculiar institution. Strange to say, given his often-gloomy disposition, Adams was generally more optimistic. Despite the numerous comments on slave power impositions that darkened the pages of his diary, he never stopped believing that history was on the side of freedom; he could see it in events such as the abolition of slavery in Britain's colonies. Providence, too, was on the side of emancipation. His Puritan forebears had expected periodic visitations of God's anger on a sinful people, and Adams never doubted that slavery was a sin. As a frustrated poet who had composed large quantities of fair-to-middling verse during his long life, he would have greeted the sentiments expressed in Julia Ward Howe's "Battle Hymn of the Republic" with appreciative envy:

> Mine eyes have seen the glory of the coming of the Lord:
> He is trampling out the vintage where the grapes of wrath are stored;
> He hath loosed the fateful lightning of His terrible swift sword:
> His truth is marching on.

"We know the day of your redemption must come," Adams told an 1843 gathering of African Americans in Pittsburgh. "The time and manner of its coming we know not: It may come in peace, or it may come in blood; but *whether in peace or in blood*, LET IT COME." Appalled as he would have been by the terrible slaughter taking place on Civil War battlefields, the Bay congressman would have been perfectly happy to let Howe have the last word on the conflict's meaning:

> In the beauty of the lilies Christ was born across the sea,
> With a glory in His bosom that transfigures you and me:
> As He died to make men holy, let us die to make men free,
> While God is marching on.[9]

Notes

Abbreviations

Calhoun Papers	Robert L. Meriwether, et al., eds., *The Papers of John C. Calhoun,* 28 vols. Columbia: University of South Carolina Press, 1959–2003.
JCC	John C. Calhoun
JQA	John Quincy Adams
JQA Diary	The Diaries of John Quincy Adams: A Digital Collection, Massachusetts Historical Society, Boston, MA.
MHS	Massachusetts Historical Society, Boston, MA
Writings of JQA	Worthington Chauncey Ford, ed. *Writings of John Quincy Adams.* New York: Macmillan, 1913–1917.

Introduction

1. James Oakes, *Freedom National: The Destruction of Slavery in the United States, 1861–1865* (New York: W. W. Norton, 2013), 41.

2. James Oakes, *The Crooked Path to Abolition: Abraham Lincoln and the Antislavery Constitution* (New York: W. W. Norton, 2021).

3. JQA Diary, 43: January 2, 1843.

Chapter 1: Background

1. Fred Kaplan, *John Quincy Adams: American Visionary* (New York: HarperCollins, 2014), 6–64, quotation on p. 61.

2. John Niven, *John C. Calhoun and the Price of Union* (Baton Rouge: Louisiana State University Press, 1988), 6–25.

3. JQA, *The New England Confederacy of MDCXLIII: A Discourse Delivered before the Massachusetts Historical Society, at Boston, on the 25th of May, 1843, in Celebration of the Second Centennial Anniversary of That Event* (Boston: Charles C. Little & James Brown, 1843), 6.

4. Niven, *Calhoun,* 10, 14; Margaret L. Coit, *John C. Calhoun: American Portrait* (1950; repr. Columbia: University of South Carolina Press, 1991), 11–12, 16.

5. Quotation in Charles M. Wiltse, *John C. Calhoun: Nationalist, 1782–1828* (Indianapolis: Bobbs-Merrill, 1944), 105; Coit, *Calhoun,* 2–6; William M. Meigs, *The Life of John Caldwell Calhoun,* 2 vols. (New York: Neale Publishing, 1917), 1:45–47.

6. Abigail Adams to JQA, July 21, 1786; Abigail Adams 2d to JQA, May 3, 1782, in *Adams Family Correspondence,* ed. L. H. Butterfield et al., 13 vols. (Cambridge, MA: Harvard University Press, 1963–), 7:276, 4:320.

7. John Adams to JQA, December 14, 1781, May 14, 1783; Abigail Adams to JQA, March 2, 1780; JQA to Thomas Boylston Adams, May 3, 1788, in *Adams Family Correspondence,* ed. Butterfield et al., 4:263, 5:160, 3:293, 8:257–58.

8. Abigail Adams to JQA, January 21, 1781, December 26, 1783, November 20, 1783, in *Adams Family Correspondence,* ed. Butterfield et al., 4:66, 5:284, 274.

9. Abigail Adams to JQA, March 20, 1780, January 21, 1781; John Adams to JQA, February 12, 1781, in *Adams Family Correspondence,* ed. Butterfield et al., 3:311, 4:68, 80; *Diary of John Quincy Adams, 1779–1788,* ed. Robert J. Taylor et al., 2 vols. (Cambridge, MA: Harvard University Press, 1981), 1:368; JQA Diary, 28:August 2, 1812; final quotation in Lynn H. Parsons, "The 'Splendid Pageant': Observations on the Death of John Quincy Adams," *New England Quarterly* 53 (December 1980): 473.

10. JQA to Thomas Boylston Adams, July 2, 1786, in *Adams Family Correspondence,* ed. Butterfield et al., 7:230–31; Salmon P. Chase to Thomas Sparhawk, January 2, 1828, in *The Salmon P. Chase Papers,* ed. John Niven, 5 vols. (Kent, OH: Kent State University Press, 1993–1998), 2:21; Memorandum by Francis Wharton, February 18, 20, 1845, in *Calhoun Papers,* 21:323; third quotation in William J. Plumer Jr., to William Plumer, January 1, 1821, in *The Missouri Compromises and Presidential Politics, 1820–1825: From the Letters of William Plumer, Junior,* ed. Everett Somerville Brown (St. Louis: Missouri Historical Society, 1926), 64; JQA to Louisa Catherine Adams, August 11, 1821, in *Writings of JQA,* 7:170–71.

11. First quotation in Joshua R. Giddings, *History of the Rebellion: Its Authors and Causes* (New York: Follett, Foster, 1864), 167 note; [South Carolina General Assembly], *The Death and Funeral Ceremonies of John Caldwell Calhoun, Containing the Speeches, Reports and Other Documents Connected Therewith, the Oration of the Honorable R. B. Rhett, before the Legislature, &c.* (Columbia: A. S. Johnston, 1850), 167; William C. Preston, *The Reminiscences of William C. Preston,* ed. Minnie Clare Yarborough (Chapel Hill: University of North Carolina Press, 1933), 7–8; JQA Diary, 30:January 6, 1818; Salmon P. Chase journal, April 10, 1830, in *Chase Papers,* ed. Niven, 1:49; James H. Hammond, *Letters and Speeches of the Hon. James H. Hammond, of South Carolina* (New York: John F. Trow, Printers, 1866), 295.

12. Italics in the original. Josiah Quincy, *Figures of the Past: From the Leaves of Old Journals* (Boston: Roberts Brothers, 1883), 263–64; Rachel Shelden, *Washington Brotherhood: Politics, Social Life, and the Coming of the Civil War* (Chapel Hill: University of North Carolina Press, 2013), 34; William J. Grayson, *Witness to Sorrow: The Antebellum Autobiography of William J. Grayson,* ed. Richard J. Calhoun (Columbia: University of South Carolina Press, 1990), 91, 143, quotation on p. 91; Thomas Sergeant Perry, *The Life and Letters of Francis Lieber* (Boston: James R. Osgood, 1882), 123; Dixon H. Lewis to R. K. Crallé, March 20, 1840, in "Calhoun as Seen by His Political Friends: Letters of Duff Green, Dixon H. Lewis and Richard K. Crallé during the Period from 1831 to 1848," ed. Francis W. Moore, *Publications of the Southern Historical Association,* 7 (September 1903): 355.

13. JQA to John D. Heath, January 7, 1822, in *Writings of JQA,* 7:193.

14. John Adams to JQA, October 23, 1790, in *Adams Family Correspondence,* ed. Butterfield et al., 9:139; JQA Diary, 31: March 4, 1820, February 25, 1821.

15. William Earl Weeks, *John Quincy Adams and American Global Empire* (Lexington: University Press of Kentucky). 106–17, 139–46, quotation on p. 117.

16. JQA Diary, 34: May 24, 1824; William J. Cooper, *The Lost Founding Father: John Quincy Adams and the Transformation of American Politics* (New York: Liveright, 2017), 176–77.

17. Quincy, *Figures from the Past*, 78; John Adams to Benjamin Rush, May 21, 1807, in *John Adams: Writings from the New Nation, 1784–1826*, ed. Gordon S. Wood (New York: Library of America, 2016), 467; JQA Diary, 27:December 4, 1803; excerpt from poem quoted in Charles N. Edel, *Nation Builder: John Quincy Adams and the Grand Strategy of the Republic* (Cambridge, MA: Harvard University Press, 2014), 253.

18. JQA Diary, 37:February 23, 1828; Charles M. Wiltse, "John Quincy Adams and Party System: A Review Article," *Journal of Politics*, 4 (August 1942): 412–13; William Plumer Jr., to William Plumer, January 27, 1821, in *Missouri Compromises and Presidential Politics*, ed. Brown, 64; Norma Lois Peterson, *Littleton Waller Tazewell* (Charlottesville: University Press of Virginia, 1983), 132; Eric H. Walther, *The Fire-Eaters* (Baton Rouge: Louisiana State University Press, 1992), 27; "A Southerner" to JCC, October 1844, in *Calhoun Papers*, 20:128.

19. JCC to Micah Sterling, January 28, 1828; JCC to Charles Tait, May 20, 1820; JCC to Joseph Swift, September 2, 1826; JCC to James Edward Colhoun, February 7, 1844, May 29, 1846; in *Calhoun Papers*, 10:340, 5:132, 10:40, 17:771–72, 18:152.

20. Irving H. Bartlett, *John C. Calhoun: A Biography* (New York: W. W. Norton, 1993), 338; Gerald M. Capers, *John C. Calhoun—Opportunist: A Reappraisal* (Gainesville: University of Florida Press, 1960); Grayson, *Witness to Sorrow*, ed. Calhoun, 129.

21. JCC to Mrs. Floride Calhoun, April 13, 1806, in *Calhoun Papers*, 1:28; Robert Elder, *Calhoun: American Heretic* (New York: Basic Books, 2021), 45, 186–87; Wiltse, *Calhoun: Nationalist*, 268–69.

22. Entries for December 15, 1785, August 8, 1788, in *Diary of JQA*, ed. Taylor et al., 1:373, 2:440; JQA to George Sullivan, January 20, 1821, in *Writings of JQA*, 7:90; Wiltse, *Calhoun: Nationalist*, 268–69.

23. James H. Hammond to JCC, August 18, 1845; JCC to James H. Hammond, August 30, 1845, in *Calhoun Papers*, 22:82, 101; JQA Diary, 42:April 26, 1840, 33:December 13, 1838, April 19, 1837.

24. JQA, *An Oration, Delivered at Plymouth, December 22, 1802: At the Anniversary Commemoration of the First Landing of Our Ancestors, at That Place* (Boston: Printed by Russell & Cutler, 1802), 13–14; JQA, *A Discourse on Education, Delivered at Braintree, Thursday, Oct. 24, 1839* (Boston: Perkins & Marvin, 1840), 25–28, quotation on p. 28. Also see his remarks in *An Address, Delivered at the Request of the Committee for Arrangements for Celebrating the Anniversary of Independence, at the City of Washington on the Fourth of July 1821, upon the Occasion of the Reading of the Declaration of Independence* (Cambridge: Printed at the Univ. Press, by Hilliard & Metcalf, 1821), 6–7; and *The Social Compact, Exemplified in the Constitution of the Commonwealth of Massachusetts* (Providence, RI: Knowles & Vose, 1842), 21–23.

25. Keith Wrightson, *Earthly Necessities: Economic Lives in Early Modern England* (New Haven, CT: Yale University Press, 2000), 128–30, 147–49, 182–90, 198–200; C. G. A. Clay, *Economic Expansion and Social Change: England, 1500–1700*, 2 vols (Cambridge: Cambridge University Press, 1984), 1:49–52, 216–20; Francis J. Bremer, *John Winthrop: America's Forgotten*

Founding Father (New York: Oxford University Press, 2003), 144–46, 157–59. This and succeeding paragraphs draw heavily on an argument developed more fully in an unpublished manuscript, "From Winthrop to Shays: The Politics of Conditional Deference in Massachusetts, 1630–1790."

26. For a particularly good account of the tensions within seventeenth-century Bay society, see Bernard Bailyn, *The Peopling of North America: The Barbarous Years: The Conflict of Civilizations, 1600–1675* (New York: Alfred A. Knopf, 2012), ch. 12.

27. William V. Wells, *The Life and Public Services of Samuel Adams*, 3 vols. (1865; repr. Freeport, NY: Books for Libraries Press, 1969), 3:407.

28. Wallace Notestein, *The English People on the Eve of Colonization, 1603–1660* (New York: Harper & Brothers, 1954), ch. 18; T. H. Breen, *The Character of the Good Ruler: A Study of Puritan Political Ideas in New England* (New Haven, CT: Yale University Press, 1970), 58–86.

29. Robert Zemsky, *Merchants, Farmers, and River Gods: An Essay on Eighteenth-Century American Politics* (Boston: Gambit, 1971), 28–38; Michael Zuckerman, *Peaceable Kingdoms: New England Towns in the Eighteenth Century* (1970; repr. New York: W. W. Norton, 1978), 146–49.

30. Kevin Joseph MacWade, "Worcester County, 1750–1774: A Study of a Provincial Patronage Elite" (PhD diss., Brown University, 1974), ch. 2, 71–80, 84; Hendrik Hartog, "The Public Law of a County Court: Judicial Government in Eighteenth-Century Massachusetts," *American Journal of Legal History*, 20 (October 1976): 282–329; John M. Murrin, "Review Essay," *History and Theory*, 11 (1972): 244, 250–57, 261–62; L. Kinvin Wroth, "Possible Kingdoms: The New England Town from the Perspective of Legal History," *American Journal of Legal History*, 15 (October 1971): 318–30.

31. Ray Raphael, *The First American Revolution: Before Lexington and Concord* (New York: New Press, 2002).

32. Van Beck Hall, *Politics without Parties: Massachusetts, 1780–1791* (Pittsburgh: University of Pittsburgh Press, 1971).

33. Entries for September 7, November 26, 1786, in *Diary of JQA*, ed. Taylor et al., 2:92. 131–32; JQA to John Adams, December 30, 1786, in *Adams Family Correspondence*, ed. Butterfield et al., 7:418.

34. *Writings of JQA*, 1:65–110; JQA to Thomas Boylston Adams, February 1, 1792, in *Adams Family Correspondence*, ed. Butterfield et al. 8:254–55. For Adams's response to Austin's earlier attack on the legal profession, see JQA to Abigail Adams, December 23, 1787, ibid., 8: 214.

35. Paul Goodman, *The Democratic-Republicans of Massachusetts: Politics in a Young Republic* (Cambridge. MA: Harvard University Press, 1964), 75–78; James M. Banner Jr., *To the Hartford Convention: The Federalists and the Origins of Party Politics in Massachusetts, 1789–1815* (New York: Alfred A. Knopf, 1970), 217–18, 225; J. R. Pole, *Political Representation in England and the Origins of the American Republic* (New York: MacMillan, 1966), 545–46.

36. Banner, *To the Hartford Convention*, 221–67; David Hackett Fischer, *The Revolution of American Conservatism: The Federalist Party in the Era of Jeffersonian Democracy* (New York: Harper & Row, 1965), 29–109.

37. William F. Hartford, *Money, Morals, and Politics: Massachusetts in the Age of the Boston Associates* (Boston: Northeastern University Press, 2001), 10–11, first two quotations on p. 10; final quotation in *Writings of JQA*, 3:10.

38. First quotation in *Writings of JQA*, 3:10; second quotation from Fisher Ames to Christopher Gore, February 24, 1803, in *Works of Fisher Ames*, ed. Seth Ames and W. B. Allen, 2 vols. (1859; repr. Indianapolis: Liberty Fund, 1983), 2:1459; Abigail Adams to JQA, September 6, 1785, in *Adams Family Correspondence*, ed. Butterfield et al., 6:345; Hartford, *Money, Morals, and Politics*, 11–12; Publius Valerius, *The Repertory*, October 30, 1804, in *Writings of JQA*, 3:59; Final quotation from JQA, Reply to the Appeal of the Massachusetts Federalists (1829), in *Documents Relating to New England Federalism*, 1800–1815, ed. Henry Adams (Boston: Little, Brown, 1905), 148.

39. Hartford, *Money, Morals, Politics*, 13–18.

40. JQA to James Sullivan, January 10, 1808, in *Writings of JQA*, 3:186; JQA, Reply to the Massachusetts Federalists, in *Documents Relating to New England Federalism*, ed. Adams, 172; first quotation from JQA to Orchard Cook, in *Writings of JQA*, 3:241; Pickering characterization in JQA, *Parties in the United States*, ed. Charles True Adams (New York: Greenberg 1941), 83; JQA to Harrison Gray Otis, March 31, 1808, in *Writings of JQA*, 3:189–223, quotations on pp. 202, 220–221; JQA, *American Principles: A Review of Works of Fisher Ames, compiled by a Number of His Friends* (Boston: Everett & Munroe, 1809), 34, Preface, 6.

41. George A, Lipsky, *John Quincy Adams: His Theory and Ideas* (New York: Thomas Y. Crowell, 1950), 171–76; Rufus King to Christopher Gore, November 22, 1816, in *The Life and Correspondence of Rufus King: Comprising His Letters, Private and Official, His Public Documents and His Speeches*, ed. Charles R. King, 6 vols. (New York: G. P. Putnam's Sons, 1894–1900), 6:36; Peter C. Brooks to Edward Everett, January 17, 1832, in reel 5, Edward Everett Papers, MHS.

42. Sources for this and the next two paragraphs include L. H. Roper, *Conceiving Carolina: Proprietors, Planters, and Plots, 1662–1729* (New York: Palgrave/Macmillan, 2004); M. Eugene Sirmans, *Colonial South Carolina: A Political History, 1663–1763* (Chapel Hill: University of North Carolina Press, 1966), chs. 2–6; Jack P. Greene, "Colonial South Carolina and the Caribbean Connection," in *Imperatives, Behaviors, and Identities: Essays in Early American Cultural History* (Charlottesville: University Press of Virginia, 1992), 68–86; John J. Navin, *The Grim Years: Settling South Carolina, 1670–1720* (Columbia: University of South Carolina Press, 2020); Robert M. Weir, *Colonial South Carolina: A History* (1983; repr. Columbia: University of South Carolina Press, 1997), chs. 4–5; Walter Edgar, *South Carolina: A History* (Columbia: University of South Carolina Press, 1998), chs. 3, 6.

43. [Francis Yonge], *A Narrative of the Proceedings of the People of South Carolina in the Year 1719* (1726), in *Historical Collections of South Carolina; Embracing Many Rare and Valuable Pamphlets, and Other Documents, Relating to the History of That State from Its First Discovery to its Independence in the Year 1776*, ed. Bartholomew Rivers Carroll (New York: Harper & Brothers, 1836), 160–61.

44. Pauline Maier, *American Scripture: Making the Declaration of Independence* (New York: Alfred A. Knopf, 1997), 226–34; Peter H. Wood, *Black Majority: Negroes in Colonial South Carolina from 1670 through the Stono Rebellion* (1974; repr. New York: W. W. Norton, 1975), ch. 5.

45. *A Short Description of the Province of South Carolina: With an Account of the Air, Weather, and Diseases at Charlestown, Written in the Year 1763* (1763), in *Historical Collections of South Carolina*, ed. Carroll, 479; John Drayton, *A View of South Carolina, as Respects Her Natural and Civil Concerns* (Charleston: W. P. Young, 1802), 144, 146; Charles Cotesworth Pinckney, *An Address Delivered in Charleston, before the Agricultural Society of South Carolina, on Tuesday, the 18th August, 1829* (Charleston: A. E. Miller, 1829), 15; [William Drayton]. *The South Vindicated from the Treason and Fanaticism of the Northern Abolitionists* (Philadelphia: H. Manly, 1836), 115, 119.

46. *A Short Description of the Province of South Carolina* (1763), in *Historical Collections of South Carolina*, ed. Carroll, 480; Wood, *Black Majority*, chs. 8, 12, quotation on p. 308; Donald D. Wax, "'The Great Risque We Run': The Aftermath of Slave Rebellion in Stono, South Carolina, 1739–1745," *Journal of Negro History*, 67 (Summer 1982): 136–47; Ryan A. Quintana, *Making a Slave State: Political Development in South Carolina* (Chapel Hill: University of North Carolina Press, 2018), 32–38, 44–47, 104–15, 166–82.

47. Wood, *Black Majority*, 323–26; Robert L. Meriwether, *The Expansion of South Carolina, 1729–1765* (Kingsport, TN: Southern, 1940), chs. 2, 10–12, 16; Rachel N. Klein, "Ordering the Backcountry: The South Carolina Regulators," *William and Mary Quarterly*, 30 (October 1981): 363–68.

48. Charles Woodmason, *The Carolina Backcountry on the Eve of the Revolution: The Journal and Other Writings of Charles Woodmason, Anglican Itinerant*, ed. Richard J. Hooker (Chapel Hill: University of North Carolina Press, 1953), 27, 228.

49. Ibid., 60, 222, 28; Richard Maxwell Brown, *The South Carolina Regulators* (Cambridge, MA: Harvard University Press, 1963), 46–51; Klein, "Ordering the Backcountry," 678.

50. Marjoleine Kars, *Breaking Loose Together: The Regulator Rebellion in Pre-Revolutionary North Carolina* (Chapel Hill: University of North Carolina Press, 2002); Rachel N. Klein, *Unification of a Slave State: The Rise of the Planter Class in the South Carolina Backcountry* (Chapel Hill: University of North Carolina Press, 1990), 64–68; 77; Brown, *South Carolina Regulators*, ch. 5; James Haw, "Political Representation in South Carolina, 1669–1794: Evolution of a Lowcountry Tradition," *South Carolina Historical Magazine*, 10 (April 2002): 112.

51. Woodmason, *Carolina Backcountry*, ed. Hooker, 221; Jerome Nadelhaft, *The Disorders of War: The Revolution in South Carolina* (Orono: University of Maine at Orono Press, 1981), 136–38, 200–02, 209–11; Edgar, *South Carolina*, 254–57; William A. Schaper, "Sectionalism and Representation in South Carolina," *Annual Report of the American Historical Association for 1900* (Washington, DC: Government Printing Office, 1901), 140–44; Appius [Robert Goodloe Harper], *An Address to the People of South Carolina, by the General Committee of the Representative Reform Association, at Columbia* (Charleston, SC: W. P. Young, 1794), iii, 5, iv.

52. Haw, "Political Representation in South Carolina," 125–28, quotation on p. 128; Klein, *Unification of a Slave State*, 246–58; Schaper, "Sectionalism and Representation," 199–201.

53. JCC to Andrew Pickens Jr., May 23, 1803; JCC to Mrs. Floride Calhoun, April 6, 1809, in *Calhoun Papers*, 1:9–10, 41; Kaplan, *American Visionary*, 130–31.

54. Edgar, *South Carolina*, 261–64; Klein, *Unification of a Slave State*, 1–6, 63–64, 179, 144, quotation on p. 144.

55. JCC to James L. Orr, William Sloan, Alexander Evans, and Frederick W. Symmes, November 1846, in *Calhoun Papers*, 23:510–18; Lacy K. Ford, "Recovering the Republic:

Calhoun, South Carolina, and the Concurrent Majority," *South Carolina Historical Magazine,* 80 (June 1988): 153–54; Ford, *The Origins of Southern Radicalism: The South Carolina Upcountry, 1800–1860* (New York: Oxford University Press, 1988), 284–303.

56. Klein, *Unification of a Slave State,* 305; Niven, *Calhoun,* 31.

Chapter 2: Nationalism and Empire

1. JQA to Abigail Adams, August 10, 1812, in *Writings of JQA,* 4:388; JQA to George Washington Adams, April 3, 1813, in "Letters of John Quincy Adams," *Proceedings of the Massachusetts Historical Society,* 2nd series, 10 (1895–1896): 387.

2. First quotation in JQA to Abigail Adams, March 30, 1812, in *Writings of JQA,* 4:304. Subsequent quotations in JQA to John Adams, January 12, 1813, ibid., 4:425; JQA to Abigail Adams, January 30, 1813, in *Correspondence of John Quincy Adams, 1811–1814,* ed. Charles Francis Adams (Worcester, MA: American Antiquarian Society, 1913), 31; JQA to Levett Harris, November 15, 1814; JQA to William Plumer, October 5, 1815, in *Writings of JQA,* 4:187–88, 5:401.

3. JQA to William Eustis, October 26, 1811, in *Writings of JQA,* 4:262; JQA Diary, 29:December 14, 1814; JQA to Abigail Adams, April 30, 1812, in *Writings of JQA,* 4:321; JQA to John Adams, November 5, 1812, in *Correspondence, 1811–1814,* ed. Adams, 16–17; John Adams to Richard Rush, July 15, 1813, in *John Adams: Writings from the New Nation, 1784–1826,* ed. Gordon S. Wood (New York: Library of America, 2016), 565; JQA to Thomas Boylston Adams, August 7, 1813, in *Correspondence, 1811–1814,* ed. Adams, 49.

4. Charles N. Edel, *Nation Builder: John Quincy Adams and the Grand Strategy of the Republic* (Cambridge, MA: Harvard University Press, 2014). 60–63, 81–83, 95–96; JQA to Thomas Boylston Adams, February 4, 1801; JQA to William Vans Murray, June 7, 1798; JQA to Abigail Adams, June 20, 1811; JQA to Samuel Dexter, April 14, 1816, in *Writings of JQA,* 2:499–502, 301, 4:127–28, 6:15, quotations on pp. 2:499, 6:15.

5. JQA to John Adams, May 26, 1816; JQA to Joseph Hall, September 9, 1815; JQA to William Harris Crawford, September 14, 1814; JQA to Abigail Adams, January 1, 1812, in *Writings of JQA,* 6:38, 5:375, 140, 4:286, quotations on pp. 6:38, 5:140; *Documents Relating to New-England Federalism,* ed. Henry Adams (Boston: Little, Brown, 1905), 171–72; JQA to Peter Paul Francis De Grand, April 29, 1815, in *Writings of JQA,* 5:314.

6. First quotation in JCC to Dr. James McBride, February 16, 1812, in *Calhoun Papers,* 1:90; *Annals of Congress,* 12th Cong., 1st sess., Part 2 (May 1812): 1397, 1399.

7. Roger H. Brown, "The War Hawks of 1812: A Historical Myth," *Indiana Magazine of History,* 60 (June 1964): 146; *Calhoun Papers,* 1:150–61, 228–29, first quotation on p. 153; final quotation in William M. Meigs, *The Life of John Caldwell Calhoun,* 2 vols. (New York: Neale Publishing, 1917), 1:217.

8. JQA to John Adams, May 29, 1816, in *Writings of JQA,* 6:38; John Niven, *John C. Calhoun and the Price of Union: A Biography* (Baton Rouge: Louisiana State University Press, 1988), 46–47.

9. *Calhoun Papers,* 1:314–15, 317–18, 325, 329–30, quotations on pp. 314–15.

10. *Annals of Congress,* 14th Cong., 1st sess. (April 1816): 1331–38, quotations on pp. 1331–32; Brian Schoen, "Calculating the Price of Union: Republican Economic Nationalism and the Origins of Southern Sectionalism," *Journal of the Early Republic,* 23 (Summer 2003): 201–02.

11. First and third quotations in *Annals of Congress,* 14th Cong., 1st sess. (April 1816): 1335–36; second and final quotations ibid., 14th Cong., 2d sess. (February 1817): 852, 854; Robert Elder, *Calhoun: American Heretic* (New York: Basic Books, 2021), 141–47.

12. John Lauritz Larson, "'Bind the People Together': The National Union and the Struggle for a System of Internal Improvement," *Journal of American History,* 74 (September 1987): 377–85, first quotation on p. 383; Larson, *Internal Improvement: National Public Works and the Promise of Popular Government in the Early United States* (Chapel Hill: University of North Carolina Press, 2001), 64–69; remaining quotations in *Annals of Congress,* 14th Cong., 2d sess. (February 1817): 855–56. South Carolina's strong commitment to internal improvements during the postwar period doubtless influenced Calhoun as well. Ryan A. Quintana, *Making A Slave State: Political Development in South Carolina* (Chapel Hill: University of North Carolina Press, 2018), 152–65.

13. Alan Taylor, *The Internal Enemy: Slavery and War in Virginia, 1772–1832* (New York: W. W. Norton, 2013), 398; JCC, speech at Abbeville, South Carolina, May 27, 1825, in *Calhoun Papers,* 10:22–23.

14. Edel, *Nation Builder,* 116–17; Niven, *Calhoun,* 58–61; [R. M. T. Hunter], *Life of John C. Calhoun, Presenting a Condensed History of Political Events from 1811 to 1843* (New York: Harper & Brothers, 1843), 73.

15. JQA Diary, 32: October 15, 1821, 31:March 20, 1821.

16. JQA to Abigail Adams, April 26, 1814, in *Correspondence, 1811–1814,* ed., Adams, 61; Napoleon quotation from JQA to Samuel Dexter, April 14, 1816, in *Writings of JQA,* 6:15; JQA, *An Address, Delivered at the Request of the Committee of Arrangements for Celebrating the Anniversary of Independence, at the City of Washington on the Fourth of July 1821, upon the Reading of the Declaration of Independence* (Cambridge: Printed at the Univ. Press, by Hilliard & Metcalf, 1821), 32.

17. First quotation in George Wilson Pierson, *Tocqueville and Beaumont in America* (New York: Oxford University Press, 1938), 420; JQA Diary, 31:November 16, 1819; JQA, *The New England Confederacy of MDCXLIII: A Discourse Delivered before the Massachusetts Historical Society, at Boston, on the 29th of May, 1843, in Celebration of the Second Centennial of That Event* (Boston: Charles C. Little & James Brown, 1843), 46. Also see Walter LaFeber's convenient compilation of Adams's statements on continentalism, *John Quincy Adams and American Continental Empire: Letters, Papers and Speeches* (Chicago: Quadrangle Books, 1965).

18. David J. Weber, *The Spanish Frontier in North America* (New Haven, CT: Yale University Press, 1992), 275, 29–97.

19. Weber, *Spanish Frontier,* 280–81; Frank Lawrence Owsley Jr., and Gene A. Smith, *Filibusters and Expansionists: Jeffersonian Manifest Destiny, 1800–1821* (Tuscaloosa: University of Alabama Press, 1978), 7–9, 63.

20. JCC to Charles Tait, January 20, 1820, in *Calhoun Papers,* 4:616–617; JQA Diary, 31:February 22, 1821.

21. William Earl Weeks, *John Quincy Adams and American Global Empire* (Lexington: University Press of Kentucky, 1992), 128–30.

22. Ibid., 53–54, 57–58, 107–12.

23. JCC to James Monroe, September 12, 1818, in *Calhoun Papers,* 3:121; Niven, *Calhoun,* 70; Elder, *Calhoun,* 172–73; Gerald M. Capers, *John C. Calhoun—Opportunist: A Reappraisal*

(Gainesville: University of Florida Press, 1960), 68–69; JQA Diary, 30:July 15, 1818; JCC to Andrew Jackson, September 8, 1818; JCC to Charles Tait, July 20, 1818, in *Calhoun Papers,* 3:110–11, 2:408. For a contrary view of Calhoun's motives that characterizes his readiness to censure Jackson as "an act of utter cynicism" calculated "to neutralize a potential political rival," see Weeks, *Adams and American Global Empire,* 114–15. Weeks's argument would be more persuasive if the Florida invasion had occurred four or five years later. There is no evidence that the South Carolinian believed that Jackson was likely to block his path to the presidency as early as 1818.

24. William Earl Weeks, *The New Cambridge History of American Foreign Relations, Volume 1: Dimensions of the Early American Empire, 1754–1865* (Cambridge: Cambridge University Press, 2013), 109.

25. JQA Diary, 30:July 21, 1818, July 15, 1818, July 17, 1818, July 20, 1818, quotations in first two entries; Edel, *Nation Builder,* 144–50.

26. JQA to George W. Erving, November 28, 1818, in *Writings of JQA,* 474–502, quotations on pp. 488, 502; William Earl Weeks, "John Quincy Adams's 'Great Gun' and the Rhetoric of American Empire," *Diplomatic History,* 83 (Winter 1990): 25–42.

27. Deborah A. Rosen, *Border Law: The First Seminole War and American Nationhood* (Cambridge, MA: Harvard University Press, 2015), 36; Weeks, *Adams and American Global Empire,* 122–24, 161–66; JQA Diary, 31:February 22, 1819.

28. JQA Diary, 34:November 23, 7, 1823, quotations in the two entries; Weeks, *New Cambridge History of American Foreign Relations, Volume 1,* 115–16; Edel, *Nation Builder,* 171–74.

29. James D. Richardson, comp., *A Compilation of the Messages and Papers of the Presidents, 1789–1897,* 20 vols. (New York: Bureau of National Literature, 1897), 2:787–88.

30. Quotations in JQA Diary, 31:April 13, 1820; William Plumer Jr., to his father, April 7, 1820, in *The Missouri Compromises and Presidential Politics, 1820–1825: From the Letters of William Plumer, Junior,* ed. Everett Somerville Brown (St. Louis: Missouri Historical Society, 1820), 16.

31. JQA Diary, 31:July 5, 1819, January 16, 1820, February 28, 1821, March 31, 1820, February 20, 1820, February 24, 1820, March 3, 1820, quotations in first, second, fifth, sixth, and seventh entries; Edel, *Nation Builder,* 158–59.

32. Robert Pierce Forbes, *The Missouri Compromise and Its Aftermath: Slavery and the Meaning of America* (Chapel Hill: University of North Carolina Press, 2007), 102–03; JCC to Henry W. DeSaussure, April 20, 1820; JCC to Virgil Maxcy, August 17, 1820; JCC to Charles Tait, October 20, 1820, in *Calhoun Papers,* 27:366–67, 5:327, 413–14; Meigs, *Calhoun,* 1:340–43; final quotation in JCC to Andrew Jackson, June 1, 1820, in *Calhoun Papers,* 5:164.

33. JQA Diary, 31:February 24, 1820, 35:March 9, 1824.

34. [Hunter], *Life of Calhoun,* 24–25; Irving H. Bartlett, *John C. Calhoun: A Biography* (New York: W. W. Norton, 1993), 89–90.

35. JCC to Virgil Maxcy, September 9, 1825, in *Calhoun Papers,* 10:43; Bartlett, *Calhoun,* 91–93; Elder, *Calhoun,* 157–62.

36. JQA, *Parties in the United States,* ed. Charles True Adams (New York: Greenberg, 1941), 127–29; [Hunter], *Life of Calhoun,* 25–26; Elder, *Calhoun,* 157–62.

37. JQA Diary, 32:October 15, 1821; JCC to Charles G. Haines, November 1, 1822; JCC to Henry Clay, January 7, 1819; JCC to James Monroe, December 3, 1824, in *Calhoun Papers,*

27:407, 3:469, 9:424–29, closing quotations on p. 428; Larson, *Internal Improvement,* 161–73; *Annals of Congress,* 14th Cong., 2d sess. (February 1817): 854.

38. JCC to Thomas A. Smith, March 16, 1818; JCC to John Floyd, April 19, 1824, in *Calhoun Papers,* 2:195, 9:38.

39. Colin G. Calloway, *The Scratch of a Pen: 1763 and the Transformation of North America* (New York: Oxford University Press, 2006), chs. 2–4, quotation on p. 55.

40. Reginald Horsman, *Expansion and American Indian Policy, 1783–1812* (1967; repr. Norman: University of Oklahoma Press, 1992).

41. Donald R. Hickey, *The War of 1812: A Forgotten Conflict* (Urbana: University of Illinois Press, 1989), 135–39, 146–51; Anthony F. C. Wallace, *The Long, Bitter Trail: Andrew Jackson and the Indians* (New York: Hill & Wang, 1993), 50–51; Hickey, *War of 1812,* 289–91.

42. JQA, *An Oration, Delivered at Plymouth, December 22, 1802: At the Anniversary Commemoration of the First Landing of Our Ancestors at That Place* (Boston: Printed by Russell & Cutler, 1802), 23–24; Fred Kaplan, *John Quincy Adams: American Visionary* (New York: HarperCollins), 192–93; JQA to Benjamin Waterhouse, October 24, 1813, in *Writings of JQA,* 4:526; JQA Diary, 29:September 1, 1814; JQA to James Monroe, September 5, 1814; JQA, Answer to the British Commissioners, in *Writings of JQA,* 5:115–16, 98.

43. JCC to Robert Carter Nicholas, February 22, 1821; JCC to David B. Mitchell, December 29, 1818; JCC to James Monroe, February 8, 1822; JCC to Henry Clay, January 18, 1820, in *Calhoun Papers,* 5:641, 3:170–71, 6:681, 4:577, quotations on pp. 3:170–71, 4:577.

44. JCC to the Piankashaw delegation, August 1, 1824, in *Calhoun Papers,* 9:258; Jefferson quotation in Bernard W. Sheehan, *Seeds of Extinction: Jeffersonian Philanthropy and the American Indian* (Chapel Hill: University of North Carolina Press, 1973), 149; third quotation in JCC to Benjamin O'Fallon, December 18, 1819; JCC to Col. Henry Leavenworth, December 29, 1819; JCC to Col. Henry Atkinson, August 18, 1819; final quotation in JCC to Lewis Cass, June 27, 1823, in *Calhoun Papers,* 4:501, 518, 255, 7:137.

45. JCC to William Ward, July 8, 1823; Thomas L. McKenney to John Johnston, May 11, 1824; JCC to Col. Henry Leavenworth, July 11, 1820; JCC to Henry Atkinson, December 19, 1820; JCC to Richard Graham, May 11, 1820, in *Calhoun Papers,* 8:160, 9:84, 5:250, 505, 110–11, quotation on pp. 5:110–11.

46. Lewis Cass to JCC, September 14, 1818; Thomas L. McKenney to JCC, August 19, 1818, in *Calhoun Papers,* 3:124–27, 47–53, quotations on pp. 124, 49–50.

47. JCC to Henry Clay, December 5, 1818, in *Calhoun Papers,* 3:345–54, quotations on pp. 347, 353, 354. Also see Col. Henry Atkinson to JCC, November 26, 1819; JCC to Col. Henry Atkinson, February 7, 1820; JCC to Walter Leake, January 31, 1820, ibid., 4:433–34, 646, 621–22.

48. Bartlett, *Calhoun,* 98.

49. Theda Perdue and Michael D. Green, *The Cherokee Nation and the Trail of Tears* (New York: Penguin Books, 2007), ch. 2.

50. JCC to Joseph McMinn, July 29, 1818; JCC to the Cherokee delegation, February 11, 1819, in *Calhoun Papers,* 2:436–39, 3:565–66, quotation on p. 2:439; Perdue and Green, *Cherokee Nation,* 50–52. Also see JCC to Henry Clay, December 5, 1818; Return J. Meigs to JCC, February 10, 1819; JCC to Lewis Cass, March 27, 1819, in *Calhoun Papers,* 3:250, 561–62, 696.

51. John Ross, Major Ridge, and Elijah Hicks to James Monroe, January 19, 1824; John Ross and other members of the Cherokee National Committee to JCC, October 24, 1822;

John Ross, George Lowrey, Major Ridge, and Elijah Hicks to JCC, February 11, 1824, in *Calhoun Papers,* 8:488–89, 7:316–17, 8:535.

52. First quotation in JCC to John Forsyth, April 12, 1824, in *Calhoun Papers,* 9:28; Michael D. Green, *The Politics of Indian Removal: Creek Government and Society in Crisis* (Lincoln: University of Nebraska, 1982), 48; Sheehan, *Seeds of Extinction,* 264–65; Claudio Saunt, *Unworthy Republic: The Dispossession of Native Americans and the Road to Indian Territory* (New York: W. W. Norton, 2020), 16–18, 22–24, 34–35; JCC to James Monroe, March 29, 1824; Levi Colbert and other members of the Chickasaw delegation to JCC, December 7, 1824, in *Calhoun Papers,* 8:608, 9:433; JQA Diary, 35:March 29, 1824; JCC to Joseph Gales Jr., and William W. Seaton, July 1838, in *Calhoun Papers,* 14:364.

53. JCC to James Monroe, January 24, 1825, in *Calhoun Papers,* 9:516–17; JQA Diary, 37:February 7, 1826; Reginald Horsman, *Race and Manifest Destiny: The Origins of Racial Anglo-Saxonism* (Cambridge, MA: Harvard University Press, 1981), 197–200; Green, *Politics of Indian Removal,* 133–34, 139; James Traub, *John Quincy Adams, Militant Spirit* (New York: Basic Books, 2016), 319–22; first quotation in JQA Diary, 37:December 23, 1825; Jackson quotation in Horsman, *Race and Manifest Destiny,* 202; JQA, *New England Confederacy,* 12–16, quotation on p. 14. Lynn Hudson Parsons provides an able summary of Adams's changing views on Native Americans in "'A Perpetual Harrow upon My Feelings': John Quincy Adams and the American Indian," *New England Quarterly,* 46 (September 1973): 339–79.

54. JQA, *New England Confederacy,* 15; JQA Diary, 37:January 23, 1828, 34:January 8, 1824; final quotation in JQA to inhabitants of the twelfth congressional district, August 13, 1838, in *Niles' National Register,* 55 (September 22, 1838): 55.

55. JQA, *Oration at Plymouth,* 23; JQA Diary, 31:March 3, 1820.

56. JCC to Henry M. Brackenridge, October 21, 1821, in *Calhoun Papers,* 6:454–55.

Chapter 3: Sectionalism and Nullification

1. JQA Diary, 32:July 8, 1822; JCC to Major John A. Dix, October 5, 1828, in *Calhoun Papers,* 10:429; William Plumer Jr., to William Plumer, January 3, 1822, December 3, 1823, in *The Missouri Compromises and Presidential Politics, 1820–1825: From the Letters of William Plumer, Junior* (St. Louis: Missouri Historical Society, 1926), 71–73, 86–87, second quotation on p. 86; JQA Diary, 34:February 24, 1824.

2. JCC to Joseph G. Swift, March 10, 1825; JCC to John McLean, September 3, 1827, in *Calhoun Papers,* 10:10, 307; William J. Cooper, *The Lost Founding Father: John Quincy Adams and the Transformation of American Politics* (New York: Liveright, 2017), 229–30, 246–47; Irving H. Bartlett, *John C. Calhoun: A Biography* (New York: W. W. Norton, 1993) 125–27, 132–34; "Patrick Henry" and "Onslow" letters in *Calhoun Papers,* 10:92–96, 99–104. 113–27, 135–55, 165–97, 203–22, 223–32; JCC, speech at Pendleton, South Carolina, September 7, 1826, ibid., 10:201–02; JQA, Reply to the Appeal of the Massachusetts Federalists (1829), in *Documents Relating to New England Federalism, 1800–1815,* ed. Henry Adams (Boston: Little, Brown, 1905), 140.

3. JQA Diary, 38:March 2, 1831; JQA to JCC, September 8, 1831; JCC to JQA, September 26, 1831, in *Calhoun Papers,* 11:469–70, 473; JQA, *An Oration Addressed to the Citizens of the Town of Quincy, on the Fourth of July, 1831, the Fifty-Fifth Anniversary of the Independence of the United States of America* (Boston: Richardson, Lord & Holbrook, 1831), quotation on p. 23; Fort Hill Address, in *Calhoun Papers,* 11:413–39; final quotation in JQA to A. H. Everett,

September 18, 1831, in "Letters of John Quincy Adams to Alexander Hamilton Everett, 1811–1837," *American Historical Review,* 11 (January 1906): 341.

4. JQA Diary, 31: November 30, 1824; William W. Freehling, *Prelude to Civil War: The Nullification Controversy in South Carolina, 1816–1836* (New York: Harper & Row, 1966), 32–39, 42–47, 203–04, 361–64; Walter Edgar, *South Carolina: A History* (Columbia; University of South Carolina Press, 1998), 275–77; Alfred Glaze Smith, *Economic Readjustment of an Old Cotton State: South Carolina, 1820–1860* (Columbia: University of South Carolina Press, 1958), ch. 2.

5. *State Documents on Federal Relations: The States and the United States*, ed. Herman V. Ames (Philadelphia: University of Pennsylvania, 1911), 135, 139–40; Lacy K. Ford, *Origins of Southern Radicalism: The South Carolina Upcountry, 1800–1860* (New York: Oxford University Press, 1988), 117–18; final quotation in Brutus [Robert James Turnbull], *The Crisis: or, Essays on the Usurpations of the Federal Government* (Charleston: A. E. Miller, 1827), 127.

6. Dumas Malone, *The Public Life of Thomas Cooper, 1783–1839* (New Haven, CT: Yale University Press, 1926), chs. 2, 4, quotation on p. 328; Thomas Cooper, *A Tract on the Proposed Alteration of the Tariff, Submitted for the Consideration of the Members from South Carolina in Congress* (New York: Clayton & Van Norden, 1824), 4–5, 13–19, quotations on pp. 4, 19.

7. First quotation from Thomas Cooper to Martin Van Buren, April 11, 1828, in Malone, *Cooper*, 329; Thomas Cooper, *Consolidation, an Account of Parties in the United States from the Convention of 1787, to the Present Period*, 2d ed. (1824; repr. Columbia, SC: Times & Gazette Office, 1830), 19–20, 25. It should be noted that Cooper later acknowledged Calhoun's changing views on internal improvements. See note to page 20 ibid.

8. JCC to Moses Waddell, September 15, 1821; JCC to Charles Tait, October 1, 1821; JCC to Joseph G. Swift, May 10, 1823; JCC to Micah Sterling, August 5, 1823; JCC to Jacob Brown, August 8, 1823; JCC to Micah Sterling, October 13, 1823; JCC to Joseph G. Swift, August 24, 1823; JCC to Robert S. Garnett, July 3, 1824, in *Calhoun Papers,* 3:388, 413, 8:58–59, 210, 215, 313, 243, 9:199, quotations on pp. 3:388, 8:58–59, 8:313, 243, 9:199.

9. JQA Diary, 32:October 1, 1822; JCC to Joseph G. Swift, December 11, 1825; JCC, speech, March 22, 1838; JCC to Andrew Jackson, June 4, 1826, in *Calhoun Papers,* 10:58, 14:241, 10:110; John Lauritz Larson, *Internal Improvement: National Public Works and the Promise of Popular Government in the Early United States* (Chapel Hill: University of North Carolina Press, 2001), 174–77; Cooper, *Lost Founding Father,* 226–27.

10. JCC to James Edward Colhoun, May 4, 1826, in *Calhoun Papers,* 10:382; *Niles' Weekly Register,* 33 (September 8, 1827): 27–32, Cooper quotations on p. 32.

11. First quotation in Robert Pierce Forbes, *The Missouri Compromise and Its Aftermath: Slavery and the Meaning of America* (Chapel Hill: University of North Carolina Press, 2007), 225–26; Brian C. Neumann, *Bloody Flag of Anarchy: Unionism in South Carolina during the Nullification Crisis* (Baton Rouge: Louisiana State University Press, 2022), 95–96; [Turnbull], *The Crisis,* 161, 117–21, quotation on p. 161.

12. *Register of Debates,* 19th Cong., 2d sess. (February 7, 1827): 1000–07, first quotation on p. 1007; George McDuffie, *Speech of Mr. McDuffie on Internal Improvements, with a Few Introductory Remarks in Answer to a Pamphlet Entitled "Consolidation"* (Columbia, SC: D & J. M. Faust, 1824), 15–19, second quotation on p. 18; McDuffie, *National and State Rights, Considered by the Hon. George McDuffie, under the Signature of "one of the People" in*

Reply to the "Trio" (1821; repr. Charleston Free Press, 1831), third quotation on p. 9; fourth quotation in an excerpt from an 1821 statement in *Niles' Weekly Register,* 38 (March 27, 1830): 88; [Turnbull], *The Crisis,* 75–93, quotations on p. 76. McDuffie was slow to retreat from his support for internal improvements. In a March 1828 speech deploring Southern opposition to such measures, he contended that that they provided "the only form in which the southern states can be indemnified for the tax upon them to sustain the manufactures of the eastern states." *Niles' Weekly Register,* 43 (September 8, 1832): 27.

13. Freehling, *Prelude to Civil War,* 144–45.

14. JCC to Littleton Waller Tazewell, August 25, 1827; JCC to Virgil Maxcy, July 24, 1827; JCC to Tazewell, August 25, 1827, in *Calhoun Papers,* 10:300, 27:461–62, 10:301; Charles M. Wiltse, *John C. Calhoun: Sectionalist, 1840–1850* (Indianapolis: Bobbs-Merrill, 1951), 421.

15. Robert V. Remini, "Martin Van Buren and the Tariff of Abominations," *American Historical Review,* 63 (July 1958): 903–17; William K. Bolt, *Tariff Wars and the Politics of Jacksonian America* (Nashville, TN: Vanderbilt University Press, 2017), ch. 7; JCC to Duff Green, July 1, 1828, in *Calhoun Papers,* 10:302; *Niles' Weekly Register,* 35 (September 20, 1828): 60–63; William M. Meigs, *The Life of John Caldwell Calhoun,* 2 vols. (New York: Neale Publishing, 1917), 1:370–71; Samuel Smith to JCC, July 5, 1828, in *Calhoun Papers,* 10:393; *Niles' Weekly Register,* 34 (June 28, 1828): 289; William C. Davis, *Rhett: The Turbulent Life and Times of a Fire-Eater* (Columbia: University of South Carolina Press, 2001), 38–42; JCC to John McLean, July 10, 1828; JCC to Samuel Smith, July 28, 1828; final quotation in JCC to Major John A. Dix, September 1, 1828; JCC to James Monroe, September 5, 1828, third quotation in JCC to Samuel D. Ingham, September 26, 1829; JCC to John McLean, October 4, 1828, in *Calhoun Papers,* 10:397–98, 403–04, 414, 417, 11:79; 10:428.

16. Freehling, *Prelude to Civil War,* 154; *Niles' Weekly Register,* 35 (November 22, 1828): 203–08, quotation on p. 207; Davis, *Rhett,* 43–44; JCC to William C. Preston, November 6, 1828, in *Calhoun Papers,* 10:432.

17. "Rough Draft of What Is Called the South Carolina Exposition," in *Calhoun Papers,* 10:445–534, quotations on pp. 458, 460, 480.

18. Quotations in ibid., 520, 526, 490, 492.

19. JCC to William C. Preston, January 6, 1829; JCC to Andrew Jackson, July 10, 1828; JCC, "Rough Draft of What Is Called the South Carolina Exposition," in *Calhoun Papers,* 10:546, 397, 530.

20. Ford, *Origins of Southern Radicalism,* 128–130, quotation on p. 129; Hugh S. Legaré speech, July 4, 1831, in *Writings of Hugh Swinton Legaré,* ed. Mary S. Legaré, 2 vols. (Charleston, SC: Burges & James, 1846), 1:272.

21. Freehling, *Prelude to Civil War,* 145–47, 22–24, first quotation on p. 146; George McDuffie, *Speech at Charleston, May 19, 1831,* in *The Nullification Era: A Documentary Record,* ed. William W. Freehling (New York: Harper Torchbooks, 1967), 103–19, quotations on p. 119; Charles M. Wiltse, *John C. Calhoun: Nullifier, 1829–1839* (Indianapolis: Bobbs-Merrill, 1949), 110–11.

22. Charles J. McDonald to JCC, May 30, 1831; Tomlinson Fort to JCC, July 15, 1831; Duff Green to JCC, August 1, 15, 1830, May 31, 1831, in *Calhoun Papers,* 11:396, 410–11, 210–12, 216–17, 398, 400, Green quotations on pp. 398, 400; James Hamilton Jr., to James H. Hammond, June 11, 1831, in "Letters on the Nullification Movement in South Carolina, 1830–1834," *American Historical Review,* 8 (July 1901): 747.

23. Charleston Committee of Arrangements to Andrew Jackson, June 5, 1831; Jackson to Charleston Committee of Arrangements, in *Niles' Weekly Register,* 40 (July 16, 1831): 150–51, quotations on p. 150.

24. Report of the Legislature in Reply to Jackson's Letter of June 14, December 17, 1831, in *State Documents on Federal Relations,* ed. Ames, 168; John F. Marszalek, *The Petticoat Affair: Manners, Mutiny, and Sex in Andrew Jackson's White House* (New York: Free Press, 1997); JCC to Andrew Jackson, May 29, 1830; Andrew Jackson to JCC, May 30, 1830, in *Calhoun Papers,* 11:173–80, 192–93, quotations on pp. 173, 192–93; Bartlett, *Calhoun,* 169–75.

25. JCC to James H. Hammond, January 15, 1831; JCC, toast, April 13, 1830, in *Calhoun Papers,* 11:298, 148.

26. Unionist toast quoted in Meigs, *Calhoun,* 1:435; JCC toast in *Niles' Weekly Register,* 40 (July 30, 1831): 375; JCC to Virgil Maxcy, September 11, 1830; JCC to Francis W. Pickens, August 1, 1831, in *Calhoun Papers,* 11:227, 445–46.

27. Fort Hill Address, July 26, 1831, in *Calhoun Papers,* 11:413–39, quotation on p. 427.

28. Duff Green to Richard K Crallé, August 21, 1831; JCC to Armistead Burt, December 27, 1831; JCC to Waddy Thompson, July 8, 1832, in *Calhoun Papers,* 11:459–60, 531, 604.

29. Bolt, *Tariff Wars,* 113–17; JCC to James Hamilton Jr., in Pendleton *Messenger,* September 15, 19, 1832; JCC, Draft Report on Federal Relations for the South Carolina General Assembly, November 1831; JCC, Address to the People of the United States, drafted for the South Carolina Convention, November 1832, in *Calhoun Papers,* 11:640–41, 644, 647–48, 495–500, 676, 679, quotation on p. 676; Ordinance of Nullification of South Carolina, November 24, 1832, in *State Documents on Federal Relations,* ed. Ames, p. 171.

30. JCC to Virgil Maxcy, September 11, 1830, in *Calhoun Papers,* 11:229; Wiltse, *Calhoun: Nullifier,* 88–89; JQA, *Letters from John Quincy Adams to His Constituents of the Twelfth Congressional District of Massachusetts* (Boston: Isaac Knapp, 1837), 36.

31. JCC to Littleton Waller Tazewell, April 1, 1827; JCC to William C. Preston, May 10, 1831, in *Calhoun Papers,* 10:282, 11:381; *Charleston Courier,* December 24, 1832, quoted in Richard E. Ellis, *The Union at Risk: Jeffersonian Democracy, States' Rights and the Nullification Crisis* (New York: Oxford University Press, 1987), 123. Unlike some younger and more radical proponents of states' rights who adopted a more dismissive view of the Old Dominion's influence, Calhoun maintained a strong belief in Virginia's importance throughout his political career. See Davis, *Rhett,* 276–77.

32. Allison Goodyear Freehling, *Drift toward Dissolution: The Virginia Slavery Debate of 1831–1832* (Baton Rouge: Louisiana State University Press, 1982), 17–35; *Proceedings and Debates of the Virginia State Convention, of 1829–30* (Richmond: Ritchie & Cook, 1830), 280–82, 688, 172, 307, 76, 283–84, quotation on p. 172; Joseph Clarke Robert, *The Road from Monticello: A Study of the Virginia Slavery Debate of 1832* (Durham, NC: Duke University Press, 1941); *Sons of the Fathers: The Virginia Slavery Debate of 1831–1832,* ed. Erik S. Root (Lanham, MD: Lexington Books, 2010), 56, 108.

33. Freehling, *Prelude to Civil War,* 82–86, 251; Ellis, *Union at Risk,* 133, 139; Charles H. Ambler, *The Life and Diary of John Floyd, Governor of Virginia and the Father of the Oregon Country* (Richmond: Richmond Press, 1918), 186–88, 202, 170, 83–85, quotations on pp. 202, 170; Lacy K. Ford, *Deliver Us from Evil: The Slavery Question in the Old South* (New York: Oxford University Press, 2009), 362–63; final quotation in JCC, speech on the force bill, February 15, 16, 1833, in *Calhoun Papers,* 12:66; James H. Read, *Majority Rule versus*

Consensus: The Political Thought of John C. Calhoun (Lawrence: University Press of Kansas, 2009), 75. One South Carolinian who had some understanding of what was happening in Virginia was Daniel E. Huger. See William Grayson's account of a conversation with the Charleston unionist in *Witness to Sorrow: The Antebellum Autobiography of William J. Grayson*, ed. Richard J. Calhoun (Columbia: University of South Carolina Press, 1990), 105.

34. First quotation in Nathan Appleton to R. H. Kingsbury, June 26, 1846, in Appleton Family Papers, MHS; *Register of Debates,* 22d Cong., 1st sess. (May 1832): 3191–97, 3204–05, second quotation on pp. 3204–05; William F. Hartford, *Money, Morals, and Politics: Massachusetts in the Age of the Boston Associates* (Boston: Northeastern University Press, 2001), 48–58; *Register of Debates,* 22d Cong., 1st sess. (June 1832): 3309–10.

35. Quotation in *Boston Daily Courier,* June 15, 1832. Arguments introduced in this paragraph are developed at greater length in Hartford, *Money, Morals, and Politics,* chs. 1–2.

36. JQA to John Adams, August 21, 1781, January 1, 1782; JQA to Abigail Adams, September 10, 1785, August 16, 1785; Abigail Adams to JQA, March 20, 1786, in *Adams Family Correspondence,* ed. L. H. Butterfield et al., 13 vols. (Cambridge, MA: Harvard University Press, 1963—), 4:207, 277, 5:243, 6:254, 7:97.

37. JQA Diary, 31:March 3, 1820; final quotation in George Wilson Pierson, *Tocqueville and Beaumont in America* (New York: Oxford University Press, 1938), 410.

38. JQA Diary, 28:May 15, 1812; JQA, *Parties in the United States*, ed. Charles True Adams (New York: Greenberg, 1941), 39.

39. *A Compilation of the Messages and Papers of the Presidents, 1789–1797*, comp. James D. Richardson, 20 vols. (New York: Bureau of National Literature, 1897), 3:1160–66, quotation on p. 1163; JQA to A. H. Everett, April 15, 1830, in "Letters to Everett," 335–36; Leonard L. Richards, *The Life and Times of Congressman John Quincy Adams* (New York: Oxford University Press, 1980), 62–65; JQA Diary, 39:December 5, 1832; final quotation in JQA to Samuel L. Southard, December 5, 1832, reel 151, Adams Family Papers, MHS; JQA Dairy, 39:December 31, 1832.

40. *Register of Debates*, 22d Cong., 2d sess. (February 1833): appendix, 53–54, 60, 42–43, quotations on pp. 60, 43. Adams was still denouncing Jackson's 1832 message a decade later. See JQA, *Address of John Quincy Adams, to His Constituents of the Twelfth Congressional District, September 17, 1842* (Boston: J. H. Eastburn, 1842), 21–22.

41. *Register of Debates*, 22d Cong., 2d sess. (February 1833): 57.

42. *Register of Debates*, 22d Cong., 2d sess. (February 4, 1833): 1582–83, 1613–16, quotations on pp. 1583, 1613–15.

43. Ibid., 1616–17; Benjamin Waterhouse to JQA, February 18, 1833, reel 497, Adams Family Papers, MHS; *Northampton Courier,* February 27, 1833; JQA to Charles Francis Adams, March 13, 1833, reel 151, Adams Family Papers, MHS.

44. Quotations from different parts of JQA to Benjamin F. Hallett, March 6, 1833; JQA to William Plumer Jr., April 6, 1833, both items in reel 151, Adams Family Papers, MHS.

45. Read, *Majority Rule versus Consensus*, 41–45; JQA to Charles Francis Adams, March 13, 1833, reel 151, Adams Family Papers, MHS; *Register of Debates*, 22d Cong., 2d sess. (February 1833): 1611; *Niles' Weekly Register,* 67 (March 8, 1844): 155–56, final quotation on p. 155. Richard L. Bushman provides an able summary of the interaction of protection and allegiance in English political culture in *King and People in Provincial Massachusetts* (Chapel Hill: University of North Carolina Press, 1985), 17–25.

46. *Register of Debates*, 22d Cong., 2d sess. (February 1833): appendix, 46.

47. Thomas Cooper, *Two Essays: 1. On the Foundations of Civil Government: 2. On the Constitution of the United States* (Columbia: D. & J. M. Faust, 1826), 27–29, first quotation on p. 29; Cooper, *Consolidation*, 22–30; James Hamilton Jr., to John Taylor et al., September 14, 1830, in *Charleston Mercury*, September 29, 1830, in *The Nullification Era*, ed. Freehling, 100–01; second quotation in *Register of Debates*, 22d Cong. 1st sess. (May 1832): appendix, 81; third quotation in *Niles' Weekly Register*, 46 (August 1834): 380; fourth quotation in JQA to Charles W. Upham. February 2, 1837, in "Ten Unpublished Letters of John Quincy Adams, 1796–1837," ed. Edward H. Tatum Jr., *Huntington Library Quarterly*, 4 (April 1941): 383; *Register of Debates*, 22d Cong, 2d sess. (February 1833): appendix, 44; final quotation in ibid., 22d Cong, 1st sess. (June 1832): 3256.

48. Quotations in JQA to Edward Everett, October 10, 1836, in "Jefferson and Madison and the Doctrines of Interposition and Nullification: A Letter of John Quincy Adams," ed. Ralph L. Ketcham, *Virginia Magazine of History and Biography*, 66 (April 1958): 182, 180; JQA, *The Lives of James Madison and James Monroe, Fourth and Fifth Presidents of the United States, with Historical Notices of Their Administrations* (1836, 1831; repr. Boston: Phillips, Sampson, 1850), 71, 74–75; JQA to Alexander H. Everett, May 24, 1830, September 18, 1831, in "Letters to Everett," 339–40, 342.

49. JQA, *Oration Addressed to the Citizens of Quincy*, 17–18, 22–23, first quotation on p. 22; *Register of Debates*, 22d Cong, 2d sess. (February 1833): 1612; JQA, *An Oration Delivered before the Inhabitants of Newburyport, at Their Request, on the Sixty-Fifth Anniversary of the Declaration of Independence, July 4th, 1837* (Newburyport, MA: Morss & Brewster, 1837), 42–44, final quotation on p. 43; JQA. *The Jubilee of the Constitution: A Discourse Delivered at the Request of the New York Historical Society, in the City of New York on Tuesday, the 30th of April, 1839, Being the Fiftieth Anniversary of the Inauguration of George Washington as President* (New York: Samuel Colman, 1839), 20, 30, 37–38, 41, 119.

50. First quotation in JQA Diary, 31:December 27, 1819; Charles N. Edel, *Nation Builder: John Quincy Adams and the Grand Strategy of the Republic* (Cambridge, MA: Harvard University Press, 2014), 280–84, quotation on p. 281; JQA, *Jubilee of the Constitution*, 41, 119.

51. Pauline Maier, *American Scripture: Making the Declaration of Independence* (New York: Alfred A. Knopf, 1997), 170–80; William Henry Harrison to JCC, November 29, 1831, *Ohio State Journal and Columbus Gazette*, January 2, 1832, in *Calhoun Papers*, 11:516; JQA Diary, 39:March 7, 1833; Ellwood Fisher to JCC, November 5, 1848; Robert L. Dorr to JCC, March 1. 1847, in *Calhoun Papers*, 26:123, 24:230.

52. JQA Diary, 45:February 19, 1845; JCC to Duff Green, September 20, 1834, in *Calhoun Papers*, 12:363.

53. Benjamin Waterhouse to JQA, February 18, 1833, reel 497, Adams Family Papers, MHS; JCC, speech, June 24, 1812, in *Calhoun Papers*, 1:128.

54. Freehling, *Prelude to Civil War*, 252–54, 260; Neumann, *Bloody Flag of Anarchy*, 58–61.

55. Freehling, *Prelude to Civil War*, 255–59, 82–86; JCC, draft of An Address to the People of the United States, in *Calhoun Papers*, 11:672–75, quotation on 672; [Robert Y. Hayne], Report of the Committee of Twenty-One, November 22, 1832, in Commonwealth of Massachusetts, *State Papers on Nullification* (Boston: Dutton & Wentworth, 1834), 15–17, 25–26, 21, quotations on pp. 15, 21; South Carolina Nullification Ordinance, November 24, 1832, ibid., 28–33, final quotations on pp. 30–31; Freehling, *Prelude to Civil War*, 260–64.

56. Andrew Jackson to Martin Van Buren, December 23, 1832; Jackson to Joel R. Poinsett, December 6, December 9, 1832, in *Correspondence of Andrew Jackson*, 7 vols., ed. John Spencer Bassett (Washington, DC: Carnegie Institution of Washington, 1926–1935), 4:504–05; 497–98, 493–94, quotations on pp. 497, 494; Jackson, Proclamation to the People of South Carolina, December 10, 1832, in *State Papers on Nullification*, 75–97, quotations on pp. 92, 96.

57. Andrew Jackson, Proclamation to the People of South Carolina, December 10, 1832, in *State Papers on Nullification*, 91; South Carolina's Reply to Jackson's Proclamation, December 20, 1832, in *State Documents on Federal Relations*, ed. Ames, 174–76. Conceptions of manhood among white Carolinians is one of several major themes addressed in Neumann, *Bloody Flag of Anarchy.*

58. James L Petigru to Hugh S. Legaré, December 21, 1832, in James Petigru Carson, *Life, Letters and Speeches of James Louis Petigru: The Union Man of South Carolina* (Washington, DC: W. H. Lowdermilk, 1920), 113; Freehling, *Prelude to Civil War*, 288–89; JCC, speech on the force bill, February 15, 16, 1833, in *Calhoun Papers*, 12:45–93, quotations on pp. 86, 65, 92–93.

59. Alabama and Mississippi Resolves, in *State Papers on Nullification*, 219–25, 229–31, quotation on p. 222; JCC to Samuel D. Ingham, January 17, 1833, in *Calhoun Papers*, 12:17; Bartlett, *Calhoun*, 193–96; Ellis, *Union at Risk*, chs. 5–6; Claudio Saunt, *Unworthy Republic: The Disappearance of Native Americans and the Road to Indian Territory* (New York: W. W. Norton, 2020), 167–68.

60. Freehling, *Prelude to Civil War*, 274–86; Neumann, *Bloody Flag of Anarchy*, 69–73, 78–82; *Jackson Correspondence*, ed. Bassett, 4:490–94, 497–98, 501–02; 5:5–18, 21–24, 28–29; Meigs, *Calhoun*, 2:35–36; JCC to William C. Preston, February 3, 1833, in *Calhoun Papers*, 12:38.

61. Ellis, *Union at Risk*, 174–5, first quotation on p. 174; Andrew Jackson to Joel R. Poinsett, January 18, 1833, in *Jackson Correspondence*, ed. Bassett, 5:5; Bolt, *Tariff Wars*, 134–39.

62. Porcher eulogy, July 5, 1850, in *The Carolina Tribute to Calhoun*, ed. J. P. Thomas (Columbia: Richard L. Bryan, 1857), 279; JCC, remarks during final consideration of the compromise Tariff Bill, March 1, 1833; JCC, speech at Charleston, November 22, 1833, in *Calhoun Papers*, 12:138, 181.

63. *Speeches Delivered in the Convention of the State of South-Carolina, Held in Columbia, in March 1833* (Charleston, SC: E. J. Van Brunt, 1833), 27, 36, 40–42, 52, 62, quotations on pp. 27, 40, 52; Davis, *Rhett*, 74–77.

64. First quotation in JQA to Benjamin F. Hallett, March 6, 1833; remaining quotations in JQA to Charles Francis Adams, March 26, 1833, JQA to William Ellis, March 15, 1833, reel 151, Adams Family Papers, MHS; Cooper, *Lost Founding Father*, 303.

65. JQA Diary, 38:January 10, 1832; JQA to Charles Francis Adams, March 13, 1833, reel 151, Adams Family Papers, MHS.

66. Joel R. Poinsett to Andrew Jackson, March 21, 1833, in *Jackson Correspondence*, ed. Bassett, 5:44; James L. Petigru to Hugh S. Legaré, July 18, 1833, in Carson, *Life of Petigru*, 125; William H. Pease and Jane H. Pease, *James Louis Petigru: Southern Conservative, Southern Dissenter* (Athens: University of Georgia Press, 1995), 125; JCC, speech in reply to Daniel Webster, March 1, 1833, in *Calhoun Papers*, 12:14; Niven, *John C. Calhoun and the Price of Union: A Biography* (Baton Rouge, 1988), 196–97; Gerald M. Capers, *John C. Calhoun—Opportunist: A Reappraisal* (Gainesville: University of Florida Press, 1960), 164–65.

67. JCC, remarks on the president's message on South Carolina, January 16, 1833, in *Calhoun Papers*, 12:14.

68. JQA, *Parties in the United States,* ed. Adams, 127; John G. Grove, "Binding the Republic Together: The Early Political Thought of John C. Calhoun," *South Carolina Historical Magazine,* 115 (April 2014): 100–21; Lacy K. Ford Jr., "Inventing the Concurrent Majority: Madison, Calhoun and the Problem of Majoritarianism in American Political Thought," *Journal of Southern History,* 60 (February 1994): 42–45.

Chapter 4: Slavery and Antislavery

1. There were some exceptions to the inattention paid Black abolitionists, the most notable of which was the alarmed response to David Walker's 1829 pamphlet, *Walker's Appeal, in Four Articles, Together with a Preamble, to the Coloured Citizens of the World.* See Peter P. Hinks, *David Walker's Appeal to the Coloured Citizens of the World* (University Park: Pennsylvania State University Press, 2000).

2. Don E. Fehrenbacher, *The Dred Scott Case: Its Significance in American Law and Politics* (New York: Oxford University Press, 1978), 122.

3. William J. Grayson, *Witness to Sorrow: The Antebellum Autobiography of William J. Grayson*, ed. Richard J. Calhoun (Columbia: University of South Carolina Press, 1990), 184.

4. JQA Diary, 31:April 30, 1819.

5. Lacy K. Ford, *Deliver Us from Evil: The Slavery Question in the Old South* (New York: Oxford University Press, 2009), 314–25; Brutus [Robert James Turnbull], *The Crisis: or, Essays on the Usurpations of the Federal Government* (Charleston, SC: A. E. Miller, 1827), 126–38, 148, quotations on pp. 131, 138; Charles Cotesworth Pinckney, *An Address Delivered in Charleston, before the Agricultural Society of South Carolina, on Tuesday, the 18th August, 1829* (Charleston: A. E. Miller, 1829), 8–10, quotation on p. 10; Whitemarsh Seabrook, *A Concise View of the Critical Situation and Future Prospects of the Slave-Holding States in Relation to Their Colored Population* (Charleston, SC: A. E. Miller, 1825), 8–13; William W. Freehling, *Prelude to Civil War: The Nullification Crisis in South Carolina, 1816–1836* (New York: Harper & Row, 1966), 301–03. Evidence of Calhoun's subsequent adoption of these views can be found in *Calhoun Papers,* 12:197, 13:371.

6. William Lloyd Garrison, *Thoughts on African Colonization: or, an Impartial Exhibition of the Doctrines, Principles and Purposes of the American Colonization Society, Together with the Resolutions, Addresses and Remonstrances of the Free People of Color* (Boston: Garrison & Knapp, 1832), 21; *First Annual Report of the New-England Anti-Slavery Society, Presented Jan. 9, 1833* (Boston: Isaac Knapp, 1833), 23–41, quotations on pp. 27, 31, 37; Manisha Sinha, *The Slave's Cause: A History of Abolition* (New Haven, CT: Yale University Press, 2016), 195–224.

7. Sinha, *The Slave's Cause*, 224–27, 239–52; Henry Mayer, *All on Fire: William Lloyd Garrison and the Abolition of Slavery* (New York: St. Martin's, 1998), 209–10.

8. Alfred Huger to Samuel L. Gouvernour, August 1, 1835, in "Postmaster Huger and the Incendiary Publications," ed. Frank Otto Gatell, *South Carolina Historical Magazine,* 64 (October 1963): 194–95; Brian C. Neumann, *Bloody Flag of Anarchy: Unionism in South Carolina during the Nullification Crisis* (Baton Rouge: Louisiana State University Press, 2022), 119–20.

9. *Proceedings of the Citizens of Charleston, on the Incendiary Machinations, Now in Progress, against the Peace and Welfare of the Southern States* (Charleston: A. E. Miller, 1835);

Freehling, *Prelude to Civil War*, 340–48; Neumann, *Bloody Flag of Anarchy*, 120–25; JCC, report of February 3, 1836, and speech of April 12, 1836, in *Calhoun Papers*, 13:58, 62–64, 161–65, quotations on pp. 58, 165.

10. Stanley Harrold, *American Abolitionism: The Direct Political Impact from Colonial Times into Reconstruction* (Charlottesville: University of Virginia Press, 2019), 49–51, 56–58; Julia Roy Jeffrey, *The Great Silent Army of Abolitionism: Ordinary Women in the Antislavery Movement* (Chapel Hill: University of North Carolina Press, 1998), 86–93; *Second Annual Report of the American Anti-Slavery Society* (1835), 62; Stewart quotation in *Fifth Annual Report of the American Anti-Slavery Society* (1838), 41. William Lee Miller provides a useful summary of the number of petitions presented in *Arguing about Slavery: The Great Battle in the United States Congress* (New York: Alfred A. Knopf, 1996), 305–09.

11. *Register of Debates*, 24th Cong., 1st sess. (December 18, 21, 1835): 1966–67, 1969, 2006, quotations on pp. 1967, 2006.

12. JCC, remarks and speeches on receiving abolition petitions, January 7, January 19, March 8, 1836, February 8, 1837, in *Calhoun Papers*, 13:28, 43, 92–96, 102–05, 392–93, quotations on pp. 103, 105; William W. Freehling, *The Road to Disunion: Secessionists at Bay, 1776–1854* (New York: Oxford University Press, 1990), 322–27; Daniel Wirls, "'The Only Mode of Avoiding Everlasting Debate': The Overlooked Senate Gag Rule for Antislavery Petitions," *Journal of the Early Republic*, 27 (Spring 2007): 115–38.

13. *Register of Debates*, 24th Cong., 1st sess. (February 8, 1836): 2491–93, 2496–97, quotations on pp. 2492–93, 2496; Drew Gilpin Faust, *James Henry Hammond and the Old South: A Design for Mastery* (Baton Rouge: Louisiana State University Press, 1982), 178; Ford, *Deliver Us from Evil*, 502–03; Francis W. Pickens to Patrick Noble, March 7, 1836, in "Five Letters from Francis W. Pickens to Patrick Noble, 1835–1836," ed. Alice Noble Waring, *South Carolina Historical Magazine*, 54 (April 1953): 77.

14. Henry L. Pinckney, *An Oration, Delivered in the Independent, or Congregational Church, Charleston, before the State Rights & Free Trade Party, the State Society of Cincinnati, the Revolution Society, the '76 Association, and the State Volunteers, on the 4th of July, 1833* (Charleston, SC: A. E. Miller, 1833), 50; Neumann, *Bloody Flag of Anarchy*, 42–44, 60, 128; Pinckney, *Address to the Electors of Charleston District, South Carolina, on the Subject of the Abolition of Slavery* (Washington, DC: n.p., 1836), 8–11, quotations on pp. 8, 10; *Register of Debates*, 24th Cong., 1st sess. (February 8, May 19, 1836): 2492–95, 3776–77, final quotation on p. 3777.

15. *Register of Debates*, 24th Cong., 1st sess. (May 18, 1836): 3776; Leonard L. Richards, "The Jacksonians and Slavery," in *Antislavery Reconsidered: New Perspectives on the Abolitionists*, ed. Lewis Perry and Michael Fellman (Baton Rouge: Louisiana State University Press, 1986): 99–118.

16. [Turnbull], *The Crisis*, 132–33; report and resolutions of a public meeting at Pendleton, South Carolina, September 9, 1835, in *Calhoun Papers*, 12:551–53; Edmund Bellinger Jr., *Speech on the Subject of Slavery, Delivered 7th Sept'r, 1835, at a Public Meeting of the Citizens of Barnwell District, South Carolina* (Charleston, SC: Dan J. Dowling, Printer, 1835); *Niles' Weekly Register*, 48 (October 3, 1835): 72; 49 (January 2, 1836): 309, 318–19; resolutions of South Carolina, December 16, 1835, in *State Documents on Federal Relations: The States and the United States*, ed. Herman V. Ames (Philadelphia: University of Pennsylvania, 1911), 218–19.

17. *Register of Debates*, 24th Cong., 1st sess. (February 1, January 21, March 1, 1836): 2450–54, 2242, 672–76, quotations on pp. 2452, 2242, 676; [William Drayton], *The South Vindicated from the Treason and Fanaticism of the Northern Abolitionists* (Philadelphia: H. Manly, 1836), 198.

18. Miller, *Arguing about Slavery*, 34; *Register of Debates*, 24th Cong, 1st sess. (December 18, 1835): 1986; Faust, *James Henry Hammond*, 171–74; Harriet Martineau, *Retrospect of Western Travel*, 3 vols. (London: Saunders & Otley, 1838), 1:244.

19. JCC, remarks in debate on the reception of abolition petitions, February 12, 1836; speech at Pendleton, South Carolina, August 12, 1836; speech on abolition petitions, March 9, 1836; remarks on receiving abolition petitions, February 6, 1837, in *Calhoun Papers*, 13:77, 275, 103–05, 394, quotations on pp. 275, 103–05. Calhoun's slippery slope argument was not new. For an earlier statement of it, see Whitemarsh Seabrook's observations in *Concise View*, 13–14.

20. JCC, remarks in debate on the reception of abolition petitions, February 12, 1836; speech at Pendleton, South Carolina, August 12, 1836; remarks on receiving abolition petitions, February 6, 1837, in *Calhoun Papers*, 13:77, 275, 394, quotations on pp. 275, 394; Pickens quotation in *Niles' National Register*, 67 (January 4, 1845): 282. Calhoun's observations on the rising generation in the North made a sufficiently strong impression on Robert Barnwell Rhett that the Carolina fire-eater later included an extensive quotation from them in his eulogy to Calhoun. See [South Carolina General Assembly]. *The Death and Funeral Ceremonies of John Caldwell Calhoun, Containing the Speeches, Reports, and Other Documents Connected Therewith; the Oration of the Hon. R. B. Rhett, before the Legislature, &c.* (Columbia, SC: A. B. Johnston, 1850), 153. Also see Leonard L. Richards's observations on slaveholder concern about "the 'machinery' of organized antislavery" in *"Gentlemen of Property and Standing": Anti-Abolition Mobs in Jacksonian America* (New York: Oxford University Press, 1970), 47–49.

21. William G. Simms to P. C. Pendleton, February 1, 1841, in *The Letters of William Gilmore Simms*, ed. Mary C. Simms Oliphant et al., 6 vols. (Columbia: University of South Carolina Press, 1952–1982), 1:226–27; David Moltke-Hansen, "The Expansion of Intellectual Life: A Prospectus," in *Intellectual Life in Antebellum Charleston*, ed. Michael O'Brien and David Moltke-Hansen (Knoxville: University of Tennessee Press, 1986), 3–44; Simms to P. C. Pendleton, February 1, 1841, in *Simms Letters*, ed. Oliphant et al., 1:224.

22. William G. Simms to P. C. Pendleton, December 1, 1840, February 1, 1841; Simms to Benjamin F. Perry, October 13, 1843; prospectus of the *Southern Quarterly Review*, October 1, 1843, in *Simms Letters*, ed. Oliphant et al., 1:196–200, 215–28, 370, 373–74, quotations on pp. 200, 374; William R. Taylor, *Cavalier and Yankee: The Old South and American National Character* (New York: Harper Torchbooks, 1957), 269–70. Following Simms's 1854 departure from the editorship, the *Review* entered a period of decline that ended in its liquidation three years later. John McCardell, *The Idea of a Southern Nation: Southern Nationalists and Southern Nationalism, 1830–1860* (New York: W. W. Norton, 1979), 171.

23. JCC, speech on abolition petitions, March 9, 1836; remarks on the right of petition, February 13, 1840, in *Calhoun Papers*, 13:103–05, 15:102–03, quotation on p. 15:103; Freehling, *Road to Disunion: Secessionists at Bay*, 323–24.

24. *Register of Debates*, 24th Cong., 1st sess. (January 21, 1836): 2243; William Harper, *Anniversary Oration; Presented by the Hon, William Harper, in the Representative Hall, Columbia,*

S.C., Dec. 9, 1835 (Washington, DC: Duff Green, Printer, 1836), 8; *Register of Debates*, 24th Cong., 1st sess. (February 1, 1836): 2460–61.

25. A South-Carolinian [Edwin C. Holland], *A Refutation of the Calumnies Circulated Against the Southerly & Westerly States, Respecting the Institution and Existence of Slavery among Them, To Which Is Added a Minute and Particular Account of the Actual State and Condition of Their Negro Population* (Charleston: A. E. Miller, 1822), 43–45; Thomas Cooper, *Two Essays: 1. On the Foundation of Civil Government: 2. On the Constitution of the United States* (Columbia: D. & J. M. Faust, 1826), 44–47; [Edwin Brown], *Notes on the Origin and Necessity of Slavery* (Charleston: A. E. Miller, 1826), 5–6, 29–32; Ford, *Deliver Us from Evil*, 618, n. 24; Bellinger, *Speech on the Subject of Slavery*, 12–31, 34, quotation on p. 34; [Drayton], *The South Vindicated*, 304; Register of Debates, 24th Cong., 1st sess. (February 1, 1836): 2456–57.

26. Irving H. Bartlett, *John C. Calhoun: A Biography* (New York: W. W. Norton, 1991), 217; JCC to John McLean, August 4, 1828, in *Calhoun Papers*, 10:406–07; Freehling, *Prelude to Civil War*, 307.

27. JCC, remarks in debate on his fifth resolution on abolition and the Union, January 10, 1838; remarks on receiving abolition petitions, February 6, 1837; report and resolutions of a public meeting at Pendleton, SC, September 8, 1835; JCC to William C Brown, November 14, 1844; JCC to James T Austin, December 28, 1837; report by Horace Binney of a conversation with Calhoun, 1834, in *Calhoun Papers*, 14:84–85, 13:395–96, 12:550–51, 20:291, 14:34, 27:499, quotations on pp. 14:84, 13:395, 14:84–85; Ford, *Deliver Us from Evil*, 507–08, 526–27; final quotation in Elizabeth Fox-Genovese and Eugene D. Genovese, *Slavery in White and Black: Class and Race in the Southern Slaveholders' New World Order* (New York: Cambridge University Press, 2008), 4.

28. JCC to Duff Green, August 30, 1835; JCC to Armistead Burt, June 28, 1836; Robert Y. Hayne to JCC, November 1, 1838, in *Calhoun Papers*, 12:547, 13:250, 14:459; Ford, *Deliver Us from Evil*, 495–96.

29. *Register of Debates*, 24th Cong., 1st sess. (February 12, 22, 1836), 478–79, 482–84, quotations on pp. 479, 482, 484.

30. Ibid., 24th Cong., 2d sess. (February 6, 1637): 719–23, quotations on pp. 719, 721, 722.

31. H. B. Bascom, *Methodism and Slavery: with Other Matters in Controversy between the North and the South* (Frankfort: Hodges, Todd & Pruett, 1845); JCC to Thomas G. Clemson, June 23, 1845; JCC to James H. Hammond, July 7, 1845; JCC to Thomas B. Stevenson, July 7, 1845; Hammond to JCC, July 20, 1845, August 18, 1845; JCC to Hammond, August 30, 1845; Hammond to JCC, September 26, 1845; JCC to Hammond, September 28, 1845, in *Calhoun Papers*, 21:598, 22:12, 13, 31–32, 79–82, 100–01, 172, 177, quotations on pp. 21:598, 22:31, 172, 82, 177; Hammond diary entry for September 6, 1845, in *Secret and Sacred: The Diaries of James Henry Hammond. A Southern Slaveholder*, ed. Carol Blesser (New York: Oxford University Press, 1988), 152–53.

32. JCC, resolutions on abolition and the Union, December 27, 1837; JCC, remarks on his resolutions on abolition and Union, December 28, 1837; JCC, remarks against referring his resolutions on abolition and the Union to a select committee, January 5, 1838, in *Calhoun Papers*, 14:31–32, 41, 57–58, 61, quotation on p. 57; James H. Read, *Majority Rule versus Consensus: The Political Thought of John C. Calhoun* (Lawrence: University Press of Kansas, 2009), 96–102; Bartlett, *Calhoun*, 240–42.

33. JCC, remarks on his resolutions on abolition and the Union, December 28, 1838; JCC, further remarks in debate on his fifth resolution on abolition and the Union, January 10, 1838; JCC to Littleton W. Tazewell, January 24, 1836; JCC, remarks on receiving abolition petitions, December 12, 1837; JCC to James Edward Colhoun, January 8, 1838; JCC to John R. Matthewes, February 24, 1838, in *Calhoun Papers,* 14:36–37, 83, 13:50; 14:11–12, 70, 158–159, quotations on pp. 14:36–37, 83, 70; Read, *Majority Rule versus Consensus,* 102–03.

34. Resolutions of the legislature of Massachusetts, April 12, 1837, in *State Documents on Federal Relations: The States and the United States,* ed. Herman V. Ames (Philadelphia University of Pennsylvania, 1911), 222–23; JCC to Richard Peters, April 25, 1837; JCC to James Edward Colhoun, December 20, 1837, in *Calhoun Papers,* 13:502, 14:15, quotation on p. 13: 502.

35. JQA Diary, 33:April 2, 1837; Leonard L. Richards, *The Life and Times of Congressman John Quincy Adams* (New York: Oxford University Press, 1986), 60–65; JQA Diary, 36:February 28, 1829; JQA to A. H. Everett, May 10, 1836, in "Letters of John Quincy Adams to Alexander Hamilton Everett, 1811–1837," *American Historical Review,* 11 (January 1906): 351; JQA to Charles Francis Adams, March 23, 1837, reel 506, Adams Family Papers, MHS.

36. JQA Diary, 42:May 24, 1840, 36:June 1, 1830, 39:March 10, 1834, final quotations in 42:June 24, 1840; 41:July 21, 1842.

37. JQA to S. Sampson, May 21, 1836, in Charles Francis Adams, "John Quincy Adams and Martial Law," *Proceedings of the Massachusetts Historical Society,* 2d series, 15 (1901–1902): 448–49; JQA Diary, 42:July 15, 1839; James G. Birney to Salmon P. Chase, February 2, 1842; Birney to Leicester King, January 1, 1844, in *Letters of James Gillespie Birney, 1831–1857,* ed. Dwight L. Dumond, 2 vols. (1938; repr. Gloucester, MA: Peter Smith, 1968), 2:671, 768–72, quotation on p. 772. It should be added that Adams had an equally poor opinion of Birney, describing him as "the sport of envious, bitter, ambitious and malignant passions," whose "head is turned by the greatness thrust upon him of a party candidate for the presidency." JQA Diary, 44:September 23, 1844.

38. JQA Diary, 38:January 10, 1831, 40:August 11, 12, 18, 1835, quotations in entries for August 11, 12; Richards, *Congressman John Quincy Adams,* 110–12; Henry F. Benson to Amos A. Phelps, August 27, 1835, in Antislavery MSS., Boston Public Library; *Boston Courier,* September 9, 1835.

39. William F. Hartford, *Money, Morals, and Politics: Massachusetts in the Age of the Boston Associates* (Boston: Northeastern University Press), 105–06; William Ellery Channing, *Slavery* (1835), in *The Works of William Ellery Channing,* 6 vols. (Boston: American Unitarian Association, 1903), 2:145; JQA Diary, 40:January 8, 1836; *Liberator,* February 27, 1836; William Lloyd Garrison to Samuel J. May, December 5, 1835, in *The Letters of William Lloyd Garrison,* ed. Walter M. Merrill and Louis Ruchames, 6 vols. (Cambridge, MA: Harvard University Press, 1971–1981), 1:572. The Garrisonian Massachusetts Anti-Slavery Society followed the Boston editor's lead, criticizing Channing's treatment of abolitionists, but stating that "we are not behind others in our approbation of a very large proportion of his work." *Fourth Annual Report of the Massachusetts Anti-Slavery Society, with Some Account of the Annual Meeting, January 20, 1836* (Boston: Isaac Knapp, 1836), 30–38, quotation on p. 37.

40. Pickens and Hammond quotations in *Register of Debates,* 24th Cong., 1st sess. (January 21, February 1, 1836): 2243, 2453; JCC, remarks on receiving abolition petitions, January 7, 1836, in *Calhoun Papers,* 13:25; *Liberator,* December 8, 1837; William Ellery Channing to

Samuel E. Sewall, November 25, 1837; Channing to William Lloyd Garrison, December 9, 1837, in Garrison MSS., Boston Public Library; *Liberator,* December 8, 1837; "Jacobin" quotation in JQA Diary, 33:November 12, 1838; Aaron Hobart to JQA, March 5, 1836; Benjamin Waterhouse to JQA, May 10, 1836, reel 503, Adams Family Papers, MHS, quotation in Hobart letter; final quotations in JQA Diary, 33:April 19, 1837, November 12, 1838.

41. Hartford, *Money, Morals, and Politics,* 108–11; JQA Diary, 43:October 7, 1842; Samuel Osgood to JQA, December 20, 1837, reel 507, Adams Family Papers, MHS.

42. JQA Diary, 38:December 12, 1831, January 10, 1832; Richards, *Congressman John Quincy Adams,* 105–06; William J. Cooper, *The Lost Founding Father: John Quincy Adams and the Transformation of American Politics* (New York: Liveright, 2017), 322–23; *Register of Debates,* 24th Cong., 1st sess. (December 21, 1835, January 25, 1836): 2000–02, 2316–17, quotation on p. 2002; *Congressional Globe,* 26th Cong., 1st sess. (January 22, 1840): appendix, 746–48.

43. David C. Frederick, "John Quincy Adams, Slavery, and the Disappearance of the Right of Petition," *Law and History Review,* 9 (Spring 1991): 127, 129–30, first quotation on p. 130; JQA, *Speech of John Quincy Adams, of Massachusetts: Upon the Right of the People, Men and Women, to Petition . . . and the Petitions of More Than One Hundred Thousand Petitioners, Relating to the Annexation of Texas* (Washington, DC: Gales & Seaton, 1838), 19–26; final quotation in *Register of Debates,* 24th Cong. 2d sess. (January 23, 1837): 1427.

44. *Register of Debates,* 25th Cong., 3d sess. (February 25, 1839): 205; Robert P. Ludlum, "The Antislavery 'Gag Rule': History and Argument," *Journal of Negro History,* 28 (April 1941): 217–18; *Congressional Globe,* 25th Cong., 3d sess. (January 7, 1839): 99; ibid., 27th Cong., 2d sess. (June 3, 1842): 570; final quotation in JQA Diary, December 22, 1837; *Congressional Globe,* 27th Cong., 1st sess. (June 8, 1841): 38.

45. Frederick, "John Quincy Adams," 134–37; *Register of Debates,* 24th Cong., 2d sess. (February 6, 8, 9, 1837): 1603, 1673–75, 1680, quotations on pp, 1603, 1674, 1680.

46. *Register of Debates,* 24th Cong., 2d sess. (February 6, 7, 1837): 1599, 1633; JQA, *Letters from John Quincy Adams to His Constituents in the Twelfth Congressional District of Massachusetts. To Which Is Added His Speech in Congress, Delivered February 9, 1837* (Boston: Isaac Knapp, 1837), 25–26.

47. JCC to James H. Hammond, February 18, 1838; JCC to John R. Mathewes, February 12, 1837, in *Calhoun Papers,* 13:443, 420.

48. JCC to Col. James Edward Colhoun, February 1, 1840, in *Calhoun Papers,* 15:67; *Congressional Globe,* 27th Cong., 2d sess. (January 21, 25, 1842): 158, 168, 170.

49. *Congressional Globe,* 27th Cong., 2d sess. (February 3, 1842): 208; Joshua R. Giddings to his wife, February 6, 1842, in George W. Julian, *The Life of Joshua R. Giddings* (Chicago: A. C. McClurg, 1892), 110; Leonard L. Richards, *The Slave Power: The Free North and Southern Domination, 1780–1860* (Baton Rouge: Louisiana State University Press, 2000), 24; second Giddings quotation in Corey M. Brooks, *Liberty Power: Third Parties and the Transformation of American Politics* (Chicago: University of Chicago Press, 2016), 66; Theodore Dwight Weld to Angelina G. Weld, February 22, 1842, in *Letters of Theodore Dwight Weld, Angelina Grimké Weld and Sarah Grimké, 1822–1844,* ed. Gilbert H. Barnes and Dwight L. Dumond, 2 vols. (1934; repr. Gloucester, MA: Peter Smith, 1965), 2:935.

50. Richards, *Congressman John Quincy Adams,* 124–25, quotation on p. 124; JQA Diary, 43:February 6, 1843; *Congressional Globe,* 27th Cong., 2d sess. (January 28, 1842): 192–93;

Brooks, *Liberty Power*, 66; James M. McPherson, "The Fight Against the Gag Rule: Joshua Leavitt and Antislavery Insurgency in the Whig Party, 1839–1842," *Journal of Negro History*, 48 (July 1963): 190–91.

51. William Lee to JQA, February 22, 1837; Joseph Paine to JQA, February 6, 1837, reel 505; Anthony Collamore to JQA, March 10, 1837, reel 506; John Marston to JQA, February 25, 1837, reel 505, all four items in Adams Family Papers, MHS; Ludlum, "Antislavery 'Gag Rule,'" 242–43.

52. Richards, *Congressman John Quincy Adams*, 176–78; Frederick, "John Quincy Adams," 139; Joshua R. Giddings, *History of the Rebellion: Its Authors and Causes* (New York: Follett, Foster, 1864), 237; William G. Simms to Armistead Burt, January 1, 1845, in *Simms Letters*, ed. Oliphant et al., 2:7; Botts and Rives quotations in Russell B. Nye, *Fettered Freedom: Civil Liberties and the Slavery Controversy, 1830–1860* (1963; repr. Urbana: University of Illinois Press, 1972), 65.

53. JQA Diary, 39:February 6, 1834; Barton H. Wise, *The Life of Henry A. Wise, 1806–1876* (New York: MacMillan, 1899), 62; JQA Diary, 44:December 3, 1844, August 12, 1843.

54. Wise, *Life of Henry A. Wise*, 61; second quotation in William M. Wiecek, *The Sources of Antislavery Constitutionalism in America, 1760–1848* (Ithaca, NY: Cornell University Press, 1977), 245; Publius Valerius [JQA] articles in *The Repertory*, October 26, November 6, 1804; proposed amendment to the Constitution, December 1804, all three items in *Writings of JQA*, 3:48–50, 70–76, 87–100; JQA to Asa Walker, Charles A. Stackpole, and F. M. Sabine, July 4, 1843, in *Niles' National Register*, 64 (August 26, 1843): 411.

55. JQA, *An Oration Delivered to the Inhabitants of Newburyport, at Their Request, on the Sixty-First Anniversary of the Declaration of Independence, July 4th, 1837* (Newburyport, MA: Charles Whipple, 1837), 50–53, 15–17, 25, 42–44, quotations on pp. 51, 15, 25; final quotation in JQA, *Speech of John Quincy Adams, upon the Right of the People, Men and Women, to Petition . . .*, 84; also see JQA, *Argument of John Quincy Adams, before the Supreme Court of the United States, in the Case of the United States, Apellanats, vs. Cinque, and Others, Africans, Captured in the Schooner Amistad . . .* (New York: S. W. Benedict, 1841), 87–89; William Goodell, *Views of American Constitutional Law, in Its Bearing upon American Slavery* (Utica, NY: Jackson & Chaplin, 1844), 137–39; JQA, *The Jubilee of the Constitution: A Discourse Delivered at the Request of the New York Historical Society, in the City of New York on Tuesday, the 30th of April, 1839, Being the Fiftieth Anniversary of the Inauguration of George Washington as President* (New York: Samuel Colman, 1839), 20, 30, 37–38, 41, 119.

56. JQA to Asa Walker, Charles A. Stackpole, and F. M. Sabine, July 4, 1843, in *Niles' National Register*, 64 (August 26, 1843): 411; JQA Diary, 43:July 10, 1842. Also see Adams's remarks on abolition as the fulfillment of scriptural prophecy in *An Oration Delivered before the Inhabitants of Newburyport*, 53–64.

57. Alvan Stewart, *Writings and Speeches of Alvan Stewart, on Slavery*, ed. Luther Rawson Marsh (New York: A. B. Burdick, 1860), 260.

58. Wendell Phillips, *Speeches, Lectures, and Letters* (Boston: Lee & Shepard, 1884), 153; JCC to Samuel D. Ingham, February 27, 1834; JCC to Christopher Van Deventer, January 25, 1834; JCC to James Edward Colhoun, February 5, 1834, in *Calhoun Papers*, 12:242, 230, 231–32, quotation on p. 242; Charles M. Wiltse, *John C. Calhoun: Nullifier, 1829–1839* (Indianapolis: Bobbs-Merrill, 1949), 319.

59. Ellis G. Loring to William Ellery Channing, March 17, 1838, reel 3, William Ellery Channing Papers, MHS; *Sixth Annual Report of the Board of Managers of the Massachusetts Anti-Slavery Society, Presented January 24, 1838, with an Appendix* (Boston: Isaac Knapp, 1838), iii; *Congressional Globe*, 28th Cong., 1st sess. (December 22, 1843): 65; Joshua Leavitt to James G. Birney, February 10, 1843, in *Birney Letters*, ed. Dumond, 2:715–16.

60. *Third Annual Report of the American Anti-Slavery Society* (1836), 85; *Fifth Annual Report of the Board of Managers of the Massachusetts Anti-Slavery Society, with Some Account of the Annual Meeting, January 25, 1837* (Boston: Isaac Knapp, 1837), 34–35; JCC to Augustin S. Clayton, August 5, 1836, in *Calhoun Papers*, 13:263. Garrison biographer Henry Mayer has written that the Boston editor considered Calhoun "the perfect satanic antihero." *All on Fire*, 218.

61. *Fifth Annual Report of the Massachusetts Anti-Slavery Society*, 35; Rives quotation in Bartlett, *Calhoun*, 241; William J. Cooper Jr., *The South and the Politics of Slavery, 1828–1856* (Baton Rouge: Louisiana State University Press, 1978), 58–97, quotation on p. 68; Neumann, *Bloody Flag of Anarchy*, ch. 6.

62. Freehling, *Road to Disunion: Secessionists at Bay*, 326; *Mary Chesnut's Civil War*, ed. C. Vann Woodward (New Haven, CT: Yale University Press, 1981), 377; Cooper, *The South and the Politics of Slavery*, 104–12.

Chapter 5: Party, Politics, and the Expansion of Slavery

1. Martin Van Buren to Thomas Ritchie, January 13, 1827, in *The Age of Jackson*, ed. Robert V. Remini (Columbia: University South Carolina Press, 1972), 8; Donald B. Cole, *Martin Van Buren and the American Political System* (Princeton, NJ: Princeton University Press, 1984), ch. 5.

2. Joel H. Silbey, *The Partisan Imperative: The Dynamics of American Politics before the Civil War* (New York: Oxford University Press, 1985).

3. George A. Lipsky, *John Quincy Adams: His Theory and Ideas* (New York: Thomas Y. Crowell, 1950), 152; JQA to Thomas Boylston Adams, July 11, 1800, in *Writings of JQA*, 2:464; JQA Diary, 35:August 24, 1824, 37:December 11, 1827, 41:October 1, 1840.

4. Mary W. M. Hargreaves, *The Presidency of John Quincy Adams* (Lawrence: University Press of Kansas, 1985), 47–61; William J. Cooper, *The Lost Founding Father: John Quincy Adams and the Transformation of American Politics* (New York: Liveright, 2017), 250–54; JQA Diary, 33:May 13, 1825, second quotation in 31:September 7, 1820, 37:April 26, 1827.

5. JQA Diary, 27:December 31, 1803; William F. Hartford, *Money, Morals, and Politics: Massachusetts in the Age of the Boston Associates* (Boston: Northeastern University Press, 2001), ch. 1; JQA to William Plumer, August 16, 1809, in *Niles' Weekly Register*, 36 (March 6, 1829): 17–18; JQA to Orchard Cook, August 22, 1808, in *Writings of JQA*, 3:239.

6. JQA, Reply to the Appeal of the Massachusetts Federalists, in *Documents Relating to New-England Federalism, 1800–1815*, ed. Henry Adams (Boston: Little, Brown, 1905), 107–329; Richard Hofstadter, *The Idea of a Party System: The Rise of Legitimate Opposition in the United States, 1780–1840* (Berkeley: University of California Press, 1969), 194–98, 200, 203–04.

7. JQA Diary, 35:August 31, 1824, 24:January 28, 1802, 33:January 31, 1825; JQA, *The Lives of James Madison and James Monroe, Fourth and Fifth Presidents of the United States, with*

Historical Notices of Their Administrations (1836, 1831; repr. Boston: Phillips, Sampson, 1850), 313–14.

8. JQA, *Letters and Opinions of the Masonic Institution* (Cincinnati: Lorenzo Stratton, 1851), 249–50, 235–40, 263–64, quotations on pp. 237, 264. My interpretation of this phase of Adams's political life draws heavily on observations in Leonard L. Richards, *The Life and Times of Congressman John Quincy Adams* (New York: Oxford University Press, 1986), 43–54; and Sean Wilentz, *The Politicians & the Egalitarians: The Hidden History of American Politics* (New York: W. W. Norton, 2016), 135–46.

9. JQA, *Letters and Opinions of the Masonic Institution,* 213–14; JQA Dairy, 39:January 13, 1834; Wilentz, *The Politicians & the Egalitarians,* 128.

10. Richards, *Congressman John Quincy Adams,* 52–54; JQA, *The Social Compact . . .* (Providence, RI: Knowles & Vose, 1842), 31–32; First quotation in *Congressional Globe,* 27th Cong., 2d sess. (June 13, 1842): 621; John Adams to Elbridge Gerry, November 4, 1779, in *The Works of John Adams,* ed. Charles Francis Adams, 10 vols. (1850–1856; repr. Freeport, NY: Books for Libraries Press, 1969), 8:276; third quotation in JQA Diary, 33:April 8, 1837; *Congressional Globe,* 27th Cong., 2d sess. (August 17, 1842): 906.

11. JQA Diary, 33:December 27, 1838, 41:February 8, 1841, 42:February 13, June 29, 1840.

12. JQA to A. H. Everett, December 1, 1835, in "Letters of John Quincy Adams to Alexander H. Everett, 1811–1837," *American Historical Review,* 11 (January 1906): 349; JQA to Nicholas Biddle, June 10, 1836, in Charles Francis Adams, "John Quincy Adams and Martial Law," *Proceedings of the Massachusetts Historical Society,* 2d series, 15 (1901–1902): 454; JQA Diary, 42:October 28, 1839; Richards, *Congressman John Quincy Adams,* 56–57; JQA to Thomas Boylston Adams, April 10, 1811; JQA to William Plumer, October 6, 1810, in *Writings of JQA,* 4:68, 3:511.

13. Richards, *Congressman John Quincy Adams,* 75–84; JQA, *Speech [Suppressed by the Previous Question] of Mr. John Quincy Adams, on the Removal of the Public Deposites, and Its Reasons* (Washington, DC: Gales & Seaton, 1834), 32, 37, 41–43, first quotation on p. 32; remaining quotations in *Register of Debates,* 23d Cong., 1st sess. (April 9, 1834): 3506–07.

14. Abbott Lawrence to Leverett Saltonstall, January 28, 1842, in "The Saltonstall Papers, 1816–1845," ed. Robert F. Moody, *Collections of the Massachusetts Historical Society,* 82–86 (1978–1992), 85:23; Abbott Lawrence to Daniel S. Baker et al., August 20, 1844, in *Boston Courier,* September 24, 1844; John Davis, "The Influence of Slavery upon Free Labor," MS. speech, ca. 1840, in John Davis Papers, American Antiquarian Society, Worcester, MA; *Congressional Globe,* 27th Cong., 1st sess. (June 23, 1841): 98; quotation in JQA Diary, 43: March 26, 1842.

15. Brooks Adams, "The Heritage of Henry Adams," in Henry Adams, *The Degradation of the Democratic Dogma,* intro. Brooks Adams (New York: MacMillan, 1919), 20–28; first quotation in JQA to Charles W. Upham, February 2, 1837, in "Ten Unpublished Letters of John Quincy Adams, 1796–1837," ed. Edward H. Tatum Jr., *Huntington Library Quarterly,* 4 (April 1941): 382; JQA, Chesapeake and Ohio Canal groundbreaking speech, July 4, 1828, in *Niles' Weekly Register,* 34 (July 12, 1828): 327.

16. JQA Diary, 39:January 7, 1833; Daniel Feller, *The Public Lands in Jacksonian Politics* (Madison: University of Wisconsin Press, 1984). 190; *Register of Debates,* 22d Cong., 2d sess. (February 1833): appendix, 46–48; JQA, *Address of John Quincy Adams, to His Constituents of the Twelfth Congressional District, at Braintree, September 17, 1842* (Boston: J. H. Eastburn,

Printer, 1842), 40–53, 23, quotations on pp. 51, 23; JQA, address at Weymouth, in *Niles' National Register*, 67 (March 9, 1844): 155.

17. JQA Diary, 42: March 27, 1840; William J. Cooper Jr., *The South and the Politics of Slavery, 1828–1856* (Baton Rouge: Louisiana University Press, 1978), 113–18, quotation on p. 118.

18. JQA, *Speech [Suppressed by the Previous Question] on the Removal of the Public Deposits*, 38–40, quotation on p. 38; JQA Diary, 33:December 5, 1837; JQA, *Address of John Quincy Adams to His Constituents at Braintree, September 17, 1842*, 52; JQA Diary, 41:April 6, 1841.

19. Joshua R. Giddings, *History of the Rebellion: Its Authors and Causes* (New York: Follett, Foster, 1864), 133–34; JQA Diary, 47:March 7, 1838, 43:January 19, 1842, February 9, 1843, second quotation in 33:December 13, 1838; Richards, *Congressman John Quincy Adams*, 55–57, 124–25; Martin Van Buren to Thomas Ritchie, January 13, 1827, in *Age of Jackson*, ed. Remini, 8; JQA Diary, 41:November 20, 1841, final quotation in 45:January 1, 1845, 43:June 13, 17, 1843.

20. JQA Diary, 33:November 24, 1838, 44:October 2, 1844.

21. [R. M. T. Hunter], *Life of John C. Calhoun, Presenting a Condensed History of Political Events from 1811 to 1843* (New York: Harper & Brothers, 1843), 11.

22. JCC, speech on the dangers of a "factious opposition," January 15, 1814; JCC to James Monroe, June 23, 1826; JCC to Micah Sterling, December 16, 1826; JCC to Boling Hall, January 12, 1833; final quotation in JCC to Samuel D. Ingram, February 11, 1832, in *Calhoun Papers*, 1:195, 199–200, 10:132, 237, 12:8, 11:547.

23. Lacy K. Ford Jr., *Origins of Southern Radicalism: The South Carolina Upcountry, 1800–1860* (New York: Oxford University Press, 1988), 193–94; Richard W. McCormick, *The Second American Party System: Party Formation in the Jacksonian Era* (1966; repr. New York: W. W. Norton, 1973), 7, 343–44; Lacy K. Ford, "Recovering the Republic: Calhoun, South Carolina and the Concurrent Majority," *South Carolina Historical Magazine*, 80 (July 1988): 148; Mark Kaplanoff, "Charles Pinckney and the American Republican Tradition," in *Intellectual Life in Antebellum Charleston*, ed. Michael O'Brien and David Moltke-Hansen (Knoxville: University of Tennessee Press, 1986), 115–16; Kenneth S. Greenberg, *Masters and Statesmen: The Political Culture of American Slavery* (Baltimore: Johns Hopkins University Press, 1985), 54–57; JCC to James H. Hammond, April 2, 1840, in *Calhoun Papers*, 15:173.

24. Rachel N. Klein, *Unification of a Slave State: The Rise of the Planter Class in the South Carolina Backcountry, 1760–1808* (Chapel Hill: University of North Carolina Press, 1990), 262–68; William W. Freehling, *Prelude to Civil War: The Nullification Controversy in South Carolina, 1816–1836* (New York: Harper & Row, 1966), 89–91.

25. JCC, *A Discourse on the Constitution and Government of the United States*; James H. Hammond to JCC, April 28, 1840; JCC to James H. Hammond, May 16, 1840, in *Calhoun Papers*, 28:239, 15:189, 228–29; Brian C. Neumann, *Bloody Flag of Anarchy: Unionism in South Carolina during the Nullification Crisis* (Baton Rouge: Louisiana State University Press, 2022).

26. JCC, *A Discourse on the Constitution*; JCC, *A Disquisition on Government*; quotation in JCC, second speech on the bill for the admission of Michigan, January 5, 1837; JCC to William Smith, July 3, 1843, in *Calhoun Papers*, 28:234–39, 29–35, 13:349, 17:284–85; Ford, "Recovering the Republic," 153–58. Also see James H. Read, *Majority Rule versus Consensus: The Political Thought of John C. Calhoun* (Lawrence: University Press of Kansas, 2009), which

provides an extended analysis of what the doctrine of the concurrent majority meant to Calhoun.

27. JCC, *A Disquisition on Government*, in *Calhoun Papers*, 28:32–33; Read, *Majority Rule versus Consensus*, 144–45, 171; Manisha Sinha, *The Counter-Revolution of Slavery: Politics and Ideology in Antebellum South Carolina* (Chapel Hill: University of North Carolina Press, 2000), 13–14, 86–91; final quotation in Freehling, *Prelude to Civil War*, 89. It should be noted that some historians reject Hamilton's description of Palmetto politics. Lacy K. Ford Jr., has argued that Carolina yeomen exercised considerable influence in a democratic political process. My own position is closer to that of Rachel Klein, who "see[s] planters maintaining power and authority through their accommodations (sometimes grudging) to the yeomanry." Ford, *Origins of Southern Radicalism*; Klein, *Unification of a Slave State*, 305, n. 3.

28. JCC to Albert H. Pemberton, November 19, 1838; JCC to James L. Orr et al., November 1846, in *Calhoun Papers*, 14:473–74. 23:510–18, quotations on pp. 14:473, 23:518; Ford, *Origins of Southern Radicalism*, 284–303.

29. Ker Boyce to JCC, December 13, 1844, in *Calhoun Papers*, 20:535–36; Alfred Huger to William Porcher Miles, June 1, 1860, in Steven A. Channing, *Crisis of Fear: Secession in South Carolina* (1970; repr. New York: W. W. Norton, 1974), 168, n. 1; William J. Grayson, *Witness to Sorrow: The Antebellum Autobiography of William J. Grayson*, ed. Richard J. Calhoun (Columbia: University of South Carolina Press, 1990), 131; Daniel Huger to Benjamin Perry, April 10, 1833, in Lillian Adele Kibler, *Benjamin F. Perry: South Carolina Unionist* (Durham, NC: Duke University Press, 1946), 160; Ford, *Origins of Southern Radicalism*, 166–68; William Gilmore Simms to James H. Hammond, March 28, 1847, in *The Letters of William Gilmore Simms*, ed. Mary C. Simms Oliphant et al., 6 vols. (Columbia: University of South Carolina Press, 1952–1982), 2:291; James Henry Hammond, *Secret and Sacred: The Diaries of James Henry Hammond, a Southern Slaveholder*, ed. Carol Blesser (New York: Oxford University Press, 1988), 95–96, 141, 145, 223 quotations on pp. 145, 141; Benjamin F. Perry, *Reminiscences of Public Men, by Ex-Gov. B. F. Perry* (Philadelphia: J. D. Avil, 1883), 297–98.

30. JCC to Francis W. Pickens, July 17, 1835, in *Calhoun Papers*, 12:543–44.

31. JCC to Dr. William C. Daniell[?], October 28, 1838; JCC, speech on the bill to prevent the interference of certain federal officers in elections, February 22, 1839; JCC to Nathaniel Bailey and others, September 1840, in *Calhoun Papers*, 14:447, 572–74, 15:353–54, quotations on pp. 14:447, 572, 15:353–54.

32. JCC, speech on amendment to separate the government and the banks, October 9, 1837; JCC to Calvin Graves and others, September 6, 1838; JCC to James Montgomery Calhoun, October 13, 1837; JCC to B. G. Wright and others, April 1838; JCC to John Bauskett and others, November 3, 1837, in *Calhoun Papers*, 13:630, 14:419, 13:621, 14:256; 13:636–39, quotations on pp. 13:630, 14:419, 13:621, 14:256.

33. Ford, *Origins of Southern Radicalism*, 159–75; Irving H. Bartlett, *John C. Calhoun: A Biography* (New York: W. W. Norton, 1993), 238–40, 242–47; John Niven, *John C. Calhoun and the Price of Union* (Baton Rouge: Louisiana State University Press, 1988), 230–34.

34. JQA to A. H. Everett, November 7, 1837, in "Letters to Everett," 354; JQA to inhabitants of the twelfth congressional district, August 13, 1838, in *Niles' National Register*, 55 (November 22, 1838): 56.

35. Read, *Majority Rule versus Consensus*, 140–45; Richard N. Current, *John C. Calhoun* (New York: Washington Square Press, 1966), 86–102; JCC to Robert L. Alexander and

others, September 12, 1844; JCC, speech on the Oregon bill, June 27, 1848, in *Calhoun Papers,* 19:758, 25:532–33, quotations on pp. 19:758, 25:533. Also see Richard Hofstadter's dated but insightful essay, "John C. Calhoun: the Marx of the Master Class," in *The American Political Tradition and the Men Who Made It* (New York: Alfred A. Knopf, 1948), ch. 4.

36. JCC, speech before the passage of the tariff bill, August 5, 1842; Address of the South Carolina Democratic Convention, May 22, 1843; Virgil Maxcy to JCC, December 3, 10, 31, 1843; George McDuffie to JCC, January 3, 1844; Duff Green to JCC, January 6, 1844; "The Address of Mr. Calhoun to His Political Friends and Supporters" (published version), *Charleston Mercury,* January 29, 1844; JCC to Franklin H. Elmore, January 16, 1844, in *Calhoun Papers,* 16:360–75, 17:197–98, 586, 601–02, 651, 671, 676, 739–40, 710–11, quotations on pp. 16:360, 17:739–40, 711.

37. William C. Davis, *Rhett: The Turbulent Life and Times of a Fire-Eater* (Columbia: University of South Carolina Press, 2001), 197–201; *Niles' National Register,* 66 (August 13, 1844): 409–10.

38. JCC to Henry W. Conner, July 24, 1844; James A. Black for R. M. Saunders to JCC, June 1844; John A. Hogan to JCC, June 29, 1844; Unknown, Greene County, AL, to JCC, July 12, 1844; Francis W. Pickens to JCC, September 9, August 10, November 27, December 2, 1844; Francis W. Pickens to James Edward Colhoun, December 7, 1844, Ker Boyce to JCC, November 28, 1844, in *Calhoun Papers,* 19:430, 162–63, 221–22, 325–26, 728–29, 552, 20:380–81, 446, 502–03, 382–83, first two quotations on pp. 19:430, 552, 20:380; Robert B. Rhett to R. M. T. Hunter, August 30, 1844, in "Correspondence of Robert M. T. Hunter, 1826–1878," ed. Charles Henry Ambler, *Annual Report of the American Historical Association for the Year 1916,* 2 vols. (Washington, DC: Government Printing Office, 1918), 2:71.

39. Davis, *Rhett,* 203–04, 270; *Charleston Courier,* in *Niles' National Register,* 66 (August 24, 1844): 420; *Mary Chesnut's Civil War,* ed. C. Vann Woodward (New Haven, CT: Yale University Press, 1981), xxxvii–xxxviii, 68, 410, quotation on p. 410.

40. Memorandum by James H. Hammond, March 18, 1831, in "Letters on the Nullification Movement in South Carolina, 1830–1834," in *American Historical Review,* 8 (July 1901): 743–44; JCC to Augustin S. Clayton, August 5, 1836; JCC to Wilson Lumpkin, February 4, 1842; James Gadsden to JCC, October 9, 1845, in *Calhoun Papers,* 13:264, 15:108, 22:217.

41. JCC, address on taking the chair of the Southwestern Convention at Memphis, November 13, 1845; "Memorial from the Memphis Convention to the Honorable Senate of the U.S. of America," January 22, 1846; JCC, remarks on presenting the Memphis memorial, February 3, 1846; JCC, Report on the Memphis Memorial, June 26, 1846, in *Calhoun Papers,* 22:279–83, 479–93, 23:201–27, quotation on p. 22:280.

42. "The Memphis Convention," *Southern Quarterly Review,* 10 (October 1846): 377–417; Ker Boyce to JCC, November 28, 1844, in *Calhoun Papers,* 20:392–83; Charles M. Wiltse, *John C. Calhoun: Sectionalist, 1840–1850* (Indianapolis: Bobbs-Merrill 1951), 240–42; Hammond diary entry for November 26, 1846, in *Secret and Sacred,* ed. Blesser, 163; Drew Gilpin Faust, *James Henry Hammond and the Old South: A Design for Mastery* (Baton Rouge: Louisiana State University Press, 1982), 248–50.

43. JCC to Thomas G. Clemson, July 11, 1846, in *Calhoun Papers,* 23:300–01; "The Memphis Convention," 417; Daniel Feller, *The Public Lands in Jacksonian Politics,* 119–25, quotation on p. 120.

44. Cooper, *The South and the Politics of Slavery,* 228–31, quotation on p. 229.

45. William Cronon, *Changes in the Land: Indians, Colonists, and the Ecology of New England* (New York: Hill & Wang, 1983), 56–57; *Congressional Globe,* 29th Cong., 1st sess. (February 7, April 13, 1846): 340–42, 663–64, "great nation" quotation on p. 342; David M. Pletcher, *The Diplomacy of Annexation: Texas, Oregon, and the Mexican War* (Columbia: University of Missouri Press, 1973), 329–30; Cooper, *The Lost Founding Father,* 420–21.

46. James Craig Hammond, *Slavery, Freedom, and Expansion in the Early American West* (Charlottesville: University of Virginia Press, 2007), 39–40, 44–45; Don E. Fehrenbacher, *The Dred Scott Case: Its Significance in American Law and Society* (New York: Oxford University Press, 1978), 92–94, quotation on p. 94; *Register of Debates,* 24th Cong., 1st sess. (May 7, 13, 1836): 3522, 3701–05; William Earl Weeks, *John Quincy Adams and American Global Empire* (Knoxville: University Press of Kentucky, 1992), 123–24, 167–68, 197; Cooper, *The Lost Founding Father,* 371–73, 414–16.

47. *Register of Debates,* 24th Cong., 1st sess. (May 25, 1836): 4044–47, quotation on p. 4044; JQA Dairy, 41:December 24, 1836; second quotation in JQA to Nicholas Biddle, June 10, 1836, in Adams, "John Quincy Adams and Martial Law," 454; JQA Diary, 33:June 6, 1838; JQA to inhabitants of the twelfth congressional district, August 13, 1838, in *Niles' National Register,* 55 (September 22, 1838): 58; JQA, *Address of John Quincy Adams, to His Constituents of the Twelfth Congressional District, at Braintree, September 17, 1842* (Boston: J. H. Eastburn, Printer, 1842), 10–16, third quotation on p. 16; *Congressional Globe,* 27th Cong., 2d sess. (April 15, 1842): 429.

48. JQA and others, "to the people of the free states of the union," March 3, 1843, in *Niles' National Register,* 63 (May 13, 1843): 173–75; Frederick Merk, with the collaboration of Lois Bannister Mark, *Slavery and the Annexation of Texas* (New York: Alfred A. Knopf, 1972), 205–11; first quotation in JQA Diary, 44:April 22, 1844; JQA, address before the Boston Young Men's Whig Club, in *Niles' National Register,* 67 (October 19, 1844): 105–11, quotation on p. 111; JQA, address at Weymouth, October 30, 1844, in ibid., 67 (November 9, 1844): 154–59, final quotation on p. 156. Leonard L. Richards provides a more expansive treatment of Adams and the slave power conspiracy in *Congressman John Quincy Adams,* 151–70; Also see Richards, *The Slave Power and Southern Domination, 1780–1860* (Baton Rouge: Louisiana State University Press, 2000), ch. 1.

49. JQA Diary, 31:March 3, 1820; JQA to Kiah Bailey, March 27, 1837, in Adams, "John Quincy Adams and Martial Law," 466; JQA to Thomas Loring, August 8, 1842, reel 154, Adams Family Papers, MHS; *Congressional Globe,* 28th Cong., 1st sess. (December 22, 1843, March 22, 1844): 64–66, 425; next to last quotation on p. 425; JQA Diary, 44:October 17, 1844. For a particularly bitter expression of Southern opposition to Adams's position on the three-fifths compromise, see Henry St. George Tucker to Thomas Walker Gilmer, January 6, 1844, in Merk, *Slavery and the Annexation of Texas,* 265.

50. Richards, *Congressman John Quincy Adams,* 153–54, 168–70; JQA Diary, 43:February 27, 1843, 44:January 4, 1844; Pletcher, *The Diplomacy of Annexation,* 87–88, 205, 119.

51. JCC to Samuel D. Ingham, June 21, 1836; JCC, remarks at Charleston, March 17, 1837; Abel Upshur to JCC, August 16, 1843; JCC to Abel Upshur, August 27, 1843; Virgil Maxcy to JCC, December 3, 10, 1843; James Gadsden to JCC, May 3, 1844, in *Calhoun Papers,* 13:247–48, 498, 17:356–57, 381–82, 586, 601–02, 18:411, quotations on pp. 13:498, 17:382, 18:411.

52. JQA, address before the Boston Young Men's Whig Club, in *Niles' National Register,* 67 (October 19, 1844): 111; Matthew Karp, *This Vast Southern Empire: Slaveholders at the Helm of American Foreign Policy* (Cambridge, MA: Harvard University Press, 2016), 93–97; JCC to Richard Packenham, April 18, 1844, in *Calhoun Papers,* 18:274–78, quotations on pp. 275, 276, 278.

53. JQA Diary, 44:May 27, 1844; Joel H. Silbey, *Storm over Texas: The Annexation Controversy and the Road to Civil War* (New York: Oxford University Press, 2005), 43–46; James H. Hammond to JCC, June 7, 1844, in *Calhoun Papers,* 18:739–40, quotation on p. 740; Richards, *The Slave Power*, 140–45; Kinley J. Brauer, *Cotton versus Conscience: Massachusetts Whig Politics and Southwestern Expansion, 1843–1848* (Lexington: University of Kentucky Press, 1967), chs. 4–7; Charles Francis Adams Diary, March 21, 1844, reel 67, Adams Family Papers, MHS.

54. Pletcher, *The Diplomacy of Annexation*, ch. 12; Martin Van Buren to George Bancroft, February 15, 1845, in "Van Buren-Bancroft Correspondence," *Proceedings of the Massachusetts Historical Society,* 42 (June 1909): 439; Eric Foner, "The Wilmot Proviso Revisited," *Journal of American History,* 56 (September 1969): 274–77.

55. Congressional Globe, 29th Cong., 1st sess. (August 8. 1846): 1215–16; *Acts and Resolves of Massachusetts,* April 26, 1847, in *State Documents on Federal Relations: The States and the United States,* ed. Herman V. Ames (Philadelphia: University of Pennsylvania, 1911), 242.

56. JCC to Thomas G. Clemson, November 6, 1846, in *Calhoun Papers,* 23:527–28, quotation on p. 527; Michael F. Holt, *The Fate of Their Country: Politicians, Slavery Extension, and the Coming of the Civil War* (New York: Hill & Wang, 2004), 22–28; Silbey, *Storm over Texas,* 125–26; Ellwood Fisher, Cincinnati, to JCC, December 2, 1846; JCC to David Johnson, January 13, 1847; JCC to Anna Maria Calhoun, December 27, 1846, in *Calhoun Papers,* 23:554, 24:67, 43, final two quotations on pp. 23:554, 24:67

57. JCC, speech and resolutions on the restriction of slavery from the territories, February 19, 1847, in *Calhoun Papers,* 24:169–76, quotations on pp. 175, 172, 175–76.

58. JCC to Thomas G. Clemson, July 30, 1846, in *Calhoun Papers,* 23:147; *Congressional Globe*, 29th Cong., 2d sess. (February 8, 1847): 356–60; Brian DeLay, *War of a Thousand Deserts: Indian Raids and the U.S.-Mexican War* (New Haven, CT: Yale University Press, 2007).

59. JCC to Thomas G. Clemson, July 30, 1846, February 17, 1847; JCC, speech on the war with Mexico, January 4, 1848; JCC, first speech on the bill for an additional military force, March 16, 1848; JCC, speech on his slavery resolutions in reply to James F. Simmons, February 20, 1847, in *Calhoun Papers,* 23:376–77, 24:160, 25:93–94, 86, 241–44, 24:188, quotations on pp. 23:376–77, 25:244, 24:188.

60. JCC, speech on the war with Mexico, January 4, 1848, in *Calhoun Papers,* 25:81–82, 85–89, quotations on p. 85; Reginald Horsman, *Race and Manifest Destiny: The Origins of American Racial Anglo-Saxonism* (Cambridge, MA: Harvard University Press, 1981), 236–47; DeLay, *War of a Thousand Deserts*, 291–93.

61. Entry for January 23, 1847, *The Diary of James K. Polk during His Presidency, 1845 to 1849*, ed. Milo M. Quaife, 4 vols. (Chicago: A. C. McClurg, 1910), 2:350; JCC, speech on war with Mexico, February 9, 1847, in *Calhoun Papers,* 24:118; Ernest McPherson Lander Jr., *Reluctant Imperialists: Calhoun, the South Carolinians, and the Mexican War* (Baton Rouge: Louisiana State University Press, 1980), 174–76.

62. JCC, speech and resolutions on the restriction of slavery from the territories, February 19, 1847; JCC, speech on the proposal to extend the Missouri Compromise line to the Pacific, August 10, 1848, in *Calhoun Papers,* 24:174, 25:667.

63. Chaplain W. Morrison, *Democratic Politics and Sectionalism: The Wilmot Proviso Controversy* (Chapel Hill: University of North Carolina Press, 1967), 88–90; Christopher Childers, *The Failure of Popular Sovereignty: Slavery, Manifest Destiny, and the Radicalization of Southern Politics* (Lawrence: University Press of Kansas, 2012), 131–33; Thompson quotation in Lander, *Reluctant Imperialists,* 153; JCC to Henry Bailey, June 15, 1848; JCC to Col. Nathaniel R. Eaves, July 9, 1848, in *Calhoun Papers,* 25:484–85, 580, quotation on p. 484; Childers, *The Failure of Popular Sovereignty,* 147–49.

64. Quotation in Robert W. Johannsen, *Stephen A. Douglas* (1973; repr. Urbana: University of Illinois Press, 1997), 670; Fehrenbacher, *The Dred Scott Case,* ch. 20; Childers, *The Failure of Popular Sovereignty,* 142, 148, 270–72.

65. JCC to Wilson Lumpkin, April 21, 1848; JCC to Edmund S. Dargan, May 24, 1847; JCC to Joseph W. Lesesne, July 19, 1847; JCC, speech on the proposal to extend the Missouri Compromise line to the Pacific, August 10, 1848; JCC to Henry W. Connor, October 18, 1848, in *Calhoun Papers,* 25:350–51, 24:358–59, 463–64, 25:660–63, 26:94, quotations on pp. 25: 350, 661–62, 26:94.

66. *Boston Daily Whig,* July 7, August 7, 1846, first quotation in August 7th edition; Martin Duberman, *Charles Francis Adams, 1807–1886* (Boston: Houghton Mifflin, 1961), 90–91, 113; Charles Francis Adams Diary, September 14, 1848, reel 71, Adams Family Papers, MHS.

67. George W. Julian, *The Life of Joshua R. Giddings* (Chicago: A. C. McClurg, 1892), 306; first quotation in Charles Francis Adams to Joshua R. Giddings, October 18, 1847; Adams to John G. Palfrey, December 17, 1847, both items in reel 159, Adams Family Papers, MHS; second quotation in Henry B. Stanton, *Random Reflections* (New York: Harper & Brothers, 1887), 183; Charles Francis Adams to John G. Palfrey, December 12, 1848, reel 160, Adams Family Papers, MHS.

68. Salmon P. Chase to Joshua R. Giddings, February 15, 1842, in *The Salmon P. Chase Papers,* ed. John Niven, 5 vols. (Kent, OH: The Kent State University Press, 1993–1998), 2:86; Eric Foner, *Free Soil, Free Labor, Free Men: The Ideology of the Republican Party before the Civil War* (New York: Oxford University Press, 1970), 73–87; Julian, *Giddings,* 212–13, 241, second quotation on p. 241; Thomas Hudson McKee, *The National Conventions and Platforms of all Political Parties, 1789 to 1904: Conventions, Popular and Electoral Vote,* 5th ed. (Baltimore: Friedanwald, 1904), 67–68; James Oakes, *Freedom National: The Destruction of Slavery in the United States, 1861–1865* (New York: W. W. Norton, 2013), 22–34. My debt to Oakes here and in the succeeding paragraphs will be immediately apparent to anyone who has read his fine work.

69. JQA Diary, 31:March 3, 1820.

70. Oakes, *Freedom National,* 19–20; *Congressional Globe,* 28th Cong., 1st sess. (December 22, 1843): 65.

71. JCC to Henry S. Foote, August 3, 1849; JCC, The Address of the Southern Delegates in Congress to Their Constituents, January 22, 1849, in *Calhoun Papers,* 27:10–11, 26:234–42, quotations on pp. 27:10, 26:238, 241–42. James Oakes provides illuminating context for Calhoun's remarks in *The Scorpion's Sting: Antislavery and the Coming of the Civil War* (New York: W. W. Norton, 2014), ch. 1.

72. Robert Toombs to John J. Crittenden, September 27, 1848, January 22, 1849; Hopkins Holsey to Howell Cobb, February 24, 1849, in "The Correspondence of Robert Toombs, Alexander H. Stephens, and Howell Cobb," ed. Ulrich B. Phillips, *Annual Report of the American Historical Association for the Year 1911,* 2 vols. (Washington, DC: Government Printing Office, 1913), 129, 141, 154–56, quotations on pp. 129, 141, 154; Cooper, *The South and the Politics of Slavery,* 287–89; Wiltse, *John C. Calhoun: Sectionalist,* 398; proceedings of a public meeting at Accomac Country, VA, March 26, 1849; proceedings of a meeting of the citizens of Greene County, MO, May 28, 1849, both items in *Calhoun Papers*, 26:359–62, 411–14, final quotation on p. 360.

73. JCC. *A Discourse on the Constitution*; JCC, speech on the Oregon bill, June 27, 1848; JCC to the people of the Southern States, July 5, 1849, in *Calhoun Papers*, 28:220–24, 25:527–28, 26:487–88; Childers, *The Failure of Popular Sovereignty*, 115–18; Don E. Fehrenbacher, *The Dred Scott Case,* 140; JCC, speech on the slavery question, March 4, 1850, in *Calhoun Papers,* 27:189–98, 209–10, quotation on p. 210.

74. David Potter, completed and edited by Don E. Fehrenbacher, *The Impending Crisis, 1848–1861* (New York: Harper Colophon Books, 1976), 113; Oakes, *Freedom National,* 42–48.

Conclusion

1. William G. Simms to Nathaniel Beverly Tucker, March 12, 1851, in *The Letters of William Gilmore Simms*, ed. Mary C. Simms Oliphant et al., 6 vols. (Columbia: University of South Carolina Press, 1952–1982), 3:99; Steven A. Channng, *Crisis of Fear: Secession in South Carolina* (1970; repr. New York: W. W. Norton, 1974), 168, n. 1, n. 3; Francis Lieber to Judge Thayer, February 1, 1864, in Thomas Sergeant Perry, *The Life and Letters of Francis Lieber* (Boston: James R. Osgood, 1882), 338; *Mary Chesnut's Civil War*, ed. C. Vann Woodward (New Haven, CT: Yale University Press, 1981), 758.

2. Thomas W. Ward to Joshua Bates, April 7, 1848, copy, Thomas Wren Ward Papers, MHS; Theodore Parker, "A Discourse occasioned by the death of John Quincy Adams, delivered at the Melodeon, in Boston, March 5th, 1848," *Massachusetts Quarterly Review,* 3 (June 1848): 331–76, quotations on pp. 358, 364, 345; Lynn Hudson Parsons, "The 'Splendid Pageant': Observations on the Death of John Quincy Adams," *New England Quarterly,* 53 (December 1980): 464–82.

3. Parker, "A Discourse occasioned by the death of John Quincy Adams," 366; Benjamin Perry journal entry, April 28, 1850, in Lillian Adele Kibler, *Benjamin F. Perry: South Carolina Unionist* (Durham, NC: Duke University Press, 1946), 243; Francis Lieber to George S. Hilliard, 1850, in Perry, *Life and Times of Francis Lieber,* 244; Parker, "A Discourse occasioned by the death of John Quincy Adams," 375.

4. Parker, A Discourse occasioned by the death of John Quincy Adams," 375; entry for January 2, 1851, in *Secret and Sacred: The Diaries of James Henry Hammond, a Southern Slaveholder*, ed. Carol Blesser (New York: Oxford University Press, 1988), 299.

5. Virginia Mason, *The Public Life and Diplomatic Correspondence of James Murray Mason, with Some Personal History* (New York: Neale, 1906), 72–73.

6. Paul D. Escott, *Jefferson Davis and the Failure of Confederate Nationalism* (Baton Rouge: Louisiana State University Press, 1978), 4; William J. Cooper Jr., *Jefferson Davis, American* (New York: Vintage Books, 2000), 105, 192, 210, 339–48; quotation from Roy Franklin Nichols, *The Disruption of American Democracy* (New York, 1948), 283, in Don E.

Fehrenbacher, *The Dred Scott Case: Its Significance in American Law and Politics* (New York: Oxford University Press, 1978), 531.

7. Declaration of Causes Which Induced the Secession of South Carolina, in *The Rebellion Record: A Diary of American Events, with Documents, Narratives, Illustrative Incidents, Poetry, Etc.*, vol. 1, ed. Frank Moore (New York: G. P. Putnam, 1864), document 3; James H. Read, *Majority Rule versus Consensus: The Political Thought of John C. Calhoun* (Lawrence: University Press of Kansas, 2009), 111–12.

8. *Register of Debates,* 24th Cong., 1st sess. (May 25, 1836): 4039–40; JQA to Robert Walsh, June 3, 1836, in Charles Frances Adams, "John Quincy Adams and Martial Law," *Proceedings of the Massachusetts Historical Society,* 2d series, 15 (1901–1902): 451; first quotation in *Congressional Globe,* 27th Cong., 1st sess. (June 9, 1841): 38; second quotation ibid., 27th Cong., 2d sess. (April 15, 1842): 429; JQA Diary, 43:March 3, 1842; James Oakes, *Freedom National: The Destruction of Slavery in the United States, 1861–1865* (New York: W. W. Norton, 2013), 36–41; Oakes, *The Crooked Road to Abolition: Abraham Lincoln and the Antislavery Constitution* (New York: W. W. Norton, 2021), 136–38, 141–42.

9. JQA Diary, 33:April 19, 1837, December 13, 1838, 42:April 26, 1840; JQA, *An Oration Delivered before the Inhabitants of Newburyport, at Their Request, on the Sixty-Fifth Anniversary of the Declaration of Independence, July 4th, 1837* (Newburyport, MA: Charles Whipple, 1837), 53–64; John Stauffer and Benjamin Soskis, *The Battle Hymn of the Republic: A Biography of the Song That Marches On* (New York: Oxford University Press, 2013), 298–99; Adams quotation in Joshua R. Giddings, *History of the Rebellion: Its Authors and Causes* (New York: Follett, Foster, 1864), 217.

Bibliography

Primary Sources

Manuscript Collections

Boston, MA. Boston Public Library. Antislavery Collection.

———. Garrison MSS.

Boston, MA. Massachusetts Historical Society. Adams Family Papers. Microfilm ed.

———. Appleton Family Papers.

———. The Diaries of John Quincy Adams: A Digital Collection.

———. Edward Everett Letters. Microfilm ed.

———. Thomas Wren Ward Papers.

———. William Ellery Channing Papers. Microfilm ed.

———. Winthrop Family Papers. Microfilm ed.

Cambridge, MA. Houghton Library, Harvard University. Ellis Gray Loring Letterbook.

Worcester, MA. American Antiquarian Society. John Davis Papers.

Newspapers

Boston Daily Courier

Boston Daily Whig

Liberator (Boston)

Niles' National Register (Baltimore)

Niles' Weekly Register (Baltimore)

Published Primary Sources

Adams, Charles Francis. *Diary of Charles Francis Adams*. Edited by Aida Dipace Donald et al. 8 vols. Cambridge, MA: Harvard University Press, 1964–1986.

Adams, Henry, ed. *Documents Relating to New England Federalism, 1800–1815*. Boston: Little, Brown, 1905.

Adams, John. *John Adams: Writings from the New Nation, 1784–1826*. Edited by Gordon S. Wood. New York: Library of America, 2016.

———. *The Works of John Adams, the Second President of the United States*. Edited by Charles Francis Adams. 10 vols. 1850–1856. Reprint, Freeport, NY: Books for Libraries, 1969.

Adams, John Quincy. *An Address, Delivered at the Request of the Committee for Arrangements for Celebrating the Anniversary of Independence, at the City of Washington on the Fourth of July, 1821, upon the Occasion of Reading the Declaration of Independence*. Cambridge, MA: University Press by Hillard & Metcalf, 1821.

———. *Address of John Quincy Adams, to His Constituents of the Twelfth Congressional District at Braintree, September 11, 1842*. Boston: J. H. Eastburn, Printer, 1842.

———. *American Principles: A Review of Works of Fisher Ames, compiled by a Number of His Friends*. Boston: Everett & Munroe, 1809.

———. *Argument of John Quincy, before the Supreme Court of the United States, in the Case of the United States, Appellants vs. Cinque, and Others, Africans, Captured in the Schooner Amistad, by Lieut. Gedney, Delivered on the 24th of February and 1st of March, 1841. With a Review of the Case of the Antelope, Reported in the 10th, 11th, and 12th Volumes of Wheaton's Reports*. New York: S. W. Benedict, 1841.

———. *Correspondence of John Quincy Adams, 1811–1814*. Edited by Charles Francis Adams. Worcester, MA: American Antiquarian Society, 1913.

———. *A Discourse on Education, Delivered at Braintree, Thursday, Oct. 24, 1839*. Boston: Perkins & Marvin, 1840.

———. "Jefferson and Madison and the Doctrines of Interposition and Nullification: A Letter of John Quincy Adams." Edited by Ralph L. Ketcham. *Virginia Magazine of History and Biography* 66 (April 1958): 178–82.

———. *John Quincy Adams and American Continental Empire: Letters, Papers and Speeches*. Edited by Walter LaFeber. Chicago: Quadrangle Books, 1965.

———. *John Quincy Adams and the Politics of Slavery: Selections from the Diary*. Edited by David Waldstreicher and Matthew Mason. New York: Oxford University Press, 2017.

———. *The Jubilee of the Constitution: A Discourse Delivered at the Request of the New York Historical Society, in the City of New York on Tuesday, the 30th of April, 1839, Being the Fiftieth Anniversary of the Inauguration of George Washington as President*. New York: Samuel Colman, 1839.

———. "Letter of John Quincy Adams." *Proceedings of the Massachusetts Historical Society* 4, second series (1887–1889): 61–65.

———. *A Letter to the Hon. Harrison Gray Otis, a Member of the Senate of Massachusetts, on the Present State of Our National Affairs, with Remarks upon Mr. Pickering's Letter to the Governor of the Commonwealth of Massachusetts*. New Haven, CT: Sydney's Press, 1808.

———. *Letters and Opinions of the Masonic Institution*. Cincinnati: Lorenzo Stratton, 1851.

———. *Letters from John Quincy Adams to His Constituents of the Twelfth Congressional District of Massachusetts. To Which Is Added His Speech in Congress, Delivered February 9, 1837*. Boston: Isaac Knapp, 1837.

———. "Letters of John Quincy Adams." *Proceedings of the Massachusetts Historical Society* 10, second series (1895–1896): 374–92.

———. "Letters of John Quincy Adams to Alexander Hamilton Everett, 1811–1837." *American Historical Review* 11 (January 1906): 332–54.

———. *Letters of John Quincy Adams to His Son, on the Bible and Its Teachings*. Auburn, NY: James M. Alden, 1850.

———. *Life in a New England Town, 1787, 1788: Diary of John Quincy Adams, While a Student in the Office of Theophilus Parsons at Newburyport*. Edited by Charles Francis Adams. Boston: Little, Brown, 1903.

———. *The Lives of James Madison and James Monroe, Fourth and Fifth Presidents of the United States, with Historical Notices of the Their Administrations*. 1836, 1831. Reprint, Boston: Sampson, 1850.

———. *Memoirs of John Quincy Adams, Comprising Portions of His Diary from 1795 to 1848.* Edited by Charles Francis Adams. 12 vols. Philadelphia: J. B. Lippincott, 1874–77.

———. *Mr. Adams' Speech, on War with Great Britain and Mexico, with the Speeches of Messrs. Wise and Ingersoll, to Which It Is in Reply*. N.p., 1842.

———. *The New England Confederacy of MDCXLIII: A Discourse Delivered before the Massachusetts Historical Society, at Boston, on the 29th of May, 1843, in Celebration of the Second Centennial Anniversary of the Event.* Boston: Charles C. Little & James Brown, 1843.

———. *An Oration, Delivered at Plymouth, December 22, 1802: At the Anniversary Commemoration of the First Landing of Our Ancestors, at That Place.* Boston: Russell & Cutler, 1802.

———. *An Oration Delivered before the Inhabitants of the Town of Newburyport, at Their Request, on the Sixty-First Anniversary of the Declaration of Independence, July 4th, 1837.* Newburyport, MA: Charles Whipple, 1837.

———. *An Oration Delivered to the Citizens of the Town of Quincy, on the Fourth of July, 1831, the Fifty-Fifth Anniversary of the Independence of the United States of America.* Boston: Richardson, Lord & Holbrook, 1831.

———. *Parties in the United States.* Edited by Charles True Adams. New York: Greenberg, 1941.

———. *Six Letters from John Quincy Adams to Edward Livingston on Masonry*. Philadelphia: C. T. Jones, 1833.

———. *The Social Compact, Exemplified in the Constitution of the Commonwealth of Massachusetts, with Remarks on the Theories of Divine Right of Hobbes and Filmer, and the Counter Theories of Sydney, Locke, Montesquieu, and Rousseau, Concerning the Origins and Nature of Government.* Providence, RI: Knowles and Vose, 1842.

———. *Speech of John Quincy Adams, of Massachusetts: Upon the Right of the People, Men and Women, to Petition; on the Freedom of Speech and of Debate in the House of Representatives of the United States; on the Resolutions of the Seven State Legislatures, and the Petitions of More Than One Hundred Thousand Petitioners, Relating to the Annexation of Texas to This Union.* Washington, DC: Gales and Seaton, 1838.

———. *Speech of the Hon. John Quincy Adams, in the House of Representatives on the State of the Nation, Delivered May 25, 1836.* New York: H. R. Piercy, 1836.

———. *Speech [Suppressed by the Previous Question] of Mr. John Quincy Adams, of Massachusetts, on the Removal of the Public Deposites, and Its Reasons.* Washington, DC: Gales & Seaton, 1834.

———. "Ten Unpublished Letters of John Quincy Adams, 1796–1837." Edited by Edward H. Tatum, Jr. *Huntington Library Quarterly* 4 (April 1941): 369–88.

———. *Writings of John Quincy Adams.* Edited by Washington Chauncey Ford. 7 vols. New York: Macmillan, 1913–1917.

American Anti-Slavery Society. *Second Annual Report of the American Anti-Slavery Society.* New York: William S. Dorr, 1835.

———. *Third Annual Report of the American Anti-Slavery Society.* New York: William S. Dorr, 1836.

———. *Fifth Annual Report of the American Anti-Slavery Society.* New York: William S. Dorr, 1838.

Ames, Herman V., ed. *State Documents on Federal Relations: The States and the United States.* Philadelphia: University of Pennsylvania, 1911.

Annals of Congress: Debates and Proceedings, 1789–1824. Washington, DC: Gales & Seaton.

Appleton, Nathan. "Labor, Its Relations in Europe and the United States Compared." *Hunt's Merchants Magazine* 11 (September 1844): 217–23.

Bancroft, George. *The Life and Letters of George Bancroft*. Edited by M. A. DeWolfe Howe. 2 vols. New York: Charles Scribner's Sons, 1908.

Barnes, Gilbert H., and Dwight L. Dumond, eds. *Letters of Theodore Dwight Weld, Angela Grimké Weld and Sarah Grimké, 1822–1844*. 2 vols. 1934. Reprint, Gloucester, MA: Peter Smith, 1965.

Barnwell, Robert W. "Hamlet to Hotspur: Letters of Robert Woodward Barnwell to Robert Barnwell Rhett." Edited by John Barnwell. *South Carolina Historical Magazine* 77 (October 1976): 236–56.

Bellinger, Edward, Jr. *Speech on the Subject of Slavery, Delivered 7th Sept'r, 1835, at a Public Meeting of the Citizens of Barnwell District, South Carolina*. Charleston: Dan J. Dowling, 1835.

Birney, James G. *Letters of James Gillespie Birney, 1831–1857*. Edited by Dwight L. Dumond. 2 vols. 1938. Reprint, Gloucester: Peter Smith, 1965.

[Brown, Edward]. *Notes on the Origin and Necessity of Slavery*. Charleston: A. E. Miller, 1826.

Buckingham, Joseph T. *Personal Memoirs and Recollections of Editorial Life*. 2 vols. Boston: Ticknor, Reed, & Fields, 1852.

Calhoun, John C. *The Papers of John C. Calhoun*. Ed. Robert L. Meriwether et al. 28 vols. Columbia: University of South Carolina Press, 1959–2003.

Channing, William Ellery. *The Works of William Ellery Channing*. 6 vols. Boston: American Unitarian Association, 1903.

Chase, Salmon P. *The Papers of Salmon P. Chase*. Edited by John Niven. 5 vols. Kent, OH: Kent State University Press, 1993–1998.

Chesnut, Mary Boykin. *Mary Chesnut's Civil War*. Edited by C. Vann Woodward. New Haven, CT: Yale University Press, 1981.

Commonwealth of Massachusetts. *State Papers on Nullification: Including the Public Acts of the People of South Carolina, Assembled at Columbia, November 19, 1832, and March 11, 1833; the Proclamation of the President of the United States, and the Proceedings of the Several State Legislatures Which Have Acted on the Subject*. Boston: Dutton & Wentworth, 1834.

Congressional Globe, 1833–1850. Washington, DC: Blair & Rives.

Cooper, Thomas. *Consolidation, an Account of Parties in the United States from the Convention of 1787, to the Present Period*. 1824. Reprint, Columbia, SC: Times & Gazette Office, 1830.

———. "Letters of Dr. Thomas Cooper, 1825–1832." *American Historical Review* 6 (July 1901): 725–36.

———. *A Tract on the Proposed Alteration in the Tariff, Submitted to the Consideration of the Members from South Carolina in Congress*. New York: Clayton & Van Norden, 1824.

———. *Two Essays: 1. On the Foundation of Civil Government; 2. On the Constitution of the United States*. Columbia, SC: D & J. M. Faust, 1826.

Drayton, John. *A View of South Carolina, as Respects Her Natural and Civil Concerns*. Charleston, SC: C. P. Young, 1802.

[Drayton, William]. *The South Vindicated from the Treason and Fanaticism of the Northern Abolitionists*. Philadelphia: H. Manly, 1836.

Ford, Worthington C., ed. "Van Buren-Bancroft Correspondence." *Proceedings of the Massachusetts Historical Society* 42 (June 1909): 381–442.

Freehling, William W., ed. *The Nullification Era: A Documentary Record.* New York: Harper Torchbooks, 1967.

Garrison, William L. *The Letters of William Lloyd Garrison.* Edited by Walter M. Merrill and Louis Ruchames. 6 vols. Cambridge, MA: Harvard University Press, 1971–1981.

———. *Thoughts on African Colonization: or, an Impartial Exhibition of the Doctrines, Principles and Purposes of the African Colonization Society, Together with the Resolutions, Addresses and Remonstrances of the Free People of Color.* Boston: Garrison & Knapp, 1832.

Gatell, Frank Otto, ed. "Postmaster Huger and the Incendiary Publications." *South Carolina Historical Magazine* 64 (October 1963): 193–201.

Giddings, Joshua R. *History of the Rebellion: Its Authors and Causes.* New York: Follett, Foster, 1864.

Goodell, William. *Views of American Constitutional Law, in Its Bearing upon American Slavery.* Utica, NY: Jackson & Chaplin, 1844.

Grayson, William J. *Witness to Sorrow: The Antebellum Autobiography of William J. Grayson.* Edited by Richard J. Calhoun. Columbia: University of South Carolina Press, 1990.

Gregg, William. *Essays on Domestic Industry: or, an Inquiry into the Expediency of Establishing Cotton Manufactures in South Carolina.* Charleston, SC: Burges & James, 1845.

[Hamilton, James]. *An Account of the Late Intended Insurrection among a Portion of the Blacks of This City.* Charleston, SC: A. E. Miller, 1822.

Hammond, James H. *Letters and Speeches of the Hon. James H. Hammond, of South Carolina.* New York: John F. Trow, 1866.

———. *Secret and Sacred: The Diaries of James Henry Hammond, a Southern Slaveholder.* Edited by Carol Blesser. New York: Oxford University Press, 1988.

[Harper, Robert Goodloe]. *An Address to the People of South Carolina, by the General Committee of the Representative Reform Association, at Columbia.* Charleston, SC: W. P. Young, 1794.

Harper, William. *Anniversary Oration; Presented by the Hon. William Harper, in the Representative Hall, Columbia, S.C., Dec. 9, 1835.* Washington, DC: Duff Green, 1836.

[———]. *Judge Harper's Speech, before the Charleston State Rights and Free Trade Association, at Their Regular Meeting, April 1, 1832.* Charleston, SC: E. J. Van Brunt, 1832.

———. *Memoir of Slavery, Read before the Society for the Advancement of Learning, of South Carolina, at the Annual Meeting at Charleston, 1837.* Charleston, SC: James S. Burges, 1838.

———. *The Remedy by State Interposition, or Nullification, Explained and Advocated by Judge Harper, in His Speech at Columbia, (S.C.) on the Twentieth of September, 1830.* Charleston, SC: E. J. Van Brunt, 1832.

[Holland, Edwin C.]. *A Refutation of the Calumnies Circulated against the Southerly & Westerly States, Respecting the Institution and Existence of Slavery among Them. To Which Is Added a Minute and Particular Account of the Actual State and Condition of the Negro Population.* Charleston, SC: A. E. Miller, 1822.

Hunter, Robert M. T. "Correspondence of Robert M. T. Hunter, 1826–1876." Edited by Charles Henry Ambler. 2 vols. *Annual Report of the American Historical Association for the Year 1916.* Washington, DC: Government Printing Office, 1918.

[———]. *Life of John C. Calhoun, Presenting a Condensed History of Political Events from 1811 to 1843*. New York: Harper & Brothers, 1843.

Jackson, Andrew. *Correspondence of Andrew Jackson.* Edited by John Spencer Bassett. 7 vols. Washington, DC: Carnegie Institution of Washington, 1926–1935.

King, Rufus. *The Life and Correspondence of Rufus King: Comprising His Letters, Private and Official, His Public Documents and His Speeches*. Edited by Charles H. King. 6 vols. New York: G. P. Putnam's Sons, 1894–1900.

Laurens, Edward. *A Letter to the Hon. Whitemarsh Seabrook of St. John's Colleton, in Explanation and Defence of "An Act to Amend the Law in Relation to Slaves and Free People of Color."* Charleston, SC: Observer Office Press, 1835.

Legaré, Hugh S. *Writings of Hugh Swinton Legaré, Late Attorney General and Acting Secretary of State of the United States, Consisting of a Diary of Brussels, and Journal of the Rhine, Extracts from His Diplomatic Correspondence; Orations and Speeches; and Contributions to the New York and Southern Reviews*. 2 vols. Edited by Mary S. Legaré. Charleston, SC: Burges & James, 1845–1846.

"Letters on the Nullification Movement in South Carolina." *American Historical Review* 6 (July 1901): 736–65.

Lovejoy, Joseph C., and Owen Lovejoy. *Memoir of the Rev. Elijah P. Lovejoy; Who Was Murdered in Defence of the Liberty of the Press, at Alton, Illinois, Nov. 7, 1837, with an Introduction by John Quincy Adams*. New York: John S. Taylor, 1838.

Martineu, Harriet. *Retrospect of Western Travel*. 3 vols. London: Saunders & Otley, 1838.

Massachusetts Anti-Slavery Society. *Fourth Annual Report of the Board of Managers of the Massachusetts Anti-Slavery Society*. Boston: Isaack Knapp, 1836.

———. *Fifth Annual Report of the Board of Managers of the Massachusetts Anti-Slavery Society*. Boston: Isaack Knapp, 1837.

———. *Sixth Annual Report of the Board of Managers of the Massachusetts Anti-Slavery Society*. Boston: Isaack Knapp, 1838.

May, Samuel J. *Some Recollections of Our Antislavery Struggle*. Boston, Fields, Osgood, 1869.

McDuffie, George. *National and State Rights. Considered by the Hon. George McDuffie, under the Signature of "One of the People," in Reply to the "Trio."* 1821. Reprint, Charleston, SC: Free Press, 1831.

———. *Speech of Mr. McDuffie on Internal Improvements: With a Few Introductory Remarks in Answer to a Pamphlet Entitled "Consolidation."* Columbia, SC: D & J. M. Faust, 1824.

McKee, Thomas Hudson, ed. *The National Conventions and Platforms of All Political Parties, 1789 to 1904: Conventions, Popular and Electoral Vote*. Baltimore: Friedenwald, 1904.

Mood, Fulmer, and Granville Hicks, eds. "Letters to Dr. Channing on Slavery and the Annexation of Texas, 1837." *New England Quarterly* 5 (July 1932): 587–601.

Moore, Frank, ed. *The Rebellion Record: A Diary of American Events, with Documents, Narratives, Illustrative Incidents, Poetry, Etc*. New York: G. P. Putnam, 1864.

Moore, Frederick W., ed. "Calhoun as Seen by His Political Friends: Letters of Duff Green, Dixon H. Lewis and Richard K. Crallé during the Period from 1831 to 1848." *Publications of the Southern Historical Association* 7 (September 1903): 353–61.

———. "Calhoun as Seen by His Political Friends: Letters of Duff Green, Dixon H. Lewis and Richard K. Crallé during the Period from 1831 to 1848." *Publications of the Southern Historical Association* 7 (November 1903): 419–26.

New-England Antislavery Society. *First Annual Report of the Board of Managers of the New-England Anti-Slavery Society*. Boston: Isaack Knapp, 1833.

Newsome, A. R., ed. "Correspondence of John C. Calhoun, George McDuffie and Charles Fisher, Relating to the Presidential Campaign of 1824." *North Carolina Historical Review* 7 (October 1930): 477–504.

Palfrey, John G. *Papers on the Slave Power Published in the "Boston Whig."* Boston: Merrill, Cobb, 1846.

Parker, Theodore. "A Discourse Occasioned by the Death of John Quincy Adams, Delivered in the Melodeon, in Boston, March 5th, 1848." *Massachusetts Quarterly Review* 3 (June 1848): 331–76.

———. *The Slave Power*. Edited by James K. Hosmer. N.d. Reprint, New York: Arno Press & *New York Times*, 1969.

Perry, Benjamin F. *Reminiscences of Public Men, by Ex-Gov. B. F. Perry*. Philadelphia: J. D. Avil, 1883.

Petigru, James Louis. *Life, Letters and Speeches of James Louis Petigru: The Union Man of South Carolina*. Edited by James Petigru Carson. Washington, DC: W. H. Lowdermilk, 1920.

Phillips, U. B., ed. "The Correspondence of Robert Toombs, Alexander H. Stephens, and Howell Cobb." 2 vols. *Annual Report of the American Historical Association for the Year 1911*. Washington, DC: Government Printing Office, 1913.

Phillips, Wendell. *Speeches, Lectures, and Letters*. Series One. Boston: Lee & Shepard, 1884.

———. *Speeches, Lectures, and Letters*. Series Two. Boston: Lee & Shepard, 1891.

Pickens, Francis W. "Five Letters from Francis W. Pickens to Patrick Noble, 1835–1836." Edited by Alice Noble Waring. *South Carolina Historical Magazine* 54 (April 1953): 75–82.

Pinckney, Charles Cotesworth. *An Address Delivered in Charleston, before the Agricultural Society of South Carolina, at the Anniversary Meeting, on Tuesday, the 15th August, 1829*. Charleston, SC: A. E. Miller, 1829.

Pinckney, Henry L. *Address to the Electors of Charleston District, South Carolina, on the Subject of the Abolition of Slavery*. Washington, DC: n.p., 1836.

———. *An Oration, Delivered in the Independent, or Congregational Church, Charleston, before the State Rights & Free Trade Party, the State Society of Cincinnati, the Revolution Society, the '76 Association, and the State Volunteers, on the 4th of July, 1833*. Charleston, SC: A. E. Miller, 1833.

Plumer, William, Jr. *The Missouri Compromises and Presidential Politics, 1800–1825: From the Letters of William Plumer, Junior*. Edited by Everett Somerville Brown. St. Louis: Missouri Historical Society, 1926.

Polk, James K. *The Diary of James K. Polk during His Presidency*. Edited by Milo Milton Quaife. 4 vols. Chicago: A. C. McClurg, 1913.

Preston, William C. *The Reminiscences of William C. Preston*. Edited by Minnie Clare Yarborough. Chapel Hill: University of North Carolina Press, 1933.

Proceedings and Debates of the Virginia State Convention of 1829–30. Richmond, VA: Ritchie & Cook, 1830.

Proceedings of the Citizens of Charleston, on the Incendiary Machinations, Now in Progress, against the Peace and Welfare of the Southern States. Charleston, SC: A. E. Miller, 1835.

Quincy, Josiah. *Figures of the Past: From the Leaves of Old Journals*. Boston: Roberts Brothers, 1883.

Register of Debates in Congress, 1824–1837. Washington, DC: Gales & Seaton.

Remini, Robert V., ed. *The Age of Jackson*. Columbia: University of South Carolina Press, 1972.

Rhett, Robert B. "Robert Barnwell Rhett on the Biography of Calhoun." *American Historical Review* 13 (January 1908): 310–12.

[Rice, William]. *Vindex on the Liability of the Abolitionists to Criminal Punishment, and on the Duty of Non-Slaveholders to Suppress Their Efforts*. Charleston, SC: A. E. Miller, 1836.

Richardson, James D., comp. *A Compilation of the Messages and Papers of the Presidents, 1789–1897*. 20 vols. New York: Bureau of National Literature, 1897.

Rives, Bartholomew Rivers, ed. *Historical Collections of Early South Carolina: Embracing Many Rare and Valuable Pamphlets, and Other Documents, Relating to the History of That State from the First Discovery to Its Independence in the Year 1776*. New York: Harper & Brothers, 1836.

Salley, Alexander S., ed. *Narratives of Early Carolina, 1650–1707*. New York: Charles Scribner's Sons, 1911.

Seabrook, Whitemarsh B. *An Appeal to the People of the Northern and Eastern States on the Subject of Negro Slavery in South Carolina*. New York: n.p., 1834.

———. *A Concise View of the Critical Situation and Future Prospects of the Slave-holding States, in Relation to Their Coloured Population*. Charleston, SC: A. E. Miller, 1825.

———. *An Essay on the Management of Slaves, and Especially, of Their Religious Instruction, Read before the Agricultural Society of St. John's Colleton*. Charleston, SC: A. E. Miller, 1834.

Simms, William Gilmore. *The Letters of William Gilmore Simms*. Edited by Mary S. Simms Oliphant. 6 vols. Columbia: University of South Carolina Press, 1952–1982.

[South Carolina General Assembly]. *The Death and Funeral Ceremonies of John Caldwell Calhoun, Containing the Speeches, Reports, and Other Documents Connected Therewith, the Oration of the Hon. R. B. Rhett, before the Legislature, &c.* Columbia, SC: A. S. Johnston, 1850.

Speeches Delivered in the Convention of the State of South Carolina, Held in Columbia, in March 1833. Charleston, SC: E. J. Van Brunt, 1833.

Stewart, Alvan. *Writings and Speeches of Alvan Stewart*. Edited by Luther Rawson Marsh. New York: A. B. Burdick, 1860.

Sumner, Charles. *The Selected Letters of Charles Sumner*. Edited by Beverly Wilson Palmer. 2 vols. Boston: Northeastern University Press, 1990.

Thomas, J. P., ed. *The Carolina Tribute to Calhoun*. Columbia, SC: Richard L. Bryan, 1857.

[Trumbull, Robert James]. *The Crisis: or, Essays on the Usurpations of the Federal Government*. Charleston, SC: A. E. Miller, 1827.

Woodmason, Charles. *The Carolina Backcountry on the Eve of the Revolution: The Journal and Other Writings of Charles Woodmason, Anglican Itinerant*. Edited by Richard J. Hooker. Chapel Hill: University of North Carolina Press, 1953.

Secondary Sources

Books and Articles

Adams, Charles Francis. "John Quincy Adams and Martial Law." *Proceedings of the Massachusetts Historical Society* 15, second series (1901–1902): 436–78.

Adams, Henry. *The Degradation of the Democratic Dogma*. New York: Macmillan, 1919.

Ambler, Charles H. *Sectionalism in Virginia from 1776 to 1861*. Chicago: University of Chicago Press, 1910.

———. *The Life and Diary of John Floyd, Governor of Virginia, an Apostle of Secession, and the Father of the Oregon Country*. Richmond, VA: Richmond Press, 1918.

———. *Thomas Ritchie: A Study in Virginia Politics*. Richmond, VA: Bell, Book & Stationery, 1913.

Ames, Herman V. "John C. Calhoun and the Secession Movement of 1850." *Proceedings of the American Antiquarian Society* 28, new series (April 1918): 19–50.

Ammon, Harry. *James Monroe: The Quest for National Identity*. 1971. Reprint, Charlottesville: University Press of Virginia, 1990.

Bailyn, Bernard. *The Barbarous Years: The Peopling of North America: The Conflict of Civilizations, 1600–1675*. New York: Alfred A. Knopf, 2012.

Bancroft, Frederic. *Calhoun and the South Carolina Nullification Movement*. Baltimore: Johns Hopkins University Press, 1928.

Banner, James M., Jr. *To the Hartford Convention: The Foundation and the Origins of Party Politics in Massachusetts, 1789–1815*. New York: Alfred A. Knopf, 1970.

Barnwell, John. *Love of Order: South Carolina's First Secession Crisis*. Chapel Hill: University of North Carolina Press, 1982.

Barsness, Richard W. "John C. Calhoun and the Military Establishment, 1817–1825." *Wisconsin Magazine of History* 50 (Autumn 1966): 49–53.

Bartlett, Irving H. *John C. Calhoun: A Biography*. New York: W. W. Norton, 1993.

Belko, William B. "John C. Calhoun and the Creation of the Bureau of Indian Affairs: An Essay on Political Rivalry, Ideology and Policymaking in the Early Republic." *South Carolina Historical Magazine* 105 (July 2004): 170–97.

Bemis, Samuel Flagg. *John Quincy Adams and the Foundation of American Foreign Policy*. New York: Alfred A. Knopf, 1949.

———. *John Quincy Adams and the Union*. New York: Alfred. A. Knopf, 1956.

Bergeron, Paul A. "The Nullification Controversy Revisited." *Tennessee Historical Quarterly* 35 (Fall 1976): 263–75.

Blue, Frederick J. *The Free Soilers: Third Party Politics, 1848–1854*. Urbana: University of Illinois Press, 1973.

Bolt, William K. *Tariff Wars and the Politics of Jacksonian America*. Nashville, TN: Vanderbilt University Press, 2017.

Bonner, Robert E. *Mastering America: Southern Slaveholders and the Crisis of American Nationhood*. Cambridge: Cambridge University Press, 2009.

Boucher, Chauncey Samuel. *The Nullification Controversy in South Carolina*. Chicago: University of Chicago Press, 1916.

Brands, H. W. *Heirs of the Founders: Henry Clay, John C. Calhoun and Daniel Webster, the Second Generation of American Giants*. New York: Doubleday, 2018.

Brauer, Kinley J. *Cotton versus Conscience: Massachusetts Whig Politics and Southwestern Expansion, 1843–1848*. Lexington: University of Kentucky Press, 1967.

———. "The Massachusetts State Texas Committee: A Last Stand against the Annexation of Texas." *Journal of American History* 51 (September 1964): 214–31.

Breese, Donald H. "James L. Orr, Calhoun and the Cooperationist Tradition in South Carolina." *South Carolina Historical Magazine* 80 (October 1979): 273–85.

Brooke, John L. *The Heart of the Commonwealth: Society and Political Culture in Worcester County, Massachusetts, 1713–1861*. 1989. Reprint, Amherst: University of Massachusetts Press, 1992.

Brooks, Corey M. *Liberty Power: Antislavery Third Parties and the Transformation of American Politics*. Chicago: University of Chicago Press, 2016.

Brown, Richard Maxwell. *The South Carolina Regulators*. Cambridge, MA: Harvard University Press, 1963.

Brown, Roger H. "The War Hawks of 1812: A Historical Myth." *Indiana Magazine of History* 60 (June 1964): 137–51.

Bushman, Richard L. *King and People in Provincial Massachusetts*. Chapel Hill: University of North Carolina Press, 1985.

Capers, Gerald M. *John C. Calhoun—Opportunist: A Reappraisal*. Gainesville: University of Florida Press, 1960.

———. "A Reconsideration of John C. Calhoun's Transition from Nationalism to Nullification." *Journal of Southern History* 14 (February 1948): 34–48.

Capers, Henry D. *The Life and Times of C. G. Memminger*. Richmond, VA: Everett Waddey, 1893.

Channing, Steven A. *Crisis of Fear: Secession in South Carolina*. New York: W. W. Norton, 1974.

Childers, Christopher. *The Failure of Popular Sovereignty: Slavery, Manifest Destiny, and the Radicalization of Southern Politics*. Lawrence: University Press of Kansas, 2012.

Coclanis, Peter A. *The Shadow of a Dream: Economic Life and Death in the South Carolina Low Country, 1670–1920*. New York: Oxford University Press, 1989.

Coit, Margaret L. *John C. Calhoun: American Portrait*. 1950. Reprint, Columbia: University of South Carolina Press, 1991.

Cole, Donald B. *Martin Van Buren and the American Political System*. Princeton, NJ: Princeton University Press, 1984.

Conlin, Michael F. *The Constitutional Origins of the American Civil War*. New York: Cambridge University Press, 2019.

Cooper, William J. *Jefferson Davis, American*. New York: Vintage Books, 2000.

———. *The Lost Founding Father: John Quincy Adams and the Transformation of American Politics*. New York: Liveright, 2017.

———. *The South and the Politics of Slavery, 1828–1856*. Baton Rouge: Louisiana State University Press, 1978.

Crapol, Edward R. *John Tyler: The Accidental President*. Chapel Hill: University of North Carolina Press, 2006.

Cunningham, Noble E., Jr. *The Presidency of James Monroe*. Lawrence: University Press of Kansas, 1996.

Current, Richard N. *John C. Calhoun*. New York: Washington Square, 1966.

Dalzell, Robert F., Jr. *Enterprising Elite: The Boston Associates and the World They Made*. Cambridge, MA: Harvard University Press, 1987.

Darling, Arthur B. *Political Change in Massachusetts, 1824–1848: A Study of Liberal Movements in Politics*. New Haven, CT: Yale University Press, 1925.

Davis, William C. *Rhett: The Turbulent Life and Times of a Fire-Eater*. Columbia: University of South Carolina Press, 2001.

DeLay, Brian. *War of a Thousand Deserts: Indian Raids and the U.S.-Mexican War*. New Haven, CT: Yale University Press, 2008.

Delbanco, Andrew. *The War before the War: Fugitive Slaves and the Struggle for America's Soul from the Revolution to the Civil War*. New York: Penguin, 2018.

Duberman, Martin. *Charles Francis Adams, 1809–1886*. Boston: Houghton Mifflin, 1961.

Earle, Jonathan H. *Jacksonian Antislavery and the Politics of Free Soil*. Chapel Hill: University of North Carolina Press, 2004.

Edel, Charles N. *Nation Builder: John Quincy Adams and the Grand Strategy of the Republic*. Cambridge, MA: Harvard University Press, 2014.

Edgar, Walter. *South Carolina: A History*. Columbia: University of South Carolina Press, 1998.

Edmonds, John B., Jr. *Francis W. Pickens and the Politics of Destruction*. Chapel Hill: University of North Carolina Press, 1986.

Eichert, Magdalen. "John C. Calhoun's Land Policy of Cession." *South Carolina Historical Magazine* 55 (October 1954): 198–209.

Elder, Robert. *John C. Calhoun: American Heretic*. New York: Basic Books, 2021.

Ellis, Richard E. *The Union at Risk: Jacksonian Democracy, States' Rights, and the Nullification Crisis*. New York: Oxford University Press, 1987.

Ewing, Gretchen Garst. "Duff Green, John C. Calhoun, and the Election of 1828." *South Carolina Historical Magazine* 79 (April 1978): 128–37.

Faust, Drew Gilpin. *The Creation of Confederate Nationalism: Identity and Ideology in the Civil War South*. Baton Rouge: Louisiana State University Press, 1988.

———. *James Henry Hammond and the Old South: A Design for Mastery*. Baton Rouge: Louisiana State University Press, 1982.

Fehrenbacher, Don E. *Constitutions and Constitutionalism in the Slaveholding South*. Athens: University of Georgia Press, 1989.

———. *The Dred Scott Case: Its Significance in American Law and Politics*. New York: Oxford University Press, 1978.

———. *The Slaveholding Republic: An Account of the United States Government's Relations with Slavery*. Edited by Ward M. McAfee. New York: Oxford University Press, 2001.

Feller, Daniel. *The Public Lands in Jacksonian Politics*. Madison: University of Wisconsin Press, 1984.

Finkelman, Paul. *Supreme Injustice: Slavery and the Nation's Highest Court*. Cambridge, MA: Harvard University Press, 2018.

Fischer, David Hackett. *The Revolution of American Conservatism: The Federalist Party in the Era of Jeffersonian Democracy*. New York: Harper & Row, 1965.

Foner, Eric. *Free Soil, Free Labor, Free Men: The Ideology of the Republican Party before the Civil War*. New York: Oxford University Press, 1970.

———. "The Wilmot Proviso Revisited." *Journal of American History* 56 (September 1969): 262–79.

Forbes, Robert Pierce. *The Missouri Controversy and Its Aftermath: Slavery and the Meaning of America*. Chapel Hill: University of North Carolina Press, 2007.

Ford, Lacy K. *Deliver Us from Evil: The Slavery Question in the Old South*. New York: Oxford University Press, 2009.

———. "Inventing the Concurrent Majority: Madison, Calhoun, and the Problem of

Majoritarianism in American Political Thought." *Journal of Southern History* 60 (February 1994): 19–58.

———. *Origins of Southern Radicalism: The South Carolina Upcountry, 1800–1860*. New York: Oxford University Press, 1988.

———. "Recovering the Republic: Calhoun, South Carolina, and the Concurrent Majority." *South Carolina Historical Magazine* 89 (July 1988): 146–59.

———. "Republican Ideology in a Slave Society: The Political Economy of John C. Calhoun." *Journal of Southern History* 54 (August 1988): 405–24.

Ford, Worthington C. "The Recall of John Quincy Adams in 1808." *Proceedings of the Massachusetts Historical Society* 45, third series (1911–1912): 354–73.

Formisano, Ronald P. "Deferential-Participant Politics: The Early Republic's Political Culture, 1789–1840." *American Political Science Review* 68 (June 1974): 473–87.

———. "Political Character, Antipartyism and the Second Party System." *American Quarterly* 21 (Winter 1969): 683–709.

———. *The Transformation of Political Culture: Massachusetts Parties, 1790s–1840s*. New York: Oxford University Press, 1983.

Fox-Genovese, Elizabeth, and Eugene D. Genovese. *Slavery in White and Black: Class and Race in the Southern Slaveholders' New World Order*. New York: Cambridge University Press, 2008.

Frederick, David C. "John Quincy Adams, Slavery, and the Disappearance of the Right of Petition." *Law and History Review* 9 (Spring 1991): 113–55.

Freehling, Alison Goodyear. *Drift toward Dissolution: The Virginia Slavery Debate of 1831–1832*. Baton Rouge: Louisiana State University Press, 1982.

Freehling, William W. *Prelude to Civil War: The Nullification Controversy in South Carolina, 1816–1836*. New York: Harper & Row, 1966.

———. *The Reintegration of American History: Slavery and the Civil War*. New York: Oxford University Press, 1994.

———. *The Road to Disunion: Secessionists at Bay, 1776–1854*. New York: Oxford University Press, 1990.

Glick, Wendell. "The Best Possible World of John Quincy Adams." *New England Quarterly* 37 (March 1964): 3–17.

Goodman, Paul. *The Democratic-Republicans of Massachusetts: Politics in a Young Republic*. Cambridge, MA: Harvard University Press, 1964.

———. *Towards a Christian Republic: Antimasonry and the Great Transition in New England, 1826–1836*. New York: Oxford University Press, 1988.

Green, Michael D. *The Politics of Indian Removal: Creek Government and Society in Crisis*. Lincoln: University of Nebraska Press, 1982.

Greenberg, Amy S. *A Wicked War: Polk, Clay, Lincoln, and the 1846 U.S. Invasion of Mexico*. New York: Alfred A. Knopf, 2012.

Greenberg, Kenneth S. *Masters and Statesmen: The Political Culture of American Slavery*. Baltimore: Johns Hopkins University Press, 1985.

———. "Representation and the Isolation of South Carolina, 1776–1860." *Journal of American History* 64 (December 1977): 723–43.

Greene, Jack P. "Colonial South Carolina and the Caribbean Connection." In *Imperatives,*

Behaviors, and Identities: Essays in Early American Cultural History, edited by Jack P. Greene, 68–86. Charlottesville: University Press of Virginia, 1992.

Gregory, Frances W. *Nathan Appleton: Merchant and Entrepreneur, 1779–1861*. Charlottesville: University Press of Virginia, 1975.

Grove, John P. "Binding the Republic Together: The Early Political Thought of John C. Calhoun." *South Carolina Historical Magazine* 115 (April 2014): 100–21.

Hahn, Steven. *A Nation without Borders: The United States and the World in an Age of Civil Wars, 1830–1910*. New York: Viking, 2016.

Hall, Van Beck. *Politics without Parties: Massachusetts, 1780–1791*. Pittsburgh: University of Pittsburgh Press, 1964.

Hammond, John Craig. "President, Planter, Politician: James Monroe, the Missouri Compromise, and the Politics of Slavery." *Journal of American History* 105 (March 2019): 843–67.

———. *Slavery, Freedom, and Expansion in the Early American West*. Charlottesville: University of Virginia Press, 2007.

Hargreaves, Mary W. M. *The Presidency of John Quincy Adams*. Lawrence: University Press of Kansas, 1985.

Harp, Gillis J. "Taylor, Calhoun, and the Decline of a Theory of Political Disharmony." *Journal of the History of Ideas* 46 (January–March 1985): 107–20.

Harrold, Stanley. *American Abolitionism: Its Direct Political Impact from Colonial Times into Reconstruction*. Charlottesville: University of Virginia Press, 2019.

Haw, James. "Political Representation in South Carolina, 1669–1794: Evolution of a Lowcountry Tradition." *South Carolina Historical Magazine* 103 (April 2002): 106–29.

———. "The Problem of South Carolina Reexamined: A Review Essay." *South Carolina Historical Magazine* 197 (January 2006): 9–25.

Heidler, David S., and Jeanne T. Heidler. *Old Hickory's War: Andrew Jackson and the Quest for Empire*. 1996. Reprint, Baton Rouge: Louisiana State University Press, 2003.

Hietala, Thomas R. *Manifest Design: Anxious Aggrandizement in Late Jacksonian America*. Ithaca, NY: Cornell University Press, 1985.

Higginbotham, Don. "Fomentors of Revolution: Massachusetts and South Carolina." *Journal of the Early Republic* 14 (Spring 1994): 1–33.

Higham, John W. "The Changing Loyalties of William Gilmore Simms." *Journal of Southern History* 8 (May 1943): 210–23.

Hinks, Peter P. *David Walker's Appeal to the Coloured Citizens of the World*. University Park: Penn State University Press, 2000.

Hofstadter, Richard. *The American Political Tradition and the Men Who Made It*. New York: Alfred A. Knopf, 1948.

———. *The Idea of a Party System: The Rise of Legitimate Opposition in the United States*. Berkeley: University of California Press, 1969.

Holt, Michael F. *The Fate of Their Country: Politicians, Slavery Extension, and the Coming of the Civil War*. New York: Hill & Wang, 2004.

———. *The Political Crisis of the 1850s*. New York: John Wiley & Sons, 1978.

———. *The Rise and Fall of the American Whig Party: Jacksonian Politics and the Onset of the Civil War*. New York: Oxford University Press, 1999.

Holton, Woody. *Abigail Adams*. New York: Free Press, 2009.

Horsman, Reginald. *The Causes of the War of 1812*. Philadelphia: University of Pennsylvania Press, 1962.

———. *Expansion and American Indian Policy, 1783–1812*. 1967. Reprint, Norman: University of Oklahoma Press, 1992.

———. *Race and Manifest Destiny: The Origins of American Racial Anglo-Saxonism*. Cambridge, MA: Harvard University Press, 1981.

Howe, David Walker. *The Political Culture of the American Whigs*. Chicago: University of Chicago Press, 1979.

Isenberg, Nancy, and Andrew Burstein. *The Problem of Democracy: The Presidents Adams Confront the Cult of Personality*. New York: Viking, 2019.

Johannsen, Robert W. *Stephen A. Douglas*. 1973. Reprint, Urbana: University of Illinois Press, 1997.

Johnson, D. Andrew. "The Regulation Reconsidered: Shared Grievances in the Colonial Carolinas." *South Carolina Historical Magazine* 114 (April 2013): 132–54.

Julian, George W. *The Life of Joshua R. Giddings*. Chicago: A. C. McClung & Company, 1892.

Kaplan, Fred. *John Quincy Adams: American Visionary*. New York: HarperCollins, 2014.

Karp, Matthew. *This Vast Southern Empire: Slaveholders at the Helm of American Foreign Policy*. Cambridge, MA: Harvard University Press, 2016.

Kars, Marjoleine. *Breaking Loose Together: The Regulator Rebellion in Pre-Revolutionary North Carolina*. Chapel Hill: University of North Carolina Press, 2002.

Kibler, Lillian Adele. *Benjamin F. Perry: South Carolina Unionist*. Durham, NC: Duke University Press, 1946.

———. "Unionist Sentiment in South Carolina in 1860." *Journal of Southern History* 4 (August 1938): 346–66.

Klein, Rachel N. "Ordering the Backcountry: The South Carolina Regulators." *William and Mary Quarterly* 38 (October 1981): 661–80.

———. *Unification of a Slave State: The Rise of the Planter Class in the South Carolina Backcountry, 1760–1808*. Chapel Hill: University of North Carolina Press, 1990.

Lander, Ernest M., Jr. "The Calhoun-Preston Feud, 1836–1842." *South Carolina Historical Magazine* 59 (January 1958): 24–37.

———. "Dr. Thomas Cooper's Views in Retirement." *South Carolina Historical Magazine* 54 (October 1953): 173–84.

———. *Reluctant Imperialists: Calhoun, the South Carolinians, and the Mexican War*. Baton Rouge: Louisiana State University Press, 1980.

Larson, John Lauritz. "'Bind the Nation Together': The National Union and the Struggle for a System of Internal Improvements." *Journal of American History* 74 (September 1987): 363–87.

———. *Internal Improvement: National Public Works and the Promise of Popular Government in the Early Republic*. Chapel Hill: University of North Carolina Press, 2001.

———. "Liberty by Design: Freedom, Planning, and John Quincy Adams's American System." In *The State and Economic Knowledge: The American and British Experiences*, 73–102. New York: Woodrow Wilson International Center for Scholars/Cambridge University Press, 1990.

Latner, Richard B. "The Nullification Crisis and Republican Subversion." *Journal of Southern History* 43 (February 1977): 19–38.

Laurie, Bruce. *Beyond Garrison: Antislavery and Social Reform*. New York: Cambridge University Press, 2005.

———. "The 'Fair Field of the Middle Ground': Abolitionism, Labor Reform, and the Making of an Antislavery Bloc in Antebellum Massachusetts." In *Labor Histories: Class, Politics, and the Working-Class Experience*, ed. Eric Arnesen et al., 45–70. Urbana: University of Illinois Press, 1998.

———. *Rebels in Paradise: Sketches of Northampton Abolitionists*. Amherst: University of Massachusetts Press, 2015.

Levin, Phyllis Lee. *The Remarkable Education of John Quincy Adams*. New York: Palgrave/Macmillan, 2015.

Lewis, James E., Jr. *The American Union and the Problem of Neighborhood: The United States and the Collapse of the Spanish Empire, 1783–1829*. Chapel Hill: University of North Carolina Press, 1998.

Lipsky, George A. *John Quincy Adams: His Theory and Ideas*. New York: Thomas Y. Crowell, 1950.

Ludlum, Robert P. "The Antislavery 'Gag Rule': History and Argument." *Journal of Negro History* 26 (April 1941): 203–43.

MacLean, William Jerry. "The Racial Thought of John Quincy Adams." *Journal of the Early Republic* 2 (Summer 1984): 143–60.

Maier, Pauline. *American Scripture: Making the Declaration of Independence*. New York: Alfred A. Knopf, 1997.

———. "The Road Not Taken: John C. Calhoun, Nullification, and the Revolutionary Tradition in South Carolina." *South Carolina Historical Magazine* 82 (January 1981): 1–19.

Malone, Dumas. *The Public Life of Thomas Cooper, 1782–1839*. New Haven, CT: Yale University Press, 1926.

Marmor, Theodore. "Anti-Industrialism and the Old South: The Agrarian Perspective of John C. Calhoun." *Comparative Studies in Society and History* 9 (July 1967): 377–406.

Marszalek, John F. *The Petticoat Affair: Manners, Mutiny, and Sex in Jackson's White House*. New York: Free Press, 1997.

Mason, Matthew. *Slavery and Politics in the Early Republic*. Chapel Hill: University of North Carolina Press, 2006.

Mason, Virginia. *The Public Life and Diplomatic Correspondence of James Murray Mason, with Some Personal History*. New York: Neale Publishing, 1906.

May, Ernest R. *The Making of the Monroe Doctrine*. Cambridge, MA: Harvard University Press, 1976.

Mayer, Henry. *All on Fire: William Lloyd Garrison and the Abolition of Slavery*. New York: St. Martin's, 1998.

Mayfield, John. *Rehearsal for Reconstruction: Free Soil and the Politics of Anti-Slavery*. Port Washington, NY: Kennikat, 1980.

McCormick, Richard P. *The Second American Party System: Party Formation in the Jacksonian Era*. 1966. Reprint, New York: W. W. Norton, 1973.

McFaul, John M. *The Politics of Jacksonian Finance*. Ithaca, NY: Cornell University Press, 1972.

McPherson, James M. "The Fight against the Gag Rule: Joshua Leavitt and Antislavery Insurgency in the Whig Party, 1830–1842." *Journal of Negro History* 48 (July 1963): 177–93.

Meigs, William M. *The Life of John C. Calhoun*. 2 vols. New York: Neale Publishing, 1917.

Meinke, Scott R. "Slavery, Partisanship, and Procedure in the U.S. House: The Gag Rule, 1836–1845." *Legislative Studies Quarterly* 32 (February 2007): 33–57.

Mendelsohn, Jack. *Channing: Reluctant Rebel*. Boston: Little, Brown, 1971.

Mercantini, Jonathan. *Who Shall Rule at Home: The Evolution of South Carolina Political Culture, 1745–1778*. Columbia: University of South Carolina Press, 2007.

Merchant, Holt. *South Carolina Fire-Eater: The Life of Laurence Massillon Keitt, 1824–1864*. Columbia: University of South Carolina Press, 2014.

Meriwether, Robert L. *The Expansion of South Carolina, 1729–1765*. Kingsport, TN: Southern, 1940.

Merk, Frederick. *The Monroe Doctrine and American Expansionism, 1843–1849*. 1966. Reprint, New York: Vintage Books, 1972.

Merk, Frederick, with Lois Bannister Merk. *Slavery and the Annexation of Texas*. New York: Alfred A. Knopf, 1972.

Moore, Peter N. *World of Toil and Strife: Community Transformation in Backcountry South Carolina, 1750–1806*. Columbia: University of South Carolina Press, 2007.

Morison, Chaplain W. *Democratic Politics and Sectionalism: The Wilmot Proviso Controversy*. Chapel Hill: University of North Carolina Press, 1967.

Nadelhaft, Jerome J. *The Disorders of War: The Revolution in South Carolina*. Orono: University of Maine at Orono Press, 1981.

Nagel, Paul C. *Descent from Glory: Four Generations of the John Adams Family*. New York: Oxford University Press, 1983.

———. *John Quincy Adams: A Public Life, a Private Life*. Cambridge, MA: Harvard University Press, 1987.

Navin, John J. *The Grim Years: Settling South Carolina, 1670–1729*. Columbia: University of South Carolina Press, 2020.

Neumann, Brian C. *Bloody Flag of Anarchy: Unionism in South Carolina during the Nullification Crisis*. Baton Rouge: Louisiana State University Press, 2022.

Niven, John. *John C. Calhoun and the Price of Union: A Biography*. Baton Rouge: Louisiana State University Press, 1988.

———. *Martin Van Buren: The Romantic Age of American Politics*. New York: Oxford University Press, 1983.

———. *Salmon P. Chase: A Biography*. New York: Oxford University Press, 1995.

Nye, Russel B. *Fettered Freedom: Civil Liberties and the Slavery Controversy, 1830–1860*. 1963. Reprint, Urbana: University of Illinois Press, 1972.

Oakes, James. *The Crooked Road to Abolition: Abraham Lincoln and the Antislavery Constitution*. New York: W. W. Norton, 2021.

———. *Freedom National: The Destruction of Slavery in the United States, 1861–1865*. New York: W. W. Norton, 2013.

———. *The Scorpion's Sting: Antislavery and the Coming of the Civil War*. New York: W. W. Norton, 2014.

O'Brien, Michael, and David Moltke-Hansen, eds. *Intellectual Life in Antebellum Charleston*. Knoxville: University of Tennessee Press, 1966.

Ochenkowski, J. P. "The Origins of Nullification in South Carolina." *South Carolina Historical Magazine* 93 (April 1982): 121–53.

Olwell, Richard. *Masters, Slaves, and Subjects: The Culture of Power in the South Carolina Low Country, 1740–1790*. Ithaca, NY: Cornell University Press, 1998.

Owsley, Frank Lawrence, and Gene A. Smith. *Filibusters and Expansionists: Jeffersonian Manifest Destiny, 1800–1821*. Tuscaloosa: University of Alabama Press, 1997.

Parsons, Lynn Hudson. *The Birth of Modern Politics: Andrew Jackson, John Quincy Adams, and the Election of 1828*. New York: Oxford University Press, 2009.

———. "In Which the Political Becomes the Personal, and Vice Versa: The Last Ten Years of John Quincy Adams and Andrew Jackson." *Journal of the Early Republic* 23 (Autumn 2003): 421–43.

———. "'A Perpetual Harrow of My Feelings': John Quincy Adams and the American Indian." *New England Quarterly* 46 (September 1973): 339–79.

———. "'The Splendid Pageant': Observations on the Death of John Quincy Adams." *New England Quarterly* 53 (December 1980): 464–82.

Pease, William H., and Jane H. Pease. *James Louis Petigru: Southern Conservative, Southern Dissenter*. Athens: University of Georgia Press, 1995.

———. *The Web of Progress: Private Values and Public Spheres in Boston and Charleston, 1828–1843*. 1985. Reprint, Athens: University of Georgia Press, 1991.

Perdue, Theda, and Michael D. Green. *The Cherokee Nation and the Trail of Tears*. New York: Penguin, 2007.

Perkins, Bradford. *Castlereagh and Adams: England and the United States, 1812–1823*. Berkeley: University of California Press, 1964.

Perry, Thomas Sergeant. *The Life and Letters of Francis Lieber*. Boston: James R. Osgood, 1882.

Peterson, Merrill D. *The Great Triumvirate: Webster, Clay, and Calhoun*. New York: Oxford University Press, 1987.

———. *Olive Branch and Sword: The Compromise of 1833*. Baton Rouge: Louisiana State University Press, 1982.

Peterson, Norma Lois. *Littleton Waller Tazewell*. Charlottesville: University Press of Virginia, 1983.

Pierson, George Wilson. *Tocqueville and Beaumont in America*. New York: Oxford University Press, 1938.

Potter, David M. *The Impending Crisis, 1848–1861*. New York: Harper & Row, 1976.

———. *The South and the Concurrent Majority*. Baton Rouge: Louisiana State University Press, 1972.

Quintana, Ryan A. *Making a Slave State: Political Development in South Carolina*. Chapel Hill: University of North Carolina Press, 2018.

Raiford, Norman Gasque. "South Carolina and the Second Bank of the United States: Conflict in Political Principle or Economic Interest?" *South Carolina Historical Magazine* 72 (January 1971): 30–43.

Ramsdell, Charles W. "The Natural Limits of Slavery Expansion." *Southwestern Historical Quarterly* 33 (October 1929): 91–111.

Ramsey, William L. *The Yamasee War: A Study of Culture, Economy, and Conflict in the Colonial South*. Lincoln: University of Nebraska Press, 2008.

Read, James H. *Majority Rule versus Conscience: The Political Thought of John C. Calhoun.* Lawrence: University Press of Kansas, 2009.

Remini, Robert V. *Henry Clay.* New York: W. W. Norton, 1991.

———. *Martin Van Buren and the Making of the Democratic Party.* New York: Columbia University Press, 1959.

———. "Martin Van Buren and the Tariff of Abominations." *American Historical Review* 63 (July 1958): 903–17.

Richards, Leonard L. *"Gentlemen of Property and Standing": Anti-Abolition Mobs in Jacksonian America.* New York: Oxford University Press, 1970.

———. "The Jacksonians and Slavery." In *Antislavery Reconsidered: New Perspectives on the Abolitionists*, ed. Lewis Perry and Michael Fellman, 99–118. Baton Rouge: Louisiana State University Press, 1979.

———. *The Life and Times of Congressman John Quincy Adams.* New York: Oxford University Press, 1986.

———. *The Slave Power: The Free North and Southern Domination, 1780–1860.* Baton Rouge: Louisiana State University Press, 2000.

Rich, Robert. "'A Wilderness of Whigs': The Wealthy Men of Boston." *Journal of Social History* 4 (Spring 1971): 263–76.

Robert, Joseph Clarke. *The Road from Monticello: A Study of the Virginia Slavery Debate of 1832.* Durham, NC: Duke University Press, 1941.

Rogers, George C., Jr. "South Carolina Federalists and the Origins of the Nullification Movement." *South Carolina Historical Magazine* 71 (January 1970): 17–31.

Roper, L. H. *Conceiving Carolina: Proprietors, Planters, and Plots, 1662–1729.* New York: Palgrave Macmillan, 2004.

Rosen, Deborah A. *Border Law: The First Seminole War and American Nationhood.* Cambridge, MA: Harvard University Press, 2015.

Rothman, Adam. *Slave Country: American Expansion and the Origins of the Deep South.* Cambridge, MA: Harvard University Press, 2008.

Rugemer, Edward B. "The Southern Response to British Abolitionism: The Maturation of Proslavery Apologetics." *Journal of Southern History* 70 (May 2004): 221–48.

Russell, Greg. "John Quincy Adams: Virtue and the Tragedy of Statesmen." *New England Quarterly* 69 (March 1996): 56–74.

Saunt, Claudio. *Unworthy Republic: The Dispossession of Native Americans and the Road to Indian Territory.* New York: W. W. Norton, 2020.

Schaper, William August. *Sectionalism and Representation in South Carolina.* 1901. Reprint, New York: Da Capo, 1968.

Schoen, Brian. *The Fragile Fabric of Union: Cotton, Federal Politics, and the Global Origins of the Civil War.* Baltimore: Johns Hopkins University Press, 2009.

Schroeder, John H. *Mr. Polk's War: American Opposition and Dissent, 1846–1848.* Madison: University of Wisconsin Press, 1973.

Sellers, Charles. *James K. Polk, Continentalist, 1843–1846.* Princeton, NJ: Princeton University Press, 1966.

Sewell, Richard H. *Ballots for Freedom: Antislavery Politics in the United States, 1837–1860.* 1976. Reprint, New York: W. W. Norton, 1980.

Sexton, Jay. *The Monroe Doctrine: Empire and Nation in Nineteenth-Century America*. New York: Hill and Wang, 2011.

Sheehan, Bernard W. *Seeds of Extinction: Jeffersonian Philanthropy and the American Indian*. Chapel Hill: University of North Carolina Press, 1973.

Sheidley, Harlow W. *Sectional Nationalism: Massachusetts Conservative Leaders and the Transformation of America, 1815–1836*. Boston: Northeastern University Press, 1998.

Sheldon, Rachel A. *Washington Brotherhood: Politics, Social Life, and the Coming of the Civil War*. Chapel Hill: University of North Carolina Press, 2013.

Silbey, Joel H. "John C. Calhoun and the Limits of Southern Congressional Unity, 1841–1850." *The Historian* 30 (November 1967): 58–71.

———. *The Partisan Imperative: The Dynamics of American Politics before the Civil War*. New York: Oxford University Press, 1985.

———. *Storm over Texas: The Annexation Controversy and the Road to Civil War*. New York: Oxford University Press, 2005.

Simpson, Craig A. *A Good Southerner: The Life of Henry A. Wise of Virginia*. Chapel Hill: University of North Carolina Press, 1985.

Sinha, Manisha. *The Counter-Revolution of Slavery: Politics and Ideology in Antebellum South Carolina*. Chapel Hill: University of North Carolina Press, 2000.

———. *The Slave's Cause: A History of Abolition*. New Haven, CT: Yale University Press, 2016.

Sirmans, M. Eugene. *Colonial South Carolina: A Political History, 1663–1763*. Chapel Hill: University of North Carolina Press, 1966.

Skeen, C. Edward. "Calhoun, Crawford, and the Politics of Retrenchment." *South Carolina Historical Magazine* 73 (July 1972): 141–55.

Smith, Adam Glaze, Jr. *Economic Readjustment of an Old Cotton State: South Carolina, 1820–1860*. Columbia: University of South Carolina Press, 1958.

Smith, Mark M., ed. *Stono: Documenting and Interpreting a Southern Slave Revolt*. Columbia: University of South Carolina Press, 2005.

Spivak, Burton. *Jefferson's English Crisis: Commerce, Embargo, and the Republican Revolution*. Charlottesville: University Press of Virginia, 1979.

Stagg, J. C. A. *Mr. Madison's War: Politics, Diplomacy, and Warfare in the Early American Republic, 1783–1830*. Princeton, NJ: Princeton University Press, 1983.

Stauffer, John, and Benjamin Soskis. *The Battle Hymn of the Republic: A Biography of the Song That Marches On*. New York: Oxford University Press, 2013.

Stewart, James Brewer. *Joshua Giddings and the Tactics of Radical Politics*. Cleveland: The Press of Case Western Reserve University, 1970.

Sutton, Robert P. *Revolution to Secession: Constitution Making in the Old Dominion*. Charlottesville: University Press of Virginia, 1989.

Taylor, Alan. *American Republics: A Continental History of the United States, 1783–1850*. New York: W. W. Norton, 2021.

———. *The Internal Enemy: Slavery and War in Virginia, 1772–1832*. New York: W. W. Norton, 2013.

Thomas, John L. *The Liberator, William Lloyd Garrison: A Biography*. Boston: Little, Brown, 1963.

Thompson, John R. "John Quincy Adams, Apostate: 'Outrageous Federalist' to 'Republican Exile,' 1801–1809." *Journal of the Early Republic* 11 (Summer 1991): 161–83.

Tise, Larry E. *Proslavery: A History of the Defense of Slavery in America, 1701–1840*. Athens: University of Georgia Press, 1987.

Vajda, Zoltán. "Calculated Sympathies: John C. Calhoun's Sentimental Union and the South." *South Carolina Historical Magazine* 114 (July 2013): 210–30.

Van Atta, John R. *Securing the West: Politics, Public Lands, and the Fate of the Old Republic, 1785–1850*. Baltimore: Johns Hopkins University Press, 2014.

———. *Wolf by the Ears: The Missouri Crisis, 1819–1821*. Baltimore: Johns Hopkins University Press, 2016.

Van Cleve, George William. *A Slaveholders' Union: Slavery, Politics, and the Constitution in the Early American Republic*. Chicago: University of Chicago Press, 2010.

Wallace, Anthony F. C. *The Long, Bitter Trail: Andrew Jackson and the Indians*. New York: Hill & Wang, 2013.

Wallace, David Duncan. *South Carolina: A Short History, 1520–1948*. Chapel Hill: University of North Carolina Press, 1953.

Walther, Eric H. *The Fire-Eaters*. Baton Rouge: Louisiana State University Press, 1992.

Waterhouse, Richard. *A New World Gentry: The Making of a Merchant and Planter Class in South Carolina, 1670–1770*. 1989. Reprint, Charleston, SC: History Press, 2005.

Wax, Donald D. "'The Great Risque We Run': The Aftermath of Slave Rebellion at Stono, South Carolina, 1739–1745." *Journal of Negro History* 67 (Summer 1982): 138–47.

Weber, David J. *The Spanish Frontier in North America*. New Haven, CT: Yale University Press, 1992.

Weeks, William Earl. *John Quincy Adams and American Global Empire*. Lexington: University of Kentucky Press, 1992.

———. "John Quincy Adams's 'Great Gun' and the Rhetoric of American Empire." *Diplomatic History* 83 (Winter 1990): 25–42.

———. *The New Cambridge History of American Foreign Relations, Volume 1: Dimensions of the Early American Empire, 1754–1865*. Cambridge: Cambridge University Press, 2013.

Wiecek, William M. *The Sources of Antislavery Constitutionalism in America, 1760–1848*. Ithaca, NY: Cornell University Press, 1977.

Weir, Robert M. *Colonial South Carolina: A History*. 1983. Reprint, Columbia: University of South Carolina Press, 1997.

———. "'The Harmony We Were Famous For': An Interpretation of Pre-Revolutionary South Carolina Politics." *William and Mary Quarterly* 26 (October 1969): 473–501.

Wilentz, Sean. *No Property in Man: Slavery and Antislavery in the Nation's Founding*. Cambridge, MA: Harvard University Press, 2018.

———. *The Politicians & the Egalitarians: The Hidden History of American Politics*. New York: W. W. Norton, 2016.

Wilson, Major L. "'Liberty and Union': An Analysis of the Three Concepts Involved in the Nullification Controversy." *Journal of Southern History* 33 (August 1967): 331–55.

———. "A Preview of Irrepressible Conflict: The Issue of Slavery during the Nullification Controversy." *Mississippi Quarterly* 12 (Fall 1966): 164–93.

Wiltse, Charles M. *John C. Calhoun: Nationalist, 1782–1828*. Indianapolis: Bobbs-Merrill, 1944.

———. *John C. Calhoun: Nullifier, 1829–1839*. Indianapolis: Bobbs-Merrill, 1949.

———. *John C. Calhoun: Sectionalist, 1840–1850*. Indianapolis: Bobbs-Merrill, 1951.

———. "John Quincy Adams and the Party System: A Review Article." *Journal of Politics* 4 (August 1942): 407–14.

Wirls, Daniel. "'The Only Mode of Avoiding Everlasting Debate': The Overlooked Senate Gag Rule for Antislavery Petitions." *Journal of The Early Republic* 27 (Spring 2007): 115–38.

Wise, Barton H. *The Life of Henry A. Wise of Virginia, 1806–1876*. New York: Macmillan, 1899.

Wood, Peter H. *Black Majority: Negroes in Colonial South Carolina from 1670 through the Stono Rebellion*. 1974. Reprint New York: W. W. Norton, 1975.

Young, Robert Jeffrey. *Domesticating Slavery: The Master Class in George and South Carolina, 1670–1838*. Chapel Hill: University of North Carolina Press, 1999.

Zemsky, Robert. *Merchants, Farmers, and River Gods: An Essay on Eighteenth-Century American Politics*. Boston: Gambit, 1971.

Dissertations

Angelo, Theodore Angelis. "Pregnant with Future Consequences: Political Culture in Revolutionary Massachusetts, 1774–1787." PhD diss., City University of New York, 2002.

Haws, Robert James. "Massachusetts Whigs, 1833–1854." PhD diss., University of Nebraska, 1973.

Index